Xamarin Mobile Application Development

Cross-Platform C# and Xamarin.Forms Fundamentals

Dan Hermes

Apress®

Xamarin Mobile Application Development: Cross-Platform C# and Xamarin.Forms Fundamentals

ISBN-13 (pbk): 978-1-4842-0215-9

ISBN-13 (electronic): 978-1-4842-0214-2

Managing Director: Welmoed Spahr
Lead Editor: James DeWolf
Technical Reviewer: Ed Snider
Developmental Editor: Anne Marie Walker
Editorial Board: Steve Anglin, Gary Cornell, Louise Corrigan, James T. DeWolf, Jonathan Gennick, Robert Hutchinson, Michelle Lowman, James Markham, Susan McDermott, Matthew Moodie, Jeffrey Pepper, Douglas Pundick, Dominic Shakeshaft, Gwenan Spearing, Matt Wade, Steve Weiss
Coordinating Editor: Melissa Maldonado
Copy Editor: Kezia Endsley and Sharon Wilkey
Compositor: SPi Global
Indexer: SPi Global
Artist: SPi Global

Distributed to the book trade worldwide by Springer Science+Business Media New York, 233 Spring Street, 6th Floor, New York, NY 10013. Phone 1-800-SPRINGER, fax (201) 348-4505, e-mail orders-ny@springer-sbm.com, or visit www.springeronline.com. Apress Media LLC is a California LLC and the sole member (owner) is Springer Science+Business Media Finance Inc (SSBM Finance Inc). SSBM Finance Inc is a Delaware corporation.

For information on translations, please e-mail rights@apress.com, or visit www.apress.com.

Apress and friends of ED books may be purchased in bulk for academic, corporate, or promotional use. eBook versions and licenses are also available for most titles. For more information, reference our Special Bulk Sales–eBook Licensing web page at www.apress.com/bulk-sales.

Any source code or other supplementary material referenced by the author in this text is available to readers at www.apress.com. For detailed information about how to locate your book's source code, go to www.apress.com/source-code/.

To Kristina, for her unwavering love, dedication, and support

Contents at a Glance

Contents

Foreword

Dan Hermes' extraordinary book is the most intelligent work on cross-platform mobile development I've seen. He focuses on Xamarin.Forms but provides a comprehensive guide as well to Xamarin.Android and Xamarin.iOS. This puts Xamarin.Forms in context, and explains the underlying native code for those who want to know not only how to write with Xamarin.Forms but why it works and what's under the hood. I learned a lot from these parts of this excellent book.

Dan made the decision to write all the examples in C#. While I prefer writing much of the UI in Extensible Application Markup Language (XAML), his approach does make clear what is actually being created. Most important, you can download all the examples in both C# and XAML, and all the code samples are complete, well commented, and ready to run.

Another helpful feature is that the illustrations show the running example code on all three platforms (iOS, Android, and Windows Phone). I have railed and ranted against samples that are overly complex and designed to show how clever the author is, rather than making the issue crystal clear. Dan, thank goodness, gets it, and his examples are well explained and focused.

The book starts out simple, but he takes you through the fundamentals and then on to more-advanced topics such as custom control rendering to extend the Xamarin.Forms capabilities.

Code patterns can help you avoid reinventing the wheel, and Dan uses and explains in detail some of the most important patterns for mobile development, including hierarchical and modal windows, drill-down lists, tabs, creating a navigation drawer, and a good deal more.

He then tackles one of the trickier but extremely important topics in mobile development: persistence. Dan covers the three most important approaches: using SQLite, using ADO.NET, and using the repository pattern with a data access Layer (DAL). He dives into data binding and discusses Model -View- ViewModel (MVVM), perhaps the most important pattern in mobile development.

With the depth of coverage of Xamarin.iOS, Xamarin.Android, and Xamarin.Forms, you will be well placed to decide which technology to use for your particular project.

Xamarin novices will benefit greatly from this book, but don't underestimate how useful it will be for Xamarin veterans as well.

—Jesse Liberty
Director of New Technology Development, Falafel Software
Xamarin Certified Developer / Xamarin MVP

Additional Foreword

The first time I saw Xamarin.Forms, it was hardly recognizable as the powerful cross-platform framework it is today. I was visiting our San Francisco office, it was late at night, Jason Smith (the creator of Xamarin.Forms) was busily coding away, and I was packing some stuff up for the evening. I heard a sudden exclamation from Jason, and a huge grin was pasted on his face: "Wanna see something really cool?" he queried. "Absolutely," I responded. I walked around the desk to see what he wanted to show me. On his screen was an iOS simulator with a box displayed on it.

Not wanting to dampen his enthusiasm for what was obviously a really impressive feat—I mean, we're talking advanced stuff here, a box (note: sarcasm)—I replied something to the effect of, "Fantastic. What am I looking at?" I knew of Jason's project; Nat Friedman and I had knocked our heads about to solve a fundamental challenge to cross-platform mobile development, the UI layer, and Jason was doing some prototyping work to investigate the feasibility of doing a cross-platform UI framework the right way.

Xamarin was already awesome. I loved MonoTouch (the former product name of Xamarin.iOS) so much that before Xamarin was a company (and consequently, I was part of the executive team, driving it along with Nat, Miguel de Icaza, and Joseph Hill), I had penned the book on it. How cool was it that you could use the same language, C# (my favorite language on the planet), to build native mobile apps for iOS and Android (Windows Mobile was still in its infancy at that point), share all of your back-end and logic code, and do it all from a Mac (my OS of choice by then)? It was super awesome. But it wasn't without a huge opportunity; you could share a lot of code with Xamarin, but even with the MVVM frameworks, unifying your UI code was still a big challenge.

"This is a canvas drawing a box using the native UI toolkits on both iOS and Android; here's the code," said Jason. Sure enough, the same code was being used by both an iOS and an Android project to render the box. And thus Xamarin.Forms was born. We used the code name Duplo before settling on the Xamarin.Forms brand, and at the time it was fitting; Xamarin.Forms was a child's building-block toy. You could build some basic toy apps, nothing sophisticated, but even then, the value of what Jason had created was apparent. Xamarin.Forms quickly evolved to the frame that now barely resembles the prototype framework Jason showed me late that evening nearly two years ago.

Today Xamarin.Forms is an incredibly powerful framework. By extending it via custom renderers to provide native, platform-specific functionality, there's very little you can't do at a UI level.

And now, you hold in your hands (either physically or virtually), the first non-Xamarin book on Xamarin. Forms (don't worry, it also covers Xamarin.iOS and Xamarin.Android so you can get down and dirty with a bare-metal native UI).

I'm really excited about this book. When Dan first contacted me a year ago about the book, he told me his vision for it: a thorough, deep dive with a quality narrative in the same spirit of my original (and now woefully outdated) MonoTouch book. Something that did the platform justice. And after reading it, I think you'll agree that Dan's unique voice and clear appreciation for the platform has come through in a practical way; he's created a solid handbook for working with Xamarin that I think you'll come to appreciate, whether you're a brand-new Xamarin developer or an old hat at it.

This weighty book gives clear guidance that will help you build quality apps, starting with architectural considerations, and then jumping into practical code strategies. It leads with Xamarin.Forms, but it also teaches you how to punch through into the native UI toolkits, and explains not just the how of things, but the why.

And with that, I leave you in adept hands and wish you a fun journey through building apps with Xamarin via Dan's competent guidance.

—Bryan Costanich
Vice President
Xamarin

About the Author

 **Dan Hermes** is a software consultant and founder of Lexicon Systems, an award-winning Xamarin and .NET consulting firm. His clients include dozens of software-building organizations, such as Fidelity Investments, EDS, Blue Cross Blue Shield of Massachusetts, and Computerworld magazine. He speaks at conferences and teaches Xamarin, C#, and mobile development at developer user groups, colleges, and corporate training facilities. He and his company build .NET, iOS, and Android applications in sectors sfuch as biotech, finance, healthcare, retail, transportation, advertising, and sports; for blue chips and startups; and especially for software companies. Dan conducts Xamarin code reviews, delivers Xamarin workshops, and he and his team build acclaimed Xamarin apps.

Dan is a contemporary Renaissance Man who is also active in the arts. His music compositions have aired on National Public Radio (NPR). He has taught his music curriculum at the Boston Conservatory. His digital fine art exhibits internationally, resides in cataloged private collections, and has been cited by Forbes and Reuters. He has written art reviews published by Media-N and MIT Press and he served as a founding director of Art Technology New England (ATNE).

Dan mixes arguably authentic tiki cocktails and has a blue-fronted Amazon parrot named Chicken.

Firms who are passionate about serving their customers through software development call upon Dan to help lead them into the fast-growing world of mobile devices using Xamarin.

About the Technical Reviewer

 **Ed Snider** is a senior software developer at InfernoRed Technology, a speaker, and a Xamarin MVP based in the Washington, DC/Northern Virginia area. He has a passion for mobile development, regularly speaking at local user groups and community events, and is the founder and organizer of the Northern VA Mobile C# Developers Group. Ed is primarily focused on building mobile solutions on the Windows, iOS, and Android platforms for small and large organizations and has been working with .NET for over 10 years. Ed blogs at www.edsnider.net and can be found on Twitter at www.twitter.com/edsnider.

Acknowledgments

Forming a group of smart, dedicated people is a good way to get a big thing done. Some call it a collective or a mastermind, and others call it open sourcing. I want to share with you our collective for this book and thank them publicly.

James DeWolf, my senior editor at Apress, is one of the most accomplished leaders I've seen in any field. Thank you, Jim, for this opportunity and for your unfailing and well-calibrated follow-through. Anne Marie Walker, each of your developmental edits not only helped make this a better book, but also helped teach me how to write. Melissa Maldonado, thank you for your patience with my copious special requests, for keeping the trains running on time, and for herding this book home to publication. And to all the rest of the Apress editors, formatters, and staff, thank you!

Thank you thrice Ed Snider, tech reviewer and Xamarin MVP, for combing through every one of these code examples and offering your sage advice. It's a worlds-better book for it. If any errors are left in here, it's because I snuck them in after your review.

There are over 200 C# code examples in this book. All of the UI examples were also built in XAML and are available for download. Many, many thanks to the XAML developers Jason Awbrey and Alex Blount for making this possible.

The folks at Xamarin are upbeat, brilliant, and incredibly helpful in every way. They brought us a great product suite and also bring us a positive and inspiring attitude, every day. Thank you, Mike Bluestein, for stressing the importance of Xamarin.iOS and Xamarin.Android; and thank you, Bryan Costanich, for saying that Xamarin.Forms was the way forward—I followed both of your advice. Jason Smith, tech lead of Xamarin. Forms, having lunch with you at Evolve in Atlanta gave this book focus and grounding. Joseph Hill, thank you for your advice and encouragement. Thank you, Spencer Montgomery, Erik Polzin, and Matt Mason for your partner support. Thank you, James Montemagno, Mark Smith, Pierce Boggan, and many others.

And thank you, Miguel de Icaza, for cofounding Xamarin and for being your brilliant self. I am honored to be part of your collective.

Great bloggers give us guidance and humor. This book owes a debt to the great bloggers and Xamarin forum contributors who help set direction and confirm details on many topics: James Montemagno at `motzcod.es`, Adam Wolf (a.k.a. AdamKemp) at `syntaxismyui.com`, Jim Bennett at `jimbobbennett.io`, Tomasz Cielecki (a.k.a. Cheesebaron), Kevin Ford at `magenic.com`, Jesse Liberty at `jesseliberty.com`, and many others.

So many brilliant people looked at these chapters and offered their thoughts to make this a better book. Here are a few of them: Mike Bluestein, Jim Bennett, Mark Allan, Adam Wolf, David Ortineau, Jesse Liberty, William Grand, Michael Lant, and Ed Hubbell.

At Microsoft, I want to thank Dan Stolts, Mark Eisenberg, Donna Malayeri, and Michael Cummings for bringing me clarity regarding the Azure integration with Xamarin.

At IBM, thank you, Craig Porter and Philip Sacchitella, for setting me straight on IBM MobileFirst.

■ ACKNOWLEDGMENTS

At iTexico, thank you, Abhijeet Pradhan and Mathieu Clerici, for your *top-notch* Xamarin development.

Thanks to everyone here at Lexicon Systems! That means you, Jonathan LaMaster, Tom Ruane, and everyone else who's had a hand in this. Thank you, Margo Chevers, for steeling my resolve to make this book possible. And thanks to David Alexander for editing and formatting until a publisher stepped in to give you a rest.

Thanks to my parents and family for your steady and enthusiastic support.

Thanks most of all to my sweetheart, Kristina. You went above and beyond in your support of this effort, and I am grateful.

And lest I forget, a special thanks to the semicolon. Without your stalwart delimitation at the end of almost every line of the C# in this book, and, indeed, in all of our solutions, would be an unparseable blur of commands, keywords, symbols, and objects; thank you, semicolon.

Last, thanks to all of you not listed here who had a hand in or offered a word of advice or support for this book!

Introduction

This book is a hands-on Xamarin.Forms primer and a cross-platform reference for building native Android, iOS, and Windows Phone apps using C# and .NET.

If you think of the Xamarin platform as a pyramid with Xamarin.Android and Xamarin.iOS at its base and Xamarin.Forms on top, that's what this book covers with C#. Mobile UI makes up the lion's share of the pyramid, and this book explores the important concepts, elements, and recipes using Xamarin layouts, controls, and lists.

The burning question in many new Xamarin projects is this: is Xamarin.Forms right for my project? This book covers the salient considerations in the comparison of the Xamarin.Forms option vs. a platform-specific approach with Xamarin.Android or Xamarin.iOS.

When you've reached the limits of what Xamarin.Forms can do out of the box, you'll want to customize your Xamarin.Forms controls by using custom renderers to leverage platform-specific features.

You'll also learn all of the key Xamarin UI navigation patterns: hierarchical and modal, drill-down lists, tabs, navigation drawer, and others. You can use the provided navigation code to build out the skeleton of just about any business app.

This book is a guide to SQLite data access. We'll cover the most common ways to access a SQLite database in a Xamarin app and how to build a data access layer (DAL). Once you have a database set up, you'll want to bind your data to your UI. You can do this by hand or use Xamarin.Forms data binding to bind UI elements to data sources. We'll cover many techniques for read and write data binding to both data models and to view models for a Model-View-ViewModel (MVVM) architecture.

Building an app requires more than a UI and data access; you'll also need to organize your code into a professional-grade architecture. We'll explore solution-building techniques from starter to enterprise to help you decouple your functional layers, manage your platform-specific code, and share your cross-platform classes for optimal code reuse, testability, and maintainability.

Who This Book Is For

If you're a developer, architect, or technical manager who can read C# examples to learn about cross-platform mobile development using the Xamarin platform, then this book is for you. C# developers will probably be most at home with this book because that's what I am, but I've made an effort to point out when Microsoft or .NET lingo is in use. The Xamarin platform has a way of bringing technologists from different backgrounds together.

How to Download Code Examples

All of the code for this book, the C# and Extensible Application Markup Language (XAML) solutions, can be found in two places online:

Apress web page for this book, on the Source Code/Downloads tab (`www.apress.com/9781484202159`)

GitHub at `https://github.com/danhermes/xamarin-book-examples`

XAML

This book was written in the same way that the Xamarin platform is built, code-first in C#, so all of the book examples are in C#. All of the C# UI examples were ported to XAML as well, and made available in the downloadable code. Look for the XAML boxes for tips on where to find them.

XAML The XAML version of this example can be found at the Apress web site (`www.apress.com`), or on GitHub at `https://github.com/danhermes/xamarin-book-examples`. The Xamarin.Forms solution for this chapter is `ThisChapterSolution.Xaml`.

The hardest decision I made in writing this book was not including XAML examples in the book proper. Including XAML would have meant doing away with much or all of the material on Xamarin.Android and Xamarin.iOS, topics that are indispensible for a complete understanding of the Xamarin platform. I chose to adhere to my mission for this book: cross-platform C# code-first coverage of the foundations of the Xamarin platform. That said, I understand that there is a strong need for good XAML documentation and examples. So although I wish that there had been enough time and room to include XAML examples in the text of the book, I'm proud to say that we were able to provide downloadable XAML equivalents for *all* of the C# UI examples.

Get Started with Xamarin.Forms Right Now!

No time for reading? Browse Chapter 2 for ten minutes, and then download the navigation code for Chapter 6. Rip off some of my Chapter 6 navigation patterns to use immediately in your app and get started coding right now. Leave the book open to Chapter 3 so you can build some layouts inside your navigation pages. Good luck!

Chapter Contents

All of the chapters in this book are cross-platform, weighted in favor of Xamarin.Forms. The UI chapters (Chapters 3–6) are written with Xamarin.Forms, Xamarin.Android, and Xamarin.iOS elements side by side in a mini-index at the beginning of the chapter to facilitate understanding of concepts across platforms, and to make it easier to consider custom renderers when you need them. The first part of those UI chapters is Xamarin.Forms, the second part is Xamarin.Android, and the third is Xamarin.iOS.

Chapter 1—Mobile Development Using Xamarin

An introduction to the Xamarin platform covering all the key topics in this book.

Chapter 2—Building Mobile User Interfaces (Xamarin.Forms Intro)

A Xamarin.Forms primer and a comparison of Xamarin.Forms vs. platform-specific approaches, such as Xamarin.iOS and Xamarin.Android. Covers Xamarin.Forms pages, layouts, and views.

Chapter 3—UI Design Using Layouts

Layouts help us organize the positioning and formatting of controls, allowing us to structure and design the screens of our mobile app.

Chapter 4—User Interaction Using Controls (Views)

Pickers, sliders, switches, and other mobile UI controls facilitate user interaction and data entry that is unique to the mobile user interface and differs from the PC/mouse interface, largely because of the use of gestures.

Chapter 5—Making a Scrollable List

Lists are one of the simplest and most powerful methods of data display and selection in mobile apps.

Chapter 6—Navigation

Navigation lets a user traverse an app, move from screen to screen, and access features. Hierarchical, modal, navigation drawers, drill-down lists, and other key patterns make up the core of mobile UI navigation. State management is the handling of data passed between screens as the user navigates through the app.

Chapter 7—Data Access with SQLite and Data Binding

SQLite is the database of choice for many Xamarin developers. Store and retrieve data locally by using SQLite.NET or ADO.NET. Using Xamarin.Forms data binding, fuse UI elements to your data models. Use the MVVM pattern by binding to a view model.

Chapter 8—Custom Renderers

Extend the stock Xamarin.Forms controls and take advantage of platform-specific UI feature sets while maintaining a cross-platform approach using custom renderers.

Chapter 9—Cross-platform Architecture

Architect your cross-platform application by managing platform-specific code. Project-level options in Xamarin include Portable Class Libraries (PCLs) and shared projects. Cross-platform coding techniques include conditional compilation, dependency injection (DI), and file linking.

How to Read This Book

This book covers quite a breadth of material, and there are a few ways to approach it. Here are the main navigation paths built into this book and how to use them. If you are interested in

- **Cross-platform Development: Xamarin.Forms, Xamarin.Android, and Xamarin.iOS**
  Read the book from cover to cover. Every word in this book was written for you. After you read Chapters 1 and 2, peruse the first few pages of Chapters 3–6 to understand the UI material covered in the book.

- **Xamarin.Forms**
  Read Chapters 1 and 2, and then read the first third of Chapters 3–6, which covers Xamarin.Forms UI. Then read Chapters 7, 8, and 9 for data access, custom renderers, and architecture.

- **Xamarin.Android**
  First, make sure you are up to speed on Android basics. See "Prerequisites" later in this Introduction. Then read Chapter 1 and the first half of Chapter 2. Read the middle section of Chapters 3–6, which covers the Android UI. Then read Chapters 7 and 9 for data access and architecture.

- **Xamarin.iOS**
  First, make sure you are up to speed on iOS basics. See "Prerequisites" later in this Introduction. Then read Chapter 1 and the first half of Chapter 2. Read the end section of Chapters 3–6, which covers the iOS UI. Then read Chapters 7 and 9 for data access and architecture.

- **General Reference**
  Read Chapter 1 and the first half of Chapter 2 to get oriented. Then peruse the first few pages of Chapters 3–6 to understand the UI material covered in the book and how it is organized. Use the beginning of each of these UI chapters as a cross-reference.

So many paths to pick from. This is a choose-your-own-adventure book.

CODE COMPLETE

There is a "Cliff's Notes" navigation path through this book too. If you just want the bottom line on a topic, find the section you're interested in and jump right to the *CODE COMPLETE* section. This is a complete code listing at the end of many (but not all) major topics. Many times all we want is a quick code recipe on a topic, and that's how to get it here in this book. If you need explanation about the code, turn back to the beginning of the section and step through the detailed construction of that code.

What Platform Am I Reading About Now?

Stay oriented while reading about different platforms by using the *platform headings* beneath major topic headings. Here's what the headings look like:

XAMARIN.FORMS

This heading denotes Xamarin.Forms topics.

ANDROID

This heading denotes Xamarin.Android topics.

IOS

This heading denotes Xamarin.iOS topics.

WINDOWS PHONE

This heading denotes Xamarin.Forms Windows Phone topics.

CROSS-PLATFORM

this heading denotes topics that are useful for Xamarin.Forms, Xamarin.iOS, and Xamarin.Android.

Look for the platform headings beneath the major topic headings and you'll always know what platform you're reading about.

Prerequisites

If you're mainly using Xamarin.Forms, you should be able to pick up this book without much else in the way of background, besides some C#. However, if you want to get serious about using Xamarin.Android, Xamarin.iOS, or Xamarin.Forms custom renderers, please note the following:

> *This is not an Android 101 primer.* Although it provides some introduction to key topics and then moves on to "202" material, you'll need to consult other sources for mastery of Android and Xamarin.Android fundamentals. Consult a Xamarin.Android primer on topics such as the following:

- Creating a Xamarin.Android solution using Xamarin Studio or Visual Studio
- Xamarin Designer for Android
- Activities, XML layouts, and views
- The activity life cycle
- The basic UI controls: `TextView`, `EditText`, `Button`, and `ImageView`
- Fragments
- Images and screen sizes
- Local resources
- Gestures

> *This book is not an iOS 101 primer.* Although it provides some introduction to key topics and then moves on to "202" material, you'll need to consult other sources for mastery of iOS and Xamarin.iOS fundamentals. Consult a Xamarin.iOS primer on topics such as the following:

- Creating a Xamarin.iOS solution using Xamarin Studio or Visual Studio
- Xcode Interface Builder or Xamarin Designer for iOS
- Storyboards and segues
- `UIView` and `UIViewController`
- The basic UI controls: `UILabel`, `UITextField`, `UIButton`, and `UIImageView`
- Images and screen sizes
- Local resources
- Gestures

What's Not In This Book

The Xamarin platform is a monumental project, spanning technologies and APIs of several operating systems. Writing about all of it in enough detail to be useful would require not hundreds but thousands of pages, which means that not everything could be addressed in one book. There is no coverage of the following:

- *Extensible Application Markup Language* (*XAML*) for Xamarin.Forms in the book proper, but there are complete, downloadable XAML code examples.

- *Integrated development environments* (*IDEs*) including Visual Studio and Xamarin Studio.

- *UI Designer* tools including Xcode Interface Builder, Xamarin Designer for iOS, and Xamarin Designer for Android.

- *Some introductory Xamarin.Android topics* (see "Prerequisites")

- *Some introductory Xamarin.iOS topics* (see "Prerequisites")

Windows Phone

Xamarin.Forms apps will run on Windows Phone. Windows Phone projects can be built to support Silverlight or WinRT. This book was written for Windows Phone Silverlight implementations, but much of what is written here applies to WinRT as well (and some WinRT differences are pointed out).

System Requirements

Whether you're developing on a Mac or Windows workstation, you will need to download and run the Xamarin unified installer at `http://xamarin.com/download`. This will allow you to install and configure the Xamarin platform including the Xamarin Android SDK, Xamarin iOS SDK, Xamarin Studio, and Xamarin's plug-in for Visual Studio, as appropriate.

Here are the OS and software requirements for Xamarin development.

Mac

These requirements must be met to build Xamarin apps on a Mac.

- Xamarin Studio 5+ is required to use Xamarin.Forms on OS X.

- To develop iOS apps:

  - Latest Xcode version

  - Mac OS X 10.9.3+ (Mavericks) or 10.10+

- Windows Phone apps cannot be developed on a Mac.

Windows

These requirements must be met to build Xamarin apps on a Windows workstation.

- Latest Xamarin Studio or Visual Studio 2012+ (not Express)
- Windows 7+
- For iOS development, a networked Mac is required.
- For Windows Phone development, you'll need the Windows Phone SDK.
- To use PCLs, you'll need Visual Studio 2013+ or the Portable Reference Library Assemblies 4.6. For PCLs using Xamarin Studio without Visual Studio, download the Portable Library Tools 2.

Xamarin.Forms

To use Xamarin.Forms, your app builds must target the following platforms.

- iOS 6.1+
- Android 4.0+
- Windows Phone 8 (at the time of this writing, and newer versions later)

Errata

The author, the technical reviewers, and many Apress staff have made every effort to find and eliminate all errors from this book's text and code. Even so, there are bound to be one or two glitches left. To keep you informed, there's an Errata tab on the Apress book page (www.apress.com/9781484202159). If you find any errors that haven't already been reported, such as misspellings or faulty code, please let us know by e-mailing support@apress.com.

Customer Support

Apress wants to hear what you think—what you liked, what you didn't like, and what you think could be done better next time. You can send comments to feedback@apress.com. Be sure to mention the book title in your message.

Contacting the Author

You can follow me on Twitter at @lexiconsystems, read my blog at www.mobilecsharpcafe.com, or e-mail me at dan@lexiconsystemsinc.com.

If you are seeking general Xamarin product support, please use the Xamarin support page at http://xamarin.com/support or the Xamarin forums at http://forums.xamarin.com/.

Summary

That is everything you need to get started with this book: contents, prerequisites, disclaimers, trailheads, maps, and signposts. If you're new to the Xamarin platform, welcome to the community! If you're experienced with Xamarin, thanks for reading, and there is plenty in here for you as well.

I promise you that reading this book, understanding the concepts, and practicing the code techniques herein will enrich your Xamarin acumen and raise your coding skills to greater heights. I also hope to give you a deeper appreciation for the amazing accomplishment that is the Xamarin platform.

CHAPTER 1

■ ■ ■

Mobile Development Using Xamarin

Mobile development in C# is unlike anything most of us have done with the language before. We are using it to develop apps for non-Windows platforms, namely Android and iOS. This is both an opportunity and a challenge. The opportunity is to expose ourselves to the rich breadth of technology that comprises the new business application ecosystem made up of phones and tablets of different platforms and sizes. The challenge is that so much about these devices and platforms is new to many of us, and there is much to learn. Of course, we can build Windows Phone and tablet apps in C# also. The essence of cross-platform development is building apps that will work on more than one mobile operating system: for example, on Android and iOS; or on iOS and Windows Phone; or on iOS, Android, *and* Windows Phone. Using the cross-platform techniques covered in this book, you will be equipped to develop for all the major mobile platforms!

The most exciting/terrifying part of this journey is learning the ins and outs of several operating systems. Lucky for us, Xamarin shields us from many of the details, wrapping platform-specific APIs and exposing familiar .NET using C#. Conversely, exposed to us in detail are C#-wrapped user interface (UI) APIs for each platform, giving us precise control over the visual design of our app. The trick is to understand which aspects of each operating system are important during development and which can be left up to Xamarin. Although it never hurts to delve deeper in our understanding, there are only so many hours in a day, and the bottom line is that we need to ship working software.

These are the key questions: How do we approach the development of a cross-platform mobile application? Given the history and background that we already have in C# development, how do we carry forward this knowledge and leverage it in the mobile space? Finally, given the multitude of things to learn about these operating systems, what do we need to get started and help solve the important challenges?

While writing apps for more than one platform, a key goal is the reuse of code. The more we reuse, the quicker and cheaper our projects become, and the more we lower our maintenance costs. Xamarin refers to this as the *unicorn* of mobile development: *write once, deploy anywhere*. Any quest for a unicorn begins with a fair maiden to entice it to appear. Our fair maiden is cross-platform design.

Let's explore how Xamarin helps us solve our mobile puzzles while pursuing cross-platform design.

What Is Xamarin?

Xamarin is a development platform that allows us to code native, cross-platform iOS, Android, and Windows Phone apps in C#.

How does it do that? Read on.

1

Wrapped Native APIs

Descended from the open source Mono Project that brought .NET to Linux, the Xamarin platform is a port of .NET to the iOS and Android operating systems with support for Windows Phone (see Figure 1-1). Underlying Xamarin.Android is Mono for Android, and beneath Xamarin.iOS is MonoTouch. These are C# bindings to the native Android and iOS APIs for development on mobile and tablet devices. *This gives us the power of the Android and iOS user interface, notifications, graphics, animation, and phone features such as location and camera—all using C#.* Each new release of the Android and iOS operating systems are matched by a new Xamarin release that includes bindings to their new APIs. Xamarin's port of .NET includes features such as data types, generics, garbage collection, Language-Integrated Query (LINQ), asynchronous programming patterns, delegates, and a subset of Windows Communication Foundation (WCF). Libraries are managed with a linker to include only the referenced components. Xamarin.Forms is a layer on top of the other UI bindings and the Windows Phone API, which provides a fully cross-platform UI library.

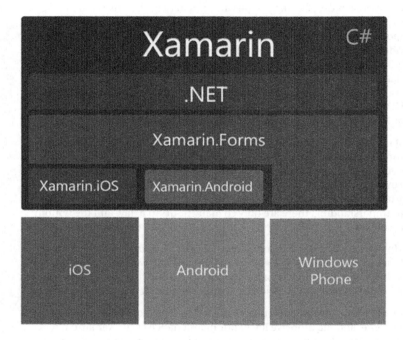

Figure 1-1. Xamarin C# libraries bind to native OS SDKs as well as .NET

So we have a .NET environment with iOS and Android C#-bound libraries with support for Windows Phone running on the mobile OS of our choice. Fantastic. Now how do we build UIs and write code using these libraries to build mobile apps? By using development environments and UI designers, of course.

Development Environments

Xamarin provides development environments and designers to help us build mobile apps on Windows or Mac. The two main choices for Xamarin development environments are Xamarin Studio on Mac or Windows, or Visual Studio on Windows with the Xamarin for Windows plug-in. A Mac is always required for the compilation of iOS apps, even if Visual Studio is used as the development environment.

UI Designers

The tools we use to create mobile user interfaces are called designers. These generate Extensible Markup Language (XML) files in their respective proprietary file formats. Two designers are available from Xamarin:

- Xamarin Designer for Android

- Xamarin Designer for iOS

With the availability of these designers, the need for the original, native XML editors has diminished. Anything you might need to build Android or iOS UIs can be found in Xamarin's tools. However, iOS developers still frequently use the Xcode Interface Builder, and Android developers (less frequently) use XML editors such as the Android Development Tools (ADT) plug-in for Eclipse. An XML layout is an XML layout, and the tool is largely a matter of taste and personal preference, even the decision to use a designer tool at all. Some Xamarin developers are opting to code UIs by hand in C# for all platforms with no designer use whatsoever. I recommend the designers to help learn the file formats, UI elements, and their properties. At the very least, use a designer tool like training wheels until you're ready to ride freestyle.

■ **Note** This book focuses on code rather than tools. Refer to the Xamarin online docs for more information on the designers and development environments at `http://developer.xamarin.com`.

What's Old: Familiar C# and .NET Techniques

Xamarin development allows us to leverage many things that we already know about C# development. We can use our high-level knowledge of the following:

- HTML-based pages

- Extensible Application Markup Language (XAML)

- UI controls

- Event-driven logic

- View life cycles

- State management

- Data binding

- Web services

We also can use many .NET-specific techniques directly and immediately, including these:

- .NET data types

- C# classes, methods, and properties

- Lambda expressions

- WCF (a subset)

- Generics (a subset)

- Local file access

- Streams

- Async/Await

- ADO.NET (a subset)

I've named just a few, so you can see there's plenty of familiar ground for the C# developer to help us make the leap into this new territory.

What's New: Mobile Development Techniques

Throughout this book, you will explore common C# techniques and patterns in mobile development. Some of them are exactly the same as the approaches we are accustomed to in traditional .NET development, some changed a little, and a few changed a lot. Here are the key topics:

- *Mobile UI* is the largest area of new learning for C# mobile development. Xamarin.Forms provides a cross-platform UI toolkit containing ready-to-use forms, pages, layouts, views, and controls. Xamarin.iOS and Xamarin.Android provide bindings to their respective native UIs. (See Chapters 2–6 and Chapter 8.)

- The *Data Access Layer* in a mobile app typically binds controls and pages to data models populated from a local database that is synced with a remote data server using web services. (See Chapter 7.)

- *Local database access* via SQLite is a change from the usual database vendors, though ADO.NET access provides a familiar inroad and the SQLite.NET component is a featureful option. (See Chapter 7.)

- *Data binding* is central to Xamarin.Forms development and is often accomplished using the Model-View-ViewModel (MVVM) pattern. (See Chapter 7.)

- *Cross-platform architecture* is a collection of code-sharing strategies to further our goal of *write once, run anywhere*. These include Portable Class Libraries (PCLs) with dependency injection, shared files and projects, and conditional compilation. (See Chapter 9.)

Let's touch on each of these topics.

Mobile UI

You have a formidable amount of new material to absorb when moving from web development to cross-platform mobile development, mostly in the area of the user interface. There is first the issue of new operating system UI APIs. Xamarin helps with this by providing platform-specific C# bindings to the major OSs with Xamarin.Android and Xamarin.iOS, while Xamarin.Forms provides cross-platform bindings to both of these plus Windows Phone. The other set of challenges involves the design differences between web apps and mobile apps. The compact screen, touch sensitivity, and handheld form factor team up to offer a fundamentally novel user experience (UX). This requires a fundamentally novel approach to design and development, leading us to explore mobile UI design.

Xamarin.Forms and Platform-Specific UI

There are two main approaches to mobile UI development using C#, which we can use separately, interchangeably, or in tandem:

- *Xamarin.Forms* is a cross-platform UI toolkit for Android, iOS, and Windows Phone.
- *Platform-specific UI* uses Xamarin.Android, Xamarin.iOS, and Windows Phone SDK.

Xamarin.Forms contains a fully cross-platform toolkit providing a single set of UI controls, layouts, and pages that map cleverly to respective native UI bindings on iOS, Android, and Windows Phone. Since Xamarin.Forms is newer than platform-specific libraries, it is also less full-featured. Each release brings us closer to full-featured cross-platform goodness, but sometimes we need more than the out-of-the-box Xamarin.Forms classes have to offer. In those cases, we use the platform-specific libraries, either for the entire page or for just parts of a page using Xamarin.Forms custom renderers called PageRenderers.

The platform-specific approach is older and more established and therefore quite detailed and full-featured. This involves libraries that bind directly to platform-specific UI APIs: Xamarin.Android for Android, and Xamarin.iOS for iOS. For Windows Phone, we use the Windows Phone SDK, a native API requiring no Xamarin bindings. These platform-specific libraries give us deep access to native UIs for providing a visually stunning, interactively rich user experience. This comes at a cost: platform-specific code requiring a separate UI project for each platform with little code reusability.

■ **Note**   Xamarin.Forms is the thrust of this book, augmented by custom renderers, which use platform-specific UI. However, developers creating platform-specific UI projects using Xamarin.iOS and Xamarin.Android without Xamarin.Forms can make excellent use of the iOS and Android sections in Chapters 2–7. If you are taking the platform-specific approach, be sure to consult other sources (such as the Xamarin online documentation) for Xamarin.Android and Xamarin.iOS solution setup and fundamentals.

Mobile UI Design

UI techniques make up the core of most mobile software development. Current hardware limitations of small devices encourage us to leave the heavy lifting to the PCs and servers on the far end of our web services. Most of the components running in a mobile business application are there to support the visible user interface. Mobile business and data access layers are often abbreviated versions of their server-side brethren. That means that what we need most often are UI components to help us design screens using layouts, implement controls for data entry and selection, build lists and tables for data display and editing, create user navigation, and use images for backgrounds and icons. The UI topics in this book cover the functions used most frequently in mobile app development. In each chapter, we start with the simplest, most cross-platform approaches available, and then delve into platform-specifics for granularity and detail. These are the mobile UI topics are covered in this book:

- *Screens, views, or pages* are similar to the web and desktop equivalents in C#, using controls with methods and properties and firing events that we handle in our controllers. (See Chapter 2.)
- *Layouts* help us organize the positioning and formatting of controls, allowing us to structure and design the screens of our mobile app. (See Chapter 3.)

- *Controls* facilitate user interaction and data entry which is unique to the mobile user interface and differs substantially from the PC/mouse interface, largely due the use of gestures. (See Chapter 4.)

- *Lists* are one of the most powerful methods of data display and selection in mobile apps. (See Chapter 5.)

- *Navigation* lets a user traverse an app, move from screen to screen, and access features. Hierarchical navigation, modal screens, navigation drawers, alerts, drilldown lists, and other key patterns make up the core of mobile UI navigation. (See Chapter 6.)

- *State Management* is the handling of data passed between screens as the user navigates through the app. (See Chapter 6.)

- *Images* are central to the mobile experience, in menus, lists, grids, carousels, and other layouts. (See Chapters 2, 4, 6.)

Xamarin.Forms Custom Renderers

Custom Renderers allow us to go deeper than the out-of-the-box Xamarin.Forms UI controls and take advantage of platform-specific UI feature sets while keeping a cross-platform approach. Xamarin.Forms applications are inherently cross-platform, running on all three major platforms using the same code base. This works well for basic designs and using certain controls. However, many projects will develop a need to go deeper with the UI, such as design nuances on a single control, native modal dialog boxes, additional graphics or animations on a page, or any requirements that go beyond the scope of what Xamarin.Forms provides in the current release. This is accomplished by subclassing native controls and implementing PageRenderers to create custom controls that give full access to platform-specific UI functionality using Xamarin.iOS and Xamarin.Android. These platform-specific controls can be employed within Xamarin. Forms pages to help maintain a cross-platform architecture.

Data Access Layer

The mobile data access layer departs from the designs we are accustomed to in web apps and more closely resembles those found in desktop apps. Approaches range in sophistication from the popular MVVM pattern to Model-View-Controller (MVC) to basic CRUD (Create/Insert/Update/Delete). Data-bound pages typically feed into a local database on the device, which syncs with a remote data server using web services.

Web services in C# mobile development are a foundational aspect of code reuse. Many of these service patterns remain the same for mobile applications as what we are accustomed to when building web apps. However, mobile web services more closely resemble those found in desktop applications, differing from web app services primarily in the importance of data synchronization and offline use. Create, Update, and Delete interfaces are exposed online for RESTful calls from a multitude of platforms and devices. The fairest of maidens dwell here in mobile web service patterns, a perfect place for *cross-platform, write-once* code.

The server-side component of web services remains the same for mobile applications, compared to what we are accustomed to with web apps—except for the addition of data synchronization with local mobile data stores for both online and offline use. Offline use requires a basic data set to be kept on hand in the local database and synced when a connection is available. Not all apps support offline use.

Recounting our experiences with data access layers in older, related technologies, we will explore the architectural options for the data access layer in C# mobile apps.

Local Data Access Using SQLite

SQLite holds the title as the most stable and reliable cross-platform database product for mobile development, an open source project that works on iOS, Android, and Windows devices. Xamarin recommends it over a number of other third-party projects, and it is the one covered in this book. Xamarin provides access to and creation of SQLite databases within the development environment, provisions ADO.NET with support for SQLite. There is also a SQLite.NET Xamarin component, a C# wrapper around the C-based SQLite data layer offering low-level access to a SQLite database which includes async transactions. All this makes it easy and painless to connect to the database, create and index tables, and read and write rows.

Data Binding

Data binding is consistent and cross-platform when using Xamarin.Forms. Modeled after data binding in Windows Presentation Foundation (WPF), the MVVM pattern is central to its implementation. In code we bind control fields to our data model and the binding mechanism is automatic. A manual implementation of a PropertyChanged event allows your code to stay in sync with the data source. Binding is done in code or in Extensible Application Markup Language XAML and can be one- or two-way. Controls, lists, and text are tethered to a data source or to one another's properties. A growing number of third party vendors are providing Xamarin. Forms control suites which include data-bound charts and grids, such as Telerik, Infragistics, Syncfusion, and DevExpress.

Data-binding is not built into Xamarin.Android and Xamarin.iOS. Platform-specific implementations of data binding are typically achieved using open-source third party libraries such as MvvmCross and MVVM Light.

Cross-platform Development

In the same way that .NET provided a unifying infrastructure spanning many operating systems and languages, Xamarin bridges the gaps between mobile operating systems and their respective development languages: iOS and Objective-C, Android and Java, and Windows Phone and tablets and C#. In this way, Xamarin extends .NET into the mobile realm, far beyond Windows operating systems. Aside from the fact that this is eminently cool, the real value here is the opportunity to share and reuse code between and across projects and platforms. The greatest benefits of Xamarin tools are found in the cross-platform code; therefore, a cross-platform approach to mobile patterns will produce the highest yield. Xamarin tools have provided us with the means to catch a glimpse of the unicorn of *write once, deploy anywhere*.

The greatest foe we face in our quest for cross-platform implementation is platform-specific code. This code must be implemented differently depending on the platform, whether iOS, Android, or Windows Phone. Cross-platform patterns are the same regardless of operating system. Cross-platform code is sometimes referred to as *shared code*, or *core code*, as it is shared between projects for different mobile operating systems.

Xamarin.Forms addresses the thorniest cross-platform challenge: the user interface. Developers using Xamarin have a fully cross-platform data solution, which is local data access using ADO.NET or SQLite.NET with SQLite and then web services. Even so, there will always be platform-specific code, as follows:

- In the UI
- Device-specific functionality, such as camera and location
- Graphics and animations
- Security, file, and device permissions

Once we've identified the platform-specific and cross-platform code, the question is then how to organize it into a cross-platform architecture.

We have quite a few options, ranging from PCLs, shared projects, and linked files, interfaces, abstraction, and conditional compilation. PCLs provide the means for a C# component to be built with a limited, platform-specific subset of the .NET library to be compiled into a Dynamic Link Library (DLL) that can be used in a Xamarin project for any platform specified by the PCL's profile. Data access layers, client-side web services, and platform-independent business logic live happily here. Platform-specific functionality can still be introduced into these libraries by using dependency injection with interfaces. A looser, more flexible approach is to use shared files or projects that contain core files recompiled for each platform. Conditional compilation, an ancient technique well-suited to small platform-specific customizations, permits blocks of code within a shared file to be included in a platform-specific compile.

We will delve into these techniques and their related patterns as they bear the mark of the unicorn, helping us to maximize our code's cross-platform footprint.

Summary

Business applications are undergoing a sea change in hardware transformation; we have not seen this magnitude of change since the commercialization of the personal computer. The momentum of consumer mobile devices has reached a tipping point, affecting the devices upon which business applications must now function. With the battle continuing to rage between mobile operating systems, it is no longer enough to just get a mobile app up and working on a single platform.

We must think cross-platform from the get-go.

Within the world of .NET, Xamarin has provided us with the tools to make cross-platform development the norm instead of a special case, so we have no excuse. If the proper approach is taken, business logic, data access layer, and, increasingly, even the UI are mostly platform-independent. So whether you are building an Android, Windows Phone, or iOS app, the approach can be largely the same for many components of the app.

Let's take a look at the code!

■ ■ ■

CHAPTER 2

Building Mobile User Interfaces

In mobile UI development using Xamarin, our screens and their controls, images, animations, and user interactions run natively on a handheld device. Various synonyms for mobile UI *screens* exist, such as *views* and *pages*, and these are used interchangeably here. A *view* can mean a *screen* but can also refer to a *control* in certain contexts.

Two standard approaches apply to building mobile UIs with Xamarin:

- *Xamarin.Forms* is a cross-platform UI library for Android, iOS, and Windows Phone.

- A *platform-specific (or native) UI* approach uses Xamarin.Android, Xamarin.iOS, and the Windows Phone SDK.

This chapter covers both approaches and defines the platform-specific components that make up each of them. We will talk about when Xamarin.Forms is useful and when a more platform-specific approach might be better. Then we'll delve into building a Xamarin.Forms UI using pages, layouts, and views. We will create a Xamarin.Forms solution containing shared projects and platform-specific ones. While adding Xamarin. Forms controls to a project, we will touch upon basic UI concepts such as image handling and formatting controls in a layout.

Let's start by discussing Xamarin.Forms.

Understanding Xamarin.Forms

Xamarin.Forms is a toolkit of cross-platform UI classes built atop the more foundational platform-specific UI classes: Xamarin.Android and Xamarin.iOS. Xamarin.Android and Xamarin.iOS provide mapped classes to their respective native UI SDKs: iOS UIKit and Android SDK. Xamarin.Forms also binds directly to the native Windows Phone SDK. This provides a cross-platform set of UI components that render in each of the three native operative systems (see Figure 2-1).

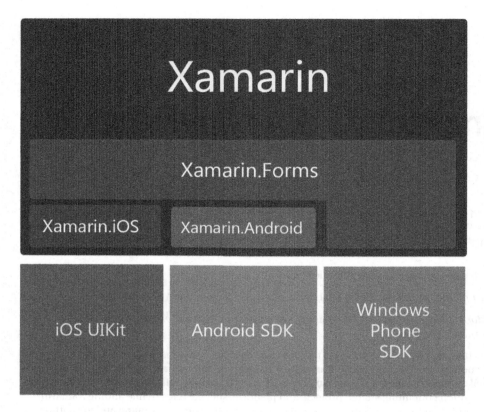

Figure 2-1. *Xamarin libraries bind to native OS libraries*

Xamarin.Forms provides a cross-platform toolkit of pages, layouts, and controls and is a great place to start to begin building an app quickly. These Xamarin.Forms elements are built with Extensible Application Markup Language (XAML) or coded in C#, using Page, Layout, and View classes. This API provides a broad range of built-in cross-platform mobile UI patterns. Beginning with the highest-level Page objects, it provides familiar menu pages such as NavigationPage for hierarchical drilldown menus, and TabbedPage for tab menus, a MasterDetailPage for making navigation drawers, a CarouselPage for scrolling image pages, and a ContentPage, a base class for creating custom pages. Layouts span the standard formats we use on various platforms including StackLayout, AbsoluteLayout, RelativeLayout, Grid, ScrollView, and ContentView, the base layout class. Used within those layouts are dozens of familiar controls, or views, such as ListView, Button, DatePicker, and TableView. Many of these views have built-in data binding options.

Xamarin.Forms comprises platform-independent classes that are bound to their native platform-specific counterparts. This means we can develop basic, native UIs for all three platforms with almost no knowledge of iOS and Android UIs. Rejoice but beware! Purists warn that trying to build apps for these platforms without an understanding of the native APIs is a reckless undertaking. Let's heed the spirit of their concerns. We must take a keen interest in Android and iOS platforms, their evolution, features, idiosyncrasies, and releases. We can also wallow in the convenience and genius of the amazing cross-platform abstraction that is Xamarin.Forms!

■ **Note** Basic pages such as login screens, simple lists, and some business apps are well-suited to out-of-the-box Xamarin.Forms at the time of this writing. Platform-specific code can be utilized in Xamarin. Forms projects for added functionality but each subsequent release of this library will allow us to build more complex screens without utilizing platform-specific code.

Xamarin.Forms Solution Architecture

One of the greatest benefits of Xamarin.Forms is that it gives us the ability to develop native mobile apps for several platforms simultaneously. Figure 2-2 shows the solution architecture for a cross-platform Xamarin.Forms app developed for iOS, Android, and Windows Phone. In the spirit of good architecture and reusability, a Xamarin.Forms cross-platform solution often uses shared C# application code containing the business logic and data access layer, shown as the bottom level of the diagram. This is frequently referred to as the Core Library. The cross-platform Xamarin.Forms UI layer is also C# and is depicted as the middle layer in the figure. The thin, broken layer at the top is a tiny amount of platform-specific C# UI code in platform-specific projects required to initialize and run the app in each native OS.

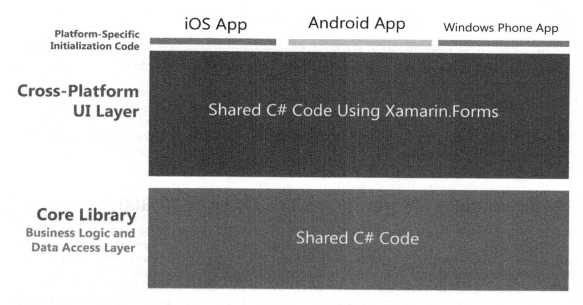

Figure 2-2. Xamarin.Forms solution architecture: One app for three platforms

Figure 2-2 is simplified to communicate the fundamentals of Xamarin.Forms. The reality is that hybridization between Xamarin.Forms and platform-specific code is possible, useful, and encouraged. It can happen at a number of levels. First, within a Xamarin.Forms Custom Renderer, which is a platform-specific class for rendering platform-specific features on a Xamarin.Forms page. Hybridization can also happen within platform-specific Android activities and iOS view controllers that run alongside Xamarin.Forms pages, or within platform-specific classes that are called as-needed to handle native functionality such as location, camera, graphics, or animation. This sophisticated approach can lead to a more complex architecture, such as Figure 2-3, and must be handled carefully. Note the addition of the Platform-specific UI Layer.

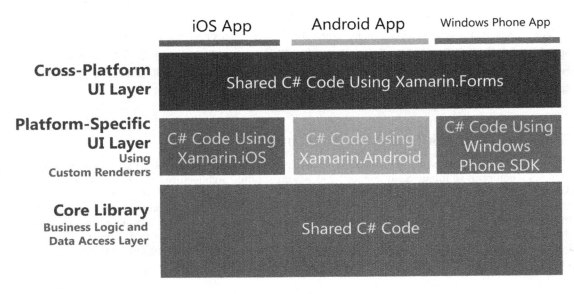

Figure 2-3. Xamarin.Forms architecture with custom renderers

> ■ **Note** Chapter 8 provides more on the use of custom renderers and platform-specific code in Xamarin. Forms solutions.

When are Xamarin.Forms appropriate to use and when do we consider other Xamarin options? I'll address this key question a bit later in the chapter, but first let's define Xamarin's platform-specific UI options.

Understanding the Platform-Specific UI Approach

Before Xamarin.Forms, there were the platform-specific (or native) UI options, which consist of the Xamarin.Android, Xamarin.iOS, and Windows Phone SDK libraries. Building screens using platform-specific UIs requires some understanding of the native UIs exposed by these libraries. We don't need to code directly in iOS UIKit or Android SDK, as we're one layer removed when using Xamarin bindings in C#. Using the Windows Phone SDK is, of course, coding natively in C# against the Windows Phone SDK, a C# library. The advantage of using Xamarin's platform-specific UIs is that these libraries are established and full-featured. Each native control and container class has a great many properties and methods, and the Xamarin bindings expose many of them out-of-the-box.

> ■ **Note** We're not talking about native UI development using Objective-C or Java here but use of Xamarin C# platform-specific bindings to native UI libraries. To avoid such confusion, this book favors the term *platform-specific* over *native* when referring to Xamarin libraries but Xamarin developers will sometimes use the term *native* to refer to the use of platform-specific libraries Xamarin.iOS and Xamarin.Android.

Platform-specific UI Solution Architecture

Figure 2-4 shows how a platform-specific solution designed to be cross-platform shares C# application code containing the business logic and data access layer, just like a Xamarin.Forms solution. The UI layer is another story: It's all platform-specific. UI C# code in these projects uses classes that are bound directly to the native API: iOS, Android, or the Windows Phone API directly sans binding.

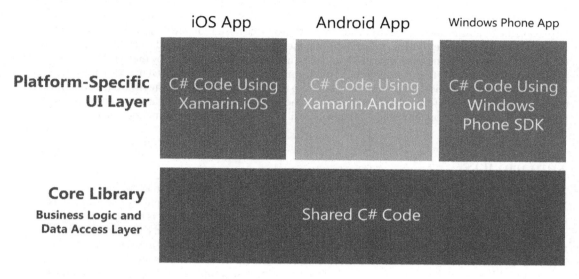

Figure 2-4. *Platform-specific UI solution architecture*

If you compare this diagram to the Xamarin.Forms diagram in Figure 2-2, you'll see that there's a lot more coding to be done here: a UI for every platform as opposed to one for all. Why would anyone bother to do it this way? There are quite a few good reasons why some or even all of the code might be done better this way. To address the burning question *Which do I use, Xamarin.Forms or Xamarin platform-specific UIs?*, see the section "Choosing Xamarin.Forms or a Platform-Specific UI" later in this chapter.

But first let's delve into the Android and iOS bindings and then look at the Windows Phone SDK.

Xamarin.Android

The Xamarin.Android C# bindings tie us into the Android API. Android apps are made up of layouts and activities, roughly translated as views and controllers. Layouts are typically XML files (.axml) edited using a UI designer that define the controls displayed on a screen. An `Activity` is a class that typically manages the life cycle of a single layout, although smaller layouts, called fragments, can be combined to comprise a screen.

Controls are called *views* in Android-ese: `Buttons`, `TextViews`, `ListViews`, and so forth. We place these on another kind of layout, controls that contain controls, which work like `<div>` in HTML: `LinearLayout`, `RelativeLayout`, `FrameLayout`, and `WebViews`. These layouts, inherited from the `ViewGroup` class are assembled manually or generated dynamically using data-binding classes called *adapters*. Inheriting from `AdapterView`, widgets such as `ListView` and `GridView` are populated by data-binding.

■ **Note** Android parlance uses "layout" to mean two different things: an XML file containing a UI screen (.axml) and a container control that houses and formats other controls, such as LinearLayout.

There are two ways to build Android layouts: using XML resource files or coding them in C# by hand. XML files (.axml) are highly readable and elegant, which encourages direct editing of the XML code, even when also using the Xamarin Designer for Android, the XML resource file editor. Most mobile developers prefer Android XML resource files (.axml) to hand-coding the UI in C#. Coding Android UI by hand in C# is not as comfortable, because the necessary methods and parameters have been deemed by the developer community to be clumsy and difficult to use. Additionally, most online examples of Android UI use XML resource files, even in the Xamarin online documentation. Those are the reasons that most of the Android development community is using XML for UI development. This practice has extended to the Xamarin development community, not to mention that using XML resource files is the Xamarin-recommended method.

Xamarin.iOS

The Xamarin.iOS C# bindings hook us up with the iOS native UI API, called UIKit. Views and ViewControllers are the equivalent of views and controllers in iOS. Views are typically constructed using a designer tool and result in an XML file (.xib or .storyboard). ViewController is a controller class that manages the views. In iOS we work with layers: tab bar view, navigation view, and images overlaying our main view, all nested inside a UIWindow. Controls include UILabel, UIButton, UITextField, and UISlider. These controls reside in a view class called UIView, which is inherited to create useful data-bound views such as UITableView for lists and UICollectionView for grids and groupings. iOS layouts are built using a technique called *AutoLayout*, based on constraints between views that move and size dynamically depending on the display context. The older layout approach, *AutoSizing*, involves creating frames and masking them, also called *springs and struts*. This is all part of UIKit, the development framework of the iOS user interface.

■ **Tip** Why the UI in UILabel, UIButton, UIThis, and UIThat? iOS's Objective-C has no namespaces, so they are concatenated with the class name.

There are two ways to build screens in iOS: the first is using a designer tool, such as the Xamarin Designer for iOS or the Xcode Interface Builder, and the second is hand-coding in C#. The designer tools create a storyboard XML file or .xib (pronounced and written: *nib*), and hand-coding is done straight in the iOS view-controller C# classes (these are then called *nib-less views*). Storyboards and nibs are sometimes difficult to read. This tightly couples them to the tools we use to construct them and discourages manual editing. Nibs are useful for simple forms such as modals and login pages, and the storyboard is the workhorse for prototyping, complex transitions, and multiple interconnected pages. Dynamic data-binding, data flow between pages, and visual effects and complexity are often best accomplished with hand-coded C#.

■ **Important Tip** The focus of this book is Xamarin.Forms and cross-platform code-first development with some of the most useful platform-specific techniques available. That's a lot to cover in one book, so the discussion of some Android and iOS basics and all designer tools is out of scope. *If you're doing platform-specific development on Android or iOS for the first time, you'll need to consult additional sources.* See the Introduction of this book for Prerequisites and consult the Xamarin, Google, and Apple online docs or one of the many fine platform-specific books to fill you in.

Windows Phone SDK

The Windows Phone SDK is a C# library with a built-in .NET API. Screens are defined by Frame classes that handle navigation and contain pages, loaded and unloaded like conventional views. Within these are layout containers called *panels*, such as Canvas for absolute positioning, and StackPanel and Grid for relative layout with autosizing. There are familiar controls such as TextBox for editing and TextBlock for labels, and Button, Image, and MediaElement for videos and music. For lists there is LongListSelector and the older ListBox. We build the UI using C#, XAML, Blend, and/or the Visual Studio UI designer.

■ **Tip** Because the Windows Phone SDK is already using C# and .NET, the Xamarin platform is not necessary to code a Windows Phone app in C#. Cross-platform development is the primary consideration that brings Xamarin together with Windows Phone: A Xamarin.Forms app can run on a Windows Phone.

Xamarin.Forms currently supports Windows Phone Silverlight, WinRT and Windows Store support have been announced.

Choosing Xamarin.Forms or a Platform-Specific UI

As developers, we are faced with this decision:

Which do I use, Xamarin.Forms or a Xamarin platform-specific UI?

The trade-off is portability of Xamarin.Forms versus the full-featured functionality of Xamarin's platform-specific UIs, namely Xamarin.Android and Xamarin.iOS. At the time of this writing, the platform-specific Xamarin APIs have considerably more features than Xamarin.Forms. The answer to our question will range from one, to the other, to both, depending on your needs. Here are suggested guidelines:

Use Xamarin.Forms for the following:

Learning Xamarin: If you're new to mobile development using C# then Xamarin. Forms is a great way to get started!

Cross-platform scaffolding: When building cross-platform apps, Xamarin.Forms is useful to build out the scaffolding of your app, as a rapid-application development toolset.

Basic Business Apps: Xamarin.Forms does these things well: basic data display, navigation, and data entry. This is a good fit for many business apps.

Basic design: Xamarin.Forms provides controls with baseline design features, facilitating basic visual formatting.

Simple cross-platform screens: Xamarin.Forms is great for creating fully functional basic screens. For more complex screens, leverage Xamarin.Forms custom renderers for platform-specific details.

Use a platform-specific UI (Xamarin.iOS or Xamarin.Android) for:

Complex screens: When an entire screen (or an entire app) requires a nuanced and complex design and UI approach, and Xamarin.Forms isn't quite up to the task, go with a platform-specific UI using Xamarin.Android and Xamarin.iOS.

Consumer Apps: Platform-specific UI has everything a developer needs to create a consumer app with complex visual design, nuanced gesture sensitivity, and high-end graphics and animation.

High-design: This approach provides complete native UI APIs with low-level access to design properties on each control, allowing for a high visual standard of design. Native animation and graphics are also available with this approach.

Single-platform apps: If you're building for only one platform, and a cross-platform approach for your app is not important in the foreseeable future (a rare case even if you're starting with one platform), consider using a platform-specific UI.

Unsupported platforms: Mac OS X, Windows Store, and WinRT apps are not currently supported by Xamarin.Forms at this time.

However, Xamarin moves fast, and these recommendations are likely to change. Here's how: With each new release of Xamarin.Forms, more properties and methods will be included in the bindings, bringing this library closer to the platform-specific ones and giving us increased control over our cross-platform UI. Also, third-party vendors and open source projects such as Xamarin Forms Labs are swiftly extending the options available with added controls, charts, and datagrids. Currently, there is no visual designer for Xamarin. Forms, but I expect there will be one soon.

When complex tasks or high design are required by Xamarin.Forms, virtually anything is possible using Custom Renderers.

Use Both Approaches with Custom Renderers

Custom Renderers provide access to the lower-level, platform-specific, screen-rendering classes called Renderers, which use platform-specific controls to create all Xamarin.Forms screens. Any Xamarin. Forms screen can be broken into platform-specific screens and classes using this approach. This means we can write a Xamarin.Forms page or app, and customize it by platform whenever necessary. More about this in Chapter 8.

Use Custom Renderers sparingly, or risk a fragmented UI code base that probably should have been written entirely as a platform-specific UI.

In each of the following chapters, we will explore the Xamarin.Forms options and then examine platform-specific implementations of the same functionality. You will be able to see how they compare at the time of this writing and how to use them together using custom renderers. As time marches on, Xamarin.Forms may progress from a scaffolding technology to fully featured building blocks for cross-platform apps. If it does not, or until it does, the platform-specific approach will remain necessary to build highly functional apps without heavy reliance on Xamarin.Forms custom renderers.

Yesterday's award-winning Xamarin apps were created using the platform-specific approach, but the key question is, What will *you* create today?

Let's explore the building blocks of the C# mobile user interface.

Exploring the Elements of Mobile UIs

Xamarin is a unifying tool serving several platforms, many of which can have different names for the same things. Here are some unifying terms, weighted heavily in the direction of Xamarin.Forms:

> *Screens, views, or pages in mobile apps are made up of several basic groups of components*: pages, layouts, and controls. Pages can be full or partial screens or groups of controls. In Xamarin.Forms, these are called pages because they derive from the Page class. In iOS, they are views; and in Android, they're screens, layouts, or sometimes loosely referred to as activities.

> *Controls are the individual UI elements we use to display information or provide selection or navigation. Xamarin.Forms calls these views, because a* View *is the class that controls inherit from. Certain controls are called widgets in Android. More on these shortly and in Chapter 4.*

> *Layouts are containers for controls that determine their size, placement, and relationship to one another. Xamarin.Forms and Android use this term, while in iOS everything is a view. More on this in Chapter 3.*

> *Lists, typically scrollable and selectable, are one of the most important data display and selection tools in the mobile UI. More on these in Chapter 5.*

> *Navigation provides the user with a way to traverse the app by using menus, tabs, toolbars, lists, tappable icons, and the up and back buttons. More on this in Chapter 6.*

> *Modals, dialog boxes, and alerts are usually popup screens that provide information and require some response from the user. More on these in Chapter 6.*

Now that we have context and some terminology to work with, let's get started with Xamarin.Forms!

Using the Xamarin.Forms UI

Pages, layouts, and views make up the core of the Xamarin.Forms UI (Figure 2-5). Pages are the primary container, and each screen is populated by a single Page class. A page may contain variations of the Layout class, which may then hold other layouts, used for placing and sizing their contents. The purpose of pages and layouts is to contain and present views, which are controls inherited from class View.

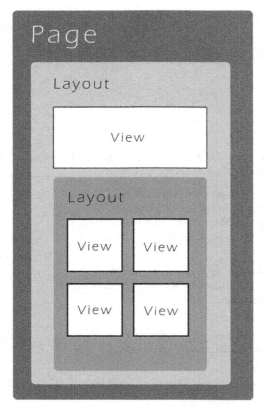

Figure 2-5. *Page, layouts, and views on a Xamarin.Forms screen*

Page

The Page class is the primary container of each main screen in the app. Derived from Xamarin.Forms.VisualElement, Page is a base class for the creation of other top-level UI classes. Here are the primary pages:

- ContentPage
- MasterDetailPage
- NavigationPage
- TabbedPage
- CarouselPage

In addition to serving as containers for layouts and views, pages provide a rich menu of prefabricated screens with useful functionality that includes navigation and gesture responsiveness. More on these in Chapters 6.

Layout

Views are placed and sized by their container class, Layout. Layouts come in a variety of flavors with different features for formatting their views. These containers allow views to be formatted precisely, loosely, absolute to the coordinate system, or relative to one another. Layouts are the soft tissue of the page, the cartilage that holds together the solid, visible aspects of the page(views). Here are the main layouts:

- StackLayout
- AbsoluteLayout
- RelativeLayout
- Grid
- ScrollView
- Frame
- ContentView

The layout's Content and/or Children properties contain other layouts and views. Horizontal and vertical alignment is set by the properties HorizontalOptions and VerticalOptions. Rows, columns, and cells within a layout can be padded with space, sized to expand to fill available space, or shrunk to fit their content. More on layouts in the next chapter.

■ **Tip** Xamarin.Forms layouts are derived from the View class, so everything contained by a page is actually some form of a view.

View

Views are controls, the visible and interactive elements on a page. These range from the basic views like buttons, labels, and text boxes to the more advanced views like lists and navigation. Views contain properties that determine their content, font, color, and alignment. Horizontal and vertical alignment is set by properties HorizontalOptions and VerticalOptions. Like layouts, views can be padded with space, sized to expand to fill available space, or shrunk to fit their content. Later in this chapter, we'll code some views, then visit them again in Chapter 4 and throughout the book. These are the primary views grouped by function:

- Basic – fundamental views
  - Label
  - Image
  - Button
  - BoxView
- List – make a scrollable, selectable list
  - ListView
- Text Entry – user entry of text strings using a keyboard
  - Entry
  - Editor

- Selection – user choice of a wide range of fields
  - `Picker`
  - `DatePicker`
  - `TimePicker`
  - `Stepper`
  - `Slider`
  - `Switch`
- User Feedback – notify the user of app processing status
  - `ActivityIndicator`
  - `ProgressBar`

■ **Tip**   Be careful not to confuse the Xamarin.Forms `View` class with a view meaning screen or presentation layer. Also, iOS refers to screens as views.

Creating a Xamarin.Forms Solution

XAMARIN.FORMS

Xamarin provides templates that contain the necessary projects to create a Xamarin.Forms app. A cross-platform solution usually contains these projects:

> *Xamarin.Forms*: Cross-platform UI code called by one of the platform-specific projects. This can be accomplished using a shared project, Portable Class Library (PCL), or shared files. The example we'll be creating in this chapter uses a PCL.

> *Xamarin.Android*: Android-specific code, including Android project startup.

> *Xamarin.iOS*: iOS-specific code, including iOS project startup.

> *Windows Phone application*: Windows Phone–specific code, including Windows Phone project startup.

> *Core Library*: Shared app logic such as business logic and data access layer using a PCL, or a shared project.

Figure 2-6 shows the main projects usually found in a Xamarin.Forms solution.

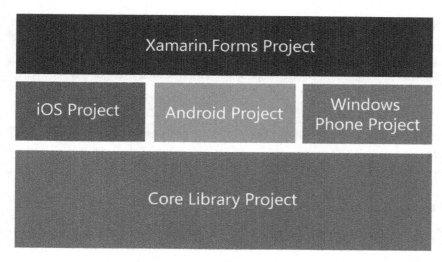

Figure 2-6. Xamarin.Forms solution

■ **Tip** The Core Library project is not added by solution templates and must be created manually, either as a shared project or PCL. If you are just getting started with Xamarin. Forms you can skip the core library for now and put all your shared files in the Xamarin.Forms project.

Let's create a simple demo app to help us explore the foundations of Xamarin.Forms and many of its commonly-used features.

Create a Xamarin.Forms solution. In Visual Studio, create a New Solution and select project type C# ➤ Mobile Apps ➤ Blank App (Xamarin.Forms Portable). In Xamarin Studio, select project type C# ➤ Mobile Apps ➤ Blank App (Xamarin.Forms Portable). Name it FormsExample.

This will create multiple projects: one for Xamarin.Forms code, and then platform-specific projects including Android, iOS, and/or Windows Phone. The platform-specific projects available depend on whether you're on a PC or a Mac, whether you're in Visual Studio or Xamarin Studio, and the licenses you own. A Mac with Xamarin Studio will give you an iOS project and an Android project. A PC with Xamarin Studio will give you Android. Solutions created in Xamarin Studio do *not* include a Windows Phone project, as Visual Studio is required to create that project, though projects created in Visual Studio can be browsed in Xamarin Studio without being compiled there. A PC with Visual Studio with both iOS and Android licenses activated will create four projects: one PCL and one for each of the three platforms.

■ **Tip** Xamarin.Forms is currently available with all licenses except the Starter license. You'll need an Indie or higher-level purchased license or trial license to use Xamarin.Forms.

More on PCLs, shared projects, and other cross-platform solution architecture options in Chapter 9.

The following sections provide each of the projects in the solution and the code they contain.

Xamarin.Forms Shared Code

When using Visual Studio, the Xamarin.Forms shared code project contains App.cs (Listing 2-1), which defines and returns the main page of the app. Xamarin.Forms 1.3 introduced the Application object which serves as the base class of App and provides the MainPage property as well as life cycle events OnStart, OnSleep, and OnResume.

■ **Tip** When using Xamarin Studio, the name of the file in Listing 2-1 is the same as your project name, FormsExample.cs in this case.

Listing 2-1. App.cs in the FormsExample project

```
namespace FormsExample
{
    public class App : Application
    {
        public App()
        {
            MainPage = new ContentPage
            {
                Content = new StackLayout
                {
                    VerticalOptions = LayoutOptions.Center,
                    Children = {
                        new Label {
                            XAlign = TextAlignment.Center,
                            Text = "Welcome to Xamarin Forms!"
                        }
                    }
                }
            };
        }

        protected override void OnStart()
        {
        }

        protected override void OnSleep()
        {
        }

        protected override void OnResume()
        {
        }
    }
}
```

Each platform-specific project creates an instance of App to set the main page, in this case a ContentPage object with its Content property populated with a friendly Label, centered horizontally and vertically. The Content property only holds one child view. Multiple views must be contained within a child Layout, a container for views, or using a ContentPage. The MainPage property is set to the root page of the application using an inline ContentPage class.

Soon we will replace this ContentPage with our own ContentPage class and place controls on it.

■ **Tip** A static Application.Current property references the current application object anywhere in your app.

The OnStart, OnSleep, and OnResume method overrides created for us are used to manage our app when it is moved to and from the background.

Application Lifecycle Methods: OnStart, OnSleep, and OnResume

When the user clicks the Back or Home (or App Switcher) buttons on their device, an app moves into the background. When they reselect the app again, it resumes and moves back into the foreground. The starting of an app, the progression of the app from the foreground into a background state then back into the foreground again, until termination, is called the application *lifecycle*. The Application class includes three virtual methods to handle lifecycle events:

- **OnStart** – Called when the app is first started
- **OnSleep** – Called each time the app is moved into the background
- **OnResume** – Called when the app is resumed after being in the background

OnSleep is also used for normal application termination (not a crash). Any time an app moves into a background state, it must be assumed that it may never return from that state.

■ **Tip** Use the Properties dictionary for disk persistence in these methods when an app is backgrounded. See Chapter 6 for more on State Management.

Building Pages Using ContentPage

The ContentPage class in App.cs (Listing 2-1), inherited from Xamarin.Forms.Page, is the generic page used in Xamarin.Forms when a page is custom-built. It contains one child, assigned to its Content property, such as the preceding Label. Placing multiple controls on a ContentPage requires the use of a custom class inherited from ContentPage, which contains a container such as a Layout.

ContentPage has properties that affect the appearance of the page. The Padding property creates space around the margins of the page to improve readability and design. BackgroundImage can contain an image that is displayed on the background of the page.

Several of ContentPage's members are useful for navigation and state management. The Title property contains text and the Icon property contains an image that display at the top of the page when NavigationPage is implemented. Lifecycle methods OnAppearing and OnDisappearing can be overridden to handle initialization and finalization of a ContentPage. The ToolBarItems property is useful for creating a drop-down menu. All of these navigation-related members are covered in Chapter 6.

Xamarin.Android

ANDROID

The Android project contains a startup file called `MainActivity.cs`, which defines an activity class inherited from `Xamarin.Forms.Platform.Android.FormsApplicationActivity` as seen in Listing 2-2.

Listing 2-2. MainActivity.cs in the FormsExample.Droid project

```
namespace FormsExample.Droid
{
    [Activity(Label = "FormsExample", Icon = "@drawable/icon", MainLauncher = true,
     ConfigurationChanges = ConfigChanges.ScreenSize | ConfigChanges.Orientation)]
    public class MainActivity : global::Xamarin.Forms.Platform.Android.
    FormsApplicationActivity
    {
        protected override void OnCreate(Bundle bundle)
        {
            base.OnCreate(bundle);
            global::Xamarin.Forms.Forms.Init(this, bundle);
            LoadApplication(new App());
        }
    }
}
```

In the `OnCreate` method, Xamarin.Forms is initialized and `LoadApplication` sets App as the current page.

Xamarin.iOS

iOS

The iOS project contains a startup file called `AppDelegate` (Listing 2-3) which inherits from `Xamarin.Forms.Platform.iOS.FormsApplicationDelegate`.

Listing 2-3. AppDelegate.cs in the FormsExample.iOS project

```
namespace FormsExample.iOS
{
    [Register("AppDelegate")]
    public partial class AppDelegate : global::Xamarin.Forms.Platform.iOS.
    FormsApplicationDelegate
    {
        public override bool FinishedLaunching(UIApplication app, NSDictionary options)
        {
            global::Xamarin.Forms.Forms.Init();
            LoadApplication(new App());
            return base.FinishedLaunching(app, options);
        }
    }
}
```

Xamarin.Forms is initialized in the `Init()` method and `LoadApplication` sets App as the current page.

Windows Phone Application

WINDOWS

The Windows Phone project contains a `Mainpage.xaml.cs` class (Listing 2-4) which inherits from `Xamarin.Forms.Platform.WinPhone.FormsApplicationPage`:

Listing 2-4. MainPage.xaml.cs in the WinPhone project

```
namespace FormsExample.WinPhone
{
    public partial class MainPage : global::Xamarin.Forms.Platform.WinPhone.
    FormsApplicationPage
    {
        public MainPage()
        {
            InitializeComponent();
            SupportedOrientations = SupportedPageOrientation.PortraitOrLandscape;
            global::Xamarin.Forms.Forms.Init();
            LoadApplication(new FormsExample.App());
        }
    }
}
```

Xamarin.Forms is initialized in the `Init()` method and `LoadApplication` sets Xamarin.Forms App as the current page.

■ **Note** Since Windows Phone applications have their own App class, use of the application namespace is good practice when referencing the Xamarin.Forms App object.

Windows Phone apps also require a reference in the `MainPage.xaml`.

```
<winPhone:FormsApplicationPage
    ...
    xmlns:winPhone="clr-
    namespace:Xamarin.Forms.Platform.WinPhone;assembly=Xamarin.Forms.Platform.WP8"
    ... >
</winPhone:FormsApplicationPage>
```

All three of our platform-specific initializers, the Android `MainActivity` the iOS `AppDelegate`, and the Windows Phone `MainPage` get the starting page from the Xamarin.Forms App class, which, by default, returns a stubbed demo page.

Core Library

The core library is a project in a Xamarin.Forms solution for the business and/or data layer of an app which should be largely platform independent. Although *not explicitly created* as part of the Xamarin.Forms solution templates, a core library project is standard practice. Create one yourself and add it to your solution. This can contain data models, shared files or resources, data access, business logic, or references to PCLs. This is the place for platform-independent middle-tier or back-end non-UI code. It is referenced by any or all of the other projects in the solution. Use it to optimize code reuse and to decouple the UI projects from the data source and business logic.

Now we need to build out the pages of our app. Time to code!

Setting the App's Main Page

XAMARIN.FORMS

First we create a custom page in the Xamarin.Forms core project and set it to be the app's main page. Create a class inherited from `ContentPage` and call it `ContentPageExample`:

```
namespace FormsExample
{
    class ContentPageExample : ContentPage
    {
        public ContentPageExample()
        {
        // views/controls will go here
```

Then back in the Xamarin.Forms `App.cs`, we update the App constructor to set an instance of our new `ContentPageExample` class as the `MainPage`:

```
namespace FormsExample
{
    public class App : Application
    {
        public App()
        {
            MainPage = new ContentPageExample();
        }
```

Now we have the custom page class ready and can load up our `ContentPageExample` constructor with controls.

Adding Xamarin.Forms Views

XAMARIN.FORMS

View is the term for *control* in Xamarin.Forms, the smallest unit of UI construction. Most views inherit from the View class and provide basic UI functions, such as a label or a button. From this point on, we will use the terms *view* and *control* interchangeably.

■ **Tip** All example code solutions, *including the XAML versions of these C# examples*, can be found under the title of this book on Apress.com in the Source Code/Downloads tab, or on GitHub at https://github.com/danhermes/xamarin-book-examples.

Let's start simply and put some views into the ContentPageExample class.

Label View

Labels display single or multiline text. Here are some examples:

```
Label labelLarge = new Label
{
    Text = "Label",
    FontSize = 40,
    HorizontalOptions = LayoutOptions.Center
};

Label labelSmall = new Label
{
    Text = "This control is great for\n" +
            "displaying one or more\n" +
            "lines of text.",
    FontSize = 20,
    HorizontalOptions = LayoutOptions.CenterAndExpand
};
```

Multiline text happens *implicitly* when enough text is used that it wraps, or *explicitly* when specifying line breaks with \n.

A Label view has two types of alignment, view-justification and text-justification. The entire view is justified within a layout using the HorizonalOptions and VerticalOptions properties assigned using LayoutOptions. Label text is justified within a Label using Label's XAlign and YAlign properties, where XAlign sets the horizontal and YAlign sets the vertical justification of text.

```
XAlign = TextAlignment.End
```

The TextAlignment enumeration has three values: Start, Center, and End. In this example we use the defaults.

Next, the labels must be assigned to a layout for placement on the page.

Placing Views Using StackLayout
XAMARIN.FORMS

A Layout view acts as a container for other views. Since a ContentPage can have only one child, all the views on our page must be placed in a single container that is made the child of the ContentPage. Here we employ StackLayout, a subclass of Layout that can "stack" child views vertically:

```
StackLayout stackLayout = new StackLayout
{
    Children =
    {
        labelLarge,
        labelSmall
    },
    HeightRequest = 1500
};
```

We place all the child views onto the parent view by using the Children property of this StackLayout and set the requested height with HeightRequest.   HeightRequest has been set larger than the visible page so later we can make it scroll.

■ **Note**   StackLayout child views are laid vertically unless horizontal order is specified using
Orientation = StackOrientation.Vertical.

To get the StackLayout to display on our page, we must assign it to the Content property of the ContentPage:

```
this.Content = stackLayout;
```

Compile and run the code. Figure 2-7 shows our labels on the StackLayout for iOS, Android, and Windows Phone, respectively.

If you're using iOS and want your Xamarin.Forms projects to look more like examples in this book that have a black background and white text, or you're using another platform and want more of an iOS look, setting background color and font color can help you.

Figure 2-7. *Xamarin.Forms* `Labels` *on a* `StackLayout`

Background Color and Font Color

XAMARIN.FORMS

Page background color and view font color can be changed using the `ContentPage's` `BackgroundColor` property and the `TextColor` property found on text-based `Views`.

If you are working on an iOS project and want your work to look more like the book examples with black backgrounds, add this line to your page:

```
this.BackgroundColor = Color.Black;
```

If you want it to look more classically iOS then set it to `Color.White`.

Text color will then be set automatically to a lighter color. However, you can control text color manually on text controls with the `TextColor` property.

```
TextColor = Color.White,
```

We use fonts in many controls, so let's do a quick overview of those.

Using Fonts

XAMARIN.FORMS

Format text on controls by using these properties:

> *FontFamily*: Set the name of the font in the `FontFamily` property, otherwise, the default system font will be used. For example, `label.FontFamily = "Courier";`

> *FontSize*: The font size and weight are specified in the `FontSize` property using a double value or a `NamedSize` enumeration. Here is an example using a double: `label.FontSize = 40;`. Set a relative size by using `NamedSize` values such as `NamedSize.Large`, using `NamedSize` members `Large`, `Medium`, `Small`, and `Micro`. For example, `button.FontSize = Device.GetNamedSize (NamedSize.Large, typeof(Button));`

> *FontAttributes*: Font styles such as bold and italics are specified using the `FontAttributes` property. Single attributes are set like this: `label.FontAttributes = FontAttributes.Bold`. `FontAttribute` options are `None`, `Bold`, and `Italic`. Multiple attributes are concatenated using the "|", for example, `label.FontAttributes = FontAttributes.Bold | FontAttributes.Italic;`

■ **Tip**   Some controls support the use of different `FontAttributes` on different parts of a string using the `FormattedString` class.

■ **Note**   The `FontSize` property using `NamedSizeo` can be declared two ways:

1.   `button.FontSize = Device.GetNamedSize (NamedSize.Large, `***button***`);`

2.   `button.FontSize = Device.GetNamedSize (NamedSize.Large, `***typeof(Button)***`);`

Use the second one for inline declarations.

Using Platform-Specific Fonts

XAMARIN.FORMS

Make sure your font name will work for all your target platforms, or your page may fail mysteriously. If you need different font names per platform, use the `Device.OnPlatform` method, which sets the a value according to the platform, like this:

```
label.FontFamily = Device.OnPlatform (
    iOS:      " Courier",
    Android:  "Droid Sans Mono",
    WinPhone: " Courier New"
);

label.FontSize = Device.OnPlatform (
    30,
    Device.GetNamedSize (NamedSize.Medium, label),
    Device.GetNamedSize (NamedSize.Large, label)
);
```

■ **Tip**   Using `Device.OnPlatform` is a handy cross-platform trick that returns a platform-specific value.

Custom fonts loaded at runtime can also be used but this requires platform-specific coding covered in the Xamarin.Forms online docs in section Working With... ➤ Fonts(1.3).

Button View

XAMARIN.FORMS

Xamarin.Forms buttons are rectangular and clickable.

Let's add a plain ole button:

```
Button button = new Button
{
    Text = "Make It So",
    FontSize = Device.GetNamedSize(NamedSize.Large, typeof(Button)),
    HorizontalOptions = LayoutOptions.Center,
    VerticalOptions = LayoutOptions.Fill
};
```

The Text property contains the text visible on the button. HorizontalOptions and VerticalOptions (discussed in the next section) determine the control's alignment and size. This NamedSize font setting makes the font Large.

■ **Tip** Buttons can be customized using the BorderColor, BorderWidth, and TextColor properties. The BorderWidth is defaulted to zero on iOS.

Add the button to our StackLayout.

```
StackLayout stackLayout = new StackLayout
{
    Children =
    {
        labelLarge,
        labelSmall,
        button
    },
    HeightRequest = 1500
};
```

Figure 2-8 shows the new button.

Figure 2-8. *Xamarin.Forms Button*

Now let's assign an event handler, either inline:

```
button.Clicked += (sender, args) =>
{
    button.Text = "It is so!";
};
```

Or by assigning a method:

```
button.Clicked += OnButtonClicked;
```

…which is called outside the page constructor:

```
void OnButtonClicked(object sender, EventArgs e)
    {
        button.Text = "It is so!";
    };
```

When you click the button the button text changes, as in Figure 2-9.

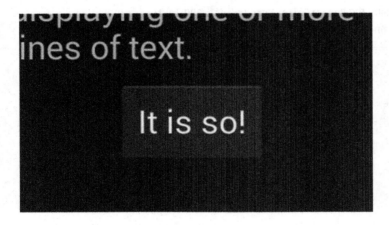

Figure 2-9. `button.Clicked` *event fired*

■ **Tip**   If you assign an event handler outside the page constructor, be sure to also define your button outside the constructor to avoid a *variable undefined* error.

BorderWidth assigns the weight of the line that draws the button.

Setting View Alignment and Size: HorizontalOptions and VerticalOptions

XAMARIN.FORMS

Horizontal and vertical alignment and, to a certain degree, the size of controls are managed by setting the HorizontalOptions and/or VerticalOptions properties to a value of the LayoutOptions class, for example:

```
Button button = new Button
{
HorizontalOptions = LayoutOptions.Center,
    VerticalOptions = LayoutOptions.Fill
}
```

Considerations in view layout are the *space provided* to the view by the layout and surrounding elements, the *padding* space around the view, and the *size* of the view itself. These types of formatting are accomplished using LayoutOptions and AndExpand.

Justification with LayoutOptions

Individual control layout is defined along a single axis by setting the HorizontalOptions or VerticalOptions property to one of the LayoutOptions classes:

- Start left or top-justifies the control (depending upon layout Orientation).
- Center centers the control.
- End right or bottom-justifies the control.
- Fill expands the size of the control to fill the space provided.

For example:

```
HorizontalOptions = LayoutOptions.Start,
```

AndExpand Pads with Space

Setting HorizontalOptions or VerticalOptions to these LayoutOptions classes provides padding space around the view:

- StartAndExpand left or top-justifies the control and pads around the control with space.
- CenterAndExpand centers the control and pads around the control with space.
- EndAndExpand right or bottom-justifies the control and pads around the control with space.
- FillAndExpand expands the size of the control and pads around the control with space.

For example:

```
HorizontalOptions = LayoutOptions.StartAndExpand
```

■ **Tip** HorizontalOptions set to Fill and FillandExpand look the same with a single control in a column.

■ **Tip** VerticalOptions set to Center or Fill is useful only if vertical space has been explicitly provided. Otherwise, these options can appear to do nothing. LayoutOptions.Fill won't make your control taller if there's no space to grow.

■ **Tip** VerticalOptions set to Expand and CenterAndExpand imposes padding space around a control in a StackLayout.

There are more formatting examples later in this chapter and a lot more on the topic of control layout and alignment in Chapter 3. Next let's create some user input.

Entry View for Text Input

XAMARIN.FORMS

The following code creates a text box for user entry of a single line of text. Entry inherits from the InputView class, a derivative of the View class.

```
Entry entry = new Entry
{
    Placeholder = "Username",
    VerticalOptions = LayoutOptions.Center,
    Keyboard = Keyboard.Text
};
```

User input goes into the Text property as a String.

Note the use of the Placeholder property, an inline label for the name of the field and a common technique in the mobile UI often preferable to space-consuming labels placed above or beside the entry control. The Keyboard property is a member of InputView and provides a range of options for the onscreen keyboard that appears for input, including Text, Numeric, Telephone, URL, and Email. Remember to add the entry to our StackLayout (see Listing 2-5 later in the chapter). Figure 2-10 shows the new entry control for username.

Figure 2-10. *Xamarin.Forms User Entry view*

■ **Tip** Use the `IsPassword` property to replace entered text letters with dots.

For multiline entry, use the `Editor` control.

BoxView

XAMARIN.FORMS

The `BoxView` control creates a colored graphical rectangle, useful as a placeholder that can be later replaced by an image or other more complex control or group of controls. This control is useful when you're waiting on the designer to get his/her act together.

```
BoxView boxView = new BoxView
{
    Color = Color.Silver,
    WidthRequest = 150,
    HeightRequest = 150,
    HorizontalOptions = LayoutOptions.StartAndExpand,
    VerticalOptions = LayoutOptions.Fill
};
```

The `Color` property can be set to any `Color` member value. The default dimensions are 40×40 pixels, which can be changed using the `WidthRequest` and `HeightRequest` properties.

■ **Tip** Be careful when setting `HorizontalOptions` and `VerticalOptions` to `LayoutOptions.Fill` and `LayoutOptions.FillAndExpand`, as this can override your `HeightRequest` and `WidthRequest` dimensions.

Add the BoxView to your StackLayout (see Listing 2-5 later in the chapter) and see the result here in Figure 2-11.

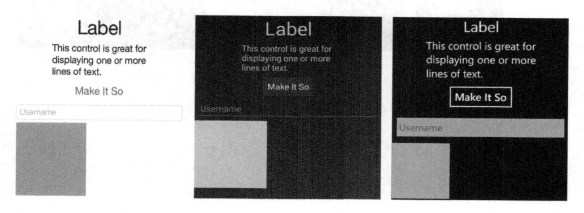

Figure 2-11. *Xamarin.Forms BoxView*

Eventually your designer will give you those promised icons and you can replace your BoxViews with real images.

Image View

XAMARIN.FORMS

The Image view holds an image for display on your page from a local or online file:

```
Image image = new Image
{
    Source = "monkey.png",
    Aspect = Aspect.AspectFit,
    HorizontalOptions = LayoutOptions.End,
    VerticalOptions = LayoutOptions.Fill
};
```

Figure 2-12 shows the monkey image at the bottom right.

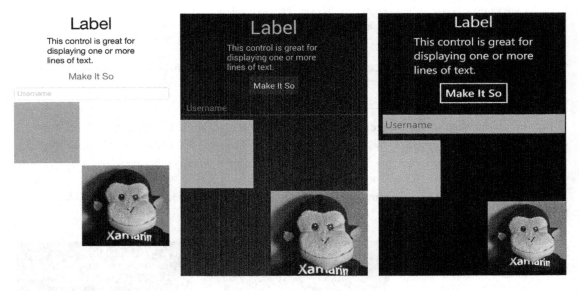

Figure 2-12. *Image view*

Let's look at how an image is handled.

Source Property

The Source property denotes the location of the image by using these ImageSource class members:

FromFile: Local image file, for example, ImageSource.FromFile("monkey.png"). The shortcut for this method when assigning the Source is to leave off the method altogether: Source = "monkey.png"

FromResource: Resource ID to an EmbeddedResource in the app or PCL, for example, ImageSource.FromResource("monkey.png").

FromUri: Online image's URI, for example, ImageSource.FromUri((new Uri(http://yourdomain.com/image.png))

■ **Tip**   You can use a FromFile shortcut to assign a local image: Source = "monkey.png"

Local Images

Local image files have platform-specific image folders in their respective projects:

Android: In the Resources/drawable folder. Don't use special characters in the filename. The Build Action must be set to Android Resource.

iOS: In the /Resources folder. Provide images for Retina displays as well, double resolution with @2x suffix on the filename before the extension. The Build Action must be set to BundleResource.

Windows Phone: In the Windows Phone project root directory. The Build Action must be set to Content.

Set Build Actions to configure images to compile properly by right-clicking image files in the project.

Image Sizing: Aspect Property

The Image.Aspect property determines image sizing and is set by using the Aspect enumerator—for example, image.Aspect = Aspect.AspectFit. These are the Aspect members:

AspectFill: Scale the image to fill the view, clipping if necessary.

AspectFit: Scale the image to fit within the view maintaining the aspect ratio with no distortion and leaving space if necessary (letterboxing).

Fill: Scale the image to fill the view entirely and exactly, possibly distorting the image.

Those are the image formatting options. Next we will make our image clickable.

Making an Image Clickable with a GestureRecognizer

Tappable images and icons are common in mobile applications for actions and navigation. Like many Xamarin.Forms views, the Image doesn't have a click or tap event and must be wired up using the GestureRecognizer class. A gesture recognizer is a class that can be added to many views to respond to user interaction. It currently supports just the tap gesture. The terms *click* and *tap* are used interchangeably in mobile UI development.

The standard gesture recognizer is declared and a handler is created to manage the Tapped event, then the gesture recognizer is added to the target view, an image in this case. Change the image's Opacity to .5 in the handler, which will fade the image slightly when tapped.

```
var tapGestureRecognizer = new TapGestureRecognizer();
tapGestureRecognizer.Tapped += (s, e) => {
    image.Opacity = .5;
};
image.GestureRecognizers.Add(tapGestureRecognizer);
```

Give that a try and make your monkey fade so you can see that the gesture recoginizer works.

■ **Tip** An alternative implementation of GestureRecognizer uses the Command property.

```
image.GestureRecognizers.Add (new TapGestureRecognizer {
    Command = new Command (()=> { /*handle tap*/ }),
});
```

User feedback is a crucial concept in mobile UI development. Any time a user does something in the UI there should be some subtle acknowledgment by the app. A tap, for instance, should respond to the user with visible feedback. Usually an image will gray out or have a white background for a sec when touched. Let's do that professionally using the image's Opacity property but adding async/await to create a slight delay in our fade without affecting the app's performance.

Replace the Tapped handler with this one that will cause the image to fade slightly for a fraction of a second. Remember to add using System.Threading.Tasks; to the top of your file for async/await.

```
tapGestureRecognizer.Tapped +=  async (sender, e) =>
{
    image.Opacity = .5;
    await Task.Delay(200);
    image.Opacity = 1;
};
```

Tapping on the image will now fade the image slightly, then back to normal, providing a responsive user experience.

In your own projects you'll use gesture recognizers (and async/await) to actually *do* something when an image is tapped. If you want to see async/await in action in this example, bump up the Delay to 2000, then click the "Make It So" button while it's awaiting and you'll see that the app is still responsive. You could do many things in this Tapped handler without interrupting the flow of the app! Often when a button or image is pressed, the result should be backgrounded using async/await for an optimal user experience.

■ **Tip** Async/await is a standard C# technique for queuing up activities in the background for simultaneous activity using the Task Parallel Library (TPL). Many Xamarin methods and functions are provisioned for background processing using `async/await`.

Finalizing the StackLayout

XAMARIN.FORMS

Now that we have our controls in place, let's pull this entire page together. Check that the stackLayout has all the views in it, as shown in Listing 2-5.

Listing 2-5. Final `StackLayout` for this chapter's Xamarin.Forms example in ContentPageExample.cs

```
StackLayout stackLayout = new StackLayout
{
    Children =
    {
        labelLarge,
        labelSmall,
        button,
        entry,
        boxView,
        image
    },
    HeightRequest = 1500
};
```

Now, we could keep our `stackLayout` assigned to `ContentPageExample.Content` and call that a page, but we have one more view to add, a container class to permit scrolling of our views.

ScrollView

XAMARIN.FORMS

The `ScrollView` layout contains a single child and imparts scrollability to its contents:

```
ScrollView scrollView = new ScrollView
{
    VerticalOptions = LayoutOptions.FillAndExpand,
    Content = stackLayout
};
```

Here we assign `stackLayout` to the `Content` property of this `ScrollView` so our entire layout of views will now be scrollable.

■ **Tip** `ScrollView` scrolls vertically by default but can also scroll sideways using the Orientation property. Ex. `Orientation = ScrollOrientation.Horizontal`

That's it for the views on this page. Now let's wire it up at the page level.

Assigning the ContentPage.Content Property

XAMARIN.FORMS

On the `ContentPage`, we must change the `Content` property assignment to the new container view, `scrollView`.

```
this.Content = scrollView;
```

The final touch will be padding around the entire page so views won't be mashed up against the sides of the screen.

Padding Around the Entire Page

XAMARIN.FORMS

The `ContentPage's` `Padding` property creates space around the entire page. Here's the property assignment:

```
this.Padding = new Thickness(left, top, right, bottom);
```

This example will place padding left, right, and bottom, but not top:

```
this.Padding = new Thickness(10, 0, 10, 5);
```

This will place equal space on all four sides:

```
this.Padding = new Thickness(10);
```

This example will slide a page just below the iOS status bar while keeping the page flush to the top of the screen for other OSes. The `Device.OnPlatform` method supplies different values or actions depending on the native OS (iOS, Android, WinPhone):

```
this.Padding = new Thickness(10, Device.OnPlatform(20, 0, 0), 10, 5);
```

This last `Padding` expression is what we use in this project and in most projects in this book.

Figure 2-13 shows a final build and run on all three platforms.

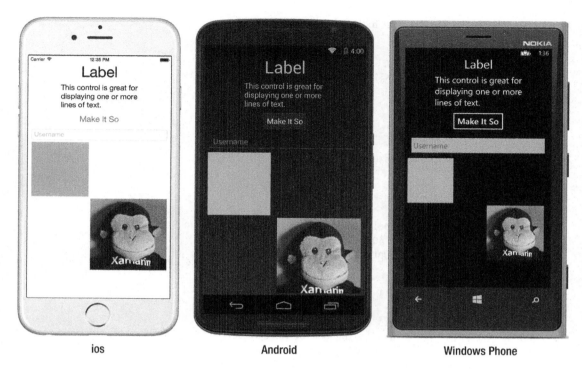

ios	Android	Windows Phone

Figure 2-13. *Final build and run of the FormsExample solution*

CODE COMPLETE: Adding Xamarin.Forms Views

XAMARIN.FORMS

Listing 2-6 provides the completed C# code for the added Xamarin.Forms views in the FormsExample solution.

■ **Xaml**   The XAML version of this example can be found under the title of this book on Apress.com in the Source Code/Downloads tab, or on GitHub at https://github.com/danhermes/xamarin-book-examples. The Xamarin.Forms solution for Chapter 2 is FormsExample.Xaml and the files are ContentPageExample.Xaml and ContentPageExample.cs.

Listing 2-6. ContentPageExample.cs in the FormsExample project

```
using System;
using Xamarin.Forms;
using System.Threading.Tasks;

namespace FormsExample
{
    class ContentPageExample : ContentPage
    {
        public ContentPageExample()
        {
            Label labelLarge = new Label
            {
                Text = "Label",
                FontSize = 40,
                HorizontalOptions = LayoutOptions.Center
            };

            Label labelSmall = new Label
            {
                Text = "This control is great for\n" +
                        "displaying one or more\n" +
                        "lines of text.",
                FontSize = 20,
                HorizontalOptions = LayoutOptions.CenterAndExpand
            };

            Button button = new Button
            {
                Text = "Make It So",
                FontSize = Device.GetNamedSize(NamedSize.Large,typeof(Button)),
                HorizontalOptions = LayoutOptions.Center,
                VerticalOptions = LayoutOptions.Fill
            };

            button.Clicked += (sender, args) =>
            {
                button.Text = "It is so!";
            };

            Entry entry = new Entry
            {
                Placeholder = "Username",
                VerticalOptions = LayoutOptions.Center,
                Keyboard = Keyboard.Text
            };

            BoxView boxView = new BoxView
            {
                Color = Color.Silver,
                WidthRequest = 150,
```

```
            HeightRequest = 150,
            HorizontalOptions = LayoutOptions.StartAndExpand,
            VerticalOptions = LayoutOptions.Fill
        };

        Image image = new Image
        {
            Source = "monkey.png",
            Aspect = Aspect.AspectFit,
            HorizontalOptions = LayoutOptions.End,
            VerticalOptions = LayoutOptions.Fill
        };

        var tapGestureRecognizer = new TapGestureRecognizer();
        tapGestureRecognizer.Tapped +=  async (sender, e) =>
        {
            image.Opacity = .5;
            await Task.Delay(200);
            image.Opacity = 1;
        };
        image.GestureRecognizers.Add(tapGestureRecognizer);

        StackLayout stackLayout = new StackLayout
        {
            Children =
            {
                labelLarge,
                labelSmall,
                button,
                entry,
                boxView,
                image
            },
            HeightRequest = 1500
        };

        ScrollView scrollView = new ScrollView
        {
            VerticalOptions = LayoutOptions.FillAndExpand,
            Content = stackLayout
        };

        // Accomodate iPhone status bar.
        this.Padding = new Thickness(10, Device.OnPlatform(20, 0, 0), 10, 5);

        this.Content = scrollView;
    }
  }
}
```

Summary

Xamarin.Forms provides a jumping-off point for cross-platform mobile app UI development, fully loaded with stock and customizable pages, layouts, and views. A Xamarin.Forms solution typically has a separate project for each of these three platforms: Android, iOS, and Windows Phone. A Xamarin.Forms project is useful for housing cross-platform UIs and a core library project contains the business logic and data layer (either can be Shared Projects or PCLs).

Developers are faced with a decision of Xamarin.Forms vs. a platform-specific UI approach with Xamarin.Android, Xamarin.iOS, and the Windows Phone SDK. The more Xamarin.Forms releases that come out, the less of a decision this may be, as Xamarin.Forms approaches the functionality of native UI APIs. For now, we need to master all the options on the table and weigh our choices carefully for each page of our app, to make sure the toolset will support our requirements. Xamarin.Forms custom renderers help us combine the two approaches.

The platform-specific UI option provides a full-featured toolset for detailed and nuanced native UI development. This is not a cross-platform approach to the presentation layer and requires the UI to be completely separated into platform-specific projects with no shared UI components. Xamarin.iOS provides bindings to the iOS UI API called UIKit. Xamarin.Android binds to the Android SDK, exposing the most important classes and their members, offering a native UI experience to the developer and user.

View is the Xamarin.Forms term for *control*, and we delved into a few of the most frequently used views: `Label`, `Entry`, `BoxView`, `Image`, `StackLayout`, and `ScrollView`.

Because layouts are some of the most powerful tools at a developer's disposal for crafting the design of an app, let's explore mobile UI layouts next.

CHAPTER 3

■ ■ ■

UI Design Using Layouts

A *layout* is a container for controls, images, text, and other layouts. Central to the creation of the mobile UIs, layouts help us to design our pages by using the placement of views and as well as nested layouts (for more views). If you've worked with HTML <div>, <table>, or <form> elements then layouts should feel familiar to you. The purpose of a layout is to indicate the location and size of each of its child elements. This is typically done three ways: relative to the individual controls in the layout, relative to the origin of the layout, or using an overlaid structure such as a grid. Each layout type has a mechanism for placing child views within it, specifying the size and location of each view, and creating space between and around the views.

In this chapter, you will build small projects to work with each of the layout types and their features. First you'll learn about the various types of layouts and explore custom controls. Xamarin.Forms, Xamarin.Android, and Xamarin.iOS use different types of layouts. Here is an overview of these types.

Xamarin.Forms Layouts

Xamarin.Forms layouts inherit from the View class and can contain views or other layouts. Xamarin.Forms layouts include the following:

- StackLayout: Stacks child views vertically or horizontally

- RelativeLayout: Uses constraints that create relationships between the elements to define the location and size of child views AbsoluteLayout: Sets the child view's location and size by using bounding rectangles or proportions to the overall layout

- Grid: Creates a table-like container with rows and columns to hold views

- Frame: Draws a frame-like border around the container

Android Layouts

Android layouts inherit from the ViewGroup class and can contain views or other layouts. Android layouts include the following:

- LinearLayout: Arranges child views vertically or horizontally

- RelativeLayout: Uses constraints that create relationships between the elements to define the location and size of child views

- TableLayout: Creates a table-like container with rows and columns to hold views

- GridLayout: Creates another table-like container with rows and columns to hold views with several options for view flow: row first, column first, or specific row/column assignment

- FrameLayout: Arranges child views vertically and provides nesting, swapping, sliding, and padding, much like a traditional .NET panel, as well as control over z-order (layer depth)

iOS Layouts

Most iOS layouts are created with designer tools such as the Xcode Interface Builder and Xamarin Designer for iOS. iOS layouts use a simple approach from a class standpoint, using a single class called UIView with two techniques. iOS layout techniques include the following:

- *AutoLayout*: Uses constraints that create flexible, relative relationships between the elements to define the location and size of child views

- *Frames*: Uses bounding rectangles called frames to indicate absolute placement and size of child views (which can be sized according to context using masks, a technique called *AutoSizing*)

When building layouts, a related topic that arises is the creation of custom controls, used as components for building layouts.

Understanding Custom Controls

Custom controls in Xamarin are partial layouts that can be included in larger layouts on an as-needed basis, that can be created on all platforms, and that can be made to function like user controls, custom controls, or panels in .NET. Custom controls are barely touched upon in this book, but the topic bears mentioning in the context of constructing professional-grade layouts.

In Xamarin.Forms, ContentView is a base class for creating custom views for nesting, padding, and reuse. Custom controls should not be confused with *customized controls*, which are usually individual Xamarin.Forms views with enhanced platform-specific functionality that are built using a custom renderer (see Chapter 8). Even so, developers will sometimes refer to a single customized control as a custom control. Also, a customized control has the capacity to contain multiple controls and might then actually become a custom control.

In Android, we have two options for creating custom controls: subclassed views and fragments. Subclassing views allows us to create custom views that can be added as child views to ViewGroups such as layouts. Subclassed views are lightweight and simple to implement. Sometimes we need access to activity features in our custom control, however, such as the navigation stack and life-cycle events. Fragments are dynamic mini-layouts with features of activities that are built using the base class Android.App.Fragment. Because of their strength and versatility as building-block UI classes, many Android apps are created entirely using fragments. They are commonly used to build apps that must work well on both phones and tablets as they help to customize the layout according to screen size.

In iOS, custom controls are often created using a designer tool, though subclassing UIView also works.

■ **Note** This chapter explores a static, manual approach to layouts. Many of these layouts, such as the Xamarin.Forms ones, contain bindable properties and can be bound to data sources and constructed dynamically at run-time. You'll learn about data -binding in later chapters (Chapter 5 and Chapter 7).

Using Xamarin.Forms Layouts

XAMARIN.FORMS

Layouts in Xamarin.Forms are containers that hold and format views. Each layout has its own set of constraints and behaviors to suit a range of design needs. You can format simple pages with a few controls quickly and easily by using StackLayout. RelativeLayout is useful when you know the coordinate relationships between controls. Use AbsoluteLayout when you know only in which quadrants and areas of the page your controls should appear, and when you need layering. Grid provides a table-like container. ContentView is a base class for building custom layout views, like such as custom controls, which can contain multiple layouts and other views, useful as a reusable component. A Frame layout provides a visible, rectangular frame around its contents.

StackLayout

XAMARIN.FORMS

Views in a StackLayout are stacked vertically unless horizontal placement is specified. StackLayout is a quick, loose layout useful for prototyping and simple screens. You add views as children to the parent view and arrange them by using HorizontalOptions and VerticalOptions, which can also be used to expand views and provide spacing between views. Useful for all Xamarin.Forms layouts, the Padding property creates space around the edges of the entire layout.

Add a StackLayout to the constructor of your ContentPage like this:

```
StackLayout stackLayout = new StackLayout {
    Spacing = 0,
    VerticalOptions = LayoutOptions.FillAndExpand,
    Children = {
        // Add Views here
        }
};
```

The Spacing property creates padding of the specified size between each view. The VerticalOptions declaration using FillAndExpand pads the end of the layout with space, pushing other views to the bottom of the page.

■ **Tip** All example code solutions, *including the XAML versions of these C# examples,* can be found on Apress.com (from the Source Code/Downloads tab, access the title of this book) or on GitHub at https://github.com/danhermes/xamarin-book-examples.

Listing 3-1 is an inline declaration of child views assigned the Children property.

Listing 3-1. StackLayoutHorizontal.cs in LayoutExample Project

```
StackLayout stackLayout = new StackLayout {
    Spacing = 0,
    Children = {
        new Label {
            Text = "Start is flush left",
            HorizontalOptions = LayoutOptions.Start,
        },
        new Label {
            Text = "Center",
            HorizontalOptions = LayoutOptions.Center
        },
        new Label {
            Text = "End is flush right",
            HorizontalOptions = LayoutOptions.End
        }
    }
};

this.Content = stackLayout;
```

In Figure 3-1, note the HorizontalOptions placement for LayoutOptions.Start, Center, and End.

Figure 3-1. StackLayout HorizontalOptions

■ **Tip** The inline declaration of child views by assigning the Children property used in Listing 3-1 is useful when building layouts quickly. The Add method works just as well:

```
stackLayout.Children.Add(View item);
```

Padding Around the Entire Layout

XAMARIN.FORMS

Much like page padding, the layout's Padding property creates space around the entire layout. Here's the inline property assignment:

```
Padding = new Thickness(left, top, right, bottom),
```

The following example places padding to the left, right, and bottom, but not on top:

```
Padding = new Thickness(10, 0, 10, 5),
```

This places equal space on all four sides:

```
Padding = new Thickness(10),
```

Stacking with Vertical Orientation

XAMARIN.FORMS

Vertical stacking, the default orientation, places each view beneath the previous one. There are four horizontal positions: Start, Center, End, and Fill. These are fields of the LayoutOptions class.

Let's make the default vertical orientation explicit, so you can see it, and add a few views to the first example (Listing 3-2).

Listing 3-2. StackLayoutVertical.cs

```
public StackLayoutVertical ()
{
    StackLayout stackLayout = new StackLayout {
        Spacing = 0,
        Orientation = StackOrientation.Vertical,
        VerticalOptions = LayoutOptions.FillAndExpand,
        Children = {
            new Label {
                Text = "Start is flush left",
                HorizontalOptions = LayoutOptions.Start,
            },
            new Label {
                Text = "Start 2",
                HorizontalOptions = LayoutOptions.Start,
            },
            new Label {
                Text = "Center",
                HorizontalOptions = LayoutOptions.Center
            },
            new Label {
                Text = "Center2",
                HorizontalOptions = LayoutOptions.Center
            },
            new Label {
                Text = "End1",
                HorizontalOptions = LayoutOptions.End
            },
            new Label {
                Text = "End is flush right",
                HorizontalOptions = LayoutOptions.End
            }
        }
    }

    this.Content = stackLayout;

};
```

Figure 3-2 shows how each view is placed lower than its sibling with vertical orientation and how each view is justified horizontally using HorizontalOptions.

Figure 3-2. *Top-to-bottom stacking with vertical orientation*

There's a fourth horizontal position: `Fill`. This causes the view to consume the available area:

```
HorizontalOptions = LayoutOptions.Fill
```

Later in this section we'll cover the `Expand` layout options (such as `FillAndExpand`), which cause views to expand and pad the available area around the view with space.

■ **Tip**　Make sure you have enough space in your layout or these alignments won't be visible.

If you have more than three views to be positioned horizontally, the horizontal orientation is preferable.

Stacking with Horizontal Orientation

XAMARIN.FORMS

Views can also be stacked horizontally by setting the `Orientation` property to `StackOrientation. Horizontal`, as shown in Listing 3-3. All views are on the same horizontal axis.

Listing 3-3. StackLayoutHorizontal.cs Continued

```
StackLayout stackLayoutHorizontal = new StackLayout {
    Spacing = 0,
    Orientation = StackOrientation.Horizontal,
    Children = {
        new Label {
            Text = "Start------"
        },
        new Label {
            Text = "------Center------",
            HorizontalOptions = LayoutOptions.CenterAndExpand
        },
        new Label {
            Text = "------End"
        }
    }
};
```

Figure 3-3 shows how each view is placed to the right of its sibling.

Figure 3-3. *Left-to-right stacking with horizontal orientation*

Horizontal padding from the expanded LayoutOptions separates views. Setting the center view's HorizontalOptions to LayoutOptions.CenterAndExpand provides space to the left and right of a centered view.

You can order views horizontally by setting Orientation to StackOrientation.Horizontal, though exact placement is impossible. Views are stacked left to right in the order added to the Children collection, with cues from HorizontalOptions.

Figure 3-4 shows what the StackLayout looks like if we were to add a few more views to the right of the previous views.

Figure 3-4. *Six views stacked left to right*

Listing 3-4 is the code with those extra views. In the online code examples, I'm moving back and forth between StackLayoutHorizontal.cs, which contains the simpler examples, and StackLayoutVertical.cs, which adds extra views.

Listing 3-4. StackLayoutVertical.cs with Views Using HorizontalOptions

```
StackLayout stackLayoutHorizontal = new StackLayout {
    Spacing = 0,
    Orientation = StackOrientation.Horizontal,
    Children = {
        new Label {
            Text = "Start 1 ---"
        },
        new Label {
            Text = "Start 2 ---"
        },
        new Label {
            Text = "---Center 1 ---",
            HorizontalOptions = LayoutOptions.CenterAndExpand
        },
        new Label {
            Text = "---Center 2 ---",
            HorizontalOptions = LayoutOptions.CenterAndExpand
        },
        new Label {
            Text = "---End 1 "
        },
        new Label {
            Text = "---End 2 "
        }
    }
};
```

51

If you want to combine your child layouts into a parent layout, consider nesting layouts.

Nesting Layouts

Layouts can contain other layouts within the Children property.

A complex page with multiple rows of horizontally oriented views is accomplished with nested StackLayouts:

```
this.Content = new StackLayout
{
    Children =
    {
        stackLayout,
        stackLayoutHorizontal
    }
};
```

■ **Tip** If more than one nested StackLayout is used, other layouts should be considered, such as RelativeLayout, AbsoluteLayout, or Grid, which lend themselves better to complexity.

Controlling the size of views in a layout and the spacing between them is important to formatting.

Expanding and Padding Views by Using LayoutOptions

XAMARIN.FORMS

Use the Expand layout option to cause views to expand or to pad the available area with space. FillAndExpand causes views to grow without creating padding space around them. All other expand options pad around the view with space.

■ **Tip** These features are easier to see if you set a background color for the view by using the BackgroundColor property.

The following are HorizontalOptions left-to-right formatting options:

- **FillAndExpand** expands the view to the right:

    HorizontalOptions = LayoutOptions.FillAndExpand;

- **StartAndExpand** pads to the right with space:

    HorizontalOptions = LayoutOptions.StartAndExpand;

- **EndAndExpand** - pads to the left with space:

    HorizontalOptions = LayoutOptions.EndAndExpand;

- **CenterAndExpand** pads to the left and right with space:

    HorizontalOptions = LayoutOptions.CenterAndExpand;

The following top-to-bottom formatting options are available for VerticalOptions:

- **FillAndExpand** - expands the view to the bottom:

  VerticalOptions = LayoutOptions.FillAndExpand;

- **StartAndExpand** - pads to the bottom with space:

  VerticalOptions = LayoutOptions.StartAndExpand;

- **EndAndExpand** - pads to the top with space:

  VerticalOptions = LayoutOptions.EndAndExpand

- **CenterAndExpand** - pads to the top and bottom with space:

  VerticalOptions = LayoutOptions.CenterAndExpand;

■ **Note** Expand layout options are only useful only if there are sibling views in the layout.

CODE COMPLETE: StackLayout

XAMARIN.FORMS

Listing 3-5 shows our full StackLayout example with a vertical and horizontal layout, the use of HorizontalOptions, and the Expand layout option, as shown in Figure 3-5.

Figure 3-5. *Two StackLayouts: one vertical and one horizontal*

■ **XAML** The XAML version of these examples can be found on Apress.com (from the Source Code/Downloads tab, access the title of this book) or on GitHub at https://github.com/danhermes/xamarin-book-examples. The Xamarin.Forms solution for Chapter 3 is LayoutExample.Xaml.

Listing 3-5. StackLayoutHorizontal.cs Code Complete

```
using System;
using Xamarin.Forms;

namespace LayoutExample
{
    public class StackLayoutHorizontal : ContentPage
    {
    public StackLayoutHorizontal()
        {
            StackLayout stackLayout = new StackLayout {
                Spacing = 0,
```

```csharp
            Children = {
                new Label {
                    Text = "Start is flush left",
                    HorizontalOptions = LayoutOptions.Start,
                },
                new Label {
                    Text = "Center",
                    HorizontalOptions = LayoutOptions.Center
                },
                new Label {
                    Text = "End is flush right",
                    HorizontalOptions = LayoutOptions.End
                }
            }

        };

        StackLayout stackLayoutHorizontal = new StackLayout {
            Spacing = 0,
            Orientation = StackOrientation.Horizontal,
            Children = {
                new Label {
                    Text = "Start------"
                },
                new Label {
                    Text = "------Center------",
                    HorizontalOptions = LayoutOptions.CenterAndExpand
                },
                new Label {
                    Text = "------End"
                }
            }
        };

        // Padding on edges and a bit more for iPhone top status bar
        this.Padding = new Thickness(10, Device.OnPlatform(20, 0, 0), 10, 5);

        this.Content = new StackLayout
        {
            Children =
            {
                stackLayout,
                stackLayoutHorizontal
            }
        };

        }
      }
    }
```

RelativeLayout

XAMARIN.FORMS

RelativeLayout auto-scales its elements to different screen sizes. Made up of the parent layout view and its child views, this layout is defined by the relationships between views. Each child view is tied to its sibling views or to the parent layout view by using constraints. A constraint can bind view locations and sizes: x/y coordinates and width/height dimensions. RelativeLayout allows us to create an interconnected web of views that stretch like rubber bands to fit the screen, providing built-in responsive design or auto-layout.

■ **Tip** RelativeLayout is useful for apps that must present well on widely varying resolutions, such as on phones and tablets.

Let's start with a fresh ContentPage, create a RelativeLayout instance, and place a label at 0,0 in the upper-left corner of the layout, as shown in Listing 3-6.

Listing 3-6. Starting RelativeLayoutExample.cs

```
public class RelativeLayoutExample : ContentPage
{
    public RelativeLayoutExample ()
    {
        RelativeLayout relativeLayout = new RelativeLayout();

        Label upperLeft = new Label
        {
            Text = "Upper Left",
            FontSize = 20
        };

        relativeLayout.Children.Add (upperLeft,
            Constraint.Constant (0),
            Constraint.Constant (0));

        // add more views here

        Content = relativeLayout;
    }
}
```

The Upper Left label is added with a location constraint to the parent layout; using Constraint.Constant(0) for both x and y places the label in the upper-left corner, at the origin: 0,0. Next we want to add more views in relation to the existing parent and child views.

Setting View Location and Size

XAMARIN.FORMS

Each time we add a view to RelativeLayout, we ask: Do we want to set the *location* of the view, the *size* of the view, or both?

Specify *location* with this Add method:

```
relativeLayout.Children.Add(view, xLocationConstraint,
    yLocationConstraint)
```

Specify both *size and location* with this one:

```
relativeLayout.Children.Add(view, xLocationConstraint,
    yLocationConstraint, widthConstraint, heightConstraint)
```

All these x/y coordinates, widths, and heights ultimately become absolute values. Data typing, however, restricts us to the use of Constraint classes. This encourages calculations based on the values of sibling and parent views, keeping things relative.

Using Constraints

XAMARIN.FORMS

Size and location are specified by using constraints. The Constraint object has three enumerations:

- Constant, for absolute x/y assignments of location and/or size
- RelativeToParent, for relative x/y calculations of location and/or size to the parent layout
- RelativeToView, for relative x/y calculations of location and/or size between child(sibling) views

The following sections discuss each in more detail.

Absolute Location and Size

Constant is used for absolute location or size.

Here is a *location* example, which places the upperLeft label at coordinates 0,0 within the layout:

```
relativeLayout.Children.Add (upperLeft,
                    Constraint.Constant (0),
                    Constraint.Constant (0));
```

This is a *size* example, creating a view at 100,100 with dimensions 50 units wide and 200 units high:

```
Label constantLabel = new Label
{
    Text = "Constants are Absolute",
    FontSize = 20
};
```

```
relativeLayout.Children.Add (constantLabel,
    Constraint.Constant (100),
    Constraint.Constant (100),
    Constraint.Constant (50),
    Constraint.Constant (200));
```

■ **Tip**   The numeric screen units used in many Xamarin.Forms views are relative units of measure that do not represent pixels, and their results vary according to screen size.

This new label is shown in Figure 3-6, with the text wrapping at 50 units wide.

Figure 3-6. *Label with a Constant contraint*

RelativeToParent Constraint

The RelativeToParent constraint ties a view's location/size to the parent RelativeLayout view. This is useful for placing and sizing views in relation to the entire page or section.

Instantiate another child view, such as Label, and add that to the child collection by using a RelativeToParent constraint. This example places the location of the new child view halfway down the length and width of the parent layout:

```
Label halfwayDown = new Label
{
    Text = "Halfway down and across",
    FontSize = 15
};

relativeLayout.Children.Add (halfwayDown ,
    Constraint.RelativeToParent((parent) =>
        {
            return parent.Width / 2;
        }),
    Constraint.RelativeToParent((parent) =>
        {
            return parent.Height / 2;
        })
);
```

These calls to `RelativetoParent` pass the parent view, `RelativeLayout`, into the lambda parameter, returning an x coordinate equal to half the width of the parent layout and a y coordinate equal to half of the height of the layout (see Figure 3-7).

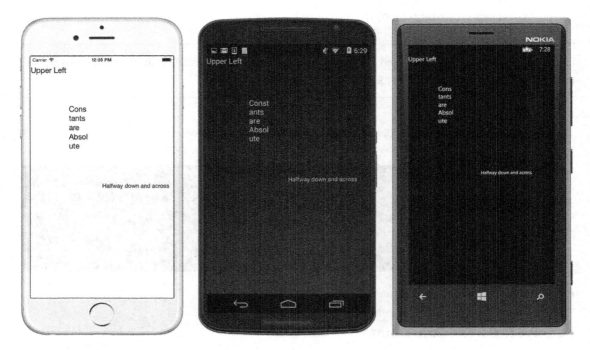

Figure 3-7. *RelativeToParent with a Height and Width calculation*

Here's the `Constraint.RelativeToParent` method in the general case:

```
Constraint.RelativeToParent ((parent) =>
    {
        return calculatedValue
    })
```

Use parent properties `X`, `Y`, `Width`, and `Height` to calculate the returned value.

Here are examples of useful calculated values to return for *location*:

- `parent.X + parent.Width;` locates the view to the right of the parent.

- `parent.X + parent.Width /2;` locates the view halfway across the width of the parent.

- `parent.Y + parent.Height;` locates the view below the parent.

- `parent.Y + parent.Height/2;` locates the view halfway down the height of the parent.

The following are values for size:

- `parent.Width;` makes the width the same as that of the parent layout.
- `parent.Width / 2;` makes the width half that of the parent layout.
- `parent.Height;` makes the height the same as that of the parent layout.
- `parent.Height / 2;` makes the height half that of the parent layout.

Create a BoxView halfway down the page that is half the height and half the width of the parent view by passing RelativeToParent calculations into the Add parameters:

```
BoxView boxView = new BoxView {
    Color = Color.Accent,
    WidthRequest = 150,
    HeightRequest = 150,
    HorizontalOptions = LayoutOptions.Center,
    VerticalOptions = LayoutOptions.CenterAndExpand
};

relativeLayout.Children.Add (boxView,
    Constraint.Constant (0),
    Constraint.RelativeToParent((parent) =>
        {
            return parent.Height / 2;
        }),
    Constraint.RelativeToParent((parent) =>
        {
            return parent.Width / 2;
        }),
    Constraint.RelativeToParent((parent) =>
        {
            return parent.Height / 2;
        })
);
```

The result looks like Figure 3-8.

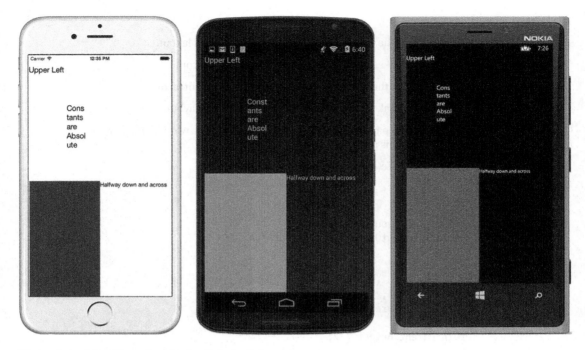

Figure 3-8. *A BoxView placed using RelativeToParent*

RelativeToView Constraint

RelativeToView constrains a view's location/size to that of another view. Instantiate another child view, such as a Label, and add that to the child collection by using a RelativeToView constraint. This example places the location of the new child view beneath the sibling view:

```
Label below = new Label
{
    Text = "Below Upper Left",
    FontSize = 15
};

relativeLayout.Children.Add (below,
    Constraint.Constant (0),
    Constraint.RelativeToView(upperLeft, (parent, sibling) =>
      {
          return sibling.Y + sibling.Height;
      })
    );
```

This call to RelativetoView passes the sibling view in the first parameter, upperLeft, and then passes the parent and sibling into the lambda parameter, returning a calculated y coordinate equal to the y value below the sibling, as shown in Figure 3-9 (for Android).

Upper Left
Below Upper Left

Figure 3-9. *Place one label below another by using RelativetoView*

Here's the Constraint.RelativeToView method in the general case:

```
Constraint.RelativeToView(siblingView, (parent, sibling) =>
    {
        return calculatedValue
    })
```

You now have three views: the new child view, the anchoring sibling view, and the parent view, or layout. Use parent or sibling properties X, Y, Width, and Height to calculate the returned value to assign to the child. Here are examples of useful calculated values to return for location:

- sibling.X + sibling.Width; locates the view to the right of the sibling.

- sibling.X + sibling.Width /2; locates the view halfway across the width of the sibling.

- sibling.Y + sibling.Height; locates the view below the sibling.

- sibling.Y + sibling.Height/2; locates the view halfway across the height of the sibling.

Here are similar values for size:

- sibling.Width; makes the width the same as the sibling.

- sibling.Width / 2; makes the width half that of the sibling.

- sibling.Height; makes the height the same as the sibling.

- sibling.Height / 2; makes the height half that of the sibling.

■ **Tip** The sibling and parent objects contain all of the properties available in these views. Properties other than those mentioned here may come in handy for your calculations, so be certain to explore.

61

CODE COMPLETE: RelativeLayout

XAMARIN.FORMS

Listing 3-7 is our full code example for RelativeLayout using Constraints: Constant, RelativeToParent, and RelativeToView (see Figure 3-10).

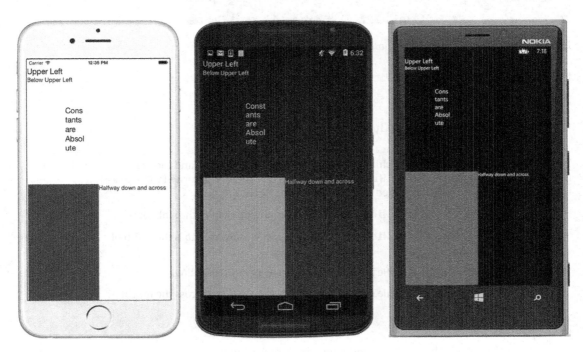

Figure 3-10. *RelativeLayoutExample.cs using all the constraint types*

■ **XAML**   The XAML version of these examples can be found on Apress.com (from the Source Code/Downloads tab, access the title of this book), or on GitHub at `https://github.com/danhermes/xamarin-book-examples`. The Xamarin.Forms solution for Chapter 3 is `LayoutExample.Xaml`.

Listing 3-7. RelativeLayoutExample.cs Code Complete

```
using System;
using Xamarin.Forms;
namespace LayoutExample
{
public class RelativeLayoutExample : ContentPage
    {
        public RelativeLayoutExample ()
        {
            RelativeLayout relativeLayout = new RelativeLayout();
```

```
    Label upperLeft = new Label
    {
        Text = "Upper Left",
        FontSize = 20,
    };

relativeLayout.Children.Add (upperLeft,
                            Constraint.Constant (0),
                            Constraint.Constant (0));

    Label below = new Label
    {
        Text = "Below Upper Left",
        FontSize = 15,
    };

relativeLayout.Children.Add (below,
        Constraint.Constant (0),
        Constraint.RelativeToView(upperLeft, (parent, sibling) =>
                        {
                                    return sibling.Y + sibling.Height;
                        })
        );

    Label constantLabel = new Label
    {
        Text = "Constants are Absolute",
        FontSize = 20
    };

relativeLayout.Children.Add (constantLabel,
        Constraint.Constant (100),
        Constraint.Constant (100),
        Constraint.Constant (50),
        Constraint.Constant (200));

    Label halfwayDown = new Label
    {
        Text = "Halfway down and across",
        FontSize = 15
    };

relativeLayout.Children.Add (halfwayDown ,
        Constraint.RelativeToParent((parent) =>
            {
                return parent.Width / 2;
            }),
        Constraint.RelativeToParent((parent) =>
            {
                return parent.Height / 2;
            })
    );
```

```
            BoxView boxView = new BoxView {
                Color = Color.Accent,
                HorizontalOptions = LayoutOptions.Start,
                VerticalOptions = LayoutOptions.StartAndExpand
            };

            relativeLayout.Children.Add (boxView,
                Constraint.Constant (0),
                Constraint.RelativeToParent((parent) =>
                    {
                        return parent.Height / 2;
                    }),
                Constraint.RelativeToParent((parent) =>
                    {
                        return parent.Width / 2;
                    }),
                Constraint.RelativeToParent((parent) =>
                    {
                        return parent.Height / 2;
                    })
            );

            Content = relativeLayout;
        }
    }
}
```

AbsoluteLayout

XAMARIN.FORMS

AbsoluteLayout is a collection of views placed at x/y coordinates ranging from 0 to 1 and bounded in size. Positions are not typically absolute, because we seldom use device-dependent x or y coordinates. Positions are usually relative to 0 being at the origin and 1 at the furthest point along a single axis. The layout is absolute in that views will go exactly where you put them, even on top of other views, so this can be useful for layering.

Using SetLayoutBounds, views in AbsoluteLayout are each bound to a bounding object, which can be a point or a rectangle. Using SetLayoutFlags, bounding points can determine location, while bounding rectangles can determine location and size.

Listing 3-8 provides an example of AbsoluteLayout.

Listing 3-8. Starting AbsoluteLayoutExample.cs

```
AbsoluteLayout absoluteLayout = new AbsoluteLayout
{
    VerticalOptions = LayoutOptions.FillAndExpand
};

// Add Views here

this.Content = absoluteLayout;
```

Now we'll add some views. First, a Label control.

```
Label firstLabel = new Label
{
    Text = "FirstLabel"
};
```

In order to assign a view to AbsoluteLayout, the control is added to the AbsoluteLayout collection and then LayoutFlags and LayoutBounds are set to define the position and size of the view. A single statement can accomplish all of these things. Here is the method and parameter to do it:

```
absoluteLayout.Children.Add (firstLabel, new Rectangle (xCoordinate,
    yCoordinate, xWidth, xHeight), AbsoluteLayoutFlags);
```

The Rectangle parameters are all doubles ranging from 0 to 1, and will be discussed more in depth soon. Here is a code example:

```
absoluteLayout.Children.Add (firstLabel, new Rectangle (0, 0,
    AbsoluteLayout.AutoSize, AbsoluteLayout.AutoSize),
    AbsoluteLayoutFlags.PositionProportional);
```

This adds the label view as a child to the layout collection and defines a bounding rectangle object that contains two pieces of information: the location and size of the view. It also ties the view to the rectangle with LayoutFlags, to specify the relationship between the bounding box and its view. Here is the longhand version:

```
absoluteLayout.Children.Add(firstLabel);
AbsoluteLayout.SetLayoutFlags(firstLabel,
    AbsoluteLayoutFlags.PositionProportional);
AbsoluteLayout.SetLayoutBounds(firstLabel,
    new Rectangle(0, 0, AbsoluteLayout.AutoSize, AbsoluteLayout.AutoSize));
```

In the longhand code, you can see the steps: add the child view to the collection, set the flags, and then set the bounds. Figure 3-11 shows the result (for Android).

Figure 3-11. *Add a label to AbsoluteLayout*

■ **Tip** AbsoluteLayout.AutoSize adjusts the height or width to the content within the view.

■ **Note** HorizontalOptions, VerticalOptions, and Expand layout options are overridden by absolute positioning.

Creating Bounding Objects with SetLayoutBounds

XAMARIN.FORMS

Views in `AbsoluteLayout` can be placed at points or bounded by rectangles (invisible ones). Points come in handy when only a location without a sized area is needed. Rectangles and points are the bounding objects specified in `SetLayoutBounds`.

Let's continue with another rectangle example. Create a second label, add it to the layout, and then set layout flags and bounds to place it at the bottom-left corner of the page:

```
Label secondLabel = new Label
{
    Text = "SecondLabel"
};

absoluteLayout.Children.Add(secondLabel);
AbsoluteLayout.SetLayoutFlags(secondLabel,
    AbsoluteLayoutFlags.PositionProportional);
AbsoluteLayout.SetLayoutBounds(secondLabel,
    new Rectangle(0, 1, AbsoluteLayout.AutoSize,
    AbsoluteLayout.AutoSize));
```

Figure 3-12 shows the result.

Figure 3-12. *secondLabel placed at the bottom of the screen with y set to 1*

Setting Location and Size by Using Rectangles

Rectangles provide AbsoluteLayout with the location and size of a bounded area in which to place a view. This is the constructor of Xamarin.Forms.Rectangle:

```
Rectangle (double locationX, double locationY, double width, double height)
```

All parameters are doubles ranging from 0 to 1. Here are a few examples of instantiated rectangles and how the parameters affect location:

- Located at the origin with maximum width and height: new Rectangle (0, 0, 1, 1)

- Horizontally centered in the space provided: new Rectangle (.5, 0, 1, 1)

- Vertically centered in the space provided: new Rectangle (0, .5, 1, 1)

- Horizontally and vertically centered in the space provided: new Rectangle (.5, .5, 1, 1)

The following are examples of parameters affecting size:

- Located at the origin with maximum width and height: new Rectangle (0, 0, 1, 1)

- Located at the origin at 20% width: new Rectangle (0, 0, .2, 1)

- Located at the origin at 20% height: new Rectangle (0, 0, 1, .2)

- Located at the origin at 20% width and height: new Rectangle (0, 0, .2, .2)

■ **Tip** The AbsoluteLayout examples in this chapter show relative units because that is the generally recommended cross-platform approach. AbsoluteLayout can also use device-specific units. Be certain you know what you're doing, as device-specific units can cause inconsistent results across different platforms and devices. Specify AbsoluteLayoutFlags.None and then use device-specific units with float values greater than 1:

```
AbsoluteLayout.SetLayoutFlags(secondLabel,AbsoluteLayoutFlags.None);
AbsoluteLayout.SetLayoutBounds(secondLabel,
new Rectangle (250f, 250f, 200f, 50f));
```

Setting Location by Using Points

Points can specify the location of a view when the size is not needed. Views can be added to AbsoluteLayout very simply by using a point:

```
absoluteLayout.Children.Add (firstLabel, new Point(0,0));
```

Points work just like the location portion of a rectangle, defining the x and y position by using doubles ranging from 0 to 1. Here's the Point constructor:

```
Point( double locationX, double locationY)
```

Points and rectangles are just geometric objects until they're bound to a view's location or size by using SetLayoutFlags.

Binding to the Bounding Object by Using SetLayoutFlags

XAMARIN.FORMS

Layout flags describe the relationship between the view and the bounding object in regards to location and size. The definition of a bounding object has *no impact* on the associated view unless a relationship is created using layout flags. This relationship creates a correlation between the child view and the bound rectangle or point. The following line of code associates the firstLabel view with the location of its bounding object:

```
AbsoluteLayout.SetLayoutFlags(firstLabel,
    AbsoluteLayoutFlags.PositionProportional);
```

Relationships between views and bounding objects are made by AbsoluteLayoutFlags in the second parameter of SetLayoutFlags. This can be done by location, by size, or by both location and size.

■ **Tip**   The most commonly used layout flags are PositionProportional and All because we are usually either placing a view or both placing and sizing it.

■ **Tip**   Images size well this way:

```
absoluteLayout.Add (image, new Rectangle (0, 0, 1, 1),
    AbsoluteLayoutFlags.All);
```

Binding Location

Bind the x/y location of the bounding object to the view by using these flags:

- PositionProportional associates a rectangle or a point's x/y location with the location of the view:

  ```
  AbsoluteLayout.SetLayoutFlags(firstLabel,
      AbsoluteLayoutFlags.PositionProportional);
  ```

  If the rectangle or point is at 0,0, the view will be at 0,0.

- XProportional associates a rectangle or a point's x coordinate with the location of the view:

  ```
  AbsoluteLayout.SetLayoutFlags(firstLabel,
      AbsoluteLayoutFlags.XProportional);
  ```

- YProportional associates a rectangle or point's y coordinate with the location of the view:

  ```
  AbsoluteLayout.SetLayoutFlags(firstLabel,
      AbsoluteLayoutFlags.YProportional);
  ```

Binding Size

Bind the size of the bounding object to the view by using these flags:

- SizeProportional associates the rectangle size with the size of the view:

  ```
  AbsoluteLayout.SetLayoutFlags(firstLabel,
          AbsoluteLayoutFlags.SizeProportional);
  ```

  If the rectangle is size .2,.5, the view will be sized to .2, .5.

- WidthProportional associates the rectangle width with the width of the view:

  ```
  AbsoluteLayout.SetLayoutFlags(firstLabel,
          AbsoluteLayoutFlags.WidthProportional);
  ```

- HeightProportional - associates the rectangle height with the height of the view:

  ```
  AbsoluteLayout.SetLayoutFlags(firstLabel,
          AbsoluteLayoutFlags.HeightProportional);
  ```

Binding Both Location and Size

Connect (or disconnect) both location and size with a rectangle or point by using All or None.

- All associates the rectangle or point's x/y location and size with the location and size of the view:

  ```
  AbsoluteLayout.SetLayoutFlags(firstLabel,
          AbsoluteLayoutFlags.All);
  ```

- None disassociates the rectangle or point from the view:

  ```
  AbsoluteLayout.SetLayoutFlags(firstLabel,
          AbsoluteLayoutFlags.None);
  ```

CODE COMPLETE: AbsoluteLayout

XAMARIN.FORMS

Listing 3-9 uses AbsoluteLayout to add labels to the top and bottom of the screen shown previously in Figure 3-12. This example uses bounding rectangles with a few different ways to add the first Label(such as using the abbreviated Add overload and using points instead of bounding rectangles).

Listing 3-9. AbsoluteLayoutExample.cs Using Rectangles and Points

```
using System;
using Xamarin.Forms;

namespace LayoutExample
{
    public class AbsoluteLayoutExample : ContentPage
    {
        public AbsoluteLayoutExample ()
        {
```

```
AbsoluteLayout absoluteLayout = new AbsoluteLayout
{
    VerticalOptions = LayoutOptions.FillAndExpand
};

Label  firstLabel = new Label
{
    Text = "FirstLabel"
};

absoluteLayout.Children.Add(firstLabel);
AbsoluteLayout.SetLayoutFlags(firstLabel,
    AbsoluteLayoutFlags.PositionProportional);
AbsoluteLayout.SetLayoutBounds(firstLabel,
    new Rectangle(0, 0, AbsoluteLayout.AutoSize,
    AbsoluteLayout.AutoSize));

// OR
//absoluteLayout.Children.Add (firstLabel, new Rectangle (0, 0,
//AbsoluteLayout.AutoSize, AbsoluteLayout.AutoSize),
//AbsoluteLayoutFlags.PositionProportional);

 // OR
//absoluteLayout.Children.Add (firstLabel, new Point(1,0));
//AbsoluteLayout.SetLayoutFlags(firstLabel,
//AbsoluteLayoutFlags.PositionProportional);


Label  secondLabel = new Label
{
    Text = "SecondLabel"
};
absoluteLayout.Children.Add(secondLabel);
AbsoluteLayout.SetLayoutFlags(secondLabel,
    AbsoluteLayoutFlags.PositionProportional);
AbsoluteLayout.SetLayoutBounds(secondLabel,
    new Rectangle(0, 1,
        AbsoluteLayout.AutoSize, AbsoluteLayout.AutoSize));

this.Content = absoluteLayout;
        }
    }
}
```

■ **XAML**   The XAML version of these examples can be found on Apress.com (from the Source Code/Downloads tab, access the title of this book) or on GitHub at `https://github.com/danhermes/xamarin-book-examples`. The Xamarin.Forms solution for Chapter 3 is `LayoutExample.Xaml`.

Grid

XAMARIN.FORMS

Grid is a table-like container of views. It is organized into rows and columns, each with a height and width, placed at specific row/column coordinates called *cells*. GridUnitType provides options for sizing rows and columns, while the grid.Children.Add method allows both single-cell and multicell views. ColumnSpacing and RowSpacing provide padding between cells.

■ **Tip** TableView is another cell-based view but is not technically a layout. It is useful for building simple groups of items such as settings dialog boxes and grouped menus. Chapter 6 has a TableView example.

Create a Grid object and define a single row and column, as shown in Listing 3-10.

Listing 3-10. Starting GridExample1.cs

```
Grid grid = new Grid
{
    VerticalOptions = LayoutOptions.FillAndExpand,
    RowDefinitions =
    {
        new RowDefinition { Height = GridLength.Auto }
    },
    ColumnDefinitions =
    {
        new ColumnDefinition { Width = GridLength.Auto }
    }
};

this.Content = grid;
```

Specify Height in each RowDefinition, and Width in each ColumnDefinition. GridLength.Auto autosizes cells for either Height or Width.

■ **Tip** The default GridLength setting for Height and Width, GridLength(1, GridUnitType.Star), expands the dimension of a row or column as much as possible.

Add a view at column and row 0, the only cell in our table:

```
grid.Children.Add(new Label
    {
        Text = "I'm at 0,0",
        FontSize = 30
    }, 0, 0);
```

This is the general-case Add for single- cell views:

```
Grid.Children.Add( view, indexColumn, indexRow)
```

Now let's crank this table up to four rows by three columns:

```
Grid grid = new Grid
{
    VerticalOptions = LayoutOptions.FillAndExpand,
    RowDefinitions =
    {
        new RowDefinition { Height = GridLength.Auto },
        new RowDefinition { Height = GridLength.Auto },
        new RowDefinition { Height = GridLength.Auto },
        new RowDefinition { Height = GridLength.Auto }
    },
    ColumnDefinitions =
    {
        new ColumnDefinition { Width = GridLength.Auto },
        new ColumnDefinition { Width = GridLength.Auto },
        new ColumnDefinition { Width = GridLength.Auto }
    }
};
```

Then add three more views at (1,1), (2,2), and (0,3). Add a little label formatting to makes things more exciting:

```
grid.Children.Add(new Label
    {
        Text = "Me? 1,1",
        FontSize = 30,
        FontAttributes = FontAttributes.Bold,
        TextColor = Color.Black,
        BackgroundColor = Color.Lime
    }, 1, 1);

grid.Children.Add(new Label
    {
        Text = "2,2 here",
        FontSize = 25,
        FontAttributes = FontAttributes.Bold,
        TextColor = Color.White,
        BackgroundColor = Color.Red
    }, 2, 2);

grid.Children.Add(new Label
    {
        Text = "I'm at 0,3",
        FontSize = 30,
        FontAttributes = FontAttributes.Bold
    }, 0, 3);
```

72

Figure 3-13 shows our `Grid` with four labels, completing the code in `GridExample1.cs`.

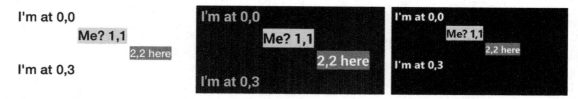

Figure 3-13. *Grid containing four views*

`GridLength.Auto` took care of column widths and row heights for us, expanding to accommodate view content.

■ **Tip** Empty cells can impact your grid. A row set to `Height = GridLength.Auto` that contains no views will have a height of zero. A column set to `Width = GridLength.Auto` that contains no views will have zero width.

■ **Tip** Here's a row and column definition shortcut. The `RowDefinition()` and `ColumnDefinition()` constructors use `GridUnitType.Star` by default, so new `RowDefinition { Height = GridLength(1, GridUnitType.Star) }` can be accomplished by

```
new RowDefinition()
```

and new `ColumnDefinition { Width = GridLength(1, GridUnitType.Star) }` is the same as this:

```
new ColumnDefinition()
```

To follow along with the online examples, save your current example, `GridExample1.cs`, and then create a new class called `GridExample2.cs`. Copy the contents of the constructor from `GridExample1.cs` into `GridExample2.cs` and continue working with `GridExample2.cs`. Remember to update your application class (such as `App.cs`) with the new `MainPage` reference to `GridExample2`.

Sizing Rows and Columns

XAMARIN.FORMS

The size of rows and columns is determined by `GridLength`. You can autosize, expand, or set specific heights and widths on rows or columns. `GridLength` is defined by its `GridUnitType`, of which there are three:

- `Auto` sizes the dimension of a row or column to its content.

- `Absolute` indicates a numeric dimension of the row or column.

- `Star` is the default setting, which expands the dimension of a row or column as much as possible, pushing subsequent rows or columns to the edge.

Assign a GridLength object to Height in RowDefinitions:

```
new RowDefinition { Height = new GridLength(200, GridUnitType.Absolute)
```

or to Width in ColumnDefinition:

```
new ColumnDefinition { Width = GridLength.Auto }
```

Sizing to Fit Views

XAMARIN.FORMS

The Auto value of GridUnitType sizes the row or column to the size of the contained views. Our Grid example is made up entirely of Auto sized rows, which we assign using a shorthand GridLength constructor:

```
GridLength.Auto
```

That returns a GridLength of type GridUnitType.Auto. Here is the longhand method:

```
new GridLength(1, GridUnitType.Auto)
```

The first parameter, with double value 1, is ignored for GridUnitType.Auto. Now let's add Absolute and Star, which use the longhand GridLength method.

■ **Tip** Small views used with UnitType.Auto can make it seem like rows or columns are missing. GridUnitType.Star is used to expand the grid to its proper proportions. See "Expanding Views Proportionally" later in this chapter.

Setting Exact Size

XAMARIN.FORMS

The Absolute value of GridUnitType sets the exact height or width of a row or column. This is the general- case method:

```
new GridLength(unitSize, GridUnitType.Absolute)
```

Change the second RowDefinition Height to an absolute size of 200 units:

```
RowDefinitions =
{
    new RowDefinition { Height = GridLength.Auto },
    new RowDefinition { Height = new GridLength(200,
        GridUnitType.Absolute) },
    new RowDefinition { Height = GridLength.Auto },
    new RowDefinition { Height = GridLength.Auto }
},
```

The second row is set to an absolute height of units, stretching it vertically, as shown in Figure 3-14. This code is found in GridExample2.cs.

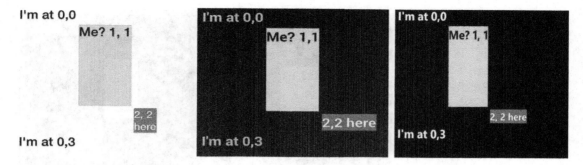

Figure 3-14. *Using GridUnitType.Absolute to set a tall row height at 1,1*

Width assigned using GridUnitType.Absolute works in a manner similar to the Height assignment:

```
new RowDefinition { Width = new GridLength(200, GridUnitType.Absolute) }
```

Expanding Views to Fit Available Space

XAMARIN.FORMS

GridUnitType.Star, the default setting for both Height and Width, expands a view within rows or columns to fill the available space. This is useful for filling the screen horizontally with columns or vertically with rows to the edge of the screen, especially when views are small. It behaves similarly to the FillAndExpand layout option, inserting padding space into the specified row or column.

Expand vertically by setting the Height of a RowDefinition. Change the third RowDefinition to use GridUnitType.Star:

```
RowDefinitions =
{
    new RowDefinition { Height = GridLength.Auto },
    new RowDefinition { Height = new GridLength(200, GridUnitType.Absolute) },
    new RowDefinition { Height = new GridLength(1, GridUnitType.Star) },
    new RowDefinition { Height = GridLength.Auto }
},
```

GridUnitType.Star expands to push the row beneath it all the way to the bottom of the screen, as shown in Figure 3-15. Remember that in many of these examples, the Padding property is being used to create space around the outside edges of the page (see Listing 3-11). This completes the code in GridExample2.cs.

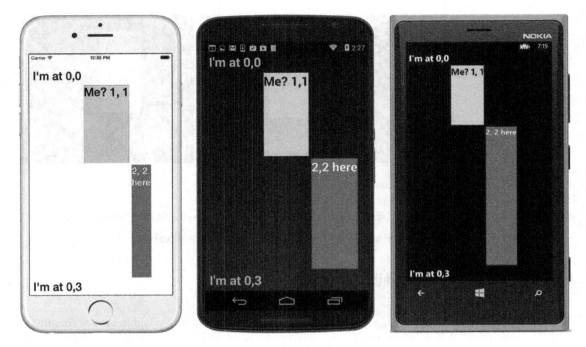

Figure 3-15. *Filling available vertical space by using GridUnitType.Star in the Height*

Expand horizontally by setting the width of ColumnDefinition. Width assigned using GridUnitType.Star works in a manner similar to the Height assignment, expanding the column to the right, pressing the grid to the right edge of the screen:

```
new ColumnDefinition { Width = new GridLength(1, GridUnitType.Star) }
```

Expanding Views Proportionally

You can control the proportions of cell sizes to one another in GridUnitType.Star cells by using the first parameter in GridLength. This technique is particularly useful with small views.

In this first example, the first parameters in all rows add up to 3 (1 + 2), breaking the row into three equal parts. This results in the first row expanding to one-third of the space and the second row expanding to two-thirds of the space:

```
new RowDefinition { Height = new GridLength(1, GridUnitType.Star) },
new RowDefinition { Height = new GridLength(2, GridUnitType.Star) },
```

In this next example, the first parameters in all rows add up to 4 (1 + 3), breaking the row into four equal parts. This results in the first row expanding to one-quarter of the space and the second row expanding to three-quarters of the space:

```
new RowDefinition { Height = new GridLength(1, GridUnitType.Star) },
new RowDefinition { Height = new GridLength(3, GridUnitType.Star) },
```

The first parameter represents a share of the total space among the Star rows or columns. If all of these parameters are specified as 1, the space will be evenly divided.

■ **Tip** Large grids can run off the visible screen. Consider using `GridLengthType.Star` to expand only to the available screen width paired with a vertical `ScrollView`. Scrolling grids vertically is commonplace, but scrolling horizontally is rare in mobile apps without a visible indicator of offscreen content (page dots, arrows, and so forth).

Creating Multicell Views

XAMARIN.FORMS

Single views can be sized to span multiple cells in the grid by using the Add method:

```
grid.Children.Add( view, indexLeftColumn, indexRightColumn,
    indexTopRow, indexBottomRow)
```

Still using a zero-based index, span columns with a view by specifying the leftmost and rightmost column indexes. Span rows by using the top and bottom row indexes.

Spanning Columns

Expand a view from left to right across multiple columns by using the second and third parameters of the Add method, `indexLeftColumn` and `indexRightColumn`, to specify the columns to span.

To follow along with the online examples, save your current example, `GridExample2.cs`, and then create a new class called `GridExample3.cs`. Copy the constructor from `GridExample2.cs` into `GridExample3.cs` and continue with `GridExample3.cs`. Remember to update `App.cs` with the new `MainPage` reference to `GridExample3`.

Let's expand our (1,1) view into the column to the right and the (2,2) cell down into the row below it. Add a Star-typed `GridLength` to the second column so it will expand horizontally:

```
ColumnDefinitions =
{
    new ColumnDefinition { Width = GridLength.Auto },
    new ColumnDefinition { Width = new GridLength(1, GridUnitType.Star) },
    new ColumnDefinition { Width = GridLength.Auto }
}
```

Change both views to use the multicell Add method. Start with the view at (1,1):

```
grid.Children.Add(new Label {
        Text = "Me? 1, 1",
        FontSize = 30,
        FontAttributes = FontAttributes.Bold,
        TextColor = Color.Black,
        BackgroundColor = Color.Lime
    }, 1, 3, 1, 2);
```

From left to right, this view spans the left side of column 1 to the left side of column 3 - a distance of two columns. (Yes, it's a little strange that there is no visible column 3, but the notation requires an endpoint, and that happens to be the beginning of the column or row we are expanding to.) See the result in Figure 3-16.

From top to bottom, this view spans from the top of row 1 to the top of row 2 (a distance of only one row).

Spanning Rows

Expand a view from a cell down through multiple rows by specifying rows to span in the Add method's last two parameters: indexTopRow and indexBottomRow.

Now change the view at (2,2):

```
grid.Children.Add(new Label {
        Text = "2, 2 here",
        FontSize = 25,
        FontAttributes = FontAttributes.Bold,
        TextColor = Color.White,
        BackgroundColor = Color.Red
    }, 2, 3, 2, 4);
```

From left to right, this view spans the left side of column 2 to the left side of column 3. From top to bottom, this view spans from the top of row 2 to the top of row 4 (a distance of two rows) and yields what you see in Figure 3-16. (There's no visible row 4; it's just an endpoint.) This completes the code in GridExample3.cs.

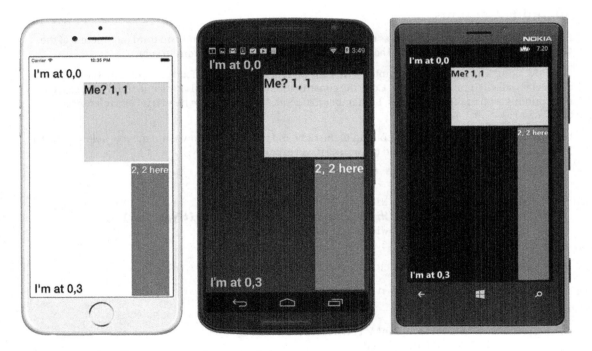

Figure 3-16. *The cell at 1,1 spans columns, and 2,2 spans rows*

■ **Tip** View formatting within a grid cell often requires use of that view's formatting properties in addition to grid properties, for example, centering text in a `Label` view:

```
XAlign = TextAlignment.Center,
YAlign = TextAlignment.Center,
```

Consult the properties of the view you're working with to help place it precisely within the cell.

Padding Between Cells

You can add space between cells by using `RowSpacing` and `ColumnSpacing`. `RowSpacing` provides padding between rows, while `ColumnSpacing` provides space between columns. Here's an example that provides 20 units of padding for each:

```
Grid grid = new Grid
{
    VerticalOptions = LayoutOptions.FillAndExpand,
    RowSpacing = 20,
    ColumnSpacing = 20,
```

CODE COMPLETE: Grid

XAMARIN.FORMS

Listing 3-11 is our Grid example shown previously in Figure 3-15 sporting four labels, two of which span multiple rows or columns.

Listing 3-11. GridExample2.cs Code Complete

```
using System;

using Xamarin.Forms;

namespace LayoutExample
{
    public class GridExample2 : ContentPage
    {
        public GridExample2()
        {
            Grid grid = new Grid
            {
                VerticalOptions = LayoutOptions.FillAndExpand,
                RowDefinitions =
                {
                    new RowDefinition { Height = GridLength.Auto },
                    new RowDefinition { Height = new GridLength(200, GridUnitType.
                    Absolute) },
                    new RowDefinition { Height = new GridLength(1, GridUnitType.Star) },
                    new RowDefinition { Height = GridLength.Auto }
                },
```

```
            ColumnDefinitions =
            {
                new ColumnDefinition { Width = GridLength.Auto },
                new ColumnDefinition { Width = new GridLength(1, GridUnitType.Star) },
                new ColumnDefinition { Width = GridLength.Auto }
            }
    };

    grid.Children.Add(new Label
        {
            Text = "I'm at 0,0",
            FontSize = 30,
            FontAttributes = FontAttributes.Bold,
    }, 0, 0);

    grid.Children.Add(new Label
        {
            Text = "Me? 1, 1",
            FontSize = 30,
            FontAttributes = FontAttributes.Bold,
            TextColor = Color.Black,
            BackgroundColor = Color.Lime
        }, 1, 3, 1, 2);

    grid.Children.Add(new Label
        {
            Text = "2, 2 here",
            FontSize = 25,
            FontAttributes = FontAttributes.Bold,
            TextColor = Color.White,
            BackgroundColor = Color.Red
        }, 2, 3, 2, 4);

    grid.Children.Add(new Label
        {
            Text = "I'm at 0,3",
            FontSize = 30,
            FontAttributes = FontAttributes.Bold
        }, 0, 3);

    // Padding on edges and a bit more for iPhone top status bar
    this.Padding = new Thickness(10, Device.OnPlatform(20, 0, 0), 10, 5);

    this.Content = grid;
        }
    }
}
```

■ **XAML**   The XAML version of these examples can be found on Apress.com (from the Source Code/Downloads tab, access the title of this book) or on GitHub at `https://github.com/danhermes/xamarin-book-examples`. The Xamarin.Forms solution for Chapter 3 is `LayoutExample.Xaml`.

ContentView

XAMARIN.FORMS

The `ContentView` layout can act as a visual or virtual container class, like a custom control. `ContentView` is designed for reuse throughout your app. It's also useful for providing quick padding or formatting around another view or layout.

As a visual rectangular container, `ContentView` provides the standard Layout class properties such as `Padding`, `BackgroundColor`, `HorizontalOptions`, and `VerticalOptions`, much like a .NET panel control. As a virtual container, it can house a child layout containing multiple views for swapping in and out of a page, and for use on different pages, a lot like a .NET custom control or an Android fragment.

This is a simple `ContentView`, a soothing teal rectangle with a white text label:

```
ContentView contentView = new ContentView
{
    BackgroundColor = Color.Teal,
    Padding = new Thickness(40),
    HorizontalOptions = LayoutOptions.Fill,
    Content = new Label
    {
        Text = "a view, such as a label, a layout, or a layout of layouts",
        FontSize = 20,
        FontAttributes = FontAttributes.Bold,
        TextColor = Color.White
    }
};
```

`ContentView` can now be used like any other view and placed into a layout that is assigned to the page's `Content` property (see Listing 3-5). Figure 3-17 shows the label tucked inside `ContentView`. Note how the `ContentView` padding creates colored space around the label.

Figure 3-17. *ContentView in action*

■ **Note**   If your screenshot doesn't match Figure 3-17 and `ContentView` consumes the entire screen, add this to `ContentView`:

```
VerticalOptions = LayoutOptions.StartAndExpand,
```

CODE COMPLETE: ContentView

Listing 3-12 is the complete `ContentView` code example shown in Figure 3-17. Two kinds of padding are used here: the colored padding inside `ContentView` and the space around the edge of `ContentPage`.

Listing 3-12. ContentViewExample.cs Code Complete

```
class ContentViewExample : ContentPage
{
    public ContentViewExample()
    {
        ContentView contentView = new ContentView
        {
            BackgroundColor = Color.Teal,
            Padding = new Thickness(40),
            HorizontalOptions = LayoutOptions.Fill,
            Content = new Label
```

```
        {
            Text = "a view, such as a label, a layout, or a layout of layouts",
            FontSize = 20,
            FontAttributes = FontAttributes.Bold,
            TextColor = Color.White
        }
    };

    // Padding on edges and a bit more for iPhone top status bar
    this.Padding = new Thickness(10, Device.OnPlatform(20, 0, 0), 10, 5);

    this.Content = new StackLayout
    {
        Children =
        {
            contentView
        }
    };
    }
}
```

■ **XAML** The XAML version of these examples can be found on Apress.com (from the Source Code/Downloads tab, access this book's title) or on GitHub at `https://github.com/danhermes/xamarin-book-examples`. The Xamarin.Forms solution for Chapter 3 is `LayoutExample.Xaml`.

Frame

XAMARIN.FORMS

The Frame layout places a visible frame around itself. The `OutlineColor` property specifies the color of the frame. See Listing 3-13.

Listing 3-13. FrameExample.cs

```
class FrameExample : ContentPage
{
    public FrameExample()
    {
        this.Padding = 20;
        this.Content = new Frame {
            Content = new Label { Text = "Framed", FontSize = 40 },
            OutlineColor = Color.Red
        };
    }
}
```

HasShadow is a Boolean property specifying a shadow effect when the platform supports it. The default Padding value on a Frame layout is 20. The Content property can be assigned to another layout, such as StackLayout, to contain and frame multiple views.

Figure 3-18 shows the Frame layout.

Figure 3-18. *Frame layout*

Those are layouts in Xamarin.Forms!

At this point, you are faced with a choice. Many of these chapters cover a single topic in three ways: Xamarin. Forms, Xamarin.Android, and Xamarin.iOS. When you're finished reading about Xamarin.Forms (like right now), you can continue reading about the chapter topic in the other OSs (Android and iOS) or you can turn to the next chapter to learn more about Xamarin.Forms. Here are your choices:

- Are you ready for more Xamarin.Forms? Turn to the next chapter to read about user interaction using Xamarin.Forms controls, which are called views.

- Do you want to know about Android layouts? Then read on.

- Are you wondering about iOS layouts? Jump down to the iOS section in this chapter.

Now let's cover platform-specific layouts, starting with Android.

Using Android Layouts

ANDROID

Android layouts contain and format controls, and inherit from the Android ViewGroup class, which is similar to the Xamarin.Forms Layout class. You can format simple pages with a few controls quickly and easily by using LinearLayout. RelativeLayout is useful when you know the relationships between controls. TableLayout provides a table-like container to assign views to specific rows and columns. GridLayout is similar to TableLayout but provides features to flow views into the table more loosely. ContentView is a base class for building custom layout views that can contain multiple layouts and other views, useful as a reusable component. Fragments are a layout-related topic but not technically layouts. Developers use fragments as advanced layouts (with their own state and life cycle) to combine to build complex, interchangeable UIs.

■ **Note**   The term *layout* can mean two things in Android. It can be a layout XML (.axml) file in the Resources folder or it can be one of the control containers (used therein) to format controls, such as LinearLayout. This book distinguishes between them by using the terms *layout XML* and *layout*.

Android layouts are similar to their Xamarin.Forms counterparts, as shown in Table 3-1.

Table 3-1. *Comparison of Android and Xamarin.Forms Layouts*

Android	Xamarin.Forms
LinearLayout	StackLayout
RelativeLayout	RelativeLayout
TableLayout	Grid
GridLayout	Grid
FrameLayout	StackLayout, ContentLayout

Though the Android FrameLayout was originally designed to house and frame a single view, it is often used as a panel-like element for multiple views where z-order can be specified, giving control over layers. It also serves as a container to dynamically swap in and swap out fragments.

Fragments inherit from Android.App.Fragment and are not technically layouts. Mini-layouts with code-behinds and rules of their own, fragments are often used as the foundation of an app's layout architecture, like custom controls, as well as in tandem with other layouts. They are a mainstay of Android mobile app responsive design, especially when a phone app needs to look great on a tablet. We use them as componentized UI building blocks for creating a screen, both statically in layout XML and swapping them in and out dynamically in real time using code.

■ **Note**   The Android AbsoluteLayout option was deprecated in favor of RelativeLayout.

LinearLayout

ANDROID

LinearLayout can visually structure and arrange other elements inside it vertically or horizontally, like <div> in web development or the Xamarin.Forms StackLayout.

Add a new Android layout XML file to your project called LinearLayoutExample.axml. LinearLayout is declared in the view like this:

```
<LinearLayout xmlns:android="http://schemas.android.com/apk/res/android"
    android:orientation=  "vertical"
    android:layout_width=  "fill_parent"
    android:layout_height= "fill_parent" >

  <!-- Add views here -->

</LinearLayout>
```

The orientation is declared as vertical, causing views to cascade top to bottom. It could also be set to horizontal, causing the views to cascade left to right.

Let's add a TextView and two Buttons inside the LinearLayout tag (Listing 3-14).

Listing 3-14. LayoutExample.axml

```
<TextView
  android:id="@+id/aTextBox"
  android:text=     "A TextView"
  android:textSize=    "20pt"
  android:layout_width=    "match_parent"
  android:layout_height=   "wrap_content"
  android:layout_weight=   "4"    />
  <Button
    android:id="@+id/aButtonMe"
    android:text="Click Me!"
    android:layout_width="match_parent"
    android:layout_height="wrap_content"
    android:layout_weight=   "1"
/>
  <Button
    android:id="@+id/aButtonOrMe"
    android:text="Or Me!"
    android:layout_width="match_parentparent"
    android:layout_height="wrap_content"
    android:layout_weight=   "1"
/>
```

Layout_weight ascribes size ratios to the views. In this case, we want the text box to own most of the screen and push other controls to the bottom, so we set the text box layout_weight to 4 (out of 6), and the buttons each to 1. Six comes from the total weight: $4 + 1 + 1 = 6$. Be sure not to set numeric height or width values when using layout_weight.

Match_parent sets the view's height or width the same as the parent layout view, minus its padding. wrap_content autosizes the view to its own content, including padding.

■ **Note** Refer to the Xamarin and Android online developer docs for more detail on placement using `View` properties such as `layout_height`, `layout_width`, `layout_gravity`, and `layout_margin`.

■ **Tip** The Xamarin Android Designer can be used for laying out an Android UI and is a great way to learn the layout XML (`.axml` files). Android layout XML is highly readable and writable, however, and the XML can also be coded by hand.

Using Activities to Display Layouts

In the contemporary Model-View-Controller (MVC) pattern, Android activities are the *controllers* and make up the core executable elements in Android mobile apps. Activities display and manage the layouts, which are the equivalent of MVC *views*.

■ **Note** This book is a Xamarin.Forms primer and cross-platform guide. It is not an Android primer and, although it introduces some basic concepts, you'll need additional sources for the Android and/or Xamarin. Android fundamentals. If you need an intro to Xamarin.Android, consult the Xamarin online docs.

Many examples in this book use only a single activity, called `MainActivity`. In these simple examples, you can load your layout XML in the `OnCreate` method of `MainActivity`, called `LinearLayoutExample` here, referring to the `LinearLayoutExample.axml` file in the `Resources/layout` folder:

```
public class MainActivity : Activity
{

    protected override void OnCreate (Bundle bundle)
    {
        RequestWindowFeature(WindowFeatures.NoTitle);
        base.OnCreate (bundle);
        SetContentView (Resource.Layout.LinearLayoutExample);
    }
}
```

This `RequestWindowFeature` call hides the app title from the top of the view. Now let's run it (Figure 3-19).

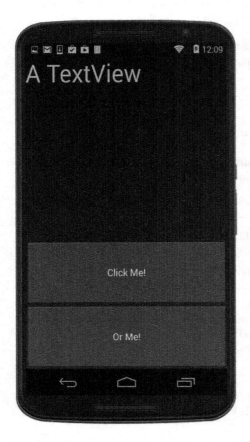

Figure 3-19. *LinearLayout using layout_weight*

Creating Layouts in Code

Layouts can be created programmatically in C# instead of using XML but, again, we recommend the Xamarin Android Designer for getting started in the Android UI. It's easy, fast, and accurate. Sometimes we need to create controls (views) in code or, more commonly, change properties on them.

Listing 3-15 is a rough C# approximation of the previous layout XML. In the main activity's OnCreate method, create a LinearLayout element and add views to the layout. Use the SetContentView method to assign the layout to the activity and display it.

Listing 3-15. LinearLayoutActivity.cs Creates a LinearLayout Using C#

```
protected override void OnCreate (Bundle bundle)
{
    RequestWindowFeature(WindowFeatures.NoTitle);
    base.OnCreate (bundle);

    var linearLayout= new LinearLayout (this);
    linearLayout.Orientation = Orientation.Vertical;

    var aTextView = new TextView (this);
    aTextView.Text = " A TextView ";
    aTextView.TextSize = 20;

    var aButtonMe= new Button (this);
    aButtonMe.Text = "Click Me!";

    var aButtonOrMe= new Button (this);
    aButtonOrMe.Text = "Or Me!";

    linearLayout.AddView (aTextView);
    linearLayout.AddView (aButtonMe);
    linearLayout.AddView (aButtonOrMe);

    SetContentView (linearLayout);
}
```

Controls are added to LinearLayout with AddView and then the layout is added as the main view with SetContentView.

Working with Nested Layouts

Multiple LinearLayout elements can define complex groupings of elements. In the following code, nodes are collapsed for readability:

```
<LinearLayout>
    <TextView/>
    <LinearLayout>
        <Button/>
        <Button/>
    </LinearLayout>
</LinearLayout>
```

If there are too many nested LinearLayout elements, performance is compromised, and RelativeLayout should be used.

RelativeLayout

ANDROID

RelativeLayout is a container of views that have a positional relationship to one another. Place views in RelativeLayout by creating constraints between individual views such a: above, below, to the right of, to the left of, with alignment, and centering.

Add a new Android layout file to your project and create RelativeLayout with our TextView and two Buttons, as shown in Listing 3-16.

Listing 3-16. RelativeLayoutExample.axml

```
<RelativeLayout xmlns:android="http://schemas.android.com/apk/res/android"
    android:layout_width="fill_parent"
    android:layout_height="fill_parent" >

    <TextView
        android:id="@+id/aTextBox2"
        android:layout_width="wrap_content"
        android:layout_height="wrap_content"
        android:text="A TextView"
    />

    <Button
        android:id="@+id/aButtonMe2"
        android:layout_width="wrap_content"
        android:layout_height="wrap_content"
        android:text="Click Me!"
        android:layout_below="@+id/aTextBox2"
    />

    <Button
        android:id="@+id/aButtonOrMe"
        android:layout_width="wrap_content"
        android:layout_height="wrap_content"
        android:text="Or Me!"
        android:layout_marginLeft="50dip"
        android:layout_alignTop="@id/aButtonMe2"
        android:layout_toRightOf="@+id/aButtonMe2"
    />

</RelativeLayout>
```

The margin is set on aButtonOrMe, using layout_marginLeft and padding between the buttons. The tops of both buttons are aligned by using layout_alignTop (see Figure 3-20). These controls use wrap_content to set their size to the size of their content, text in this case.

Figure 3-20. *RelativeLayout with three views*

■ **Tip** LinearLayout and RelativeLayout can be used to construct complex, customized views. These can, in turn, be used to create detailed list views. You'll learn more about this in Chapter 5.

■ **Note** Refer to the Xamarin and Android online developer docs for more detail on placement using RelativeLayout layout parameters such as layout_align.

TableLayout

ANDROID

You can arrange views in rows and columns with TableLayout. Declare rows and fill those rows with views. The width of a column is determined by the widest view in that column. You can stretch or shrink columns by using TableLayout properties applied top-down.

Listing 3-17 shows TableLayout with two rows, the first with two TextViews and the second row with our two Buttons.

Listing 3-17. TableLayoutExample.axml

```
<TableLayout xmlns:android="http://schemas.android.com/apk/res/android"
    android:layout_width="match_parent"
    android:layout_height="wrap_content"
    android:stretchColumns="*"
    android:shrinkColumns="*">
    <TableRow>
        <TextView
            android:layout_column="0"
            android:text="A TextView"
            android:layout_marginBottom="20dp"/>
        <TextView
            android:text="and Another!"
            android:layout_marginBottom="20dp"/>
    </TableRow>
    <TableRow>
        <Button
```

```
                android:layout_column="0"
                android:text="Click Me!" />
            <Button
                android:text="Or Me!" />
        </TableRow>
    </TableLayout>
```

stretchColumns and shrinkColumns indicate on which columns to impart the layout's width and height features (fill and wrap, in this case), with asterisk meaning all columns, the same as stretchColumns="0,1". Layout_column specifies the view's column by using a zero-based index (Figure 3-21).

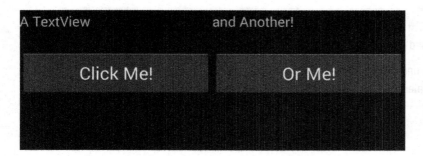

Figure 3-21. *TableLayout with two rows*

The code to accomplish almost the same thing programmatically looks like Listing 3-18.

Listing 3-18. TableViewActivity.cs

```
protected override void OnCreate (Bundle bundle)
{
    RequestWindowFeature(WindowFeatures.NoTitle);
    base.OnCreate (bundle);

    var tableLayout= new TableLayout (this);
    tableLayout.LayoutParameters = new TableLayout.LayoutParams(
        ViewGroup.LayoutParams.MatchParent,
        ViewGroup.LayoutParams.WrapContent);

    TableRow tableRow1 = new TableRow(this);
    TableRow tableRow2 = new TableRow(this);

    var aTextView1 = new TextView (this);
    aTextView1.Text = "A TextView";

    var aTextView2 = new TextView (this);
    aTextView2.Text = "and Another!";

    tableRow1.AddView (aTextView1,0); // add view to column 0
    tableRow1.AddView (aTextView2,1); // add view to column 1
```

```
var aButton1= new Button (this);
aButton1.Text = "Click Me!";

var aButton2= new Button (this);
aButton2.Text = "Or Me!";

tableRow2.AddView (aButton1,0);
tableRow2.AddView (aButton2,1);


tableLayout.AddView(tableRow1, 0); // add row 0 to layout
tableLayout.AddView(tableRow2, 1); // add row 1 to layout

SetContentView (tableLayout);
}
```

This creates two TableRows, adds views to them with the TableRow.AddView method, and then adds each TableRow to the TableLayout by using TableLayout.AddView. This sets the LayoutParameters property of the TableLayout with width and height LayoutParams. Layout parameters can be set at the layout, row, and view level.

GridLayout

ANDROID

The GridLayout class builds a table-like container for views, similarly but not identical to TableLayout. GridLayout provides the additional option of flowing views into cells as well as placing them individually. Multicell views are created by spanning several rows or columns using layout_columnSpan and layout_rowSpan. Dynamic image grids use another layout control called GridView.

There are three ways to place views in GridLayout:

- Horizontal orientation (default) - flows views into cells from left to right and then top to bottom.

- Vertical orientation flows views from top to bottom, filling each column before moving to the right to fill the next column top to bottom.

- Specify Row/Column enables each individual view to be marked with a row and column to occupy.

Filling Rows Left to Right with Horizontal Orientation

ANDROID

Horizontal orientation fills a row left -to -right with views before moving to the next row below.

Using the default horizontal orientation, create a GridLayout with two TextViews and two Buttons, as shown in Listing 3-19.

Listing 3-19. *GridLayoutExample.axml*

```
<GridLayout xmlns:android="http://schemas.android.com/apk/res/android"
        android:layout_width="match_parent"
        android:layout_height="match_parent"
        android:rowCount="2"
        android:columnCount="2">
    <TextView
            android:text="A TextView,"
            android:textSize="30dip" />
    <TextView
            android:text=" and another!"
            android:textSize="30dip" />
    <Button
            android:text="Click Me!"
            android:textSize="20dip" />
    <Button
            android:text="Or Me!"
            android:textSize="20dip" />
</GridLayout>
```

GridLayout rowCount and columnCount define the dimensions of the grid. The default orientation is horizontal, which fills cells in the row left to right before dropping down to the row below, as shown in Figure 3-22.

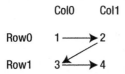

Figure 3-22. *GridLayout cells fill in a horizontal orientation*

Figure 3-23 shows the result.

Figure 3-23. *GridLayout in a horizontal orientation*

Filling Columns Top to Bottom with Vertical Orientation
ANDROID

Vertical orientation fills a column top to bottom with views before moving to the next column to the right, as shown in Figure 3-24.

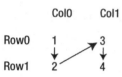

Figure 3-24. *GridLayout cells fill in a vertical orientation*

Set the GridLayout.orientation property to vertical to fill cells top to bottom before moving to the next column to the right:

```
<GridLayout xmlns:android="http://schemas.android.com/apk/res/android"
android:layout_width="match_parent"
android:layout_height="match_parent"
android:rowCount="2"
android:columnCount="2"
android:orientation="vertical">
</GridLayout>
```

Figure 3-25 shows the result.

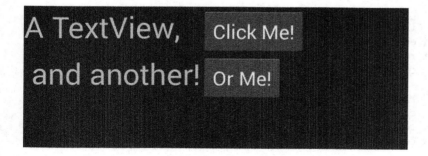

Figure 3-25. *GridLayout in a vertical orientation*

95

Specifying Rows and Columns

ANDROID

You can specify rows and columns for each and every view by removing the orientation setting and declaring layout_row and layout_column for all views in the grid.

This example purposefully crisscrosses our TextViews and Buttons to demonstrate that position is defined within each child view (Figure 3-26).

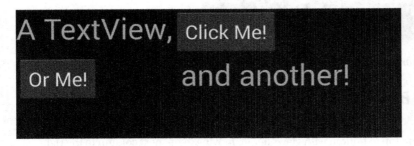

Figure 3-26. *Specify exact rows and columns in a GridLayout*

Listing 3-20 shows the code to make a GridLayout with layout_row and layout_column declared for each child view.

Listing 3-20. GridLayoutSpecifyRowCol.axml

```
<GridLayout xmlns:android="http://schemas.android.com/apk/res/android"
    android:layout_width="match_parent"
    android:layout_height="match_parent"
    android:rowCount="2"
    android:columnCount="2">
    <TextView
        android:text="A TextView,"
        android:textSize="30dip"
        android:layout_row="0"
        android:layout_column="0"/>
    <TextView
        android:text=" and another!"
        android:textSize="30dip"
        android:layout_row="1"
        android:layout_column="1" />
    <Button
        android:text="Click Me!"
        android:textSize="20dip"
        android:layout_row="0"
        android:layout_column="1" />
    <Button
        android:text="Or Me!"
        android:textSize="20dip"
        android:layout_row="1"
        android:layout_column="0" />
</GridLayout>
```

Creating Multicell Views

ANDROID

Single views can be sized to span multiple cells in the grid by setting these properties on the view.

Span *columns* as follows:

```
android:layout_columnSpan="numberOfColumnsToSpan"
```

Or you can span *rows*:

```
android:layout_rowSpan=" numberOfRowsToSpan"
```

Listing 3-21 shows an example with one of our buttons stretched to two columns.

Listing 3-21. GridLayoutMultiCellView.axml

```
<GridLayout xmlns:android="http://schemas.android.com/apk/res/android"
    android:layout_width="wrap_content"
    android:layout_height="wrap_content"
    android:rowCount="2"
    android:columnCount="2">
    <TextView
        android:text="A TextView,"
        android:textSize="30dip" />
    <TextView
        android:text=" and another!"
        android:textSize="30dip" />
    <Button
        android:text="Click Me!"
        android:textSize="20dip"
        android:layout_columnSpan="2"
        android:layout_gravity="fill"/>
</GridLayout>
```

To fill both columns with one button, its layout_gravity property is set to fill. The layout's height and width were set to wrap_content.

Figure 3-27 shows the multicelled GridLayout.

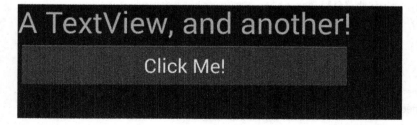

Figure 3-27. *GridLayout with a multicelled button*

■ **Tip**   Make sure that your view fills more than one cell, or changes to `layout_columnSpan` and `layout_rowSpan` may appear to have no effect. Use it or lose it.

Creating a Dynamic Grid of Images

The Android `GridView` is a two-dimensional, scrollable, grid layout useful for the display and selection of images. All cells are the same size, and their contents are populated dynamically from an `Adapter`, like a list in grid form. Chapter 7 provides more detail.

FrameLayout

ANDROID

`FrameLayout` is often used to create layered screens, because it allows the front-to-back ordering of views. It can also swap in and swap out parts of a layout dynamically by using fragments, which are explained in the next section.

`FrameLayout` was originally designed to create a single rectangular area to display a single view. However, it is typically used to achieve complex, layered screens because `FrameLayout` will accept multiple children and gives control over the view z-order (front-to-back order), placing recently added children on top. This is useful for effects such as HUD-like elements, sliding panels, and more-complex animated transitions.

Listing 3-22 is a simple example of a declared `FrameLayout` containing a `TextView`.

Listing 3-22. FrameLayout.axml

```
<LinearLayout xmlns:android="http://schemas.android.com/apk/res/android"
    android:orientation="vertical"
    android:layout_width="fill_parent"
    android:layout_height="fill_parent">
    <FrameLayout
        android:id="@+id/details"
        android:layout_weight="1"
        android:layout_width="fill_parent"
        android:layout_height="fill_parent">
        <TextView
            android:text="A TextView"
            android:layout_width="fill_parent"
            android:layout_height="wrap_content" />
    </FrameLayout>
</LinearLayout>
```

■ **Tip**   Beware of multiple nested elements on different screen sizes in this layout, as overlapping children have been reported when testing across devices.

Fragments

ANDROID

The Android Fragment is a dynamic, reusable layout built to be used on demand in our pages, much like .NET custom controls. Inherited from Android.App.Fragment, so not technically a layout, it's more like a layout on steroids because it has its own state and its own life cycle. Entire apps can be built effectively by using fragments.

Fragments are Android's solution to the variable form factor problem. We develop for devices of hundreds of different sizes, which sometimes work best with completely different layouts. Instead of building with static views and layouts on a page, fragments give us componentized, movable, and reusable elements. They are often used in apps that must look good and work well on both phones and tablets.

Fragments is a core Android UI topic, but a full exploration is beyond the scope of this book. If you think you need reusable, dynamic, custom UI components on Android, especially for phone/tablet apps, seek out more info in the Xamarin and Android online docs. Also see Chapter 6 for a good example of fragments.

Those are the Xamarin.Android layout basics. If you want to learn more about Android (or Xamarin.Forms), turn to Chapter 4, which covers user interaction via controls.

If you're ready for iOS layouts, read on.

Using iOS Layouts

iOS

Static layouts in iOS are primarily accomplished using the UIView class, the base container class for iOS controls and the *V* in iOS's MVC pattern. UIViews are typically paired with a controller class, called UIViewController, which acts like an Android activity or a Xamarin.Forms ContentPage.

■ **Tip**   Most developers create iOS layouts by using designer tools such as Xcode Interface Builder and Xamarin Designer for iOS. Since this is a code-first book and not a tool guide, there isn't much to cover here on this topic. I will touch on the fundamental concepts in code and refer you to the Xamarin online docs (http://developer.xamarin.com/guides/ios/user_interface/designer/) and Apple docs for detail on how to use the designer tools to build iOS layouts.

Views are added as subviews to UIView by using one of two techniques: AutoLayout and Frames. The AutoLayout technique uses constraints to create relative horizontal and vertical relationships between views. The Frames technique uses rectangles to bound the view, assigning them to the Frame property of the view. Location and size are absolute when using Frames and relative when using AutoLayout.

Table 3-2 compares the iOS layout approaches to those of the other platforms.

Table 3-2. *Layout Techniques and Classes by Platform*

iOS	Android	Xamarin.Forms
UIView	LinearLayout	StackLayout
AutoLayout	RelativeLayout	RelativeLayout
Frames	(deprecated)	AbsoluteLayout

> ■ **Tip** A UI designer tool is strongly recommended for getting started with layouts in nibs and storyboards, the iOS XML layout file formats. Use the Xcode Interface Builder or the Xamarin Designer for iOS. When you become familiar with the iOS UI, the hand-coding of iOS XML files is still not recommended because o the unreadbility of the files, built for configuration by design tools, not human eyes. However, I can recommend the hand-coding of C# iOS UI and skipping the XML altogether for advanced users who prefer to go without a designer tool.

Using AutoLayout

iOS

AutoLayout is a responsive layout technique, adapting to different screen sizes automatically. Within a UIViewController, views are assigned as subviews. Their placement and size can be determined by *constraints*, which are flexible, relative relationships between views.

> ■ **Note** As mentioned earlier, this book is a Xamarin.Forms primer and cross-platform guide. It is not an iOS primer and, although it introduces some basic concepts, you'll need additional sources for the iOS and/or Xamarin.iOS fundamentals. If you need an intro to Xamarin.iOS, consult the Xamarin online docs.

In your UIViewController's ViewDidLoad method, in Listing 3-23, instantiate a text box by using UITextField. Then add size and location constraints to it before adding it to the parent view.

Listing 3-23. iOSLayoutExample2ViewController.cs from Solution iOSLayoutExample2

```
public override void ViewDidLoad ()
{
    base.ViewDidLoad ();

    var textView  = new UITextField
        {
            Placeholder = "Your name",
            BorderStyle = UITextBorderStyle.RoundedRect
        };
```

Set the textView's TranslatesAutoresizingMaskIntoConstraints property to false. That property is set to true when converting the older autoresizing frame masks to the newer AutoLayout.

```
    textView.TranslatesAutoresizingMaskIntoConstraints = false;
```

Now we add constraints to the control and to the view. This is accomplished using the AddConstraints method of the control, which uses NSLayoutConstraint.

Specify the size of the text field. Build the constraints using the NSLayoutConstraint.Create method specifying the NSLayoutAttribute, in this case Height and Width. The Add method adds the textView control to the view.

```
textView.AddConstraints (new[] {
    NSLayoutConstraint.Create (textView , NSLayoutAttribute.Height,
        NSLayoutRelation.Equal, null, NSLayoutAttribute.NoAttribute,
        1, 50),
    NSLayoutConstraint.Create (textView , NSLayoutAttribute.Width,
        NSLayoutRelation.Equal, null, NSLayoutAttribute.NoAttribute,
        1, 200),
});
Add(textView);
```

Specify the location of the text field. Constrain the control to the top-level view by using the AddConstraints method on the View. NSLayoutAttribute.Left allows us to place the textView 10 points from the left, and NSLayoutAttribute.Top allows us to specify 30 points from the top.

```
View.AddConstraints (new[] {
    //Location
    NSLayoutConstraint.Create (textView, NSLayoutAttribute.Left,
        NSLayoutRelation.Equal, View, NSLayoutAttribute.Left, 1, 10),
    NSLayoutConstraint.Create (textView, NSLayoutAttribute.Top,
        NSLayoutRelation.Equal, View, NSLayoutAttribute.Top, 1, 30)
});
```

Figure 3-28 shows the text box sized and constrained to the view.

Figure 3-28. *UITextField using AutoLayout*

■ **Tip** Explore the values of NSLayoutAttribute to understand the full range of constraints available. They include Left, Right, Top, Bottom, Leading, Trailing, Width, Height, CenterX, CenterY, LeftMargin, RightMargin, TopMargin, BottomMargin, and others.

Add Constraints by Using Visual Format Language

Another way to add constraints in code is to use *Visual Format Language (VFL)*, a declarative iOS syntax for representing common constraints, including standard spacing and dimensions, vertical layout, and constraints with different priorities. This concise, human-readable grammar can be used in the AddConstraints method. Here are some code snippets to give you the flavor of VFL syntax.

This example sets a minimum width of 50 points on the text field:

```
var viewsDictionary = NSDictionary.FromObjectsAndKeys(new NSObject[]
    {textView}, new NSObject[] { new NSString("textView")});
textView.AddConstraints(NSLayoutConstraint.FromVisualFormat
    ("H:|[textView(>=50)]|", 0, null, viewsDictionary));
```

The H: specifies the horizontal orientation. For vertical constraints, add V: to the start of the VFL string. The colon specifies the control's relationship to the superview (the top-level view). This button is 50.0 points high and the standard spacing from the top of the superview.

```
var viewsDictionary = NSDictionary.FromObjectsAndKeys(new NSObject[]
    {button}, new NSObject[] { new NSString("button")});
textView.AddConstraints(NSLayoutConstraint.FromVisualFormat
    ("V:|-[button(50.0)]", 0, null, viewsDictionary));
```

VFL also allows the creation of constraints between views. The following example creates four buttons, setting the width of each to be the same as the width of the next by using parentheses, so they are all the width of buttonFourth:

```
var viewsDictionary = NSDictionary.FromObjectsAndKeys(new NSObject[]
    {buttonFirst, buttonSecond, buttonThird, buttonFourth},
    new NSObject[] { new NSString("buttonFirst"),
    new NSString("buttonSecond"), new NSString("buttonThird"),
    new NSString("buttonFourth ")});
this.View.AddConstraints( NSLayoutConstraint.FromVisualFormat
    ("H:|-[buttonFirst(buttonSecond)]-[ buttonSecond(buttonThird)]-[ " +
    "buttonThird(buttonFourth)]-[buttonFourth]-|",
    NSLayoutFormatOptions.AlignAllTop |
    NSLayoutFormatOptions.AlignAllBottom,
    height, viewsDictionary));
```

The dashes indicate a standard amount of space between views, which can also have point values to specify the exact space value. For example, [buttonFirst]-10-[buttonSecond] places 10 points between the buttons. The syntax with brackets and dashes is meant to visually represent how the controls look on the screen.

■ **Tip**   These examples are just snippets to give you the gist of VFL. The iOS Developer Guide contains a full VFL definition.

Using Frames

iOS

An absolute approach to iOS layout involves the specification of the bounds and center location of an iOS view by a RectangleF assigned to the Frame property of the superview.

■ **Note**   Note AutoSizing (or autoresizing), an older approach to iOS relative layout than AutoLayout described earlier, couples frames with `UIViewAutoResizingMasks` to create responsive 'springs and struts'. AutoSizing is not covered here because Apple has replaced it with AutoLayout using constraints. Some iOS developers feel that AutoSizing is still preferable for simple layouts.

Here's an example of absolute layout using `Frames`. Create a text field called `textView` and place and size it with a `RectangleF` assigned to the `Frame` property. Then add the `textView` to the parent view, as shown in Listing 3-24.

Listing 3-24. iOSLayoutExamplesViewController.cs from Solution iOSLayoutExamples

```
public override void ViewDidLoad ()
{
    base.ViewDidLoad ();

    var textView = new UITextField
    {
        Placeholder = "Your name",
        BorderStyle = UITextBorderStyle.RoundedRect,
        Frame = new RectangleF(10, 30, 200, 50)
    };
    Add (textView);
}
```

Figure 3-29 shows the result.

Carrier 📶   ▭

┌──────────────────────────────────┐
│ Your name   │
│   │
└──────────────────────────────────┘

Figure 3-29. *UITextField using AutoSizing*

■ **Tip**   Here's a shorthand view constructor that assigns the `Frame` property inline:

```
var textView = new UITextField(new RectangleF(10, 30, 200, 50));
```

Summary

Layouts are a fine example of just how similar these different platforms can be. Names change, but concepts don't, and for added continuity, Xamarin strives to incorporate the most useful aspects of these various platforms into Xamarin.Forms. Here are some of the universal terms related to layouts:

- *Stacked* layouts are the simplest, great for easy pages and quick prototyping and wireframing, like Xamarin.Forms `StackLayout` and Android `LinearLayout`.

- *Rectangles* frame views and their size and coordinate location.

- *Constraints* bind views together like elastic that contextually determines size and location.

- *Relative* placement gives us responsiveness to screen size at the cost of precision, and is the norm in mobile UIs.

- *Layout options* handle alignment and formatting across platforms with `HorizontalOptions` and `VerticalOptions` in Xamarin.Forms, Android `LayoutOptions`, and iOS constraints.

- The *custom control* persists as a concept in mobile development, though it is achieved and named differently across platforms, such as Xamarin.Forms `ContentView` and Android `Fragment`.

- iOS rolls many of the previous concepts into one class: `UIView`.

- *Tables* yield relativity, precision, and versatility. They are found in Xamarin.Forms `GridLayout` and Android `TableLayout` and `GridLayout`. You'll learn more about iOS tables in Chapter 5.

Those are some of the fundamentals of mobile screen layout on all platforms. But enough design and layout, already. Let's move on to user interaction!

CHAPTER 4

■ ■ ■

User Interaction Using Controls

Users choose dates, times, text, integers, doubles, and other values on mobile devices by using tactile controls. Touch-sensitive screens have user interaction that differs slightly from mouse-driven UIs: most is done with the thumbs and forefingers on the touchscreen. From the user's standpoint, this results in a hands-on control-panel interface with switches, icons, sliders, keyboards, and pickers that sometimes look—but more important, feel—like physical mechanisms.

Chapter 2 covered some of the basic Xamarin.Forms views such as the Label, Button, and Image. In this chapter, you'll explore additional controls available on each platform, the gestures and events that make them work, and their outputs.

Many of the controls in this chapter are picker-style (pick a date, pick an option, pick a time, and so forth). These controls tend to look and work better when displayed in a *modal dialog box*, a pop-up box that overlays the app and maintains focus until dismissed by the user. Xamarin.Forms handles this for you by automatically placing pickers in modals. For Android and iOS, this chapter covers platform-specific ways to build modal picker dialog boxes.

This chapter is a gallery and a reference of the most commonly used selection controls.

Xamarin.Forms Views

Xamarin.Forms views can perform these basic input functions:

- Picker : A pop-up to select a value from a simple list
- DatePicker: A pop-up for selecting month, date, and year
- TimePicker: A pop-up for selecting hour, minute, and AM/PM
- Stepper: Increment/decrement buttons for discrete values
- Slider: Sliding input lever for continuous values
- Switch: Boolean on/off control

Android Controls

These are some of the primary Android selection widgets:

- Spinner: A simple drop-down list
- DatePicker: A control for selecting month, date, and year
- TimePicker: A control for selecting hour, minute, and AM/PM
- SeekBar: Sliding input lever for continuous values

- CheckBox: A standard Boolean check-box control

- Switch: A Boolean on/off switch

- RadioButton: Button groups for single or multiple selection

iOS Controls

iOS controls perform a range of user interactions:

- UIPickerView: A simple drop-down list in a spinner

- UIDatePicker: A date and/or time spinner

- UIStepper: Increment/decrement buttons for discrete values

- UISlider: Sliding input lever for continuous values

- UISwitch: Boolean on/off control

■ **Note** The iOS and Android controls for label, text view, button, scroll view, and image are out of scope for this book. Please consult an iOS or Android primer for those.

Xamarin.Forms Views

XAMARIN.FORMS

Xamarin.Forms views provide a range of controls that mimic and extend their iOS and Android counterparts. All of the views covered here allow selection and populate at least one property with a data value specified by the user, sometimes more. Let's look at each view in turn.

Xamarin.Forms views often provide the selected value in two places: a handler event property (for example, e.NewValue) provides the most recent value, and a general-use property on the view provides the selected value for use throughout the page. You will create two labels to display both of those values: eventValue and pageValue.

Create a new ContentPage called Controls and declare two Label views to hold the results of control selection:

```
public partial class Controls : ContentPage
{
    Label eventValue;
    Label pageValue;

    public Controls()
    {
        eventValue= new Label();
        eventValue.Text = "Value in Handler";
        pageValue = new Label();
        pageValue.Text = "Value in Page";
```

Create a StackLayout at the end of your Controls() constructor to assign to your page's Content property. Center all of the controls in the StackLayout by using HorizontalOptions = LayoutOptions.Center. All of the Xamarin.Forms examples in this chapter can be found in the source listing Controls.cs in the ControlExamples solution, shown in Listing 4-1 at the end of this section.

Remember to add each view to your StackLayout as you go!

■ **Tip** All example code solutions, including the XAML versions of these C# examples, can be found at the Apress web site (www.apress.com) or on GitHub at https://github.com/danhermes/xamarin-book-examples.

Picker

The Picker view provides a pop-up to select a value from a simple list.

■ **Note** The Picker view is used for quick selection of short words, phrases, or numbers. Complex lists with composite cells containing multiple strings and images are covered in the next chapter.

First, create the picker and give it a title:

```
Picker picker = new Picker
{
    Title = "Option",
    VerticalOptions = LayoutOptions.CenterAndExpand
};
```

Next, populate the list:

```
var options = new List<string> { "First", "Second", "Third", "Fourth" };

foreach (string optionName in options)
{
    picker.Items.Add(optionName);
}
```

Option names are placed into the list and then added to the Items collection in the picker.

The Entry view in Figure 4-1 starts as a data entry field, similar to Xamarin.Forms.Entry displaying the value of the Title property.

Figure 4-1. *Entry views often have inline labels instead of side labels*

When this field is tapped, a modal dialog appears, containing the list of items (Figure 4-2).

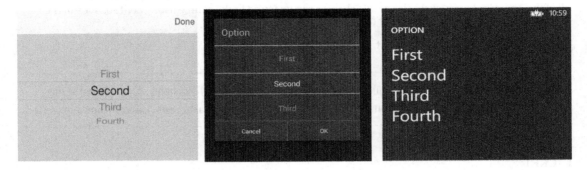

Figure 4-2. *Each picker looks a bit different, depending on the platform*

The list spins when swiped, and the highlighted value becomes the selected value. The selection is automatically populated into the original entry field so the user can see the effect of the change. The SelectedIndexChanged event also fires, which can be assigned a handler method or handled inline like this:

```
picker.SelectedIndexChanged += (sender, args) =>
{
    pageValue.Text = picker.Items[picker.SelectedIndex];
};
```

This implementation assigns the selected string to the Text property of the pageValue label.

■ **Tip** The selected index in the Picker.SelectedIndex property is a zero-based integer index. If Cancel is selected, the SelectedIndex remains unchanged.

DatePicker

XAMARIN.FORMS

The DatePicker view creates a pop-up for selection of month, date, and year. Create a DatePicker view like this:

```
DatePicker datePicker = new DatePicker
{
    Format = "D",
    VerticalOptions = LayoutOptions.CenterAndExpand
};
```

The Format property is set to D for the full month/day/year display. More date formats are provided later in this section.

The DatePicker view starts as a data entry field (Figure 4-3), similar to Xamarin.Forms.Entry displaying the value of the Date property.

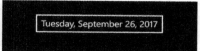

Figure 4-3. DatePicker begins as an Entry view waiting for a tap

When the date field is tapped, a modal dialog appears (Figure 4-4).

Figure 4-4. DatePicker is a modal dialog

Each column spins individually when swiped, and the highlighted values become the selected values. When Done is tapped, the selected date is automatically populated into the original entry field so the user can see the effect of the change. The DateSelected event also fires, which can be assigned a handler method or handled inline like this:

```
datePicker.DateSelected += (object sender, DateChangedEventArgs e) =>
{
        eventValue.Text = e.NewDate.ToString();
        pageValue.Text = datePicker.Date.ToString();
};
```

The properties e.OldDate and e.NewDate are available within this event to provide the old and new selected date values. In general cases, however, the value entered by the user is stored in the Date property. All of these properties use type DateTime.

The format of the Date field is customizable with the `Format` property—for example, `myDate.Format = "D"`. Other values are as follows:

- D: Full month, day, and year (Monday, March 5, 2018)

- d: Month, day, and year (3/5/2018)

- M: Month and day (March 5)

- Y: Month and year (March 2018)

- yy: Last two digits of the year (18)

- yyyy: Full year (2018)

- MM: Two-digit month (03)

- MMMM: Month (March)

- dd: Two-digit day (05)

- ddd: Abbreviated day of the week (Mon)

- dddd: Full day of the week (Monday)

You set a date range for selection by using `MaximumDate` and `MinimumDate`:

```
datePicker.MaximumDate = Convert.ToDateTime("1/1/2019");
datePicker.MinimumDate = Convert.ToDateTime("1/1/2014");
```

■ **Tip** On Android, the `Format` and `MaximumDate`/`MinimumDate` properties affect the `DatePicker` entry field but not the modal selection dialog at the time of this writing.

TimePicker

XAMARIN.FORMS

The `TimePicker` view creates a pop-up for selecting hour, minute, and AM/PM. Create a `TimePicker` view like this:

```
TimePicker timePicker = new TimePicker
{
    Format = "T",
    VerticalOptions = LayoutOptions.CenterAndExpand
};
```

The `Format` property set to T displays the full time. More time formats follow.

The `TimePicker` view starts as a data entry field similar to `Xamarin.Forms.Entry`, displaying the value of the Time property (Figure 4-5).

Figure 4-5. *TimePicker waits for a tap*

When the time field is tapped, a modal dialog appears (Figure 4-6).

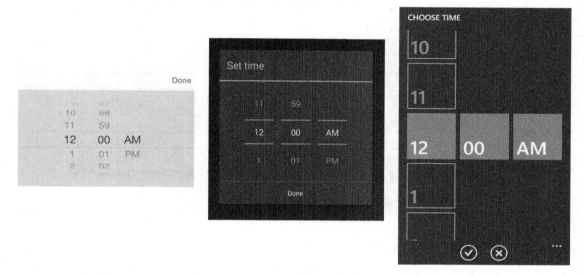

Figure 4-6. *TimePicker is a dialog box*

Each column spins individually when swiped, and the highlighted values become the selected values. When Done is tapped, the selected time is automatically populated into the original entry field so the user can see the effect of the change.

There is no TimeSelected event that triggers when a value is selected. Instead, use the PropertyChanged event in Xamarin.Forms data-binding to track changes to this view:

```
timePicker.PropertyChanged += (sender, e) =>
{
    if (e.PropertyName == TimePicker.TimeProperty.PropertyName)
    {
        pageValue.Text = timePicker.Time.ToString();
    }
};
```

The timePicker.Time property is set with the selected value as type TimeSpan.

The format of the Time field is customizable with the Format property (for example, Format = "T"). Other values are as follows:

- T: Full time with hours, minutes, seconds, and AM/PM (9:30:25 AM)

- t: Full time with hours, minutes, and AM/PM (9:30 AM)

- hh: Two-digit hours (09)

- mm: Two-digit minutes (30)

- ss: Two-digit seconds (25); seconds are not selectable in the dialog box

- tt: AM/PM designator (AM)

■ **Tip** Format affects the TimePicker entry field but not the dialog box at the time of this writing.

Stepper

XAMARIN.FORMS

The Stepper view creates increment and decrement buttons for discrete adjustments to the values:

```
Stepper stepper = new Stepper
{
    Minimum = 0,
    Maximum = 10,
    Increment = 1,
    HorizontalOptions = LayoutOptions.Center,
    VerticalOptions = LayoutOptions.CenterAndExpand
};
```

Minimum, Maximum, and Increment properties are set for the steppable value. The start value can be set in the Stepper.Value property. Here is a shortcut constructor:

```
public Stepper (Double Minimum , Double  Maximum , Double  StartValue,
                Double Increment)
```

This constructor can be implemented like this:

```
Stepper stepper = new Stepper(0 ,10 ,0 , 1);
```

Figure 4-7 shows what the Stepper view looks like.

Figure 4-7. *Plus and minus for increment and decrement*

Tapping a plus or minus button changes the adjustable value and fires the Stepper.ValueChanged event. It can be handled in a method or inline, like so:

```
stepper.ValueChanged += (sender, e) =>
{
    eventValue.Text = String.Format("Stepper value is {0:F1}", e.NewValue);
    pageValue.Text = stepper.Value.ToString();
};
```

The properties e.OldValue and e. NewValue are available within this event to provide the old and new selected values. In general cases, however, the value entered by the user is stored in the Stepper's Value property. All these properties are type Double.

Slider

XAMARIN.FORMS

The Slider view is a sliding input control providing a continuum of selection:

```
Slider slider = new Slider
{
    Minimum = 0,
    Maximum = 100,
    Value = 50,
    VerticalOptions = LayoutOptions.CenterAndExpand,
    WidthRequest = 300
};
```

Minimum and Maximum properties are set for the slidable value. The start value can be set in the Slider.Value property. The value changes by increments by one-tenth of a unit (0.1) as the slider is moved. The WidthRequest property sets the width of the view without changing minimum or maximum values. Here is a shortcut constructor:

```
public Slider (Double Minimum , Double  Maximum , Double  StartValue)
```

This constructor can be implemented like this:

```
Slider  slider = new Slider  (0 ,100 ,50);
```

Figure 4-8 shows what the Slider view looks like (with Value = 100).

Figure 4-8. *Slider view at its max value*

Sliding the slider changes the adjustable value and fires the `slider.ValueChanged` event. It can be handled inline or as a method, like so:

```
slider.ValueChanged += (sender, e) =>
{
    eventValue.Text = String.Format("Slider value is {0:F1}", e.NewValue);
    pageValue.Text = slider.Value.ToString();
};
```

The properties `e.OldValue` and `e.NewValue` are available within this event to provide the old and new selected values. In general cases, the slidable value is also stored in the `slider.Value` property. All these properties are of type `Double`.

Switch

XAMARIN.FORMS

The `Switch` view is a Boolean on/off control:

```
Switch switcher = new Switch
{
    HorizontalOptions = LayoutOptions.Center,
    VerticalOptions = LayoutOptions.CenterAndExpand
};
```

Figure 4-9 shows what the `Switch` view looks like off.

Figure 4-9. *Switch off*

And Figure 4-10 shows what the same view looks like on.

Figure 4-10. *Switch on*

Tapping the switch changes the Boolean value and fires the `Switch.Toggled` event. It can be handled inline or as a method, like so:

```
switcher.Toggled += (sender, e) =>
{
    eventValue.Text = String.Format("Switch is now {0}", e.Value);
    pageValue.Text = switcher.IsToggled.ToString();
};
```

The property e.Value is available within this event to provide the new switch value. In general cases, the value is also stored in the Switch.IsToggled property. These properties are of type Boolean.

Scale, Rotation, Opacity, Visibility, and Focus

XAMARIN.FORMS

You can alter the appearance and behavior of Xamarin.Forms views by using members of the View superclass, VisualElement.

You give focus to a view by using the Focus() method, which returns true if successful. This example sets focus on an Entry view (which pops up the keyboard):

```
var gotFocus = entry.Focus();
```

Here are some key properties that can be set on a view:

- Scale: Change the size of a view without affecting the views around it. The default value is 1.0.

```
switcher.Scale = 0.7;
```

- IsVisible: Make a view invisible, or visible again.

```
label.IsVisible = false;
```

- IsEnabled: Disable and reenable a view.

```
label.IsEnabled = false;
```

- Opacity: Fade a view in and out. The default value is 1.0.

```
label.Opacity = 0.5;
```

- Rotation: View rotation can be achieved on all axes by using the Rotation, RotationX, and RotationY properties. These rotate the view around the point set by AnchorX and AnchorY.

CODE COMPLETE: Xamarin.Forms Controls

XAMARIN.FORMS

Listing 4-1 contains the complete code listing for all Xamarin.Forms selection control examples in this chapter.

■ **XAML**   The XAML version of this example can be found at the Apress web site (www.apress.com), or on GitHub at https://github.com/danhermes/xamarin-book-examples. The Xamarin.Forms solution for Chapter 4 is ControlExamples.Xaml.

Figure 4-11 shows the full screen.

Figure 4-11. *Xamarin.Forms selection views*

Listing 4-1. Controls.cs in the ControlExamples Project of the ControlExamples Solution

```
public partial class Controls : ContentPage
    {
    Label eventValue;
    Label pageValue;

    public Controls()
    {
        eventValue= new Label();
        eventValue.Text = "Label";
        pageValue = new Label();
        pageValue.Text = "PageValue";

        Picker picker = new Picker
        {
            Title = "Option",
            VerticalOptions = LayoutOptions.CenterAndExpand
        };

        var options = new List<string> { "First", "Second", "Third", "Fourth" };
```

```csharp
foreach (string optionName in options)
{
    picker.Items.Add(optionName);
}

picker.SelectedIndexChanged += (sender, args) =>
{
    pageValue.Text = picker.Items[picker.SelectedIndex];
};

DatePicker datePicker = new DatePicker
{
    Format = "D",
    VerticalOptions = LayoutOptions.CenterAndExpand
};

datePicker.DateSelected += (object sender, DateChangedEventArgs e) =>
{
    eventValue.Text = e.NewDate.ToString();
    pageValue.Text = datePicker.Date.ToString();
};

TimePicker timePicker = new TimePicker
{
    Format = "T",
    VerticalOptions = LayoutOptions.CenterAndExpand
};

timePicker.PropertyChanged += (sender, e) =>
{
    if (e.PropertyName == TimePicker.TimeProperty.PropertyName)
    {
        pageValue.Text = timePicker.Time.ToString();
    }
};

Stepper stepper = new Stepper
{
    Minimum = 0,
    Maximum = 10,
    Increment = 1,
    HorizontalOptions = LayoutOptions.Center,
    VerticalOptions = LayoutOptions.CenterAndExpand
};
```

```
        stepper.ValueChanged += (sender, e) =>
        {
            eventValue.Text = String.Format("Stepper value is {0:F1}", e.NewValue);
            pageValue.Text = stepper.Value.ToString();
        };

        Slider slider = new Slider
        {
            Minimum = 0,
            Maximum = 100,
            Value = 50,
            VerticalOptions = LayoutOptions.CenterAndExpand,
            WidthRequest = 300
        };

        slider.ValueChanged += (sender, e) =>
        {
            eventValue.Text = String.Format("Slider value is {0:F1}", e.NewValue);
            pageValue.Text = slider.Value.ToString();
        };


        Switch switcher = new Switch
        {
            HorizontalOptions = LayoutOptions.Center,
            VerticalOptions = LayoutOptions.CenterAndExpand
        };

        switcher.Toggled += (sender, e) =>
        {
            eventValue.Text = String.Format("Switch is now {0}", e.Value);
            pageValue.Text = switcher.IsToggled.ToString();
        };

        this.Padding = new Thickness(10, Device.OnPlatform(20, 0, 0), 10, 5);

        this.Content = new StackLayout {
            HorizontalOptions = LayoutOptions.Center,
            Children = {
                eventValue,
                pageValue,
                picker,
                datePicker,
                timePicker,
                stepper,
                slider,
                switcher
            }
        };
    }
}
```

■ **Note**   Again, the two labels used in this example reflect the two ways in which selection values can be retrieved: in a handler event property (for example, e.NewValue), which provides the most recent value, or in a general-use property on the view, which provides the selected value for use throughout the page.

That completes our tour of Xamarin.Forms views!

It's time for your choice:

- If you're reading this book for *Xamarin.Forms only* and aren't yet interested in a platform-specific UI, you may want to jump to the beginning of the next chapter to continue reading about Xamarin.Forms.

- If you are ready to delve deeper into the platform-specific approach using Xamarin. Android and Xamarin.iOS, then read on!

Let's start with the Xamarin.Android controls before moving on to iOS. You can use the following controls when building Xamarin.Android platform-specific solutions or when creating Android custom renderers inside Xamarin.Forms solutions, as described in Chapter 8.

Android Controls

ANDROID

Some of the selection widgets used most often on Android are Spinner, DatePicker, TimePicker, SeekBar, CheckBox, Switch, and RadioButton. The Spinner is a simple drop-down selection picker, the SeekBar is a slider, and the rest of these controls are exactly what they sound like.

Unlike many Xamarin.Forms controls, Android views don't produce a modal dialog box by default, but produce only an inline dialog. Use the techniques described in the following sections or roll your own modals by using DialogFragments (see Chapter 6).

Create a new Android solution of type Blank App (Android) called ControlExamplesAndroid.

Spinner

A Spinner is an Android widget that provides a simple drop-down list of items to choose from.

Making a Spinner requires a few steps. You place a Spinner in your layout XML, and then create another layout that contains a TextView for binding to an Adapter to create a list to display. Next you instantiate the spinner in an activity, populate the list, and then bind the list to the Spinner.Adapter property and handle selection using the Spinner.ItemSelected event.

First, place a Spinner on a LinearLayout either using a designer or coded by hand in XML and call the layout Spinner.axml in the Resources/layout folder:

```
<Spinner
    android:layout_width="match_parent"
    android:layout_height="wrap_content"
    android:id="@+id/spinner" />
```

A Spinner is populated from an Adapter. In this example, an ArrayAdapter based on a hand-coded string array. An ArrayAdapter populates a list with strings, using a TextView for each list item.

Create a new layout to contain a TextView (also in the Resources/layout folder) that is used as a cell in the Spinner's list. Name this layout TextViewForSpinner.axml:

```
<?xml version="1.0" encoding="UTF-8"?>
<TextView xmlns:android="http://schemas.android.com/apk/res/android"
    android:id="@+id/textItem"
    android:textSize="44sp"
    android:layout_width="fill_parent"
    android:layout_height="wrap_content" />
```

Create a new activity called SpinnerActivity.cs. In the OnCreate method, point to the spinner layout by using SetContentView, and find the spinner in the layout by using FindViewById:

```
SetContentView (Resource.Layout.Spinner);
Spinner spinner = FindViewById<Spinner> (Resource.Id.spinner);
```

Populate a string array with selectable options and construct the ArrayAdapter:

```
string[] options = {"one", "two", "three", "four", "five"} ;
ArrayAdapter adapter = new ArrayAdapter (this, Resource.Layout.TextViewForSpinner,
options);
spinner.Adapter = adapter;
```

Note how the ArrayAdapter constructor uses the TextView and the string array as parameters. The ArrayAdapter is assigned to the Adapter property of the spinner.

■ **Tip** Use the default resource, SimpleSpinnerItem, instead of manually creating TextViewForSpinner.axml in the Adapter declaration:

```
ArrayAdapter adapter = new ArrayAdapter (this, Resource.Layout.SimpleSpinnerItem, options);
```

■ **Tip** You can also set a default drop-down style by using SetDropDownViewResource:

```
adapter.SetDropDownViewResource (Android.Resource.Layout.SimpleSpinnerDropDownItem);
```

The spinner looks like an Entry view at first (Figure 4-12).

Figure 4-12. *Spinner anxiously awaiting a tap*

Tap it to display the drop-down list (Figure 4-13).

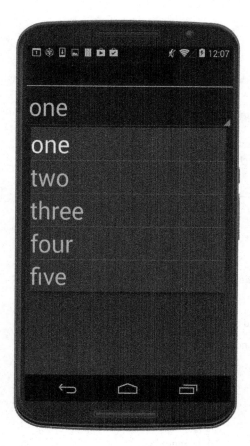

Figure 4-13. *Spinner is a dialog box*

Selecting an item fires the ItemSelected event, which can be handled inline or in a handler method like this:

```
spinner.ItemSelected += new EventHandler<AdapterView.ItemSelectedEventArgs>
(spinner_ItemSelected);
```

Here is the handler method that creates a toast to display the selected item:

```
private void spinner_ItemSelected (object sender, AdapterView.ItemSelectedEventArgs e)
{
    Spinner spinner = (Spinner)sender;

    string toast = string.Format ("Selection: {0}", spinner.GetItemAtPosition
    (e.Position));
    Toast.MakeText (this, toast, ToastLength.Long).Show ();
}
```

Selecting an item pops up the toast, displaying the selected item shown in Figure 4-14.

Figure 4-14. *A toast is Android's way of raising a glass for an important occasion*

■ **Note** Two other useful techniques for populating a spinner include an XML `<string-array>` and a data-bound adapter.

CODE COMPLETE: Spinner

ANDROID

The full `SpinnerActivity.cs` is shown in Listing 4-2. Refer to the downloadable source code for the layout XMLs.

Listing 4-2. SpinnerActivity.cs in the ControlExamplesAndroid Solution

```
[Activity (Label = "AndroidSelectionExamples", MainLauncher = true, Icon = "@drawable/icon")]
public class SpinnerActivity : Activity
{
    protected override void OnCreate (Bundle bundle)
    {
        base.OnCreate (bundle);
        SetContentView (Resource.Layout.Spinner);
        Spinner spinner = FindViewById<Spinner> (Resource.Id.spinner);
        spinner.ItemSelected += new EventHandler<AdapterView.ItemSelectedEventArgs>
        (spinner_ItemSelected);

        string[] options = {"one", "two", "three", "four", "five"} ;
        ArrayAdapter adapter = new ArrayAdapter (this,
            Resource.Layout.TextViewForSpinner, options);

        spinner.Adapter = adapter;
    }

    private void spinner_ItemSelected (object sender, AdapterView.ItemSelectedEventArgs e)
    {
        Spinner spinner = (Spinner)sender;

        string toast = string.Format ("Selection: {0}", spinner.GetItemAtPosition
        (e.Position));
        Toast.MakeText (this, toast, ToastLength.Long).Show ();
    }
}
```

DatePicker

ANDROID

The DatePicker is a spinner and/or calendar used for selecting the month, date, and year.

■ **Note** Modal dialogs are not a built-in function of Android pickers such as the DatePicker. Android pickers are inline dialogs by default. Modals must be coded by hand, in this case by using DatePickerDialog. You'll do this in the next section.

Add a DatePicker to your main layout by either using a designer or coding by hand in XML:

```
<DatePicker
    android:layout_width="match_parent"
    android:layout_height="wrap_content"
    android:id="@+id/datePicker" />
```

Instantiate a DatePicker in your activity. Match the widget ID name between the layout and activity:

```
DatePicker datePicker = FindViewById<DatePicker> (Resource.Id.datePicker);
```

The default DatePicker looks like Figure 4-15.

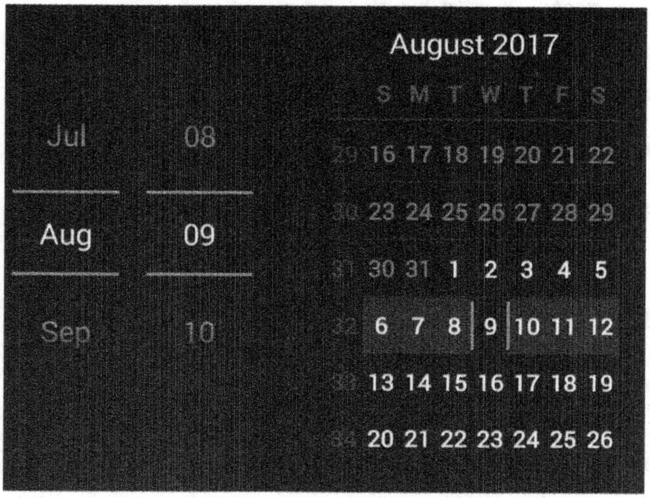

Figure 4-15. *The default DatePicker is a spinner and calendar*

Month and day columns can be scrolled and can accept a typed entry, enabling the user to search for a month or to enter the date. The calendar at right is scrollable, and the day is selectable.

This example creates an inline DatePicker, which consumes real estate and remains on the page even after the user is done with it. Typically, DatePickers are implemented as modal dialogs that allow the user to select a date value to fill a particular text field, then the dialog disappears after the selection is made.

Creating a Modal DatePicker by Using DatePickerDialog

The following example demonstrates a clickable text view that invokes the DatePicker as a modal dialog.

In a new layout called Picker.axml, add the TextView to a LinearLayout and name it textView, with the text "Pick Date":

```
<LinearLayout xmlns:android="http://schemas.android.com/apk/res/android"
    android:orientation="vertical"
    android:layout_width="fill_parent"
    android:layout_height="fill_parent">
    <TextView
        android:text="Pick Date"
        android:textAppearance="?android:attr/textAppearanceLarge"
        android:layout_width="match_parent"
        android:layout_height="wrap_content"
        android:id="@+id/textView" />
</LinearLayout>
```

In the activity, declare a date variable. Reference the textView and create a listener for the Click event that calls the ShowDialog method:

```
public class DatePickerActivity : Activity
{
    DateTime date;

    protected override void OnCreate (Bundle bundle)
    {
        base.OnCreate (bundle);
        SetContentView (Resource.Layout.Picker);

        var textView = FindViewById<TextView>(Resource.Id.textView);

        textView.Click += delegate {
            ShowDialog (0);
        };

        date = DateTime.Today;
    }
```

Add a method to the activity that fires when ShowDialog is called and that instantiates DatePickerDialog:

```
protected override Dialog OnCreateDialog (int id)
{
    return new DatePickerDialog (this, HandleDateSet, date.Year, date.Month - 1,
    date.Day);
}
```

DatePickerDialog is populated with fields from the date variable. Last, handle changes to the date in DatePickerDialog by defining HandleDateSet:

```
void HandleDateSet (object sender, DatePickerDialog.DateSetEventArgs e)
{
    var textView = FindViewById<TextView>(Resource.Id.textView);
    date = e.Date;
    textView.Text = date.ToString("d");
}
```

This assigns the entered Date to the date variable and formats this to be placed into the textView's Text property. Run the solution to see the TextView in Figure 4-16.

Figure 4-16. textView patiently awaits a click

Tap/click the TextView to pop up DatePickerDialog (Figure 4-17).

Figure 4-17. DataPickerDialog modal dialog

Spin the spinners, choose the date, and click Done. textView is updated with the selected date (Figure 4-18).

11/3/2017

Figure 4-18. *The TextView displays the selected date*

CODE COMPLETE: DatePickerExample

ANDROID

Listing 4-3 contains the activity code for the modal DatePicker dialog DatePickerDialogExample solution. Remember to add the TextView named textView to the main screen by using a designer.

Listing 4-3. DatePickerActivity.cs in the ControlExamplesAndroid Solution

```
[Activity (Label = "DatePickerDialogExample", MainLauncher = true)]
public class DatePickerActivity : Activity
    {
        DateTime date;

        protected override void OnCreate (Bundle bundle)
        {
            base.OnCreate (bundle);

            SetContentView (Resource.Layout.Picker);

            var textView = FindViewById<TextView>(Resource.Id.textView);

            textView.Click += delegate {
                ShowDialog (0);
            };

            date = DateTime.Today;
        }

        protected override Dialog OnCreateDialog (int id)
        {
            return new DatePickerDialog (this, HandleDateSet, date.Year, date.Month - 1,
            date.Day);
        }

        void HandleDateSet (object sender, DatePickerDialog.DateSetEventArgs e)
        {
            var textView = FindViewById<TextView>(Resource.Id.textView);
            date = e.Date;
            textView.Text = date.ToString("d");
        }

    }
```

TimePicker

ANDROID

The TimePicker is a spinner for selecting hour, minute, and AM/PM.

■ **Note** Modal dialog boxes are not a built-in function of pickers such as the TimePicker and must be coded manually, in this case using the TimePickerDialog class. Use the modal technique described for DatePickerDialog in the previous section. See the full code in TimePickerActivity.cs in the ControlExamplesAndroid solution.

Add a TimePicker called timePicker to your layout:

```
<TimePicker
    android:layout_width="match_parent"
    android:layout_height="wrap_content"
    android:id="@+id/timePicker" />
```

Create a TimePicker class in your activity. Match the widget ID name between the layout and activity:

```
TimePicker timePicker = FindViewById<TimePicker> (Resource.Id.timePicker);
```

Default time values can be set in the properties CurrentHour and CurrentMinute:

```
timePicker.CurrentHour = (Java.Lang.Integer) 17;
timePicker.CurrentMinute = (Java.Lang.Integer) 30;
```

The TimePicker looks like Figure 4-19.

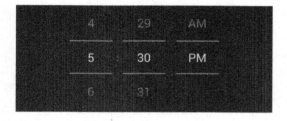

Figure 4-19. *TimePicker has columns of spinners*

All rows are scrollable. Changes to the control fire the TimeChanged event, which can be handled inline like this:

```
timePicker.TimeChanged += delegate(object sender, TimePicker.TimeChangedEventArgs e)
{
Toast.MakeText (this, "Hour: " + e.HourOfDay + " Minute: " + e.Minute, ToastLength.
Short).Show();
};
```

e.HourOfDay and e.Minute contain the selected time values. Figure 4-20 shows the toast.

Figure 4-20. *Cheers! It's that time*

SeekBar

ANDROID

A SeekBar is a sliding input lever for continuous values.

Add a SeekBar to your layout:

```
<SeekBar
    android:layout_width="match_parent"
    android:layout_height="wrap_content"
    android:id="@+id/seekBar"/>
```

Create a SeekBar class in your activity:

```
SeekBar seekBar = FindViewById<SeekBar> (Resource.Id.seekBar);
```

The SeekBar looks like Figure 4-21.

Figure 4-21. *SeekBar is a slider.*

■ **Tip** The minimum value of the SeekBar is zero.

When the SeekBar value is changed, the ProgressChanged event is fired, which can be handled inline like this:

```
seekBar.ProgressChanged += (object sender, SeekBar.ProgressChangedEventArgs e) => {
    if (e.FromUser)
    {
        Toast.MakeText (this, "Value: " + e.Progress, ToastLength.Short).Show ();
    }
};
```

The selection value is found in the e.Progress property. The e.FromUser property is true if the change was initiated by the user (not programmatically). Figure 4-22 shows the toast.

Figure 4-22. *The toast memorializes the value*

■ **Tip** The SeekBar can also be tracked with listeners by implementing the SeekBar.IOnSeekBarChange Listener interface. See http://developer.xamarin.com/recipes/android/controls/seekbar/ for details.

■ **Tip** The default SeekBar range can be changed using SeekBar.Max. The default value is 100.

CheckBox

ANDROID

CheckBox is a standard Boolean check-box control, often deployed in groups.

Add CheckBoxes to your layout:

```
<CheckBox
    android:text="Option1"
    android:layout_width="match_parent"
    android:layout_height="wrap_content"
    android:id="@+id/checkBox1" />
<CheckBox
    android:text="Option2"
    android:layout_width="match_parent"
    android:layout_height="wrap_content"
    android:id="@+id/checkBox2" />
```

These have the IDs checkBox1 and checkBox2. The Text property contains the displayed text string. Create CheckBox classes in your activity (usually in OnCreate()):

```
CheckBox checkBox1 = FindViewById<CheckBox> (Resource.Id.checkBox1);
CheckBox checkBox2 = FindViewById<CheckBox> (Resource.Id.checkBox2);
```

Check boxes look like Figure 4-23.

Figure 4-23. *Two separate, unconnected check boxes*

The Boolean selection value is stored in the CheckBox.Checked property of each CheckBox.

A Click event fires when a check box is tapped, which can be handled inline like this in the OnCreate() method:

```
checkBox1.Click += (o, e) => {
    if (checkBox1.Checked)
        Toast.MakeText (this, "Checked", ToastLength.Short).Show ();
    else
        Toast.MakeText (this, "Not checked", ToastLength.Short).Show ();
};
```

This handler displays a toast reflecting the value of checkBox1. See the rest of the code in Listing 4-4.

■ **Tip** For CheckBoxes to behave as a group (so only one can be selected at a time, for example) they must be coded by hand, by using each CheckBox's Click event and setting the value of each manually. For these situations, you should probably be considering RadioButtons, covered shortly.

Switch

ANDROID

A Switch is a Boolean on/off widget, often used to turn features on or off.

Add a Switch to your layout:

```
<Switch
        android:layout_width="wrap_content"
        android:layout_height="wrap_content"
        android:id="@+id/switch1"
        android:layout_gravity="center_horizontal" />
```

Instantiate a Switch class in your activity:

```
Switch switch1 = FindViewById<Switch> (Resource.Id.switch1);
```

A Switch looks like Figure 4-24.

Figure 4-24. *Switch is on, waiting for a tap*

The Boolean value is stored in the Switch.IsChecked property. Tapping the control fires the CheckedChange event, which can be handled like this:

```
switch1.CheckedChange += delegate(object sender, CompoundButton.
CheckedChangeEventArgs e)
{
    var toast = Toast.MakeText (this, "Selection:" + (e.IsChecked ?  "On" : "Off"),
    ToastLength.Short);
    toast.Show ();
};
```

This pops up a toast with the switch value (Figure 4-25).

Figure 4-25. *Toast displaying Switch state*

Customizing with a Title, Switch Text, and State

A text title that appears before the switch, usually a feature or question, can be added in the text property. Default text on the switch itself can be changed by using the textOn and textOff properties (for example, to indicate Yes/No instead of On/Off). The default switch on/off state can be changed with the checked property:

```
<Switch android:text="Feature activated?"
        android:id="@+id/switch1"
        android:layout_width="wrap_content"
        android:layout_height="wrap_content"
        android:checked="true"
        android:textOn="YES"
        android:textOff="NO" />
```

This results in a customized switch (Figure 4-26).

Figure 4-26. *The text property shows a label, and On/Off is now Yes/No*

RadioButton

ANDROID

A RadioButton is a selectable button widget that can be grouped with other RadioButtons by using a RadioGroup. This grouping makes selection mutually exclusive, so only one button can be selected at a time.

Create a RadioGroup containing RadioButtons in your layout:

```
<RadioGroup
  android:layout_width="fill_parent"
  android:layout_height="wrap_content"
  android:orientation="vertical">
  <RadioButton android:id="@+id/radio1"
      android:layout_width="wrap_content"
      android:layout_height="wrap_content"
      android:text="First" />
  <RadioButton android:id="@+id/radio2"
      android:layout_width="wrap_content"
      android:layout_height="wrap_content"
      android:text="Second" />
</RadioGroup>
```

Here we have two RadioButtons with the IDs radio1 and radio2. Their text properties are set to First and Second, respectively, and that is the text that will appear next to the buttons.

Create RadioButtons at the top of your activity outside OnCreate:

```
RadioButton radio1;
RadioButton radio2;
```

Inside OnCreate, find the buttons:

```
radio1 = FindViewById<RadioButton>(Resource.Id.radio1);
radio2 = FindViewById<RadioButton>(Resource.Id.radio2);
```

Figure 4-27 shows the result.

Figure 4-27. *RadioGroup of two RadioButtons*

Tapping a RadioButton fires a Click event that can be handled like this:

```
radio1.Click += RadioButtonClick;
radio2.Click += RadioButtonClick;
```

Place the handler method outside the OnCreate method:

```
private void RadioButtonClick (object sender, EventArgs e)
{
    RadioButton rb = (RadioButton)sender;
    Toast.MakeText (this, rb.Text, ToastLength.Short).Show ();
}
```

This will toast the text property of the RadioButton when tapped (Figure 4-28).

Figure 4-28. *Cheers, First!*

CODE COMPLETE: Android Controls

ANDROID

Listing 4-4 contains the activity code for the SeekBar, CheckBox, and Switch controls. For the DatePicker and TimePicker examples, see Listing 4-3 and the downloadable code solution, ControlExamplesAndroid.

Figure 4-29 displays all the selection controls covered here.

Figure 4-29. *Android selection controls*

Listing 4-4. SelectionActivity.cs in the ControlExamplesAndroid Solution

```
public class SelectionActivity : Activity
{

    RadioButton radio1;
    RadioButton radio2;

    protected override void OnCreate (Bundle bundle)
    {
        base.OnCreate (bundle);

        SetContentView (Resource.Layout.Selection);

        SeekBar seekBar = FindViewById<SeekBar> (Resource.Id.seekBar);
        seekBar.ProgressChanged += (object sender, SeekBar.ProgressChangedEventArgs e) =>
        {
            if (e.FromUser)
            {
                Toast.MakeText(this, "Value: " + e.Progress, ToastLength.Short).Show();
            }
        };

        CheckBox checkBox1 = FindViewById<CheckBox> (Resource.Id.checkBox1);
        CheckBox checkBox2 = FindViewById<CheckBox> (Resource.Id.checkBox2);
        checkBox1.Click += (o, e) =>
        {
            if (checkBox1.Checked)
                Toast.MakeText(this, "Box 1 Checked", ToastLength.Short).Show();
            else
                Toast.MakeText(this, "Box 1 Not checked", ToastLength.Short).Show();
        };
        checkBox2.Click += (o, e) =>
        {
            if (checkBox2.Checked)
                Toast.MakeText(this, "Box 2 Checked", ToastLength.Short).Show();
            else
                Toast.MakeText(this, "Box 2 Not checked", ToastLength.Short).Show();
        };

        Switch switch1 = FindViewById<Switch> (Resource.Id.switch1);
        switch1.CheckedChange += delegate(object sender, CompoundButton.
        CheckedChangeEventArgs e)
        {
            var toast = Toast.MakeText(this, "Selection:" + (e.IsChecked ? "On" : "Off"),
            ToastLength.Short);
            toast.Show();
        };
```

```
        radio1 = FindViewById<RadioButton>(Resource.Id.radio1);
        radio2 = FindViewById<RadioButton>(Resource.Id.radio2);
        radio1.Click += RadioButtonClick;
        radio2.Click += RadioButtonClick;
    }

    private void RadioButtonClick(object sender, EventArgs e)
    {
        RadioButton rb = (RadioButton)sender;
        Toast.MakeText(this, rb.Text, ToastLength.Short).Show();
    }

}
```

If you're ready to learn more about Android, then turn to Chapter 5 where you'll learn about lists.

For iOS controls, read on. Next let's explore Xamarin.iOS platform-specific controls. You can use these controls when building Xamarin.iOS platform-specific solutions or when creating iOS custom renderers inside Xamarin.Forms solutions, as described in Chapter 8.

iOS Controls

iOS

Some of most common iOS selection controls are UIPickerView, UIDatePicker, UIStepper, UISlider, and UISwitch. UIPickerView supplies a drop-down list, UIStepper gives a plus/minus button for changing numeric values, and the rest are self-explanatory.

Similar to Android, iOS controls don't produce a modal dialog box by default, but produce only an inline dialog. Use the UITextField.InputView modal dialog technique described in the following sections.

UIPickerView

The UIPickerView control provides a drop-down list for selection of a single item, typically from a short list of items obtained from a data model.

The UIPickerView is generally linked to a UITextField which, when tapped, pops up the picker. The picker is data-bound to a specialized view-model class called UIPickerViewModel, which returns rows from its contained data model and has a ValueChanged method and SelectedItem property that returns the selected value.

Let's build a drop-down that allows the user to pick a color.

Using the designer of your choice, add a UITextField to your layout (storyboard) and name it color. Then prepare the data model as a class PickerModel (Listing 4-5). Place it below the ViewDidLoad method in a UIViewController called DatePickerViewController.

Listing 4-5. PickerModel Provides Data for UIPickerView, ValueChangedEvent, and SelectedItem

```
public class PickerModel : UIPickerViewModel
{
    private readonly IList<string> items = new List<string>
    {
        "Red",
        "Blue",
        "Green",
        "Yellow",
        "Black"
    } ;

    public event EventHandler<EventArgs> ValueChanged;

    protected int selectedIndex = 0;

    public PickerModel()
    {
    }

    public string SelectedItem
    {
        get { return items[selectedIndex]; }
    }

    public override nint GetComponentCount (UIPickerView picker)
    {
        return 1;
    }

    public override nint GetRowsInComponent (UIPickerView picker, nint component)
    {
        return items.Count;
    }

    public override string GetTitle (UIPickerView picker, nint row, nint component)
    {
        return items[(int)row];
    }

    public override nfloat GetRowHeight (UIPickerView picker, nint component)
    {
        return 40f;
    }
```

```
public override void Selected (UIPickerView picker, nint row, nint component)
{
    selectedIndex = (int)row;
    if (this.ValueChanged != null)
    {
        this.ValueChanged (this, new EventArgs ());
    }
}
```

}

Components are columns in the picker. This example has only one component/column. Making a selection fires the Selected event, which stores the selected value in selectedIndex, and then fires the ValueChanged event, which later handles the chosen value.

■ **Tip** Nint and nfloat are native iOS data types that were added in the Xamarin.iOS Unified API for 32- and 64-bit support.

In your ViewDidLoad method, create a selectedColor string to store the chosen value. Then instantiate the PickerModel and wire up the model.ValueChanged event, where selectedColor is populated by the selected item:

```
public override void ViewDidLoad ()
{
        string selectedColor = "";

        PickerModel model = new PickerModel();
        model.ValueChanged += (sender, e) => {
                selectedColor = model.SelectedItem;
        } ;
```

Code the UIPickerView and set its properties, including assigning the Model and setting the default value of color.Text:

```
UIPickerView picker = new UIPickerView();
picker.ShowSelectionIndicator = true;
picker.BackgroundColor = UIColor.White;
picker.Model = model;

this.color.Text = model.SelectedItem;
```

Now let's make that picker into a pop-up.

Making a UIPickerView into a Pop-up

iOS

A modal dialog box can be created several ways, the most common using UITextField.InputView. The InputView property of UITextField supports the assignment of an alternative "keyboard," which is a UIPickerView here. This keyboard can be decorated with additional controls, such as a toolbar with a Done button.

Still in the ViewDidLoad method, create a UIToolbar. Then add the Done button that populates the textField with the color when tapped:

```
UIToolbar toolbar = new UIToolbar();
toolbar.BarStyle = UIBarStyle.Default;
toolbar.Translucent = true;
toolbar.SizeToFit();

UIBarButtonItem doneButton = new UIBarButtonItem("Done", UIBarButtonItemStyle.Done,
    (s, e) => {
        this.color.Text = selectedColor;
        this.color.ResignFirstResponder();
    } );
toolbar.SetItems(new UIBarButtonItem[]{doneButton}, true);
```

The ResignFirstResponder method dismisses the keyboard from textField.

Assign the toolbar to the textField's InputAccessoryView property.

```
this.color.InputAccessoryView = toolbar;
```

Last, associate your picker with the UITextField by using the InputView property. This causes the UIPickerView control to become a modal pop-up when the text control is tapped.

```
this.color.InputView = picker;
```

Clicking the text view pops up the picker (Figure 4-30).

Figure 4-30. *Color text field with picker pop-up*

Tapping Done executes the action, which populates the text box with the selected color (Figure 4-31), and then closes the picker by using the ResignFirstResponder() method, dismissing the keyboard from textField.

Green

Figure 4-31. *The color text field populated with the selected color*

■ **Note** See Chapter 6 for more on modals.

CODE COMPLETE: UIPickerView

iOS

Listing 4-6 shows the complete code example for UIPickerView. Remember to add the UITextField called color to your layout by using the designer tool.

Listing 4-6. PickerViewController.cs from the PickerExample solution

```
public partial class PickerViewController : UIViewController
    {
        public PickerViewController (IntPtr handle) : base (handle)
        {
        }

        public override void ViewDidLoad ()
        {
            base.ViewDidLoad ();

            string selectedColor = "";

            PickerModel model = new PickerModel();
            model.ValueChanged += (sender, e) => {
                selectedColor = model.SelectedItem;
            } ;

            UIPickerView picker = new UIPickerView();
            picker.ShowSelectionIndicator = true;
            picker.BackgroundColor = UIColor.White;
            picker.Model = model;

            this.color.Text = model.SelectedItem;

            UIToolbar toolbar = new UIToolbar();
            toolbar.BarStyle = UIBarStyle.Default;
            toolbar.Translucent = true;
            toolbar.SizeToFit();

            UIBarButtonItem doneButton = new UIBarButtonItem("Done",
            UIBarButtonItemStyle.Done,
                (s, e) => {
                    this.color.Text = selectedColor;
                    this.color.ResignFirstResponder();
                } );
            toolbar.SetItems(new UIBarButtonItem[]{doneButton}, true);

            this.color.InputAccessoryView = toolbar;
            this.color.InputView = picker;

        }
```

```csharp
public class PickerModel : UIPickerViewModel
{
    private readonly IList<string> items = new List<string>
    {
        "Red",
        "Blue",
        "Green",
        "Yellow",
        "Black"
    } ;

    public event EventHandler<EventArgs> ValueChanged;

    protected int selectedIndex = 0;

    public PickerModel()
    {

    }

    public string SelectedItem
    {
        get { return items[selectedIndex]; }
    }

    public override nint GetComponentCount (UIPickerView picker)
    {
        return 1;
    }

    public override nint GetRowsInComponent (UIPickerView picker, nint component)
    {
        return items.Count;
    }

    public override string GetTitle (UIPickerView picker, nint row, nint component)
    {
        return items[(int)row];
    }

    public override nfloat GetRowHeight (UIPickerView picker, nint component)
    {
        return 40f;
    }
```

```
public override void Selected (UIPickerView picker, nint row, nint component)
{
    selectedIndex = (int)row;
    if (this.ValueChanged != null)
    {
        this.ValueChanged (this, new EventArgs ());
    }
}
}
}
```

■ **Tip**   Modal pop-ups for iOS pickers can be produced by other methods. These require manual coding using `UIViewController` or `UIPopover`. Create a custom `UIViewController` class containing the picker, title label, and a Done button. Instantiate the modal `ViewController` and present the view with `await PresentViewCont rollerAsync(viewController, true);`.

UIDatePicker

iOS

The `UIDatePicker` is a spinner-style control used to select the date and time (Figure 4-32).

August	30	2014
September	31	2015
October	1	2016
November	**2**	**2017**
December	3	2018
January	4	2019
February	5	2020

Figure 4-32.   UIDatePicker has columns of spinners

The `UIDatePicker` is typically linked to a `UITextField` which, when tapped, pops up the picker.

Using the designer of your choice, create a `UITextField` on the layout and name it `textView`. Enter the name of the field in the Text property, in this case `Your Birthday`.

In the `ViewController`'s `ViewDidLoad` method, code the `UIDatePicker` and set the Mode property to Date, to allow date-only selection:

```
UIDatePicker datePicker = new UIDatePicker ();
datePicker.Mode = UIDatePickerMode.Date;
datePicker.BackgroundColor = UIColor.White;
```

> **Tip** We'll cover other modes, such as `Time`, `DateAndTime`, and `CountDownTimer`, in the upcoming "Specify Which Fields to Display" subsection.

Restrict the range of entries by using the `MinimumDate` and `MaximumDate` properties:

```
datePicker.MinimumDate = (NSDate)DateTime.Today.AddDays(-7);
datePicker.MaximumDate = (NSDate)DateTime.Today.AddDays(7);
```

This example limits the date to a two-week range centered on today's date. Dates outside this range can be selected with the spinner, but the spinner will then spin back within the allowable range.

Next you need to make the date picker into a pop-up.

Making a UIDatePicker into a Pop-up

Like `UIPickerView`, a modal dialog box can be created several ways, the most common using `UITextField.InputView`. The `InputView` property of the `UITextField` supports the assignment of an alternative "keyboard" that is, in this case, a `UIDatePicker`. This keyboard can be decorated with additional controls, such as a toolbar with a Done button. Create a `UIToolbar` and add the Done button, which populates the `textField` with the date when tapped:

```
UIToolbar toolbar = new UIToolbar();
toolbar.BarStyle = UIBarStyle.Default;
toolbar.Translucent = true;
toolbar.SizeToFit();

UIBarButtonItem doneButton = new UIBarButtonItem("Done", UIBarButtonItemStyle.Done,
    (s, e) => {
        DateTime dateTime = DateTime.SpecifyKind((DateTime)datePicker.Date,
        DateTimeKind.Unspecified);
        this.textField.Text = dateTime.ToString("MM-dd-yyyy");
        this.textField.ResignFirstResponder();
    } );
toolbar.SetItems(new UIBarButtonItem[]{doneButton}, true);
```

`DateTime.SpecifyKind` returns a new date/time value in the proper format. The `ResignFirstResponder` method dismisses the keyboard from `textField`.

Assign the toolbar to the `textField`'s `InputAccessoryView` property:

```
this.textField.InputAccessoryView = toolbar;
```

Last, associate your date picker with the `UITextField` by using the `InputView` property. This causes the `UIDatePicker` control to become a modal pop-up when the text control is tapped:

```
this.textField.InputView = datePicker;
```

Clicking on the text view pops up the date picker (Figure 4-33).

Figure 4-33. *textField with popped-up datePicker*

Tapping the Done option executes the action, which populates the text box with the formatted date (Figure 4-34), and closes the picker by using the `ResignFirstResponder()` method to dismiss the keyboard from `textField`.

11-02-2017

Figure 4-34. *The textField populated with a formatted date*

Various fields can appear in the `UIDatePicker` selection. Let's look at those next.

Specify Which Fields to Display

Specify the fields used in UIDatePicker with the Mode property, which uses the UIDatePickerMode enumerator. For example, datePicker.Mode = UIDatePickerMode.**Date**;

Use these UIDatePickerModes to specify the indicated fields:

- Time: Select the time only

- Date: Select the date only

- DateAndTime: Select both the date and time

- CountDownTimer: Select only hours and minutes

■ **Tip** When in CountDownTimer mode, the CountDownDuration property contains the total number of seconds of the selected time.

CODE COMPLETE: UIDatePicker

iOS

Listing 4-7 shows the complete UIDatePicker example. Remember to add textField to your layout by using the designer tool.

Listing 4-7. DatePickerViewController.cs from the DatePickerExample solution

```
public partial class DatePickerViewController : UIViewController {

public override void ViewDidLoad ()
{
    base.ViewDidLoad ();
    UIDatePicker datePicker = new UIDatePicker ();
    datePicker.Mode = UIDatePickerMode.Date;
    datePicker.BackgroundColor = UIColor.White;

    datePicker.MinimumDate = (NSDate)DateTime.Today.AddDays(-7);
    datePicker.MaximumDate = (NSDate)DateTime.Today.AddDays(7);

    UIToolbar toolbar = new UIToolbar();
    toolbar.BarStyle = UIBarStyle.Default;
    toolbar.Translucent = true;
    toolbar.SizeToFit();
```

```
UIBarButtonItem doneButton = new UIBarButtonItem("Done", UIBarButtonItemStyle.Done,
    (s, e) => {
        DateTime dateTime = DateTime.SpecifyKind((DateTime)datePicker.Date,
        DateTimeKind.Unspecified);
        this.textField.Text = dateTime.ToString("MM-dd-yyyy");
        this.textField.ResignFirstResponder();
    } );
toolbar.SetItems(new UIBarButtonItem[]{doneButton}, true);

this.textField.InputAccessoryView = toolbar;
this.textField.InputView = datePicker;
}
```

UIStepper

iOS

The UIStepper is an increment/decrement button for discrete values and is useful when slight changes to a value are needed. Add a UIStepper to the view by using your designer of choice.

Position the button and name it stepper in the Properties view. When run, it should look like Figure 4-35.

Figure 4-35. *Stepper*

Set the range of values the control will accept by using the MinimumValue and MaximumValue properties:

```
stepper.MinimumValue = 0;
stepper.MaximumValue = 11;
```

Add a UILabel named stepperLabel above the stepper to display the stepper value. Tapping the control fires the ValueChanged event, which can be handled like this:

```
stepper.ValueChanged += (object sender, EventArgs e) => stepperLabel.Text =
stepper.Value.ToString ();
```

The value of the stepper is contained in the Value property. Run it and click the plus button, clicked up from 0 to 8, to look like Figure 4-36.

8

Figure 4-36. *stepperLabel and stepper*

Keep clicking plus, and the value increases to 11.

The StepValue property will increment the stepper by the specified value. Increment by two at a time (0, 2, 4, and so forth), like this:

```
stepper.StepValue = 2;
```

The experience of using the stepper can be tweaked by using these Boolean properties:

- AutoRepeat: If true, holding down the stepper button changes the value repeatedly. Default = true.

  ```
  stepper.AutoRepeat = true;
  ```

- Continuous: If true, all value changes fire an event. If false, the event fires only when user interaction has stopped. Default = true.

  ```
  stepper.Continuous = true;
  ```

- Wraps: If true, then when the value reaches the MinimumValue, it proceeds to MaximumValue. Conversely, when it reaches MaximumValue, further increments change it to the MinimumValue. Default = false.

  ```
  stepper.Wraps = false;
  ```

UISlider

iOS

The UISlider is a sliding input button for selection across a range of values. Add a UISlider to the view by using your designer of choice.

Position the slider and stretch it to the desired width. Name it slider in the Properties view. When run, it should look like Figure 4-37.

Figure 4-37. *Slider in its native habitat*

The properties can be set in the Properties view or in code:

```
slider.MinValue = -1;
slider.MaxValue = 2;
slider.Value = 0.5f;
```

MinValue and MaxValue properties determine the endpoint values of the slider. The Value property is the default value of the slider.

Add a UILabel named sliderLabel above the stepper to display the stepper value. When the slider is moved, the ValueChanged event fires, which can be handled like this:

```
slider.ValueChanged += (sender,e) => sliderLabel.Text = ((UISlider)sender).Value.
ToString ();
```

When run, the slider looks like Figure 4-38, which shows the slider set at MinValue.

Figure 4-38. *Slider slid far left*

Figure 4-39 shows MaxValue.

Figure 4-39. *Slider slid far right*

You can customize the look of the slider by using these properties:

- MinimumTrackTintColor: Color of the slider line to the left of the button.

      slider.MinimumTrackTintColor = UIColor.LightGray;

- MaximumTrackTintColor: Color of the slider line to the right of the button.

      slider.MaximumTrackTintColor = UIColor.Green;

- ThumbTintColor: Color of the thumb button. However, this option doesn't work reliably at the time of this writing because of an Apple bug. Use the following workaround before setting ThumbTintColor to make it work:

      slider.SetThumbImage(UIImage.FromBundle("thumb.png"),UIControlState.Normal);
      slider.ThumbTintColor = UIColor.Brown;

Place a small dummy image of some kind in the Resources folder corresponding to the image name.

CheckBox: Use UISwitch or MonoTouch.Dialog
iOS

iOS doesn't have an out-of-the-box check-box control, so many developers use UISwitch, explained next. You can also use MonoTouch.Dialog, a library that makes settings UIs easy to create for cross-platform apps. (See https://github.com/migueldeicaza/MonoTouch.Dialog for more details.)

UISwitch

iOS

UISwitch has become the standard for the Boolean on/off control. Add UISwitch to the view by using your designer of choice.

Position it and name it thisSwitch in the Properties view. When run, it should look like Figure 4-40.

Figure 4-40. *UISwitch turned on*

The UISwitch.On property contains the Boolean value of the switch, which can be set or gotten. Set it to true to create a default value or set it programmatically:

```
thisSwitch.On = true;
```

Get the state from the On property, like this:

```
bool state = thisSwitch.On;
```

Add a UILabel named switchLabel above the switch to display the switch value. When the switch is moved, the ValueChanged event fires, which can be handled like this:

```
thisSwitch.ValueChanged += (sender, e) => switchLabel.Text = thisSwitch.
On.ToString();
```

Flip the switch on (Figure 4-41) to see the label change to True.

True

Figure 4-41. *It is true*

Flip the switch off (Figure 4-42) to see the label change to False.

False

Figure 4-42. *Not true at all*

You can use these properties to customize the look of the switch:

- ThumbTintColor: Color of the thumb button

      thisSwitch.ThumbTintColor = UIColor.Blue;

- TintColor: Color around the edge of the switch

      thisSwitch.TintColor = UIColor.Blue;

- OnTintColor : Color of the switch around the button when button is on

      thisSwitch.OnTintColor = UIColor.Black;

- OnImage: Image used in place of the default thumb image when the switch is on

      switch.OnImage = onImage;

- OffImage: Image used in place of the default thumb image when the switch is off

      switch.OffImage = offImage;

■ **Note** The size of the thumb image used in OnImage and OffImage must be less than or equal to 77 points wide and 27 points tall. If you specify larger images, the edges may be clipped.

CODE COMPLETE: iOS Controls
iOS

Listing 4-8 shows the complete UISlider, UIStepper, and UISwitch example in the ViewDidLoad method. Figure 4-43 shows all three selection controls.

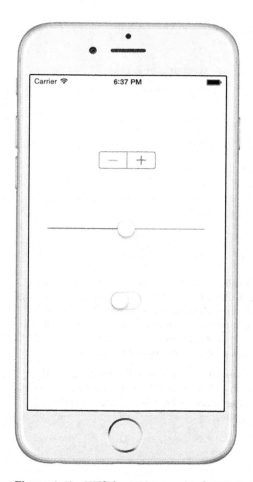

Figure 4-43. *UISlider, UIStepper, and UISwitch*

Listing 4-8. From SelectionViewController.cs in the StepperSliderSwitch solution

```
public override void ViewDidLoad ()
{
    base.ViewDidLoad ();

    slider.MinValue = -1;
    slider.MaxValue = 2;
    slider.Value = 0.5f;
    slider.SetThumbImage(UIImage.FromBundle("thumb.png"),UIControlState.Normal);
    slider.ThumbTintColor = UIColor.Brown;
    slider.MinimumTrackTintColor = UIColor.LightGray;
    slider.MaximumTrackTintColor = UIColor.Green;
    slider.ValueChanged += (sender, e) => sliderLabel.Text = ((UISlider)sender).
    Value.ToString ();
```

```
stepper.MinimumValue = 0;
stepper.MaximumValue = 11;
stepper.StepValue = 2;
stepper.ValueChanged += (object sender, EventArgs e) => stepperLabel.Text =
stepper.Value.ToString ();

thisSwitch.On = false;
thisSwitch.TintColor = UIColor.Blue;
thisSwitch.OnTintColor = UIColor.Black;
bool state = thisSwitch.On;
thisSwitch.ValueChanged += (sender, e) => switchLabel.Text =
thisSwitch.On.ToString();

}
```

Summary

Many controls share a common goal: allowing the user to pick a value. Simple selection controls require us to specify minimum and maximum values and set a default value. Pickers/spinners work best inside a modal dialog, and we use them to select from a list or choose dates and times. Xamarin.Forms handles the modal pop-ups for you, whereas Android and iOS require you to roll your own. Android provides some helpful out-of-the-box components such as DatePickerDialog and TimePickerDialog, but DialogFragment also makes a great modal. For modals in iOS, use the UITextField.InputView property (no more ActionSheets).

The selection controls in this chapter typically provide a *value changed* or click event of some kind to allow your code to respond to changes in values. While indispensable, the controls in this chapter are simple ones. In the next chapter, you'll dive deeper into the heart of mobile UI selection, where both the data and the selection can be richer and more complex when using lists and tables.

CHAPTER 5

Making a Scrollable List

Choosing quickly from a long list of items is one of the key offerings of the mobile UI. The limited real estate on mobile phone screens makes data grids a challenge and leads to extensive and creative use of lists. Grouping of items, scrolling, gesture-sensitivity, and images make lists one of the most versatile and reuseable data-bound tools available. Lists are to mobile development what the data grid is to web development.

This chapter covers the list classes available in each library to make a scrollable, selectable list. The primary considerations include binding to a data model, handling item selection, customizing the look of rows, grouping headers, and perhaps most importantly: performance.

These are the options available for creating scrollable lists on each platform:

Xamarin.Forms ListView

ListView is bound to an array or data model.

Android ListView

ListView is bound to an array or to a data model using an Adapter.

iOS UITableView

UITableView is bound to an array or to a data model using UITableViewSource.

Data Adapters

Android and iOS lists require separate adapters for data binding. In Android, we use BaseAdapter and in iOS there is UITableViewSource. In Xamarin.Forms, no additional adapter class is needed. We can bind directly to a list of Strings using the ItemsSource property with the default list template. We can also bind to data models and use custom lists with the ListView's built-in adapter class called ItemTemplate, which is configured using the SetBinding method.

Xamarin.Forms ListView

XAMARIN.FORMS

Lists in Xamarin.Forms are created using the ListView control bound to an array or data model. The Xamarin. Forms ListView class provides a scrollable, selectable list. List rows are customizable using layouts, images, and views such as buttons. ListView supports grouping, headers, footers, jump lists, and pull-to-refresh. Deleting and applying operations to list rows are supported using Context Actions.

The lists in this chapter are read-only, which means that they are bound to a data source for viewing and selecting, but the rows are not edited, deleted, or added. We touch on some editable list UI techniques in the "Context Actions and Customizing List Rows" section, but do not cover changes to the data model or two-way data binding so that these changes can be reflected in the list. For editable ListView data binding, see Chapter 7. The starting point with a ListView is data binding it to a data source.

Binding to a List of Strings

The simplest ListView implementation is binding to a List of Strings.

Instantiate a ListView class on your page and point it to a data source using the ItemsSource property, in this case a List of Strings. Using the default layout, each item in a ListView will be a single cell using the TextCell template displaying a single line of text.

```
class ListViewStrings : ContentPage
{
  public ListViewStrings()
  {
    ListView listView = new ListView();
    List<String> items = new List<String>() {"First","Second","Third"};
    listView.ItemsSource = items;
    this.Content = listView;
  }
}
```

Here's the list in Figure 5-1.

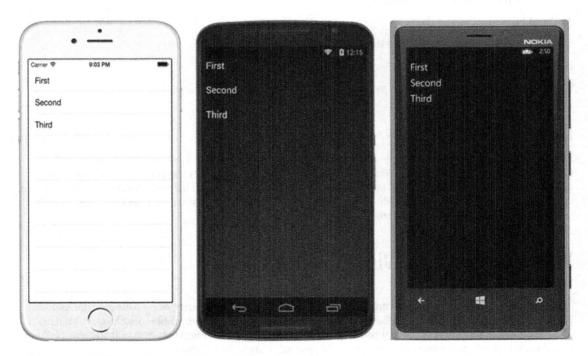

Figure 5-1. *ListView in iOS, Android, and Windows Phone*

■ **Tip** Create space around the edges of your list using the layout Padding property mentioned in Chapter 3.

```
Padding = new Thickness (0, Device.OnPlatform (20, 0, 0), 0, 0);
```

Selecting a list item fires the ItemSelected event.

Selecting an Item

XAMARIN.FORMS

There are two events for use in item selection: ItemTapped and ItemSelected. Both can happen when a user taps a cell in the ListView. The difference between them is apparent when a list permits more than just tapping and items can be selected and unselected. In simple lists where there is no unselection of rows (like the example here), there is little difference between them.

ItemTapped is the simplest. It fires as a motion event when a list row is clicked.

```
listView.ItemTapped += async (sender, e) =>
{
    await DisplayAlert("Tapped", e.Item.ToString() + " was selected.", "OK");
};
```

The ItemSelected event responds to a change in the state of row selection and happens when a row is selected or unselected.

```
listView.ItemSelected += async (sender, e) =>
{
    await DisplayAlert("Selected", e.SelectedItem.ToString()+ " was selected.", "OK");
};
```

Using async/await isn't mandatory on these event handlers, but it is a good habit when any processing is done, to avoid tying up the UI thread. Using either ItemTapped or ItemSelected to select the First item results in Figure 5-2.

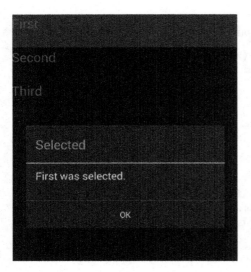

Figure 5-2. *The alert displays the selected item*

■ **Tip**   The `DisplayAlert` method is more informative than an Android toast. It provides a title and requires interaction to clear it.

Clear the selected row (removing the row highlight) by setting the `ListView`'s `SelectedItem` property to null. The easiest place to do this is inside the `ItemTapped` handler.

```
listView.ItemTapped += async (sender, e) =>
{
    await DisplayAlert("Tapped", e.Item.ToString() + " was selected.", "OK");
    ((ListView)sender).SelectedItem = null;
};
```

If you're using the `ItemSelected` event, be aware that changing the `SelectedItem` value fires the `ItemSelected` event again. You therefore need to check if `e.SelectedItem` is null prior to responding to the event.

```
listView.ItemSelected += async (sender, e) =>
{
    if (e.SelectedItem == null) return;
    await DisplayAlert("Selected", e.SelectedItem.ToString() + " was selected.", "OK");
    ((ListView)sender).SelectedItem = null;
};
```

Listing 5-1 shows the complete `ListView` example for binding to a `List` of `Strings`, selecting an item using async/await for backgrounding the `ItemTapped` event handler, and then clearing the selected row when you're done.

Listing 5-1. Binding to a List of Strings in ListViewStrings.cs

```
class ListViewStrings: ContentPage
{
    public ListViewStrings()
    {
        var items = new List<String>() {"First","Second","Third"};
        var listView = new ListView();
        listView.ItemsSource = items;

        listView.ItemTapped += async (sender, e) =>
        {
            await DisplayAlert("Tapped", e.Item.ToString() + " was selected.", "OK");
            ((ListView)sender).SelectedItem = null;
        };

        this.Padding = new Thickness(0, Device.OnPlatform(20, 0, 0), 0, 0);

        this.Content = listView;
    }
}
```

■ **Tip** Multiple row selection must be coded manually and is not covered here.

A List<String> is useful for demonstration, but in many real-world scenarios we bind to a data model.

Binding to a Data Model

XAMARIN.FORMS

Binding ListView to a data model is made easy in Xamarin.Forms through the use of ListView's built-in adapter called ItemTemplate. Prepare your data model class and assign it to the ListView.ItemsSource property. Then bind each property of your model to the list using the ItemTemplate.SetBinding method. Create a data model, or custom class, containing the list items. Call it ListItem.

```
public class ListItem {
    public string Title { get; set; }
    public string Description { get; set; }
}
```

Populate it and point the ListView's ItemsSource property to it.

```
listView.ItemsSource = new ListItem [] {
    new ListItem {Title = "First", Description="1st item"},
    new ListItem {Title = "Second", Description="2nd item"},
    new ListItem {Title = "Third", Description="3rd item"}
};
```

Format list rows using `ItemTemplate`. Create a `DataTemplate` class and pass in the cell type to display. The standard cell type is `TextCell`, which will display a title for each row plus some detail text which you'll add in a minute. Specify the property to display as the main row text by assigning it to the `TextProperty` of the list, in this case `Title`.

```
listView.ItemTemplate = new DataTemplate (typeof(TextCell));
listView.ItemTemplate.SetBinding(TextCell.TextProperty, "Title");
```

This will display the same list but from custom class `ListItem` instead of a `List` of `Strings` (Figure 5-3). No additional adapter needed!

Figure 5-3. *This ListView looks the same as Figure 5-1 but is driven by the ListItem data model*

Add a descriptive line of text to each row by binding the `DetailProperty` of the `TextCell`.

```
listView.ItemTemplate.SetBinding(TextCell.DetailProperty, "Description");
```

This binds the `Description` property of the `ListItem` class to the `DetailProperty` of the `TextCell`. Figure 5-4 shows the result.

Figure 5-4. *Title and Description properties are bound to each row using properties of TextCell*

■ **Tip**   `TextCell`'s font color can be set using its `TextColor` property and the detail font color can be set using the `DetailColor` property.

```
var template = new DataTemplate (typeof(TextCell));
template.SetValue(TextCell.TextColorProperty, Color.Red);
template.SetValue (TextCell.DetailColorProperty, Color.Blue);
listView.ItemTemplate = template;
```

When handling the item selection, remember to use the data model.

```
listView.ItemTapped += async (sender, e) =>
{
    ListItem item = (ListItem)e.Item;
    await DisplayAlert("Tapped", item.Title.ToString() + " was selected.", "OK");
    ((ListView)sender).SelectedItem = null;
};
```

CODE COMPLETE: Binding to a Data Model

XAMARIN.FORMS

Listing 5-2 shows the complete ListView example where we bind to a data model containing text and detail for each row in the list, found in the ListViewExample solution.

■ **XAML**   The XAML version of all the Xamarin.Forms examples in this chapter can be found on Apress.com (from the Source Code/Downloads tab, access the title of this book) or on GitHub at https://github.com/danhermes/xamarin-book-examples. The Xamarin.Forms XAML solution for Chapter 5 is ListViewExample.Xaml.

Listing 5-2. Binding to a Data Model ListViewDataModel.cs

```
class ListViewDataModel : ContentPage
{
    public class ListItem
    {
        public string Title { get; set; }
        public string Description { get; set; }
    }

    public ListViewDataModel()
    {
        var listView = new ListView();

        listView.ItemsSource = new ListItem[] {
        new ListItem {Title = "First", Description="1st item"},
        new ListItem {Title = "Second", Description="2nd item"},
        new ListItem {Title = "Third", Description="3rd item"}
        };

        listView.ItemTemplate = new DataTemplate(typeof(TextCell));
        listView.ItemTemplate.SetBinding(TextCell.TextProperty, "Title");
        listView.ItemTemplate.SetBinding(TextCell.DetailProperty, "Description");

        this.Padding = new Thickness(0, Device.OnPlatform(20, 0, 0), 0, 0);

        Content = listView;
```

```
        listView.ItemTapped += async (sender, e) =>
    {
        ListItem item = (ListItem)e.Item;
        await DisplayAlert("Tapped", item.Title.ToString() + " was selected.", "OK");
        ((ListView)sender).SelectedItem = null;
    };

    }
}
```

■ **Tip**   In Model View ViewModel (MVVM) apps, the data models are typically wrapped inside screen-specific classes called View Models (VM). See Chapter 7 for how to create view models that are data-bound to ListViews.

Adding an Image

XAMARIN.FORMS

Adding a single image to a ListView is easy using the ImageCell cell type. Previously, we used the TextCell cell type to display text and detail in each row. An ImageCell inherits from TextCell and adds an ImageSource property, which contains the image filename or URI. We use the bindable properties ImageSource, Text, and Detail to bind to our data model. The image is displayed left-justified, as seen in Figure 5-5.

Figure 5-5. *ImageCell in a ListView*

I'll highlight the differences from the previous TextCell data-binding example and then you can see the final result in Listing 5-3. Add a Source property of type String to the ListItem class and populate it with your images (filename or URI).

```
listView.ItemsSource = new ListItem[] {
    new ListItem {Source = "first.png", Title = "First", Description="1st item"},
    new ListItem {Source = "second.png", Title = "Second", Description="2nd item"},
    new ListItem {Source = "third.png", Title = "Third", Description="3rd item"}
};
```

Instantiate a DataTemplate containing the ImageCell and assign it to the ListView's ItemTemplate.

```
listView.ItemTemplate = new DataTemplate(typeof(ImageCell));
```

Bind the ListItem properties to the ImageCell, including text properties and image Source.

```
listView.ItemTemplate.SetBinding(ImageCell.ImageSourceProperty, "Source");
listView.ItemTemplate.SetBinding(ImageCell.TextProperty, "Title");
listView.ItemTemplate.SetBinding(ImageCell.DetailProperty, "Description");
```

Assign the listView to the Content property and that's all there is to it.

■ **Tip** The image folder will be local to each platform project (Android: Resources/drawable, iOS: /Resources, Windows Phone: WinPhone root folder). Remember to set the Build Actions by right-clicking on the image file in your project (Android: AndroidResource, iOS: BundleResource, and Windows Phone: Content).

Listing 5-3 contains the complete code to add an image to a ListView using ImageCell, as shown in Figure 5-5.

Listing 5-3. Image in a List Row in ListViewImageCell.cs

```
class ListViewImageCell : ContentPage
{
    public class ListItem
    {
        public string Source { get; set; }
        public string Title { get; set; }
        public string Description { get; set; }
    }

    public ListViewImageCell()
    {
        var listView = new ListView();
        listView.ItemsSource = new ListItem[] {
          new ListItem {Source = "first.png", Title = "First", Description="1st item"},
          new ListItem {Source = "second.png", Title = "Second", Description="2nd item"},
          new ListItem {Source = "third.png", Title = "Third", Description="3rd item"}
        };

        listView.ItemTemplate = new DataTemplate(typeof(ImageCell));
        listView.ItemTemplate.SetBinding(ImageCell.ImageSourceProperty, "Source");
        listView.ItemTemplate.SetBinding(ImageCell.TextProperty, "Title");
        listView.ItemTemplate.SetBinding(ImageCell.DetailProperty, "Description");

        this.Padding = new Thickness(0, Device.OnPlatform(20, 0, 0), 0, 0);

        Content = listView;

    }
}
```

■ **Tip**   A ListView can contain four built-in cell types: TextCell, ImageCell, SwitchCell, and EntryCell. The most useful here are TextCell and ImageCell. Although cell types can be combined using a TableView, a TableView cannot be data-bound, so TableViews are not useful for building ListViews.

Sooner or later you'll outgrow TextCell and ImageCell and will need greater control over the look of your list rows. So, you'll learn to customize them.

Customizing List Rows

XAMARIN.FORMS

Customize the list rows by creating a *custom row template*, which is basically a custom cell containing a Layout with Views. It begins with a custom class inherited from ViewCell. Then we place a layout on it and add our views. Views are more versatile than the built-in cells like TextCell and expose more properties for layout and design.

With a custom row template, you can customize your labels and add more views to your list, as shown in Figure 5-6. These three labels have their positions, font sizes, attributes, and colors customized.

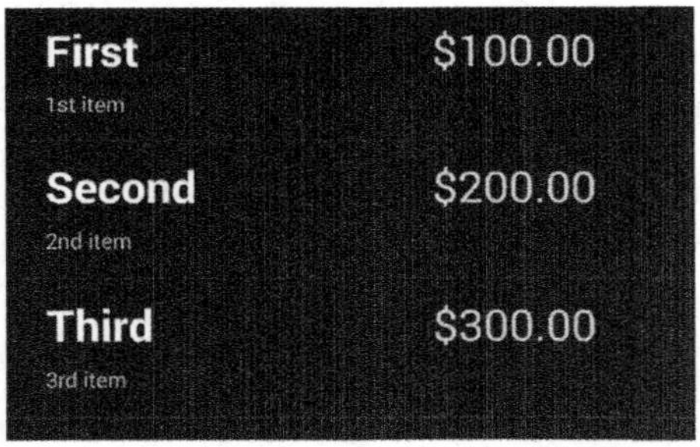

Figure 5-6. *Custom row template*

Let's walk through the code for this multi-line custom row example using three Label Views to display the title, description, and price. Figure 5-6 is an example where more control was needed over fonts and formatting than is provided for by the built-in cells.
Add Price to your ListItem data model.

```
public class ListItem
{
    public string Source { get; set; }
    public string Title { get; set; }
    public string Description { get; set; }
    public string Price { get; set; }
}
```

In the ContentPage's constructor, populate Price with values.

```
var listView = new ListView();
listView.ItemsSource = new ListItem[] {
    new ListItem {Title = "First",  Description="1st item", Price="$100.00"},
    new ListItem {Title = "Second", Description="2nd item", Price="$200.00"},
    new ListItem {Title = "Third",  Description="3rd item", Price="$300.00"}
};
```

Overerride the default list row class called ViewCell with a custom template and return a View property from the constructor. Place one or more controls or layouts within this custom template. For simple text fields in different-sized fonts, create label controls and place them on a StackLayout (or AbsoluteLayout or Grid if performance is an issue). Be careful when using Image views, as images can affect performance, particularly on older devices.

Create label controls titleLabel, descriptionLabel, and priceLabel and bind them to their respective properties in data class listView. Place titleLabel and descriptionLabel on a StackLayout called viewLayoutItem for vertical formatting and then put both the StackLayout and the priceLabel view on another StackLayout called viewLayout. Set viewLayout is set as the ViewCell's main View.

```
class ListItemCell : ViewCell
{
    public ListItemCell()
    {

        Label titleLabel = new Label
        {
            HorizontalOptions = LayoutOptions.FillAndExpand,
            FontSize = 25,
            FontAttributes = Xamarin.Forms.FontAttributes.Bold,
            TextColor = Color.White
        };
        titleLabel.SetBinding(Label.TextProperty, "Title");

        Label descLabel = new Label
        {
            HorizontalOptions = LayoutOptions.FillAndExpand,
            FontSize = 12,
            TextColor = Color.White
        };
        descLabel.SetBinding(Label.TextProperty, "Description");


        StackLayout viewLayoutItem = new StackLayout()
        {
            HorizontalOptions = LayoutOptions.StartAndExpand,
            Orientation = StackOrientation.Vertical,
            Children = { titleLabel, descLabel }
        };
```

```
            Label priceLabel = new Label
            {
                HorizontalOptions = LayoutOptions.End,
                FontSize = 25,
                TextColor = Color.Aqua
            };
            priceLabel.SetBinding(Label.TextProperty, "Price");

            StackLayout viewLayout = new StackLayout()
            {
                HorizontalOptions = LayoutOptions.StartAndExpand,
                Orientation = StackOrientation.Horizontal,
                Padding = new Thickness(25, 10, 55, 15),
                Children = { viewLayoutItem, priceLabel }
            };

            View = viewLayout;
        }


}
```

Note the use of the main StackLayout's Padding on all four sides to provide proper positioning of views within the row. LayoutOptions help with alignment (that come at a performance cost), using Start for left- or top-justified views and End for right- or bottom-justified ones. If you're on iOS, you are about to set the background color to black so you can see the white text.

Back in the ContentPage's constructor, set the ListView.ItemTemplate property to ListItemCell, the new custom template. This assigns the custom class as the template for each row in the list. Also, set the RowHeight to accommodate the extra Views.

```
listView.RowHeight = 80;
listView.ItemTemplate = new DataTemplate(typeof(ListItemCell));
```

■ **Tip** When your list rows vary in height, use ListView's HasUnevenRows property instead of RowHeight (for example, listView.HasUnevenRows = true;).

Here is the complete ContentPage Constructor.

```
public ListViewCustom()
{
    var listView = new ListView();
    listView.ItemsSource = new ListItem[] {
        new ListItem {Title = "First",  Description="1st item", Price="$100.00"},
        new ListItem {Title = "Second", Description="2nd item", Price="$200.00"},
        new ListItem {Title = "Third",  Description="3rd item", Price="$300.00"}
    };
    listView.RowHeight = 80;
    listView.BackgroundColor = Color.Black;
    listView.ItemTemplate = new DataTemplate(typeof(ListItemCell));
    Content = listView;
}
```

Customizing a list can result in a beautiful, highly-functional UI feature. Is it also one of the best ways to destroy a list's performance, so customize with caution. Use TextCell or ImageCell as well as you can before deciding to customize. Images and nested layouts are a challenge to optimize in Xamarin.Forms, particularly on older devices. If you're having difficulty with performance as you test your customized list, try the performance tips in the (Xamarin.Forms) Optimizing Performance section. If those don't work for you then consider using a custom renderer with platform-specific controls instead. (See the list views in the Android and iOS sections of this chapter and then turn to Chapter 8 to read about custom renderers.)

▓ **Tip**   ListView row separator lines are customizable using its SeparatorVisibility and SeparatorColor properties. Set the ListView's SeparatorVisibility property to None to hide the lines (the default value is Default). Set the color of the separator using SeparatorColor. Remember to define these before the ListView is loaded on Android to avoid a performance penalty.

▓ **Tip**   Headers and footers are supported by ListView. Use the Header and Footer properties for a simple text or view. For more complex layouts, use HeaderTemplate and FooterTemplate.

CODE COMPLETE: Customizing List Rows

XAMARIN.FORMS

Listing 5-4 contains the complete code for the row customization example shown in Figure 5-6, with the addition of an ItemTapped event.

Listing 5-4. Customizing List Rows in ListViewCustom.cs

```
class ListViewCustom : ContentPage
{
    public class ListItem
    {
        public string Source { get; set; }
        public string Title { get; set; }
        public string Description { get; set; }
        public string Price { get; set; }
    }

    public ListViewCustom()
    {
        var listView = new ListView();
        listView.ItemsSource = new ListItem[] {
            new ListItem {Title = "First", Description="1st item", Price="$100.00"},
            new ListItem {Title = "Second", Description="2nd item", Price="$200.00"},
            new ListItem {Title = "Third", Description="3rd item", Price="$300.00"}
        };
        listView.RowHeight = 80;
        listView.BackgroundColor = Color.Black;
        listView.ItemTemplate = new DataTemplate(typeof(ListItemCell));
        Content = listView;
```

```
        listView.ItemTapped += async (sender, e) =>
        {
            ListItem item = (ListItem)e.Item;
            await DisplayAlert("Tapped", item.Title.ToString() + " was selected.", "OK");
            ((ListView)sender).SelectedItem = null;
        };

    }

    class ListItemCell : ViewCell
    {
        public ListItemCell()
        {

            Label titleLabel = new Label
            {
                HorizontalOptions = LayoutOptions.FillAndExpand,
                FontSize = 25,
                FontAttributes = Xamarin.Forms.FontAttributes.Bold,
                TextColor = Color.White
            };
            titleLabel.SetBinding(Label.TextProperty, "Title");

            Label descLabel = new Label
            {
                HorizontalOptions = LayoutOptions.FillAndExpand,
                FontSize = 12,
                TextColor = Color.White
            };
            descLabel.SetBinding(Label.TextProperty, "Description");

            StackLayout viewLayoutItem = new StackLayout()
            {
                HorizontalOptions = LayoutOptions.StartAndExpand,
                Orientation = StackOrientation.Vertical,
                Children = { titleLabel, descLabel }
            };

            Label priceLabel = new Label
            {
                HorizontalOptions = LayoutOptions.End,
                FontSize = 25,
                TextColor = Color.Aqua
            };
            priceLabel.SetBinding(Label.TextProperty, "Price");
```

```
        StackLayout viewLayout = new StackLayout()
        {
            HorizontalOptions = LayoutOptions.StartAndExpand,
            Orientation = StackOrientation.Horizontal,
            Padding = new Thickness(25, 10, 55, 15),
            Children = { viewLayoutItem, priceLabel }
        };

        View = viewLayout;
    }
  }
}
```

■ **Tip**   Changes to list properties can be reflected in the list in real-time using an implementation of the INotifyPropertyChanged interface. See Chapter 7 for more on editable list data binding.

Among the views that can be added to a list row, Buttons require special attention due to their prevalence and unique qualities.

Adding Buttons

XAMARIN.FORMS

Buttons can be added to a list in one of two ways: as button views and as *Context Actions*. Button views are added to the custom template, while Context Actions appear when a row is swiped or long-pressed, such as for buttons hiding behind each row, which are often used for operations on the selected row such as deletion.

■ **Note**   Image Views paired with gesture recognizers (manually-coded image buttons) don't return a property containing their list row so they aren't useful as buttons.

Using Button Views

Add button views to your custom template during the customization of a ListView. Add the Button View onto a layout in a custom ViewCell and it will display on the list in every row, as shown in Figure 5-7. Set up a Button.Clicked handler using the CommandParameter property to determine which button was clicked.

Figure 5-7. *Add a Button View to a ListView*

Declare a Button view in your custom ViewCell. Bind a period (.) to the button's CommandParameter property to retrieve the clicked row.

```
var button = new Button
{
    Text = "Buy Now",
    BackgroundColor = Color.Teal,
    HorizontalOptions = LayoutOptions.EndAndExpand
};
button.SetBinding(Button.CommandParameterProperty, new Binding("."));
```

Remember to add the Button to your custom template layout as discussed in the previous section.

Handling the Clicked event requires the use of CommandParameter, which returns the data object, ListItem in this case, of the row in which the button was clicked.

```
button.Clicked += (sender, e) =>
{
    var b = (Button)sender;
    var item = (ListItem)b.CommandParameter;
  ((ContentPage)((ListView)((StackLayout)((StackLayout)b.ParentView)
      .ParentView).ParentView).ParentView).DisplayAlert("Clicked",
      item.Title.ToString() + " button was clicked", "OK");
};
```

That long ParentView expression is for climbing back up the layout tree from the button up through the nested layouts and through the ListView to retrieve the ContentPage.

Listing 5-5 contains the code excerpt where we add a Button View to the ListView, as shown in Figure 5-7.

Listing 5-5. Adding a Button to a List Row from ListViewButton.cs

```
class ListItemCell : ViewCell
{
    public ListItemCell()
    {
        // ... custom labels and layouts...

        var button = new Button
        {
```

```
            Text = "Buy Now",
            BackgroundColor = Color.Teal,
            HorizontalOptions = LayoutOptions.EndAndExpand
        };
        button.SetBinding(Button.CommandParameterProperty, new Binding("."));
        button.Clicked += (sender, e) =>
        {
            var b = (Button)sender;
            var item = (ListItem)b.CommandParameter;

            ((ContentPage)((ListView)((StackLayout)((StackLayout)b.ParentView).
            ParentView).ParentView).ParentView).DisplayAlert("Clicked", item.Title.
            ToString() + " button was clicked", "OK");
        };
```

On Android, input views like buttons have been problematic and not always selectable on Xamarin.Forms
`ListViews` due to a focus conflict between the input view and the row. Hopefully, this bug will be fixed by
the time this book hits the shelves. If not, the workaround requires creating a custom renderer for the input
control and setting the `Focusable` property to `False` (`Control.Focusable = false`). See `ListViewButton.cs`
and `ListButtonRenderer.cs` in the downloadable code for the full workaround. iOS and Windows Phone
don't have this problem.

■ **Tip**   On iOS the addition of this button can cause the title text to wrap, so set the `FontSize = 20` on `titleLabel`.

An alternative to Button Views are Context Actions.

Using Context Actions

Context Actions are bars of buttons that appear for a particular row when the row is left-swiped on iOS or
long-pressed on Android or Windows Phone, as shown in Figure 5-8.

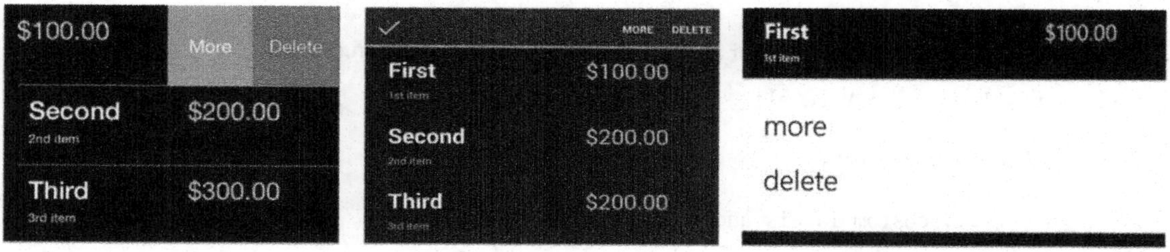

Figure 5-8. *The Context Action buttons More and Delete*

Create a MenuItem object and place it on your ViewCell subclass while customizing your list. Set the Text property to display on the contextual button and bind it like a ListView button using a period (.) and CommandParameter.

```
var moreAction = new MenuItem { Text = "More" };
moreAction.SetBinding(MenuItem.CommandParameterProperty, new Binding("."));
```

Create the Clicked event and retrieve the row data class using CommandParameter.

```
moreAction.Clicked += (sender, e) =>
{
    var mi = ((MenuItem)sender);
    var item = (ListItem)mi.CommandParameter;
    Debug.WriteLine("More clicked on row: " + item.Title.ToString());
};
```

Lastly, add the MenuItem to the ViewCell using ContextActions.Add.

```
ContextActions.Add(moreAction);
```

For a delete button, do all the same things except set the IsDestructive flag to true. On iOS this will make the button red. Set IsDestructive flag to true for only one of the buttons.

```
var deleteAction = new MenuItem { Text = "Delete", IsDestructive = true };
```

■ **Tip** if you need to find the ContentPage inside your Clicked event in this example, use the technique suggested in the previous Button View example, but use this code after the viewLayout is declared:
`((ContentPage)((ListView)viewLayout.ParentView).ParentView).DisplayAlert("More Clicked", "On row: " + item.Title.ToString(), "OK");`

Listing 5-6 contains the relevant excerpt of code for the Context Action example shown in Figure 5-8.

Listing 5-6. Creating Context Actions for a List, from ListViewContextAction.cs

```
class ListItemCell : ViewCell
{
    public ListItemCell()
    {
        // ... custom labels and layouts...

        var moreAction = new MenuItem { Text = "More" };
        moreAction.SetBinding(MenuItem.CommandParameterProperty, new Binding("."));
        moreAction.Clicked += (sender, e) =>
        {
            var mi = ((MenuItem)sender);
            var item = (ListItem)mi.CommandParameter;
            Debug.WriteLine("More clicked on row: " + item.Title.ToString());
        };
```

```
var deleteAction = new MenuItem { Text = "Delete", IsDestructive = true };
deleteAction.SetBinding(MenuItem.CommandParameterProperty, new Binding("."));
deleteAction.Clicked += (sender, e) =>
{
    var mi = ((MenuItem)sender);
    var item = (ListItem)mi.CommandParameter;
    Debug.WriteLine("Delete clicked on row: " + item.Title.ToString());
};

ContextActions.Add(moreAction);
ContextActions.Add(deleteAction);

        }
    }
```

■ **Tip** Adding and deleting rows from the list can be reflected in the UI using an `ObservableCollection`. See Chapter 7 for more on editable list data binding.

Grouping Headers

XAMARIN.FORMS

Long lists can be difficult to navigate and sometimes sorting just isn't good enough. Grouping headers create categories to help users quickly find what they're looking for. Items can be grouped using the `IsGroupingEnabled` and `GroupDisplayBinding` properties of a `ListView`.

You must first create group titles. A good way to store group headers is to create a static data model that is a collection of groups, each of which contains a collection of data items. That is, a collection of collections is created, with the group header field(s) defined in each group collection.

Create a group class that contains the group-by key and a collection for the items.

```
public class Group : List<ListItem>
{
    public String Key { get; private set; }
    public Group(String key, List<ListItem> items)
    {
        Key = key;
        foreach (var item in items)
            this.Add(item);
    }
}
```

In the ContentPage constructor, populate the groups and assign them to a master model. Create as many groups as you need with corresponding keys and their contained items. In this example there are two groups, with keys called "Important" and "Less Important".

```
List<Group> itemsGrouped = new List<Group> {
    new Group ("Important", new List<ListItem>{
        new ListItem {Title = "First", Description="1st item"},
        new ListItem {Title = "Second", Description="2nd item"},
    }),
    new Group ("Less Important", new List<ListItem>{
        new ListItem {Title = "Third", Description="3rd item"}
    })
};
```

■ **Note** This is a simplified, static data example for demonstration purposes. In the real world, you might populate a sorted data model with LINQ or with a loop, inserting grouped items with their accompanying keys.

Create the ListView, setting the IsGroupingEnabled to true and assigning the GroupDisplayBinding the property of the group-by model that contains the group header, which is the Key property here.

```
ListView listView = new ListView()
{
    IsGroupingEnabled = true,
    GroupDisplayBinding = new Binding("Key"),
    ItemTemplate = new DataTemplate(typeof(TextCell))
    {
        Bindings = {
            { TextCell.TextProperty, new Binding("Title") },
            { TextCell.DetailProperty, new Binding("Description") }
        }
    }
};
```

■ **Note** This ItemTemplate happens to contain a Title and Description, but there is no particular ItemTemplate required for the grouping of items.

Assign the group model to the ListView.ItemsSource property.

```
listView.ItemsSource = itemsGrouped;
```

Figure 5-9 shows the grouped list.

Figure 5-9. *This list of three items is grouped under two headings*

Listing 5-7 contains all code for the ListView with group headers shown in Figure 5-9.

Listing 5-7. Grouping List Items in ListViewGrouped.cs

```
class ListViewGrouped : ContentPage
{
    public class ListItem {
        public string Title { get; set; }
        public string Description { get; set; }
    }

    public ListViewGrouped()
    {
            List<Group> itemsGrouped = new List<Group> {
            new Group ("Important", new List<ListItem> {
            new ListItem {Title = "First", Description="1st item"},
            new ListItem {Title = "Second", Description="2nd item"},
                        }),

            new Group ("Less Important", new List<ListItem>{
            new ListItem {Title = "Third", Description="3rd item"}
            })
        };
```

```
            ListView listView = new ListView()
            {
                IsGroupingEnabled = true,
                GroupDisplayBinding = new Binding("Key"),
                ItemTemplate = new DataTemplate(typeof(TextCell))
                {
                    Bindings = {
                        { TextCell.TextProperty, new Binding("Title") },
                        { TextCell.DetailProperty, new Binding("Description") }
                    }
                }
            };

            listView.ItemsSource = itemsGrouped;

            Content = listView;

            this.Padding = new Thickness(0, Device.OnPlatform(20, 0, 0), 0, 0);
        }

        public class Group : List<ListItem>
        {
            public String Key { get; private set; }

            public Group(String key, List<ListItem> items)
            {
                Key = key;
                foreach (var item in items)
                    this.Add(item);
            }
        }
    }
}
```

Customizing the Group Header

XAMARIN.FORMS

When you're ready for fancier group headers than the default ones, you can create your own in a similar manner to customizing list rows, using a custom template class that implements a layout and controls. Set the custom template using a custom ViewCell called HeaderCell to the GroupHeaderTemplate property.

```
GroupHeaderTemplate = new DataTemplate(typeof(HeaderCell)),
HasUnevenRows = true,
```

This GroupHeaderTemplate assignment should follow the GroupDisplayBinding declaration in your ListView. The HasUnevenRows property helps maintain the formatting when you're handling header and item rows of different heights. On iOS the developer must then calculate (or estimate) the height of each cell manually.

Define HeaderCell as a custom template for the header cell. This example creates a white background with large black text for the header group key. Bind the Group.Key field to the title Label and place the Label inside a StackLayout.

```
public class HeaderCell : ViewCell
{
    public HeaderCell()
    {
        this.Height = 40;
        var title = new Label
        {
            FontSize = 16,
            TextColor = Color.Black,
            VerticalOptions = LayoutOptions.Center
        };

        title.SetBinding(Label.TextProperty, "Key");

        View = new StackLayout
        {
            HorizontalOptions = LayoutOptions.FillAndExpand,
            HeightRequest = 40,
            BackgroundColor = Color.White,
            Padding = 5,
            Orientation = StackOrientation.Horizontal,
            Children = { title }
        };
    }
}
```

Figure 5-10 shows the list with custom headers.

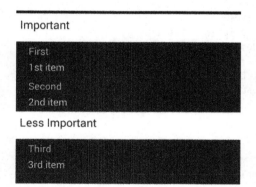

Figure 5-10. *Custom group headings can contain one or more data-bound fields*

■ **Tip** Coding for performance in Group Headers is the same as when creating custom list row templates. More detail on performance soon.

Listing 5-8 shows the `ListView` grouping template code from Figure 5-10.

Listing 5-8. Customizing List Group Headers in ListViewGroupingTemplate.cs

```
class ListViewGroupingTemplate : ContentPage
{
    public class ListItem {
        public string Title { get; set; }
        public string Description { get; set; }
    }

    public ListViewGroupingTemplate()
    {
        ListView listView = new ListView()
        {
            IsGroupingEnabled = true,
            GroupDisplayBinding = new Binding("Key"),
            GroupHeaderTemplate = new DataTemplate(typeof(HeaderCell)),
            HasUnevenRows = true,
            ItemTemplate = new DataTemplate(typeof(TextCell))
                {
                    Bindings = {
                        { TextCell.TextProperty, new Binding("Title") },
                        { TextCell.DetailProperty, new Binding("Description") }
                        }
                }
        };

        List<Group> itemsGrouped = new List<Group> {
            new Group ("Important", new List<ListItem> {
                new ListItem {Title = "First", Description="1st item"},
                new ListItem {Title = "Second", Description="2nd item"},
                    }),
            new Group ("Less Important", new List<ListItem>{
                new ListItem {Title = "Third", Description="3rd item"}
            })
        };
        listView.ItemsSource = itemsGrouped;
        Content = listView;

        this.Padding = new Thickness(0, Device.OnPlatform(20, 0, 0), 0, 0);
    }

    public class HeaderCell : ViewCell
    {
        public HeaderCell()
        {
            this.Height = 40;
            var title = new Label
```

```
            {
                FontSize = 16,
                TextColor = Color.Black,
                VerticalOptions = LayoutOptions.Center
            };
            title.SetBinding(Label.TextProperty, "Key");
            View = new StackLayout
            {
                HorizontalOptions = LayoutOptions.FillAndExpand,
                HeightRequest = 40,
                BackgroundColor = Color.White,
                Padding = 5,
                Orientation = StackOrientation.Horizontal,
                Children = { title }
            };
        }
    }

    public class Group : List<ListItem>
    {
        public String Key { get; private set; }
        public Group(String key, List<ListItem> items)
        {
            Key = key;
            foreach (var item in items)
                this.Add(item);
        }

    }
}
```

Creating a Jump List

XAMARIN.FORMS

Long lists can be unwieldy and require fast scrolling using a jump list, which is a list of keys on the right that permit quick movement through the list. These are often letters corresponding to the first letter of the items.

Assign the jump list values by binding the property in the group model to the ListView.GroupShortNameBinding property. This example binds the Group.Key property to the jump list.

```
listView.GroupShortNameBinding = new Binding("Key");
```

You'll need a fairly long grouped list to see this in action.

Let's move on to scrolling. Xamarin.Forms ListViews are automatically scrollable when they contain more elements than can fit on the screen at one time.

ListViews Scroll Automatically

XAMARIN.FORMS

No additional coding is required to get a ListView to scroll. The ScrollView is built-in and the list will scroll if it is longer than the space available on the page.

Add a few more rows to the ItemsSource in the original data-model-binding example.

```
listView.ItemsSource = new ListItem [] {
    new ListItem {Title = "First", Description="1st item"},
    new ListItem {Title = "Second", Description="2nd item"},
    new ListItem {Title = "Third", Description="3rd item"},
    new ListItem {Title = "Fourth", Description="4th item"},
    new ListItem {Title = "Fifth", Description="5th item"},
    new ListItem {Title = "Sixth", Description="6th item"} ,
    new ListItem {Title = "Seventh", Description="7th item"},
    new ListItem {Title = "Eighth", Description="8th item"},
    new ListItem {Title = "Ninth", Description="9th item"} ,
    new ListItem {Title = "Tenth", Description="10th item"},
    new ListItem {Title = "Eleventh", Description="11th item"},
    new ListItem {Title = "Twelfth", Description="12th item"} ,
    new ListItem {Title = "Thirteenth", Description="13th item"},
    new ListItem {Title = "Fourteenth", Description="14th item"},
    new ListItem {Title = "Fifteenth", Description="15th item"} ,
    new ListItem {Title = "Sixteenth", Description="16th item"},
    new ListItem {Title = "Seventeenth", Description="17th item"},
    new ListItem {Title = "Eighteenth", Description="18th item"}
};
```

Getting a ListView to scroll requires only putting enough data/rows into it to make it longer than the space on the screen (Figure 5-11).

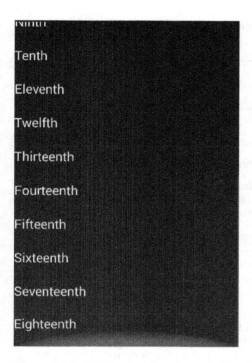

Figure 5-11. *ListView scrolls automatically when there are more rows than fit on the screen*

■ **Tip** ListView supports a pull-to-refresh feature using its IsPullToRefreshEnabled property. Set it.

    listView.IsPullToRefreshEnabled = true;

Implement the Refreshing event however you need to in order to enact a list refresh (see Chapter 7). Call the EndRefresh method and set IsRefreshing to false (it was true before).

Optimizing Performance

XAMARIN.FORMS

Cell reuse is built-in with Xamarin.Forms, giving you a leg up over iOS and Android lists. Even so, scrolling lists can become slow, laggy, or janky. This is annoying to the user and makes the app feel unprofessional.

When building ListViews, a few things to watch out for are custom template ViewCells with many views, using images on older devices, and using layouts that require a large amount of measurement calculations.

Here are some recommendations for optimizing ListView performance:

- Use the built-in cells whenever you can: TextCell and ImageCell.
- Use custom template ViewCells only when you have to.
- Use images only when necessary and keep images as small as possible.

- Use as few elements as possible. For example, consider using a single FormattedString label instead of multiple labels.

- Use AbsoluteLayout when you can, as it does no measurements.

- RelativeLayout can work well if constraints are passed directly.

- Avoid deeply nested layout hierarchies. Use AbsoluteLayout or Grid to help reduce nesting.

- Avoid specific LayoutOptions except Fill (Fill is the cheapest to compute).

As a last resort, with a complex list, use custom renderers to create the list natively (see Chapter 8).

That's it for ListView in Xamarin.Forms! At this point, you are faced with your choice. If you're finished reading about Xamarin.Forms, you can continue reading about lists in the other OSs (Android and iOS) or you can turn to the next chapter to learn more about Xamarin.Forms, where you'll read about navigation.

If you're staying with this chapter, you'll now learn about platform-specific layouts, starting with Android.

Android ListView

ANDROID

ListView is a view group that displays a scrollable list of items. ListViews are bound to an Array, List, or data model using an Adapter. They contain several built-in views containing one or two lines of text and an image. Custom views can be constructed using LinearLayout at the expense of performance. Used in its basic form, ListView is simple and fast.

These are the two most common ways to build a ListView:

- Use the ListActivity class, which is an Activity containing a ListView.

- Use the ListView tag in a layout XML, often used for customizing a list.

We'll start with the first one, ListActivity, and then talk about the second one in the "Customizing List Rows" section.

Using ListActivity

Android provides a class called ListActivity specifically designed for displaying a list. The ListActivity class inherits from the Activity class and contains a ListView. This is a convenient way to create a ListView programatically and populate it using an Adapter class. In the following example, you will code a ListView using ListActivity.

Binding to an Array of Strings

Bind a ListActivity to an array of strings to create a list.

Create an Android Activity, then change the class to inherit from ListActivity instead of Activity. Declare and assign a listItems string array, as shown in Listing 5-9.

Listing 5-9. List from an Array in ListActivityArray.cs from the ListViewExamplesAndroid Solution

```
public class MainActivity : ListActivity
{
    string[] listItems;
    protected override void OnCreate(Bundle bundle)
    {
        base.OnCreate(bundle);
        listItems = new string[] { "First", "Second", "Third"};
        ListAdapter = new ArrayAdapter<String>(this, Android.Resource.Layout.
        SimpleListItem1, listItems);
    }
}
```

Here you bind the list to an ArrayAdapter referring to the array of string's listItems using the ListActivity's ListAdapter property. SimpleListItem1 is a built-in view containing one heading per row. We will discuss other built-in layouts later.

This is all the code required to display a ListView bound to the string array (Figure 5-12).

Figure 5-12. *This ListView is bound to a string array.*

Next the user is going to want to tap one of your rows.

Selecting an Item

ANDROID

User selection of a list item is handled by overriding the OnListItemClick method in the ListActivity. The selected item index is passed in through the parameter called position.

```
protected override void OnListItemClick(ListView l, View v, int position, long id)
{
    String SelectedItem = listItems[position];
    Android.Widget.Toast.MakeText(this, SelectedItem,
        Android.Widget.ToastLength.Short).Show();
}
```

Touching a list item will now cause a toast to appear and display the Title of the ListItem (see Figure 5-13).

Figure 5-13. *Tapping "Third" will raise a Toast with that Title*

Multiple Selection

Multiple row selection is built into Android using the ListView's ChoiceMode property.

```
ListView.ChoiceMode = Android.Widget.ChoiceMode.Multiple;
```

This setting is used in tandem with another of Android's built-in list views called SimpleListItemMultipleChoice, which has checkmarks to the right of each row. You'll read about built-in views soon.

Arrays are helpful for a simple list demonstration but in the real world you'll typically bind lists to a data model.

Binding to a Data Model

ANDROID

Android ListView data binding requires an adapter between the model and the list. Create a list from a data model in three steps:

1. *Data Model*: Create a data model containing the list items.

2. *Adapter*: Create a list item adapter to specify which fields in the data model to display in the list and manage row cell reuse.

3. *Activity*: Populate the data model and pass it into the list adapter constructor. Assign the resulting adapter to the ListAdapter property of the ListActivity.

Here we go.

Data Model

Create a custom data model containing list items in a separate class file called ListItem.cs, as shown in the complete Listing 5-10.

Listing 5-10. List Data Model in ListItem.cs

```
public class ListItem
{
    public string Title { get; set; }
    public string Description { get; set; }
}
```

Adapter

To create an adapter, create a plain class called ListItemAdapter.cs (see complete Listing 5-11), which is inherited from BaseAdapter, then override Count, GetItemId, GetItem, and GetView. Declare a private copy of the data model List, called itemList. Create a ListItemAdapter constructor that receives the Activity and populated data model as parameters.

Listing 5-11. List Adapter in ListItemAdapter.cs

```
public class ListItemAdapter : BaseAdapter
{
    private List<ListItem> itemList;
    private Activity context;

    public ListItemAdapter(Activity context, List<ListItem> items) : base()
    {
        this.context = context;
        this.itemList = items;
    }
```

```
public override int Count
{
    get { return itemList.Count; }
}

public override Java.Lang.Object GetItem(int position)
{
    throw new NotImplementedException();
}

public override long GetItemId(int position)
{
    return position;
}

public override View GetView(int position, View convertView, ViewGroup parent)
{
    View view = convertView;
    if (view == null)
        view = context.LayoutInflater.Inflate(
            Android.Resource.Layout.SimpleListItem1, null);
    view.FindViewById<TextView>(Android.Resource.Id.Text1).Text =
        itemList[position].Title;
    return view;
}
}
```

GetView is the operative method here, creating individual list rows, each as a View, and returning them to the ListActivity as needed. When a list is scrolled, this method is called to create more rows to display on the screen. The Title property of ListItem is assigned to the Text property of the built-in TextView on the ListActivity, Android.Resource.Id.Text1, using the built-in list row view SimpleListItem1 (more about built-in row views soon). In GetView, always do the null cell check and use this passed-in View and Inflate method technique to construct the cells. We do this for performance reasons and will discuss it more in depth in a moment.

Activity

Back in the activity, the data model can now be bound to the list using the adapter. In the ListActivity's OnCreate method, declare listItems as data type List<ListItem>, and then populate the data model and pass it into the ListAdapter's constructor. Assign the resulting adapter to the ListActivity.ListAdapter property, as shown in the complete Listing 5-12.

Listing 5-12. List Activity in ListActivityDataModel.cs

```
public class MainActivity : ListActivity
{
    List<ListItem> listItems;
    protected override void OnCreate(Bundle bundle)
    {
        base.OnCreate(bundle);
        List<ListItem> listItems = new List<ListItem> {
```

```
            new ListItem {Title = "First", Description="1st item"},
            new ListItem {Title = "Second", Description="2nd item"},
            new ListItem {Title = "Third", Description="3rd item"}
        };
        ListAdapter = new ListItemAdapter(this, listItems);
    }
}
```

This will display the list from our data-bound model (Figure 5-14).

Figure 5-14. *This ListView is a data-bound list using an adapter*

■ **Note**   Xamarin.Android provides several cursors to bind a list directly to a SQLite data source, including `SimpleCursorAdapter` and `CursorAdapter`. These are explored in Chapter 7.

Optimizing Performance

ANDROID

When building a list adapter, it is important to code for performance which means reusing cells whenever possible. A cell is a memory location that holds a list row. The common technique used in Xamarin.Android apps is the *null cell check*, which attempts to reuse an existing cell (if it exists in memory) or creates it anew if it doesn't exist. Either way, the cell is populated with new data. This is so that cells can be recycled in memory as rows scroll off of the screen rather than be thrown away.

Here's how the null cell check works. The `GetView` method of the adapter constructs each row of the list as needed, producing new rows for display when the list is scrolled. The `View` parameter contains an existing row, if one exists. If it is null, a new row is created using the `Inflate` method. Then the row is populated with current data. We did this earlier when creating the list item adapter in Listing 5-11.

```
public override View GetView(int position, View convertView, ViewGroup parent)
{
    View view = convertView;
    if (view == null)
        view = context.LayoutInflater.Inflate(
            Android.Resource.Layout.SimpleListItem1, null);
        view.FindViewById<TextView>(Android.Resource.Id.Text1).Text =
            itemList[position].Title;
    return view;
}
```

■ **Tip** Further optimization can be attained using ViewHolder. See James Montemagno's (pronounced *mahn-teh-mahn-yo*) blog post on the topic at http://blog.xamarin.com/creating-highly-performant-smooth-scrolling-android-listviews/.

Using the Built-in Row Views

ANDROID

There are 12 built-in row views that handle basic list layouts, found in Android.Resource.Layout. Figures 5-15, 5-16, and 5-17 show the three most commonly used layouts: SimpleListItem1, SimpleListItem2, and TwoLineListItem.

Figure 5-15. *SimpleListItem1 shows a title only*

Figure 5-16. *SimpleListItem2 shows a large title and a smaller description*

Figure 5-17. *TwoLineListItem shows a large title and a description of equal size*

How the built-in list layouts are implemented depends on whether the list uses an array or binds to a data model:

- *Array*: In the activity, when assigning an ArrayAdapter to the ListAdapter, pass the built-in row view type as a parameter (see Listing 5-9):

  ```
  ListAdapter = new ArrayAdapter<String>(this,
  Android.Resource.Layout.SimpleListItem1, listItems);
  ```

- *Data Model*: In the adapter, when binding a data model and passing a ListView into an activity, set the built-in view in the GetView method by specifying the layout in the Inflate method (see Listing 5-11):

  ```
  view = context.LayoutInflater.Inflate(
    Android.Resource.Layout.SimpleListItem1, null);
  ```

Customize the chosen view in the adapter by setting the view's properties on the built-in controls: Text1 and Text2 for text strings, and Icon for an image. Use only properties that apply to the built-in view or an error will be thrown. For example:

```
view.FindViewById<TextView>(Android.Resource.Id.Text1).Text =
    itemList[position].Title;
view.FindViewById<TextView>(Android.Resource.Id.Text2).Text =
    itemList[position].Description;
view.FindViewById<ImageView>(Android.Resource.Id.Icon).
    SetImageResource(itemList[position].ImageResourceId);
```

Here are the rest of the 12 built-in row views that are members of Android.Resource.Layout :

- ActivityListItem: Image and title

- TestListItem: Small title only

- SimpleSelectableListItem: Title only supporting single or multiple selection

- SimpleListItemActivated1: Title only where background color indicates selection

- SimpleListItemActivated2: A large title and smaller description where background color indicates selection

- SimpleListItemChecked: Title only with checkmark selection

- SimpleListItemMultipleChoice: Title only with checkmark selection of multiple items

- SimpleListItemSingleChoice: Title only with radio button selection of a single item

- SimpleExpandableListItem: Titles arranged in expandable groups

Customizing List Rows

ANDROID

If none of the 12 built-in list row views suits your needs, it's time to create a custom list row view.

For this you will use the second method for creating Android ListViews: layout XML. This approach is considerably different than the previous ListActivity approach. It requires *two* XML layouts, one for the list page and the other for the row layout. An Activity is used instead of a ListActivity.

Create the main XML layout using an Android designer and call it HomeLayout.axml, as shown in Listing 5-13. It should contain a TextView called headerText and a ListView called listItems. Place the name of the list in headerText's text property, here it's called "My Items".

Listing 5-13. Layout Containing the ListView in HomeLayout.axml

```
<?xml version="1.0" encoding="utf-8"?>
<LinearLayout xmlns:android="http://schemas.android.com/apk/res/android"
    android:orientation="vertical"
    android:layout_width="fill_parent"
    android:layout_height="fill_parent">
    <TextView
        android:text="My Items"
        android:textAppearance="?android:attr/textAppearanceLarge"
        android:layout_width="match_parent"
        android:layout_height="wrap_content"
        android:id="@+id/headerText" />
    <ListView
        android:minWidth="25px"
        android:minHeight="25px"
        android:layout_width="match_parent"
        android:layout_height="wrap_content"
        android:id="@+id/listItems" />
</LinearLayout>
```

Now create another XML layout file that contains the custom row layout and name it CustomLayout.axml, as shown in Listing 5-14. Remove the default LinearLayout. Add a RelativeLayout with a LinearLayout nested within it. Add two TextViews, one named title and the other named description. Set the background color of the RelativeLayout to white and the textColor of the TextViews to black.

Listing 5-14. Custom List Row in CustomLayout.axml

```
<?xml version="1.0" encoding="utf-8"?>
<RelativeLayout xmlns:android="http://schemas.android.com/apk/res/android"
    android:layout_width="fill_parent"
    android:layout_height="wrap_content"
    android:background="#FFFFFF"
    android:padding="8dp">
    <LinearLayout
        android:orientation="vertical"
        android:layout_width="fill_parent"
        android:layout_height="fill_parent"
        android:minWidth="25px"
        android:minHeight="25px">
```

```
            <TextView
                android:text="Large Text"
                android:textAppearance="?android:attr/textAppearanceLarge"
                android:layout_width="match_parent"
                android:layout_height="wrap_content"
                android:textColor="#000000"
                android:id="@+id/title" />
            <TextView
                android:text="Small Text"
                android:textAppearance="?android:attr/textAppearanceSmall"
                android:layout_width="match_parent"
                android:layout_height="wrap_content"
                android:textColor="#000000"
                android:id="@+id/description" />
        </LinearLayout>
    </RelativeLayout>
```

Create a new Adapter called ListCustomAdapter that's based on the previous ListViewAdapter (see Listing 5-11). In the GetView method, assign the CustomLayout layout using Inflate.

```
    view = context.LayoutInflater.Inflate(Resource.Layout.CustomLayout, null);
```

Create a new main activity based on MainActivity (see Listing 5-12), but inherit from Activity instead of ListActivity and name it MainCustomListActivity. Remove the ListAdapter assignment. Create a listView variable of type ListView to hold the home layout.

```
    ListView listView;
```

In the OnCreate method, use the SetContentView method to assign the XML HomeLayout screen as the main layout, and locate the listItems ListView in the XML layout using FindViewById.

```
    SetContentView(Resource.Layout.HomeLayout);
    listView = FindViewById<ListView>(Resource.Id.listItems);
    listView.Adapter = new ListCustomAdapter(this, listItems);
```

Now we have a customizable home layout and list row layout! See Figure 5-18.

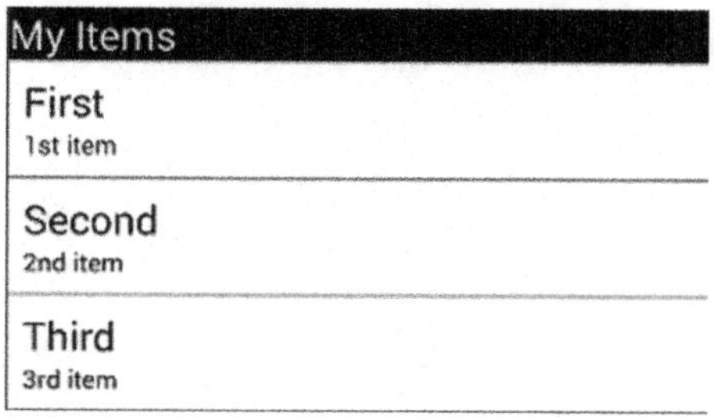

Figure 5-18. *Customized list*

■ **Tip**   Add any controls you need to the main screen and list rows, including images, binding them to properties in your data model.

Selecting an Item in a Customized Row

ANDROID

When the user selects a row on a customized layout, the click event works differently in the Activity than it did in the ListActivity. Delegate an event to handle the click.

```
listView.ItemClick += OnListItemClick;
```

Then handle the event with a non-overridden method that uses e for passing variables.

```
void OnListItemClick(object sender, AdapterView.ItemClickEventArgs e)
{
    String SelectedItem = listItems[e.Position].Title;
    Android.Widget.Toast.MakeText(this,
        SelectedItem, Android.Widget.ToastLength.Short).Show();
}
```

This will display a toast when the item is tapped.

■ **Note**   When a row is touched it should be highlighted for user feedback. When a custom view specifies a background color as CustomLayout.axml does, it also overrides the selection highlight, resulting in no visible highlight. This is a side-effect of Android ListView row customization and the solution for it is beyond the scope of this book.

CODE COMPLETE: Customizing List Rows

ANDROID

Listings 5-15 and 5-16 show the complete activity and adapter for creating custom list rows, from the ListViewExamplesAndroid solution.

Listing 5-15. Customizing a List in MainCustomListActivity.cs

```
public class MainCustomListActivity : Activity
{
    List<ListItem> listItems;
    ListView listView;
```

```
    protected override void OnCreate(Bundle bundle)
    {
        base.OnCreate(bundle);

        listItems = new List<ListItem> {
            new ListItem {Title = "First", Description="1st item"},
            new ListItem {Title = "Second", Description="2nd item"},
            new ListItem {Title = "Third", Description="3rd item"}
        };

        SetContentView(Resource.Layout.HomeLayout);
        listView = FindViewById<ListView>(Resource.Id.listItems);
        listView.Adapter = new ListCustomAdapter(this, listItems);
        listView.ItemClick += OnListItemClick;

    }

    void OnListItemClick(object sender, AdapterView.ItemClickEventArgs e)
    {
        String SelectedItem = listItems[e.Position].Title;
        Android.Widget.Toast.MakeText(this, SelectedItem, Android.Widget.ToastLength.
        Short).Show();
    }
}
```

Listing 5-16. ListCustomAdapter.cs

```
public class ListCustomAdapter : BaseAdapter
{
    private List<ListItem> itemList;
    private Activity context;

    public ListCustomAdapter(Activity context, List<ListItem> items)
        : base()
    {
        this.context = context;
        this.itemList = items;
    }

    public override int Count
    {
        get { return itemList.Count; }
    }

    public override Java.Lang.Object GetItem(int position)
    {
        throw new NotImplementedException();
    }
```

```
    public override long GetItemId(int position)
    {
        return position;
    }

    public override View GetView(int position, View convertView, ViewGroup parent)
    {
        View view = convertView;
        if (view == null)
        {
            view = context.LayoutInflater.Inflate(Resource.Layout.CustomLayout, null);
        }
        view.FindViewById<TextView>(Resource.Id.title).Text =
            itemList[position].Title;
        view.FindViewById<TextView>(Resource.Id.description).Text =
            itemList[position].Description;
        return view;
    }
}
```

Grouping Headers

ANDROID

Long lists sometimes require group headers so items can be located with ease.

There is no built-in approach for creating a list in Android with group headers. They must be coded by hand by using a custom adapter and changing the GetView method to return group headers in addition to the usual list rows. Android adapters identify rows using the index position in the list, leaving it up to the developer as to how and when to change the cell type to a group header based on this index.

■ **Note**   There are a number of different options for group list header data structures, including Dictionaries, Lists, Collections, and Classes.

Add a Boolean IsGroupHeader indicator to ListItem.cs that will be true only if the item is a group header.

```
public class ListItem
{
    public string Title { get; set; }
    public string Description { get; set; }
    public Boolean IsGroupHeader { get; set; }
}
```

Group headings will go into the Title property, intermingled with the other list item titles. Yes, it's denormalizing the data but it keeps the code simple and performance is key. Listing 5-17 shows the model population that happens in the activity's OnCreate method.

Listing 5-17. List Group Headers in MainActivityGrouped.cs

```
listItems = new List<ListItem>  {
  new ListItem {Title = "Important", Description="", IsGroupHeader=true},
  new ListItem {Title = "First", Description="1st item", IsGroupHeader=false},
  new ListItem {Title = "Less Important", Description="", IsGroupHeader=true},
  new ListItem {Title = "Second", Description="2nd item", IsGroupHeader=false},
  new ListItem {Title = "Third", Description="3rd item", IsGroupHeader=false},
  new ListItem {Title = "Fourth", Description="4th item", IsGroupHeader=false},
  new ListItem {Title = "Fifth", Description="5th item", IsGroupHeader=false},
  new ListItem {Title = "Not Important", Description="", IsGroupHeader=true},
  new ListItem {Title = "Sixth", Description="6th item" , IsGroupHeader=false},
  new ListItem {Title = "Seventh", Description="7th item", IsGroupHeader=false},
  new ListItem {Title = "Eighth", Description="8th item", IsGroupHeader=false},
  new ListItem {Title = "Ninth", Description="9th item", IsGroupHeader=false},
  new ListItem {Title = "Tenth", Description="10th item", IsGroupHeader=false},
  new ListItem {Title = "Trivial", Description="", IsGroupHeader=true},
  new ListItem {Title = "Eleventh", Description="11th item", IsGroupHeader=false},
  new ListItem {Title = "Twelfth", Description="12th item", IsGroupHeader=false},
  new ListItem {Title = "Thirteenth", Description="13th item", IsGroupHeader=false},
  new ListItem {Title = "Fourteenth", Description="14th item", IsGroupHeader=false},
  new ListItem {Title = "Fifteenth", Description="15th item" , IsGroupHeader=false},
  new ListItem {Title = "Sixteenth", Description="16th item", IsGroupHeader=false},
  new ListItem {Title = "Seventeenth", Description="17th item", IsGroupHeader=false},
  new ListItem {Title = "Eighteenth", Description="18th item", IsGroupHeader=false}
};
```

■ **Tip** When you create and collate lists from live data, you'll need to use loops or LINQ.

Assign the data model to the `ListAdapter` property of the `ListActivity` using a custom group adapter called `ListGroupAdapter`, which you'll build in just a sec.

```
ListAdapter = new ListGroupAdapter(this, listItems);
```

Let's now create the custom group adapter called `ListGroupAdapter`. Create a new adapter identical to Listing 5-16 in the previous example. In the getView method, use the `ListItem.IsGroupHeader` property to determine the style of the row: group header or list item (see Listing 5-18).

Listing 5-18. List Group Adapter in ListGroupAdapter.cs

```
public override View getView(int position, View convertView, ViewGroup parent)
{
    View view;
    if (itemList[position].IsGroupHeader) // group header view
    {
        view = context.LayoutInflater.Inflate(Android.Resource.Layout.SimpleListItem1, null);
        view.FindViewById<TextView>(Android.Resource.Id.Text1).Text = itemList[position].Title;
    }
```

```
    else // list item view
    {
        view = context.LayoutInflater.Inflate(Android.Resource.Layout.SimpleListItem2, null);
        view.FindViewById<TextView>(Android.Resource.Id.Text1).Text = itemList[position]
        .Title;
        view.FindViewById<TextView>(Android.Resource.Id.Text2).Text =
        itemList[position].Description;
    }
    return view;
}
```

This gives us a grouped list (Figure 5-19).

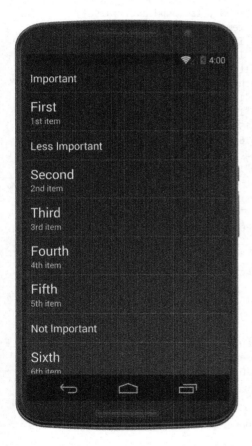

Figure 5-19. *Grouped list using conditional logic in GetView*

For demonstration purposes, this group header example uses simple built-in row styles, which are difficult to tell apart from the list item rows. Group headers look their best when the rows are customized, providing control over font, font size, color, and background. The sky is the limit with the design of rows that have been customized.

■ **Note** This group header example does not employ cell reuse and is not optimized for performance. Doing a null cell check with lists containing group headers requires the determination of the row style of the recycled view (group header or row item). This must be done by hand and is beyond the scope of this book.

■ **Tip** Expandable group headers are created using `SimpleExpandableListItem`, the built-in row list view. This requires using the `Activity` class `ExpandableListActivity` and the `Adapter` class `BaseExpandableListAdapter`. See the Xamarin GitHub example called `BuiltInExpandableViews`.

Those are the salient points about Android `ListView`. Now we'll examine the main list class on iOS, called `UITableView`.

iOS UITableView

iOS

Lists in iOS are created using the `UITableView` control bound to an array or a data model. `UITableView` provides groupings, headers, footers, images, and indexes. Each list requires a `UITableView` for the view, an adapter subclassed from `UITableSource` and assigned to the `UITableView.Source` property, and a data source, such as an array or data model.

Binding to an Array of Strings

Bind `UITableView` to an array of strings to create a list.

Create a new file of type iPhone `View Controller` called `ListArrayViewController.cs`. In this file, instantiate `UITableView` and add it to a view in the `ViewDidLoad` method of the `ViewController`.

```
public override void ViewDidLoad()
{
    base.ViewDidLoad();
    UITableView table = new UITableView(View.Bounds);
    Add (table);
}
```

For the adapter, create a new empty class called `ListSourceFromArray.cs`, subclass it from `UITableViewSource`, create a constructor, and override the `RowsInSection` and `GetCell` methods. Create an array of strings called `listItems` to bind to the list's `TextLabel.Text` property. The `RowsInSection` method returns the length of the entire list, as shown in Listing 5-19.

Listing 5-19. Using the Adapter Pattern, Subclass UITableViewSource to Create ListSourceFromArray.cs

```
using System;
using Foundation;
using UIKit;

public class ListSourceFromArray : UITableViewSource
{

    protected string[] listItems;
    protected string CellId= "TableCell";

    public ListSourceFromArray(string[] items)
    {
        listItems = items;
    }

    public override nint RowsInSection (UITableView tableview, nint section)
    {
        return listItems.Length;
    }

    public override UITableViewCell GetCell (UITableView tableView, NSIndexPath indexPath)
    {
        UITableViewCell cell = tableView.DequeueReusableCell (CellId);
        if (cell == null)  cell = new UITableViewCell (UITableViewCellStyle.Default,  CellId);
        cell.TextLabel.Text = listItems[indexPath.Row];
        return cell;
    }
}
```

Cell reuse in GetCell improves performance, thereby making scrolling faster with fewer skipped frames. As each row is retrieved, the DequeueReusableCell method checks to see if a cell (memory location for a row) already exists for that CellId. If it comes back null then instantiate a new cell, otherwise use it. When a list is scrolled, this method is called to create more rows to display on the screen, recycling cells when possible. Type NSIndexPath comes from the Foundation library in the using.

■ **Note**   There are two ways to handle list row cell reuse in iOS: this older *null cell check* method and the new way (iOS 6+). I've begun with the old way because it's simpler to demonstrate, works great with the built-in row styles, and is backward-compatible with older iOS versions. If you're targeting iOS 6+ and using customized row-styled lists, consider using the new table and cell reuse implementation explained in the "Optimizing Performance" section later in the chapter.

Finally, populate the data source. In the ViewController's ViewDidLoad method, create an array of strings and pass it into the constructor for ListSourceFromArray, and assign the new adapter to the Source property on the table. This binds the array to the UITableView. Add the completed table to your ViewController (Listing 5-20).

Listing 5-20. Creating a UITableView in ListArrayViewController.cs in the iOSListExample Solution

```
public override void ViewDidLoad()
{
    base.ViewDidLoad();
    UITableView table = new UITableView(View.Bounds);
    string[] tableItems = new string[] {"First","Second","Third","Fourth","Fifth"};
    table.Source = new ListSourceFromArray(tableItems);
    Add (table);
}
```

This will display your list (Figure 5-20).

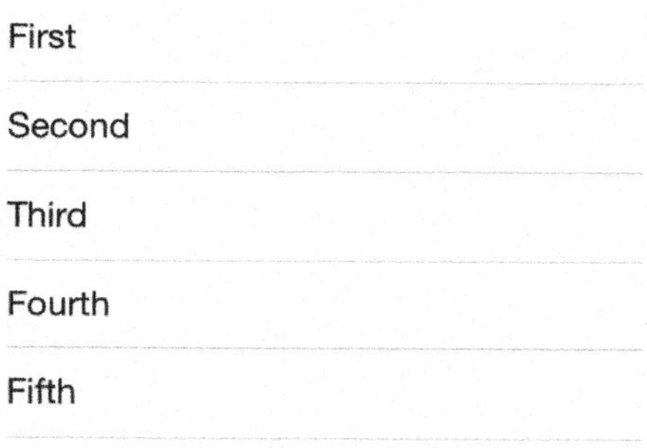

First

Second

Third

Fourth

Fifth

Figure 5-20. *UITableView list*

Selecting an Item

iOS

Selection of a list item is handled by overriding the RowSelected event in the UITableViewSource subclass, as shown in Listing 5-21.

Listing 5-21. Handling a Row Selection in ListSourceFromArray.cs

```
public override void RowSelected (UITableView tableView, NSIndexPath indexPath)
{
    new UIAlertView("Row Selected", listItems [indexPath.Row],
        null, "OK", null).Show();
    tableView.DeselectRow (indexPath, true);
}
```

indexPath denotes the index of the row. DeselectRow removes the highlight from the selected row. Figure 5-21 shows the UIAlertView displaying the selected row.

Figure 5-21. *UIAlertView with the second item selected*

Multiple Selection

Multiple row selection is achieved by setting UITableView's AllowsMultipleSelection or AllowsMultipleSelectionDuringEditing properties to true.

```
tableView.AllowsMultipleSelection = true;
```

Retrieve the results in the IndexPathsForSelectedRows property.

Binding to a Data Model

iOS

iOS UITableView data binding requires an adapter subclassed from UITableViewSource to bind the model to the list. This is similar to the approach used in Listing 5-19 to bind a string array to the list with the addition of a data model.

Create a list from a data model in three steps:

1. *Data Model*: Create a data model containing the list items.

2. *Adapter*: Create a list item adapter subclassed from UITableViewSource to specify which fields in the data model to display in the list and manage row cell reuse.

3. *View Controller*: Create a UIViewController to display the list. Instantiate the table to house the list. Populate the data model and then pass it into the list adapter constructor. Assign the resulting adapter to the Source property of the UIViewController.

Let's do each step.

Data Model

Create a custom data model containing list items in a separate class file called ListItem.cs (Listing 5-22).

Listing 5-22. Data Model in ListItem.cs.

```
public class ListItem
{
    public string Title { get; set; }
    public string Description { get; set; }
}
```

Adapter

To create an adapter, create a plain class called ListSourceFromModel.cs (see Listing 5-23), inherit from UITableViewSource, then override RowsInSection and GetCell. Declare a private copy of the data model List, called itemList. Create a constructor that receives the populated data model as a parameter. This code is almost identical to the previous example in Listing 5-19, which binds an array, so I've bolded the differences for specifying a data model.

Listing 5-23. UITableViewSource Subclass in ListSourceFromModel.cs

```
using System;
using System.Collections.Generic;
using Foundation;
using UIKit;

namespace iOSListExample
{
    public class ListSourceFromModel : UITableViewSource
    {
        protected List<ListItem> listItems;
        protected string CellId= "TableCell";

        public ListSourceFromModel (List<ListItem> items)
        {
            listItems = items;
        }
```

```
        public override nint RowsInSection (UITableView tableview, nint section)
        {
            return listItems.Count;
        }

        public override UITableViewCell GetCell (UITableView tableView,
        NSIndexPath indexPath)
        {
            UITableViewCell cell = tableView.DequeueReusableCell (CellId);
            if (cell == null)  cell = new UITableViewCell (UITableViewCellStyle.
            Default,CellId);
            cell.TextLabel.Text = listItems[indexPath.Row].Title;
            return cell;
        }
    }
}
```

The Title property of listItems is assigned to the Text property of the built-in TextLabel on the UITableViewCell, using the built-in list row view UITableViewCellStyle.Default.

GetCell is the operative method here, creating individual list rows, each as a UITableViewCell, and returning them to the UITableView. Cells are reused when possible using DequeueReusableCell. I reuse for performance reasons although the null cell check is an older implementation used here for simplicity and backward compatibility. You'll read about the newer cell reuse approach used in iOS 6+ in the "Optimizing Performance" section later in this chapter.

View Controller

In a UIViewController, the data model can be bound to the list using the adapter. Create a new file of type iPhone View Controller called ListModelViewController.cs. In the UIViewController's ViewDidLoad method, declare listItems as data type List<ListItem>, declare table as a UITableView, and then populate the data model and pass it into ListSourceFromModel's constructor. Assign the resulting adapter to the UITableView.Source property. Add the UITableView as a subview using the Add method (an alias for AddSubView). Listing 5-24 shows the complete view controller.

Listing 5-24. View Controller in ListModelViewController.cs

```
using System;
    using System.Collections.Generic;
    using Foundation;
    using UIKit;

    namespace iOSListExample
    {
        public partial class ListModelViewController : UIViewController
        {
            public ListModelViewController () : base ("ListModelViewController", null)
            {
            }

            List<ListItem> listItems;
```

```
public override void ViewDidLoad()
{
    base.ViewDidLoad();
    UITableView table = new UITableView(View.Bounds);
    listItems = new List<ListItem> {
        new ListItem {Title = "First", Description="1st item"} ,
        new ListItem {Title = "Second", Description="2nd item"} ,
        new ListItem {Title = "Third", Description="3rd item"}
    } ;
    table.Source = new ListSourceFromModel(listItems);
    Add (table);
}
}
}
```

This will display the list from the data-bound model (Figure 5-22).

First

Second

Third

Figure 5-22. *Data-bound list using UITableView*

▓ **Note** This is a simplified, static data example for demonstration purposes only. In the real world you might populate a sorted data model using LINQ or a loop.

Using Built-in Row Views

iOS

The three most common built-in row styles in UITableView are Default, Subtitle, and Value1.

Figure 5-23 shows the Default row style.

First

Second

Third

Figure 5-23. *Default row style with title only*

Figure 5-24 shows the Subtitle row style.

First
1st item

Second
2nd item

Third
3rd item

Figure 5-24. *Subtitle row style with title and description*

Figure 5-25 shows the Value1 row style.

First   1st item

Second   2nd item

Third   3rd item

Figure 5-25. *Value1 row style with title and right-justified description*

■ **Tip**   All three of these styles support images as well as text.

These styles are configured in the UITableViewSource adapter when a cell is instantiated in the GetCell method (from ListSourceStyles.cs in the downloadable examples).

```
cell = new UITableViewCell (UITableViewCellStyle.Default, cellIdentifier);
```

Text fields and images are also assigned in the GetCell method.

```
cell.TextLabel.Text = listItems[indexPath.Row].Title;
cell.DetailTextLabel.Text = listItems[indexPath.Row].Description;
cell.ImageView.Image = UIImage.FromFile("Images/" + listItems[indexPath.Row].ImageName);
```

An ImageName string field must be added to the ListItems data model and populated in order to support images.

■ **Tip**   Be careful not to assign to a property that is not present for a particular built-in row type or the compiler will throw an error.

■ **Note**   There is a fourth built-in row type called Value2 with a right-justified title and left-justified detail label. I recommend against its use because it is difficult to read.

Cell Separators

iOS

The thin line separating rows has several styles and can be turned off using the UITableView SeparatorStyle property. Color can also be set using the SeparatorColor property.

```
table.SeparatorColor = UIColor.Blue;
table.SeparatorStyle = UITableViewCellSeparatorStyle.DoubleLineEtched;
```

These are the four SeparatorStyle settings:

- *None*: Turn off the separator line
- *SingleLine*: Default single line
- *SingleLineEtched*: Grouped-style line made up of two colors
- *DoubleLineEtched*: Grouped-style thick line made up of two colors

---

■ **Note**   The SingleLineEtched and DoubleLineEtched styles only work with UITableStyle.Grouped.

Use the None SeparatorStyle to remove the separators (Figure 5-26).

```
table.SeparatorStyle = UITableViewCellSeparatorStyle.None;
```

First

Second

Third

Fourth

Fifth

Figure 5-26. *No separators with the None SeparatorStyle*

Customizing List Rows

iOS

List rows can be customized by subclassing UITableViewCell and implementing the custom cell in your adapter's GetCell method.

Create a new class called CustomCell.cs, as shown in Listing 5-25. Inherit from UITableViewCell and implement these three methods:

- Constructor: Create the controls, set their properties, and add them as subviews to the cell

- UpdateCell: Called by UITableViewSource.GetCell to set cell properties, such as title and description

- LayoutSubviews: Called automatically to set the location of the controls

Listing 5-25. A Custom UITableViewCell in Customcell.cs

```
public class CustomCell : UITableViewCell  {

    UILabel titleLabel, descriptionLabel;

    public CustomCell (NSString cellId) : base (UITableViewCellStyle.Default, cellId)
    {
        SelectionStyle = UITableViewCellSelectionStyle.Gray;
        ContentView.BackgroundColor = UIColor.FromRGB (27, 16, 117);

        titleLabel = new UILabel ()
        {
            Font = UIFont.FromName("Helvetica-Bold", 25f),
            TextColor = UIColor.White,
            BackgroundColor = UIColor.Clear
        } ;

        descriptionLabel = new UILabel ()
        {
            Font = UIFont.FromName("Helvetica-Light", 12f),
            TextColor = UIColor.FromRGB (179, 179, 186),
            TextAlignment = UITextAlignment.Center,
            BackgroundColor = UIColor.Clear
        } ;

        ContentView.AddSubviews (new UIView[] { titleLabel, descriptionLabel });

    }

    public void UpdateCell (string title, string description)
    {
        titleLabel.Text = title;
        descriptionLabel.Text = description;
    }
```

```
    public override void LayoutSubviews ()
    {
        base.LayoutSubviews ();
        titleLabel.Frame = new RectangleF(5, 4, (float)ContentView.Bounds.Width - 63, 25);
        descriptionLabel.Frame = new RectangleF(100, 18, 100, 20);
    }
}
```

This custom UITableViewCell sports the usual title and description labels with customized fonts and colors, as well as a blue background for the entire list.

■ **Tip** UITableViewCellSelectionStyle indicates the background color of the selected rows: Default (Blue), Blue, Gray, or None.

■ **Tip** LayoutSubviews can be made to customize control location depending on the cell

■ **Tip** Don't forget the references using Foundation and using UIKit.

Create a new adapter subclassed from UITableViewSource, which is virtually identical to the previous data-bound adapter shown in Listing 5-23. Here is the new GetCell implementation that instantiates your CustomCell (see Listing 5-26) with differences from the previous adapter in bold.

Listing 5-26. GetCell Method from ListSourceFromCustomCell.cs

```
    public override UITableViewCell GetCell (UITableView tableView, NSIndexPath indexPath)
    {
        var cell = tableView.DequeueReusableCell (CellId) as CustomCell;
        if (cell == null)
            cell = new CustomCell ((NSString)CellId);
        cell.UpdateCell (listItems [indexPath.Row].Title
            , listItems [indexPath.Row].Description);
        return cell;
    }
```

Note the call to UpdateCell which we implemented in our custom UITableViewCell. It updates visible properties in the cell.

Figure 5-27 shows the customized list rows.

Figure 5-27. *A UITableView with custom cells by subclassing UITableViewCell*

■ **Tip**   Images can be added to a custom cell using `UIImageView`.

Grouping Headers

iOS

Items can be grouped under headers using the `TitleForHeader` and `TitleForFooter` methods in the `UITableViewSource` adapter.

Group titles must first be created. One way to do it is to make a data model that is a collection of groups; each of which contains collections of data items. This is a collection of collections with the group header fields defined within each group collection.

Create a group class that contains the group-by key and a collection for the items (Listing 5-27).

Listing 5-27. Group Data Model in Group.cs

```
public class Group : List<ListItem>
{
    public String Key { get; private set; }
    public Group(String key, List<ListItem> items)
    {
        Key = key;
        foreach (var item in items)
            this.Add(item);
    }
}
```

In your `ViewController`, hydrate the model. Populate each `ListItem` and assign them to the master group. Create as many groups as you need with corresponding keys and their contained items. In this example there are two groups, with keys named "Important" and "Less Important".

```
List<Group> itemsGrouped;

public override void ViewDidLoad()
{
    base.ViewDidLoad();
    UITableView table = new UITableView(View.Bounds);
    itemsGrouped = new List<Group> {
        new Group ("Important", new List<ListItem> {
            new ListItem {Title = "First", Description="1st item"} ,
            new ListItem {Title = "Second", Description="2nd item"} ,
        } ),

        new Group ("Less Important", new List<ListItem>{
            new ListItem {Title = "Third", Description="3rd item"}
        } )
    } ;
```

```
    table.Source = new ListSourceFromModelGrouped(itemsGrouped);
    Add (table);
}
```

To create **headers** in your UITableViewSource, override the TitleForHeader method and return the string value relevant to each group.

```
public override string TitleForHeader (UITableView tableView, int section)
{
    return group[section];
}
```

The rest of the UITableViewSource code is shown in Listing 5-28.

■ **Note**   The iOS API refers to groups as sections.

Figure 5-28 shows the group headers returned by TitleForHeader.

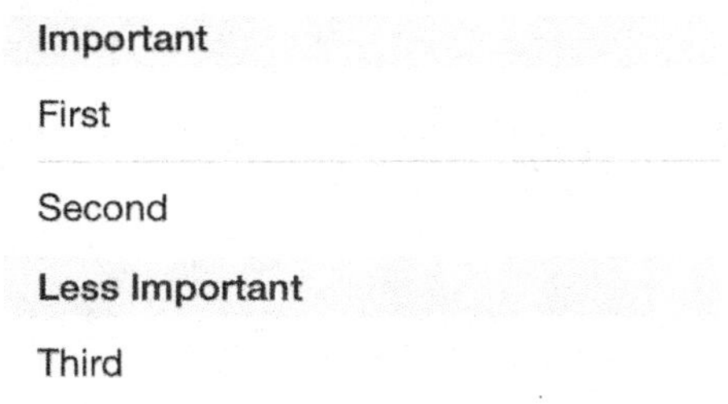

Important

First

Second

Less Important

Third

Figure 5-28. *Group headers*

For **footers**, override the TitleForFooter method and return the string value relevant to the group.

```
public override string TitleForFooter (UITableView tableView, int section)
{
    return indexedTableItems[keys[section]].Count + " items";
}
```

Let's add group footers returned by TitleForFooter.

Figure 5-29 shows headers and footers together.

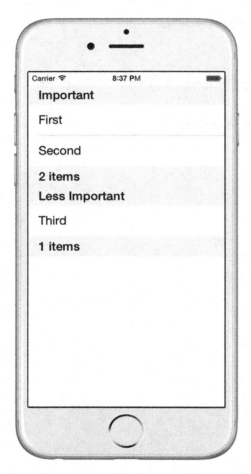

Figure 5-29. *Group headers and footers*

■ **Tip** Consider using the Grouped table style when using headers and footers, explained later in the chapter in the "Highlighting Groups Using Table Styles" section. It puts more graphical emphasis on the groupings than the default Plain table style.

CODE COMPLETE: Grouping Adapter

iOS

This is the adapter for grouping headers and footers, inherited from UITableViewSource (Listing 5-28).

Listing 5-28. Data Source for Headers and Footers in ListSourceFromModelGrouped.cs

```
public class ListSourceFromModelGrouped : UITableViewSource
{
    List<Group> groups;
    protected string cellId= "TableCell";

    public ListSourceFromModelGrouped (List<Group> items)
    {
        groups = items;
    }

    public override nint NumberOfSections (UITableView tableView)
    {
        return groups.Count;
    }

    public override nint RowsInSection (UITableView tableview, nint section)
    {
        List<ListItem> list = groups [(int)section];
        return list.Count;
    }

    public override string TitleForHeader (UITableView tableView, nint section)
    {
        return groups[(int)section].Key;
    }

    public override string TitleForFooter (UITableView tableView, nint section)
    {
        List<ListItem> list = groups [(int)section];
        return list.Count + " items";
    }

    public override void RowSelected (UITableView tableView, NSIndexPath indexPath)
    {
        List<ListItem> list = groups [indexPath.Section];
        new UIAlertView("Row Selected"
            , list[indexPath.Row].Title
            , null, "OK", null).Show();
        tableView.DeselectRow (indexPath, true);
    }
```

```
    public override UITableViewCell GetCell (UITableView tableView, NSIndexPath indexPath)
    {
        UITableViewCell cell = tableView.DequeueReusableCell (cellId);
        List<ListItem> list = groups [indexPath.Section];
        ListItem item = list[indexPath.Row];
        if (cell == null)
        { cell = new UITableViewCell (UITableViewCellStyle.Default, cellId); }
        cell.TextLabel.Text = item.Title;

        return cell;
    }
}
```

■ **Tip** Group headers and footers can be further customized by using the GetViewForHeader and GetViewForFooter method overrides on UITableViewSource.

CODE COMPLETE: Grouping View Controller

iOS

Listing 5-29 shows the UIViewController, which implements ListSourceFromModelGrouped to create a UITableView with grouped headers and footers.

Listing 5-29. Implement Grouped Headers and Footers in ListModelGroupedViewController.cs

```
    public partial class ListModelGroupedViewController : UIViewController
    {
        public ListModelGroupedViewController ()
        {
        }

        List<Group> itemsGrouped;

        public override void ViewDidLoad()
        {
            base.ViewDidLoad();
            UITableView table = new UITableView(View.Bounds);
            itemsGrouped = new List<Group> {
                new Group ("Important", new List<ListItem> {
                    new ListItem {Title = "First", Description="1st item"} ,
                    new ListItem {Title = "Second", Description="2nd item"} ,
                } ),
                new Group ("Less Important", new List<ListItem>{
                    new ListItem {Title = "Third", Description="3rd item"}
                } )
            };
```

```
        table.Source = new ListSourceFromModelGrouped(itemsGrouped);
        Add (table);
    }
}
```

Highlighting Groups Using Table Styles

iOS

Groups can be accentuated visually using the Grouped table style.

There are two table styles that can be set upon the instantiation of the UITableView: Plain and Grouped. Plain is the default style used throughout these examples. The Grouped style causes the list to contain more heavily shaded and bounded areas around the list items (Figure 5-30) and is set like this:

```
UITableView table = new UITableView(View.Bounds,
    UITableViewStyle.Grouped);
```

Figure 5-30 shows the heavier Grouped style.

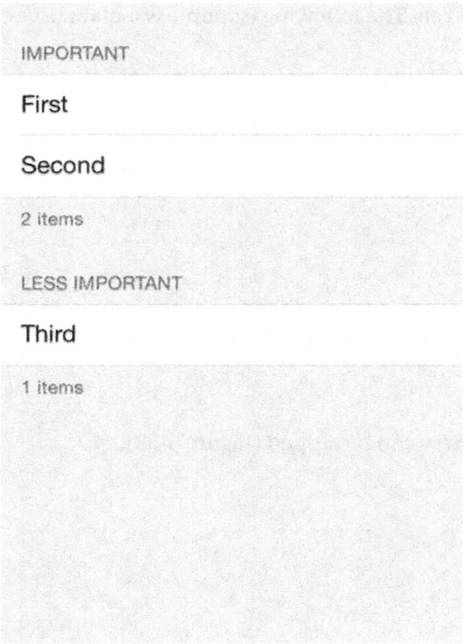

IMPORTANT

First

Second

2 items

LESS IMPORTANT

Third

1 items

Figure 5-30. *Grouped table style*

Figure 5-31 shows the lighter Plain style.

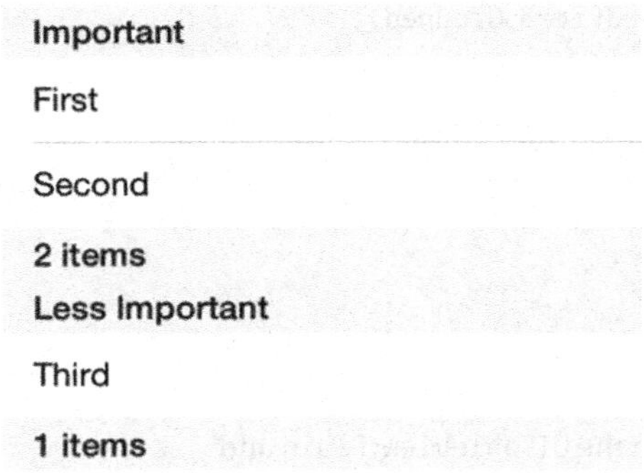

Important

First

Second

2 items

Less Important

Third

1 items

Figure 5-31. *Plain table style*

Accessorizing List Rows

iOS

Accessories are simple icons that enhance list rows. There are four accessory list row types: Checkmark, DisclosureIndicator, DetailButton, and DetailDisclosureButton. The following example is a plain list of ungrouped items.

Checkmark can indicate the selection of the row (Figure 5-32).

First	✓
Second	✓
Third	✓

Figure 5-32. *Checkmark accessory*

DisclosureIndicator is a right arrow that typically indicates the row can be tapped (Figure 5-33).

First	›
Second	›
Third	›

Figure 5-33. *DisclosureIndicator accessory*

DetailButton is a tappable info button for additional functionality, which is different than tapping the row (Figure 5-34).

First	(i)
Second	(i)
Third	(i)

Figure 5-34. *DetailButton accessory*

DetailDisclosureButton is a tappable info/right arrow button for additional functionality, which is different than tapping the row (Figure 5-35).

First	(i) >
Second	(i) >
Third	(i) >

Figure 5-35. *DetailDisclosureButton accessory*

■ **Tip** If you want the user to multi-select rows, first consider using the UITableView's AllowsMultipleSelection property described earlier in the "Multiple Selection" section, as that approach has a full multiple selection functionality baked in.

Specify accessories in the GetCell method of the UITableViewSource.

```
cell.Accessory = UITableViewCellAccessory.Checkmark;
```

Clear the accessory for a particular cell using UITableViewCellAccessory.None. This can be useful for unchecking a row.

```
cell.Accessory = UITableViewCellAccessory.None;
```

■ **Tip** Store row accessory state in your data model, *not in the view*, and use GetCell only for keeping your view in sync with the data model.

Selecting an Accessory

iOS

When a DetailButton or DetailDisclosureButton is tapped, handle the event in the UITableViewSource by overriding AccessoryButtonTapped.

```
public override void AccessoryButtonTapped (UITableView tableView, NSIndexPath indexPath)
{
    new UIAlertView("Detail Button Tapped"
        , listItems[indexPath.Row].Title , null, "OK", null).Show();
}
```

Accessory examples can be found in ListSourceStyles.cs in the downloadable code.

Optimizing Performance

iOS

As always, when building a list adapter, it is important to code for performance which means reusing cells whenever possible. A cell is a memory location that holds a list row. You want cells to be recycled in memory as rows scroll off of the screen rather than be thrown away.

A common technique used in Xamarin.iOS apps is the *null cell check,* like this one used in the UITableViewSource.GetCell method in the previous examples:

```
if (cell == null) cell = new UITableViewCell (UITableViewCellStyle.Default, CellId);
```

A new cell reuse pattern was introduced in iOS 6, doing away with the traditional *null cell check.* The cell reuse examples used previously are all backward and forward compatible, but the newer technique shown next is more efficient. This new technique is *not* backward compatible before iOS 6.

■ **Note**   The new cell reuse pattern works best with custom cells. For built-in row styles like Default, Subtitle, and Value1, I recommend using the older *null cell check* approach. At the time of this writing there is no straightforward way to use the newer pattern with built-in row styles.

To implement the new cell reuse approach, declare a CellId variable as a static variable at the top of your view controller.

```
public static NSString CellId = new NSString ("CellId");
```

After declaring your UITableView, register the class or layout file containing the cell definition using the UITableView methods RegisterClassForCellReuse or RegisterNibForCellReuse.

```
table.RegisterClassForCellReuse (typeof(CustomCell), CellId);
```

Save this new UIViewController as ListModelViewControllerCellReuse.cs and change the class and constructor name to ListModelViewControllerCellReuse. Next, make a change to your UITableViewSource subclass.

When coding GetCell in UITableViewSource, skip the null cell check. That check is now done automatically by DequeueReusableCell. Refer to the static CellId back in your view controller.

```
public override UITableViewCell GetCell (UITableView tableView,
    NSIndexPath indexPath)
{
    var cell = tableView.DequeueReusableCell
        (ListModelViewControllerCellReuse.CellId) as CustomCell;
    cell.UpdateCell (listItems [indexPath.Row].Title
        , listItems [indexPath.Row].Description);
    return cell;
}
```

Note that the view controller class is called ListModelViewControllerCellReuse in this example.

Lastly, in your custom UITableViewCell, CustomCell.cs, replace the custom cell constructor declaration with one that uses a pointer parameter instead of a string. Keep the rest of the constructor the same.

```
public CustomCell (IntPtr p):base(p)
```

These changes will implement the new cell reuse pattern and display the same list used in earlier data model bindings with the custom list rows. The entire code example is available for download in ListModelViewControllerCellReuse.cs, ListSourceFromModelCellReuse.cs, and CustomCell.cs.

An Alternative Approach to Lists: UITableViewController

iOS

The UIViewController, UITableView, and UITableViewSource classes are combined into a single class called UITableViewController. This table mega-class handles display and data logic in a single class, with many of the techniques familiar to developers such as GetCell. Developers disagree about the usefulness of this class. Many use it without difficulty or complaint, while others are bothered by the violation of Separation of Concerns (SOC), the unwieldiness of the class, and several minor design limitations over the older, more modular approach. A UITableViewController can be used to create scrolling lists with all of the features demonstrated in this chapter.

Summary

In mobile development, lists are the new data grid.

List views are bound to arrays, Lists, or data models and allow scrolling when there are more items than will fit on the screen. They usually contain text string rows but some contain images or entire layouts of controls.

Selection can be accomplished with a single row or multiple rows. Multiple-row selection must be done by hand in Xamarin.Forms. In Android, you can use ChoiceMode and iOS provides accessories like Checkmark.

Cell reuse is a common theme in performant lists and involves the economic use of already populated list rows whenever possible. In Xamarin.Forms, this is built-in but is manually coded in Android and iOS.

Grouping is often required for long lists, with *grouping headings* to help guide a user to find what they're looking for.

Built-in list row views give you layout options without having to build them from scratch. These provide a range of control layouts for list rows providing titles, descriptions, and images as well as accessories such as checkboxes and radio buttons.

Custom list rows provide versatility at the risk of slower performance. Beware when creating these, as there are often performance trade-offs. Test for performance and follow the rules of performant customization for each platform when using long lists.

Lists help us navigate an app. Let's now explore other types of navigation in Chapter 6.

CHAPTER 6

■ ■ ■

Navigation

Navigation gives users what they need to get around an app quickly, moving from screen to screen with confidence and ease. This may include menus, tappable icons, buttons, tabs, and list items, as well as many types of gesture-sensitive screens to display data, information, and options to the user.

Navigation Patterns

Navigation patterns are industry-standard templates for tying an app's screens together in an elegant and usable way. The two most common visual design patterns in mobile navigation are hierarchical and modal. An entire family of derivative patterns combine, enhance, and decorate these base navigation patterns to create the full range of mobile UI patterns. Here is an exhaustive list of the most common mobile UI navigation patterns used in Xamarin development:

- *Hierarchical*: A stack-based navigation pattern enabling users to move deeper into a screen hierarchy and then back out again, one screen at a time, by using the Up or Back buttons.

- *Modal*: A screen that interrupts hierarchical navigation, often a pop-up screen with an alert or menu that the user can complete or cancel.

- *Drill-down list*: A list of tappable items selected to display item detail.

- *Navigation drawer*: A navigation menu that slides over from the left side at the tap of an icon, typically three horizontal lines known as the *hamburger* in the upper-left corner of the screen.

- *Tabs*: A bar containing several folder-like buttons at the top or bottom of the screen, each with tappable icons or text invoking new pages.

- *Springboard*: Also referred to as a *dashboard*, this is a grid of tappable icons invoking new pages.

- *Carousel*: Screen-sized panels that slide horizontally and sometimes contain large images.

Let's explore the two most common navigation patterns, hierarchical and modal.

Hierarchical

Hierarchical is a stack-based pattern that allows users to move down into a stack of screens and then pop back out again, one screen at a time. This pattern typically uses a toolbar at the top of the screen to display an Up button in the upper-left corner when a page is selected or "drilled down into" by any means. As the user drills deeper into the menu structure, a stack is maintained, with each page pushed onto it. Two buttons—the Back and the Up button—are used in tandem to navigate backward, popping pages off the stack. The Back button is the curved arrow icon at the bottom of the screen (iOS doesn't have one). The Up button is the less-than icon in the upper-left corner. Deep navigational stacks can be traversed in this manner, with page selection requiring the use of additional UI navigation patterns such as the navigation drawer, drill-down list, or pop-up menu.

Modal

A *modal* is a single, interruptive pop-up or screen that comes in two flavors. The most common type floats on top of the main page and is usually an alert, dialog box, or menu that the user can respond to or cancel. Navigation reverts back to the originating page when the modal is dismissed. A modal informs users of an important event, such as a saved record, or gives them the opportunity to provide input or direction, such as a menu or whether to commit or cancel a transaction. The second, less common, type of modal replaces the main page entirely, interrupting the hierarchical navigation stack.

The two most common modal menus in the mobile UI are the navigation drawer and the action menu. The *navigation drawer* typically slides in from the left and is triggered by the tapping of an icon (usually the *hamburger*) in the upper-left corner of the screen and displays a list of pages to navigate to. The *action menu* typically slides in or pops up on the right side of the screen, and is invoked by tapping an icon (usually three vertical dots) in the upper-right corner of the screen and contains mostly operations (for example, Favorite This), though less frequently some navigation pages as well. To follow this established UI pattern, remember this rule: *Nav on the left, action on the right.*

Hierarchical and modal UI navigation patterns are typically used as complementary techniques, with hierarchical providing the skeleton of the navigational structure and modals giving the user choices for what they want to do and where they want to go within the app as well as informational updates along the way.

In this chapter, you will explore hierarchical, modal, and the rest of the navigation patterns on each platform.

Xamarin.Forms Navigation

Xamarin.Forms provides most of the primary navigation patterns out of the box:

- Hierarchical navigation using `NavigationPage`

- Modal using `NavigationPage`, alerts, and `ActionSheets`

- Drill-down lists using `NavigationPage`, `ListView`, and `TableView`

- Navigation drawer using `MasterDetailPage`

- Tabs using `TabbedPage`

- Springboard using images with gesture recognizers

- Carousel using `CarouselPage`

Android Navigation

Android provides many of the primary navigation patterns out of the box:

- Hierarchical navigation using `Toolbar` or `ActionBar`

- Modal using `DialogFragment`, `AlertDialog`, and `PopupMenu`

- Drill-down list using `ListView`

- Navigation drawer using `DrawerLayout`

- Tabs using `ActionBar`

iOS Navigation

iOS navigation is usually created by using designer tools, but navigation patterns can also be coded by hand.

- Hierarchical navigation using `UINavigationController`, the push segue, or the `PushViewController`

- Modal using the modal segue, the `PresentViewController`, and `UIAlertAcontroller`

- Drill-down list using `UINavigationController`

- Navigation drawer using components

- Tabs using `UITabBarController`

■ **Note** The topic of Xamarin UI navigation could fill an entire book. This chapter covers many important navigation patterns on all platforms, exhaustively in the case of Xamarin.Forms, providing code examples when possible as well as additional resources.

Before you dive into the patterns, one cross-cutting navigation topic needs to be addressed: state management. As a user navigates through an app, separate screens must appear to be part of the unified whole application, even though each screen is a separate UI with a separate controller.

State Management

State helps us maintain the illusion of consistency and continuity while the user navigates among screens, through the sharing of data on those screens. We're no longer in the world of query strings, cookies, and `Session` variables, but we must still maintain state in mobile apps. Most variables are scoped to a particular screen, so state management usually involves the explicit passing of data back and forth between screens. Parameter passing between screens is the encouraged method of state management on all mobile platforms, to minimize the risk of memory abuse and to maximize app performance.

Xamarin.Forms allows us to pass parameters into a `ContentPage` constructor. Android uses a class called `Bundle`, which is a dictionary that contains passed values, housed inside a class called `Intent`, which we use to call new activities. iOS developers favor public properties on the destination view controller, but iOS supports passing parameters into the destination page's constructor.

The static global class is a C# implementation of the Singleton pattern. It is available on all platforms but must be used with caution; be mindful of mobile-device memory limitations. Disk persistence is built into Xamarin.Forms by using the `Application` objects' `Properties`, a dictionary using ID/object pairs.

Now that you have a way to pass values between pages, let's begin with Xamarin.Forms navigation.

Xamarin.Forms Navigation

Navigation in Xamarin.Forms is based on the two primary navigation patterns: hierarchical and modal.

The *hierarchical pattern* allows the user to move down through a stack of pages, and then pop back up through them by using the Up or Back button. This is sometimes called *drill-down* or *breadcrumb* navigation.

The *modal pattern* is an interruptive screen that requires a particular action from the user but can usually be dismissed with a Cancel button. Examples include notifications, alerts, dialog boxes, and edit or new record pages.

The most common Xamarin.Forms navigation component is `NavigationPage`, which is based on the hierarchical pattern but also provides modal functionality.

■ **XAML**   The XAML version of all Xamarin.Forms examples can be found at the Apress web site (`www.apress.com`) or on GitHub at `https://github.com/danhermes/xamarin-book-examples`. The Xamarin.Forms solution for Chapter 6 is `NavigationExamples.Xaml`.

Hierarchical Navigation Using NavigationPage

XAMARIN.FORMS

`NavigationPage` creates a first-in/last-out stack of pages. Pages can be pushed onto the stack and then popped back off to return to the previous page. `NavigationPage` typically wraps the main, or home, page. It can provide a navigation bar at the top of the screen providing a current page title, icon, and an Up (<) button.

Figure 6-1 shows the navigation bar at the top of the screen for iOS and Android.

⟨ Back   **Hierarchical Navigation**   ⟨   Hierarchical Navigation

Figure 6-1. *NavigationPage*

The default text on the iOS up button is "Back." Windows Phone shows no navigation at the top of the screen using `NavigationPage`, but the Back button will work correctly, popping pages off the stack.

■ **Note**   Up and Back are different navigation buttons. Up is the less-than arrow in the top-left corner of the navigation page, and the Back button is on the bottom navigation bar provided by the OS (except in iOS).

To use NavigationPage, in your Application class's constructor, instantiate a NavigationPage object, passing in the home ContentPage as a parameter, and assign it to your MainPage:

```
public class App : Application
{
    public App()
    {
        MainPage = new NavigationPage(new HomePage());
    }
}
```

As shown in Listing 6-1, create a new ContentPage called HomePage that has a label identifying itself as Home Page and a button bringing us to the second page via the PushAsync method.

Listing 6-1. Hierarchical Navigation Home Page (in NavigationPage1.cs—See Next Tip)

```
class HomePage : ContentPage
{
    Button homeButton;
    public HomePage()
    {
        Title = "Hierarchical Navigation";

        Label homeLabel = new Label
        {
            Text = "Home Page",
            FontSize = 40
        };

        homeButton = new Button
        {
            Text = "Go to Second Page"
        };

        homeButton.Clicked += async (sender, args) =>
            await Navigation.PushAsync(new secondPage());

        StackLayout stackLayout = new StackLayout
        {
            Children = { homeLabel, homeButton }

        };

        this.Content = stackLayout;
    }
}
```

■ **Tip** If you're following along in the online code examples, notice that I simplified this example by renaming NavigationPage1 to HomePage in this text to leave out the super useful but slightly off-topic drill-down ListView home page in the downloadable code.

The home page is a simple page with your label and button, waiting to bring you to the second page, as shown in Figure 6-2.

Figure 6-2. *Home page*

Listing 6-2 contains a simple `ContentPage` called `secondPage` that labels itself Second Page.

Listing 6-2. Second Page in the Hierarchy from NavigationPage2.cs

```
class secondPage: ContentPage
{
    public secondPage()
    {
        Title = "Hierarchical Navigation";

        Label homeLabel = new Label
        {
            Text = "Second Page",
            FontSize = 40
        };

        var stackLayout = new StackLayout
        {
            Children = { homeLabel }
        };

        this.Content = stackLayout;
    }
}
```

Now that a page is pushed onto the navigation stack, the navigation bar becomes visible, as shown in Figure 6-3.

Figure 6-3. *The second page contains a navigation bar with a Back button (except on Windows Phone)*

Note that the icon in the navigation bar has been set to a blank image, as described later in the section "Customizing the Navigation Bar."

■ **Note** The navigation bar is created by `NavigationPage` automatically. When the Up button (<) is clicked, the page is popped off the stack and control is returned to the previous page.

Pushing and Popping Screens on the Navigation Stack

Three methods are used to move between pages hierarchically:

- PushAsync pushes a page onto the stack and goes there:

```
Navigation.PushAsync(new nextPage());
```

A second parameter can be added to specify whether the navigation is animated:

```
Navigation.PushAsync(new nextPage(), bool animated);
```

- PopAsync pops a page off the stack and goes to the previous page:

```
Navigation.PopAsync();
```

- PopToRootAsync pops all pages off the stack and goes to the root page:

```
Navigation.PopToRootAsync();
```

■ **Tip** Two more methods, `RemovePage` and `InsertPageBefore`, which are for changing the stack without pushing and popping.

RemovePage removes the specified page off the stack:

```
Navigation.RemovePage(page);
```

InsertPageBefore inserts a page into the stack before the specified page:

```
Navigation.InsertPageBefore(insertPage, beforePage);
```

All of these methods are generally executed inside the events of tapped icons or links, either inline, such as on our home page in Listing 6-1:

```
homeButton.Clicked += async (sender, args) =>
    await Navigation.PushAsync(new secondPage());
```

Or in delegated events:

```
private async void OnButtonClicked(object sender, EventArgs e)
{
    await Navigation.PushAsync(new nextPage());
}
```

Setting the Page Title

The Page.Title property displays a title in the navigation bar:

```
Title = "Home";
```

▪ Tip ContentPage inherits from the Page class, where a lot of the Xamarin.Forms properties discussed in this chapter reside.

Customizing the Navigation Bar

NavigationPage has several properties accessible from any child page, all of which give access to the navigation bar's elements. Navigation bar properties such as Title and Icon are set in the child page and not in the page that initiated NavigationPage. This is in keeping with native platform architectures.

In most of these Xamarin.Forms navigation examples, the icon.png file has been replaced with a blank image, so no icon is visible. This is a lean and contemporary look. The icon.png file can also be replaced with an appropriate graphic used to reflect the app, as shown in Figure 6-4.

Figure 6-4. *The icon can be changed on the navigation bar*

▪ Tip The icon.png file is platform-specific and resides in each respective platform project. See Chapter 2 for details on images.

The navigation icon can also be set dynamically to reflect the page or user context, by using SetTitleIcon and the Page.Icon property:

```
var image = "icon.png";
NavigationPage.SetTitleIcon (this, image);
```

Further customization of the navigation bar at the top of the screen is accomplished by using these NavigationPage methods:

- SetHasNavigationBar shows/hides the navigation bar on the current page:

  Ex. NavigationPage.SetHasNavigationBar(this, false);

- SetTitleIcon changes the title icon (Page.Icon property).

- SetHasBackButton shows/hides the Back button.

- SetBackButtonTitle changes the navigation title (the Page.Title property set on the calling page).

- BarBackgroundColor changes the navigation bar's color.

- BarTextColor changes the navigation bar's text color.

Handling the Back Button

Popping pages off the stack can be accomplished by either the Up or the Back button. Up is the less-than symbol (<) in the top-left corner of the navigation page, and the Back button is on the bottom navigation bar.

The Back button click event can be explicitly handled by overriding the page's OnBackButtonPressed method:

```
public override void OnBackButtonPressed()
{
    // your code here
    base.OnBackButtonPressed ();
}
```

Creating a Drop-down Menu

A drop-down menu class called ToolBarItems is built into the Page class and visible when using NavigationPage.

Instantiate NavigationPage to invoke the toolbar ContentPage, as shown in Listing 6-3.

Listing 6-3. Drop-down Menu in DropdownMenu.cs

```
class DropdownMenu: ContentPage
{
    public DropdownMenu()
    {
        ToolbarItems.Clear();
        ToolbarItems.Add(new ToolbarItem {
            Text = "Home",
            Order = ToolbarItemOrder.Secondary,
            Command = new Command(() =>
                Navigation.PushAsync(new NavigationPage1()))
        });
        ToolbarItems.Add(new ToolbarItem {
            Text = "Second",
            Order = ToolbarItemOrder.Secondary,
            Command = new Command(() =>
                Navigation.PushAsync(new NavigationPage2()))
        });
    }
}
```

This creates a drop-down menu/toolbar or tab menu with the items Home and Second. Clicking either one navigates to the respective page (see Figure 6-5). On iOS, it looks like a tab menu. On Windows Phone, it's on the bottom of the screen.

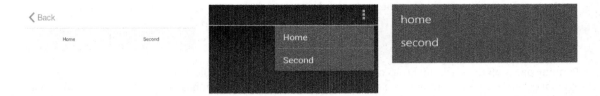

Figure 6-5. *ToolbarItems drop-down menu*

Modal

XAMARIN.FORMS

Xamarin.Forms provides three options for modal navigation:

- NavigationPage for full-page modals
- Alerts for user notifications
- Action sheets for pop-up menus

Full-Page Modal Using NavigationPage

Modal full-screen pages can be created that break the hierarchical pattern. When modal pages are raised, the hierarchy is interrupted and the navigation bar goes away. The navigation bar comes back when the modal is popped off the stack. These two methods are used to move between pages modally:

PushModalAsync pushes a page on the stack and goes there:

```
Navigation.PushModalAsync(new nextPage());
```

PopModalAsync pops a page off the stack and goes to the previous page:

```
Navigation.PopModalAsync();
```

■ **Tip** Four events on the Application object can help you manage your modal pages' life cycles: ModalPushing, ModalPushed, ModalPopping, and ModalPopped.

User Notification Using Alerts

The DisplayAlert method of the ContentPage displays a pop-up alert, as shown in Figure 6-6. This is typically used with async/await so execution will halt until the pop-up is cleared (Listing 6-4).

Figure 6-6. *DisplayAlert pop-up with title, message, and action button*

Listing 6-4. Using DisplayAlert, from Alerts.cs

```
Button button = new Button { Text = "Show Alert" };
button.Clicked += async (sender, e) =>
{
    await DisplayAlert("Hey", "You really should know about this.", "OK");
};
```

User feedback can be received by returning a value from DisplayAlert:

```
Button button = new Button { Text = "Show Alert" };
button.Clicked += async (sender, e) =>
{
    Boolean answer = await DisplayAlert("Start",
        "Are you ready to begin?", "Yes", "No");
};
```

The answer is returned as a Boolean, as shown in Figure 6-7.

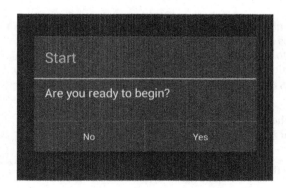

Figure 6-7. *The DisplayAlert method can return a value*

Pop-up Menu Using Action Sheets

ActionSheet provides a menu of options in a pop-up. The Xamarin.Forms version returns a string as the result.

Using DisplayActionSheet, create an action sheet activated by a button click that assigns the result to a label, as shown in Listing 6-5.

Listing 6-5. Using DisplayActionSheet from PopupMenu.cs

```
Button button = new Button { Text = "Show ActionSheet" };
button.Clicked += async (sender, e) =>
{
    String action = await DisplayActionSheet("Options",
        "Cancel", null, "Here", "There", "Everywhere");
    label.Text = "Action is :" + action;
};
```

This displays a pop-up menu in the center of the screen containing our options (Figure 6-8).

Figure 6-8. *DisplayActionSheet is a method that can return a value*

Managing State

XAMARIN.FORMS

state management is the handling and passing of data *between* pages as the user navigates through the app. There are four main approaches: passing data values directly into a page's constructor, using the static `Properties` dictionary on the `Application` object to persist key/value pairs to disk, a static data instance (*global*) available to all pages, and static properties on the `Application` object. Both the global and `Application` object techniques use the singleton pattern, and are useful for app-wide classes such as data access or business objects.

Pass data directly into pages whenever possible to keep the scope of variables narrow and manage memory prudently. The `Properties` dictionary persists when your app is backgrounded and even after your app has restarted!

Let's start with the simplest technique, passing data directly into a page.

Passing Data into Page Parameters

State is typically managed in Xamarin.Forms by passing data directly into a `Page` using its constructor. This approach scopes data objects to a single page, which is ideal from an architecture and memory use standpoint.

When calling a new page, simply pass in whatever variables were defined in your page's constructor. Define a detail page with a `ListItem` class as a constructor parameter:

```
class DetailPage : ContentPage
{
    public DetailPage(ListItem item)
    {
```

Then pass instances of the `ListItem` class directly into `DetailPage`:

```
Navigation.PushAsync (new detailPage(item));
```

Add all the parameters in your page constructors needed to pass in data from other pages. More detail on this example can be found in Listing 6-8 and Listing 6-10.

Data elements are sometimes used on many pages across an entire application, and passing them individually can become cumbersome. Frequently used data elements can be placed into a static global class so they are available app-wide.

Disk Persistence Using the Properties Dictionary

The most persistent state feature built into Xamarin.Forms is the `Properties` dictionary. Name/value pairs are stored as objects to disk and retrieved on demand from anywhere within the app, even after the app has restarted. `Properties` works a bit like cookies for your app.

Save a value to the `Properties` dictionary by using a key value, such as `id`:

```
Application.Current.Properties["id"] = 12345;
```

Retrieve the value by using a cast from the `Properties` object type:

```
var id = (int)Application.Current.Properties["id"];
```

■ **Tip** Properties are handy in the Application's `OnStart`, `OnSleep`, and `OnResume` methods for saving data between user sessions. They can also be used in a Page's `OnAppearing` and `OnDisappearing` events, which fire when a page is created or right before it is destroyed.

Using a Static Global Class

A static global class, a C# implementation of the Singleton pattern, can be used to store data across an entire application.

■ **Important Note** Implementing a Singleton is a standard C# technique that can be used across all platforms: Xamarin.Forms, Xamarin.Android, Xamarin.iOS, and Windows Phone.

Create a static class called Global and place properties within it that you desire to use across your app, such as myData, as shown in Listing 6-6.

Listing 6-6. Static Global Class in Global.cs

```
public class Global
{
    private Global ()
    {
    }

    private static Global _instance;
    public static Global Instance
    {
        get
        {
            if (_instance == null)
            {
                _instance = new Global ();
            }
            return _instance;
        }
    }

    public String myData { get; set; }
}
```

Assign values to your static global class:

```
Global.Instance.myData = "12345";
```

Access the global properties from anywhere in your application:

```
MyData myData = Global.Instance.myData;
```

■ **Caution**   Overuse of static global classes can tax memory and affect performance. Pass variables directly between pages whenever you can so they go out of scope when no longer needed.

Using a Static Property on the Application Object

A singleton can be created by using a static property on the Application object:

```
public class App : Application
{
    static Database database;
    public static Database MyDatabase {
```

```
        get {
            if (database == null) {
                database = new Database ();
            }
            return database;
        }
    }
}
```

Reference this database object anywhere in your app:

```
App.MyDatabase.DBConnect();
```

You'll use this approach in Chapter 7 for maintaining a database connection. (DBConnect is just an example method on the Database object.)

Drill-down Lists

XAMARIN.FORMS

A *drill-down list* is a list of tappable items selected to navigate to a new page. There are many ways to build them using Xamarin.Forms, and the following recipes cover the three most common types of drill-down lists: by item, by page, and grouped. A drill-down list *by item* has rows that can be selected to display more information about each item: the traditional master-detail pattern. A drill-down list *by page* is a menu of pages that can be selected to navigate to different ContentPages. Both of these recipes use a ListView to bind to a data model to provide a dynamic list of tappable items. A *grouped* drill-down list built using TableView is useful for creating categorized static menu items.

ListView is one of the most versatile tools for creating drill-down lists. Short lists can, of course, be constructed by hand by using any of the layouts filled with buttons or labels paired with gesture recognizers to handle taps. Longer lists lend themselves to data binding using ListView.

Grouping is the same as it was in the previous chapter using ListView grouping. Both items and pages can be grouped by using the IsGroupingEnabled and GroupDisplayBinding properties of ListView.

Lists of pages that require grouping can also be built by using TableView. This manual alternative to ListView uses the TextCell Command and CommandParameter properties instead of data binding.

We'll begin with the data-bound ListView menus.

Using ListView by Item

XAMARIN.FORMS

Many lists contain a bunch of items that a user wants to drill down into to reach details about each item. Use ListView to display a list of items data-bound to a data model, and then show a detail page by using PushAsync, all wrapped in NavigationPage so the user can get back to the list.

You can create your ListView by using any of the approaches discussed in Chapter 5. This implementation uses our list item class called DrilldownListViewByItem (see the full Listing 6-8). Instantiate that page in the Application class's constructor wrapped in NavigationPage (see the full Listing 6-9).

```
public class App : Application
{
    public App()
    {
        MainPage = new NavigationPage(new DrilldownListViewByItem ());
    }
}
```

This creates the list shown in Figure 6-9, with a navigation bar on iOS and Android. Windows Phone doesn't display the navigation bar.

Figure 6-9. *ListView on a page with a navigation bar*

Create a detail page called detailPage whose constructor takes ListItem as a parameter (see the full Listing 6-10). ListItem must contain either a list item ID for a detailed lookup query or all the fields needed to display on the detail page. This detail page displays a title and description.

```
class DetailPage: ContentPage
{
    public detailPage(ListItem listID) { // display detail }
}
```

Back on the list page, when an item row is tapped, pass ListItem into the detail page, which displays the detail of that particular item.

```
listView.ItemTapped += (sender, args) => {
    var item = args.Item as ListItem;
    if (item == null) return;
    Navigation.PushAsync (new detailPage(item) );
    listView.SelectedItem = null;
};
```

Tapping a list item row triggers the ItemTapped event, and the PushAsync call instantiates a detailPage and passes in ListItem to display, as shown in Figure 6-10.

Figure 6-10. *Detail page displaying title and description*

CODE COMPLETE: Drill-down List

That was a quick summary of a drill-down list by item. Listings 6-7, 6-8, 6-9, and 6-10 show the complete code listings of the drill-down list pattern using NavigationPage.

Listing 6-7. ListItem.cs

```
public class ListItem
{
    public string Title { get; set; }
    public string Description { get; set; }
}
```

Listing 6-8. DrilldownListViewByItem.cs

```
class DrilldownListViewByItem : ContentPage
{
    public DrilldownListViewByItem()
    {
        Title = "Drilldown List Using ListView";

        var listView = new ListView();
        listView.ItemsSource = new ListItem [] {
            new ListItem {Title = "First", Description="1st item"},
            new ListItem {Title = "Second", Description="2nd item"},
            new ListItem {Title = "Third", Description="3rd item"}
        };
        listView.ItemTemplate = new DataTemplate (typeof(TextCell));
        listView.ItemTemplate.SetBinding(TextCell.TextProperty, "Title");

        listView.ItemTapped += async (sender, args) =>
        {
            var item = args.Item as ListItem;
            if (item == null) return;
            await Navigation.PushAsync(new DetailPage(item));
            listView.SelectedItem = null;
        };
        Content = listView;
    }
}
```

Listing 6-9. App.cs

```
public class App : Application
{
    public App()
    {
        MainPage = new NavigationPage(new DrilldownListViewByItem ());
    }
}
```

Listing 6-10. DetailPage.cs

```
class DetailPage : ContentPage
{
    public DetailPage(ListItem item)
    {
        Label titleLabel = new Label
        {
            Text = item.Title,
            FontSize = 40
        };

        Label descLabel = new Label
        {
            Text = item.Description,
            FontSize = 40
        };

        var stackLayout = new StackLayout
        {
            Children = { titleLabel, descLabel }
        };
        this.Content = stackLayout;
    }
}
```

Using ListView by Page

XAMARIN.FORMS

Navigating a list of pages is easy with ListView. Build a menu containing a list of pages, each with their own ContentPage. Data-bind your ListView to a data model that contains ContentPages, and then drill down into each page by using NavigationPage to give the user a way to pop back to the list.

The result of Listing 6-11 looks the same on the screen as Figure 6-9 but navigates to different ContentPage types rather than just one (DetailPage).

Listing 6-11. ListView by Page in DrilldownListViewByPage.cs

```
class DrilldownListViewByPage : ContentPage
{
    public DrilldownListViewByPage()
    {
        Title = "Drilldown List Using ListView";

        var listView = new ListView();
        listView.ItemsSource = new ListItemPage [] {
            new ListItemPage {Title = "First", PageType= typeof(FirstPage)},
            new ListItemPage {Title = "Second", PageType= typeof(SecondPage)},
            new ListItemPage {Title = "Third", PageType= typeof(ThirdPage)}
        };
        listView.ItemTemplate = new DataTemplate (typeof(TextCell));
        listView.ItemTemplate.SetBinding(TextCell.TextProperty, "Title");

        listView.ItemTapped += async (sender, args) =>
        {
            var item = args.Item as ListItemPage;
            if (item == null) return;
            Page page = (Page)Activator.CreateInstance(item.PageType);
            await Navigation.PushAsync(page);
            listView.SelectedItem = null;
        };

        Content = listView;
    }

    public class ListItemPage
    {
        public string Title { get; set; }
        public Type PageType { get; set; }
    }

}
```

Using TableView for Grouping Pages

XAMARIN.FORMS

Perfect for multicategory lists of navigation items, this variation of the drill-down list pattern displays a static list by using a view called TableView. When an item is tapped, a detail screen is shown. It also uses the hierarchical pattern, which provides an option to use Back buttons. This hierarchical/drill-down list pattern is used in many of the Xamarin.Forms downloadable code projects throughout the book as the solution home page, allowing selection of the code examples in each chapter.

This recipe looks best when there are multiple categories of items to choose from, because at least one TableSection is required, even if multiple categories aren't needed, as shown in Figure 6-11.

Figure 6-11. *Grouping a list by using TableView*

If you don't want to use categories, you can keep the TableSection title blank, but that leaves a rather large gap at the top of the list. If you don't need categories, consider using ListView by page, as described in the previous section.

TableView isn't technically a layout but works much like one. This view is made up of ViewCells arranged in sections. Each TableSection denotes a different category of item, as shown in Listing 6-12.

Listing 6-12. Grouped List of Pages Using TableView in DrilldownTableView.cs

```
class DrilldownTableView : ContentPage
{
    public DrilldownTableView()
    {
        Command<Type> navigateCommand =
            new Command<Type>(async (Type pageType) =>
            {
                Page page = (Page)Activator.CreateInstance(pageType);
                await this.Navigation.PushAsync(page);
            });

        this.Title = "Drilldown List Using TableView";
        this.Content = new TableView
            {
                Intent = TableIntent.Menu,
                Root = new TableRoot
```

```
{
    new TableSection("Hindi")
    {
        new TextCell
        {
            Text = "Prathama",
            Command = navigateCommand,
            CommandParameter = typeof(FirstPage)
        },

        new TextCell
        {
            Text = "Dūsarā",
            Command = navigateCommand,
            CommandParameter = typeof(SecondPage)
        },

        new TextCell
        {
            Text = "Tīsarā",
            Command = navigateCommand,
            CommandParameter = typeof(ThirdPage)
        }
    },

    new TableSection("Español")
    {
        new TextCell
        {
            Text = "Primero",
            Command = navigateCommand,
            CommandParameter = typeof(FirstPage)
        },

        new TextCell
        {
            Text = "Segundo",
            Command = navigateCommand,
            CommandParameter = typeof(SecondPage)
        },

        new TextCell
        {
            Text = "Tercera",
            Command = navigateCommand,
            CommandParameter = typeof(ThirdPage)
        }
    },
```

```
                    new TableSection("English")
                    {
                        new TextCell
                        {
                            Text = "First",
                            Command = navigateCommand,
                            CommandParameter = typeof(FirstPage)
                        },

                        new TextCell
                        {
                            Text = "Second",
                            Command = navigateCommand,
                            CommandParameter = typeof(SecondPage)
                        },

                        new TextCell
                        {
                            Text = "Third",
                            Command = navigateCommand,
                            CommandParameter = typeof(ThirdPage)
                        }
                    }
                }
            };
        }
    }
```

Navigation Drawer Using MasterDetailPage

XAMARIN.FORMS

MasterDetailPage implements the navigation drawer pattern, which slides in a menu from the side when an icon, usually the hamburger, is tapped.

In the main page, Listing 6-13, the master and detail pages are defined. The master page is the menu drawer containing a list of menu options. Detail pages are raised when an option is tapped in the menu drawer.

Listing 6-13. Using MasterDetailPage in NavigationDrawer.cs

```
public class NavigationDrawer : MasterDetailPage
{
    public NavigationDrawer()
    {
        Title = "Navigation Drawer Using MasterDetailPage";
        string[] myPageNames = { "Home", "Second", "Third" };

        ListView listView = new ListView
        {
            ItemsSource = myPageNames,
        };
```

```
        this.Master = new ContentPage
         {
           Title = "Options",
           Content = listView,
           Icon = "hamburger.png"
         };

        listView.ItemTapped += (sender, e) =>
         {
             ContentPage gotoPage;
             switch (e.Item.ToString())
             {
                 case "Home":
                     gotoPage = new HomePage();
                     break;
                 case "Second":
                     gotoPage = new SecondPage();
                     break;
                 case "Third":
                     gotoPage = new ThirdPage();
                     break;
                 default:
                     gotoPage = new NavigationPage1();
                     break;
             }
             Detail = new NavigationPage(gotoPage);
            ((ListView)sender).SelectedItem = null;
             this.IsPresented = false;
         };

        Detail = new NavigationPage(new HomePage());
    }
}
```

When a menu item is selected, the ItemTapped event sets the Detail property to the destination page. SelectedItem is set to null to remove the highlight over the selected row, and IsPresented is set to false to remove the menu.

■ **Tip** The Title property of the Master page is required.

Because the navigation drawer already instantiates its own navigation pages, you don't need to create another NavigationPage when you call it.

```
public class App : Application
{
    public App()
    {
        MainPage = new NavigationDrawer ();
    }
}
```

This example begins as the home page set as the detail page, as shown in Figure 6-12. It hard-codes the navigation drawer pages rather than making them dynamic.

Figure 6-12. *HomePage ContentPage is the initial detail page*

Notice that the hamburger is at the bottom of the screen on Windows Phone.

■ **Important Note**   HomePage.cs contains the HomePage ContentPage shown in Figure 6-12 and is in the downloadable code but is not listed here. Be certain to download the code for this chapter and check it out, because it contains some of the most project-ready examples in this book.

When the icon is clicked, the master page is shown, containing the menu and the menu icon in the upper-left corner, as shown in Figure 6-13.

Figure 6-13. *The fly-in menu is the master page*

Change the menu icon to a hamburger by using the master page's Icon property. The icon file is taken from the local images folder for each platform.

```
this.Master = new ContentPage
{
    Title = "Options",
    Content = listView,
    Icon = "hamburger.png"
};
```

Clicking a menu item brings you to the specified new detail page.

Tabs Using TabbedPage

XAMARIN.FORMS

Having clickable folder-like tabs at the top or bottom of the screen is a common navigation pattern, implemented by TabbedPage, as shown in Figure 6-14.

Figure 6-14. *TabbedPage makes tabs that navigate to pages*

iOS tabs are at the bottom of the screen, and Android and Windows Phone tabs are at the top.

Create a class derived from TabbedPage and assign tab pages to the TabbedPage.Children property, as shown in Listing 6-14.

Listing 6-14. Tabs in TabPage.cs

```
class TabPage : TabbedPage
{
    public TabPage()
    {
        this.Title = "Tabbed Page";
        this.Children.Add (new homePage());
        this.Children.Add (new secondPage());
        this.Children.Add (new thirdPage());
    }
}
```

The Title property of each child page is where the tab titles come from. Remember to assign it wherever you create the child page or inline, as shown in Listing 6-15. Compile and run it to see the result in Figure 6-14.

■ **Tip**   In iOS, you can place icons on tabs by using the child pages' Icon property. Not so on Android.

Property assignments can take place within the Add method, as in Listing 6-15.

Listing 6-15. Inline Tab Page Property Assignments

```
this.Children.Add  (new homePage () {
  Title = "Home Page",
  Icon = "Home.png"
});
```

Creating Data-Bound Tabs

TabbedPage can be bound to a data source. Use the TabbedPage properties ItemsSource and ItemTemplate to achieve a data-bound tabbed menu.

First create a data model to hold tab information, as shown in Listing 6-16. Name and Number are the properties we use here.

Listing 6-16. TabItem class from TabPageDatabound.cs

```csharp
class TabItem
{
    public TabItem(string name, int number)
    {
        this.Name = name;
        this.Number = number;
    }
    public string Name { private set; get; }
    public int Number { private set; get; }
}
```

Create a TabbedPage with tabs assigned by using the ItemsSource property (Listing 6-17). The page destination is assigned by using ItemTemplate, dynamically creating the page with DataTemplate and bindings in the NumberPage class.

Listing 6-17. Data-Bound Tabs in TabPageDatabound.cs

```csharp
class TabPageDatabound : TabbedPage
{
    public TabPageDatabound()
    {
        this.Title = "Data-bound TabbedPage";

        this.ItemsSource = new TabItem[] {
            new TabItem ("First", 1),
            new TabItem ("Second", 2),
            new TabItem ("Third", 3),
            new TabItem ("Fourth", 4),
            new TabItem ("Fifth", 5),
            new TabItem ("Sixth", 6)
        };

        this.ItemTemplate = new DataTemplate(() =>
        {
            return new NumberPage();
        });
    }
}
```

ItemsSource allows the properties of the TabItem class to be used for binding in the specified ItemTemplate, in this case the NumberPage class.

■ **Tip** DataTemplate is commonly used for data-binding classes such as ListView and TableView. Read more about it in Chapter 7.

Create the data-bound NumberPage by calling SetBinding for the Name and Number properties, as shown in Listing 6-18. This ties the TabItem.Name property to the page's Title, and the TabItem.Number property to the label's Text property.

Listing 6-18. Data-Bound Destination Page in TabPageDatabound.cs

```
class NumberPage : ContentPage
{
    public NumberPage()
    {
        this.SetBinding(ContentPage.TitleProperty, "Name");
        Label label = new Label
        {
            HorizontalOptions = LayoutOptions.Center,
            Font = Font.SystemFontOfSize(40)
        };
        label.SetBinding(Label.TextProperty, "Number");

        this.Content = label;
    }
}
```

The result is six named tabs, as shown in Figure 6-15.

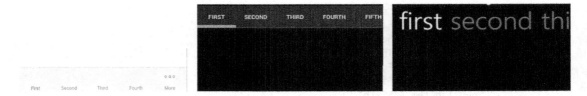

Figure 6-15. *TabbedPage with data-bound tabs*

Scroll the tab bar vertically on Android and Windows Phone or tap "More" on iOS to see the sixth tab.

When a tab is tapped, the corresponding NumberPage is created and navigated to, displaying the bound Number.

Putting NavigationPages Inside a TabbedPage

Navigation pages are used within a tabbed page by assigning them as children, creating a navigation bar when the tab is selected. Remember to assign a Title to NavigationPage to specify the name of the tab:

```
this.Children.Add (new NavigationPage (new homePage())
{
    Title = "Home",
    Icon = "Home.png"
});
```

Springboard

XAMARIN.FORMS

A *springboard* is a grid of tappable images on a home screen menu, sometimes referred to as a *dashboard*, as shown in Figure 6-16.

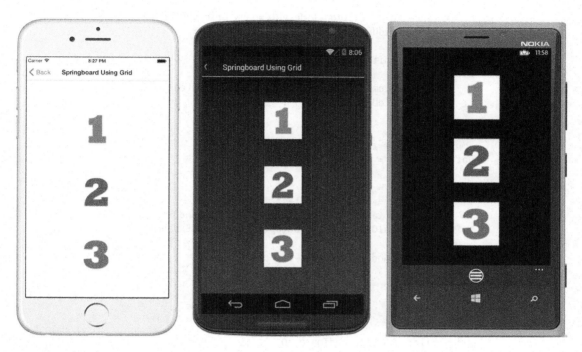

Figure 6-16. *Springboard using tap-gesture recognizers added to the images*

This springboard is implemented with a Grid layout and images provisioned with tap-gesture recognizers, as shown in Listing 6-19. This code places three images on the grid and makes them tappable. The Tapped event of each gesture handler contains a PushAsync to the requested page. I'll talk more about the tap-gesture recognizers shortly.

Listing 6-19. Springboard.cs

```
class Springboard : ContentPage
    {
        public Springboard()
        {
            Title = "Springboard Using Grid";

            Grid grid = new Grid
            {
                VerticalOptions = LayoutOptions.FillAndExpand,
                RowSpacing = 65,
                ColumnSpacing = 65,
                Padding = 60,
```

```
        RowDefinitions =
        {
            new RowDefinition { Height = new GridLength(1,
                GridUnitType.Star) },
            new RowDefinition { Height = new GridLength(1,
                GridUnitType.Star) },
            new RowDefinition { Height = new GridLength(1,
                GridUnitType.Star) }
        },
        ColumnDefinitions =
        {
            new ColumnDefinition { Width = new GridLength(1,
                GridUnitType.Star) }
        }
    };

    var firstImage = new Image
        {
            Source = "first.png",
            Aspect = Aspect.AspectFit,
            HorizontalOptions = LayoutOptions.FillAndExpand,
            VerticalOptions = LayoutOptions.FillAndExpand
        };
    grid.Children.Add(firstImage, 0 , 0);

    var secondImage = new Image
        {
            Source = "second.png"
        };
    grid.Children.Add(secondImage, 0 , 1);

    var thirdImage = new Image
    {
        Source = "third.png"
    };
    grid.Children.Add(thirdImage, 0, 2);

    var tapFirst = new TapGestureRecognizer();
    tapFirst.Tapped += async (s, e) =>
    {
        await this.Navigation.PushAsync(new FirstPage());
    };
    firstImage.GestureRecognizers.Add(tapFirst);

    var tapSecond = new TapGestureRecognizer();
    tapSecond.Tapped += async (s, e) =>
    {
        await this.Navigation.PushAsync(new SecondPage());
    };
    secondImage.GestureRecognizers.Add(tapSecond);
```

```
        var tapThird = new TapGestureRecognizer();
        tapThird.Tapped += async (s, e) =>
        {
            await this.Navigation.PushAsync(new ThirdPage());
        };
        thirdImage.GestureRecognizers.Add(tapThird);

        this.Padding = new Thickness(10, Device.OnPlatform(20, 0, 0),
            10, 5);
        this.Content = grid;
    }
}
```

Making Icons Tappable by Using Gesture Recognizers

The gesture recognizers added to each image in Listing 6-19 handle taps in the TapGestureRecognizer Tapped event, using PushAsync to push the specified page onto the navigation stack. Here a tap gesture recognizer is added to firstImage:

```
var tapFirst = new TapGestureRecognizer();
tapFirst.Tapped += async (s, e) =>
{
    await this.Navigation.PushAsync(new FirstPage());
};
firstImage.GestureRecognizers.Add(tapFirst);
```

Tappable images should be visually responsive to touch. Use the opacity trick covered back in Chapter 2 (Listing 2-6):

```
var tapFirst = new TapGestureRecognizer();
tapFirst.Tapped +=  async (sender, e) =>
{
    image.Opacity = .5;
    await Task.Delay(100);
    image.Opacity = 1;
    await this.Navigation.PushAsync(new FirstPage());
};
firstImage.GestureRecognizers.Add(tapFirst);
```

This dims the image slightly for an instant when touched to provide user feedback and let them know that their gesture did something. When using the Task class, remember to add the using statement:

```
using System.Threading.Tasks.
```

Carousel Using CarouselPage

XAMARIN.FORMS

Carousel pages scroll off the screen to reveal another page when a user slides left or right.

Create a carousel page and add child pages, as shown in Listing 6-20.

Listing 6-20. Carousel.cs

```
class Carousel :CarouselPage
{
    public Carousel()
    {
     this.Children.Add(new FirstPage());
     this.Children.Add(new SecondPage());
     this.Children.Add(new ThirdPage());
    }
}
```

This allows horizontal scrolling between child pages. Figure 6-17 shows that the home page, when slid to the left, reveals the second page.

Figure 6-17. *Sliding to the left shows the second page*

When using `CarouselPage` as a detail page in `MasterDetailPage`, set `MasterDetailPage.IsGestureEnabled` to `false` to prevent gesture conflicts between `CarouselPage` and `MasterDetailPage`.

■ **XAML**   Again, the XAML version of this entire Xamarin.Forms portion of this chapter can be found on the Apress web site at `www.apress.com` or on GitHub at `https://github.com/danhermes/xamarin-book-examples`. The Xamarin.Forms solution for Chapter 6 is `NavigationExamples.Xaml`.

You are now equipped to build the navigation outline for just about any Xamarin.Forms app you can imagine! It's choose-your-own adventure time.

- More Xamarin.Forms? Turn to Chapter 7 to read about data binding and data access.
- Ready for Android navigation? Then read on.
- Wondering about iOS navigation? Jump down to the iOS section in this chapter.

Now let's cover platform-specific navigation, starting with Android.

Android Navigation

Activities paired with XML layouts are the building blocks of Android apps. Using the MVC pattern, the layouts are the views, while the activities are the controllers that provide a code back end to each view. Activities instantiate their respective layouts (in the Resources/layout project folder) using SetContentView:

```
SetContentView(Resource.Layout.Main);
```

Building apps larger than one screen requires stringing activities together. This is typically done using Intent, a class that can create and navigate to new activities.

Hierarchical navigation is done using the toolbar, which is gradually replacing the action bar at Google's encouragement. Navigation buttons include the Up (or Home) button on the toolbar, at the top of the screen, and the Back button on the navigation bar, at the bottom of the screen. Values are passed between activities by using the Bundle class passed using Intent. A specialized layout called a fragment is used to create modals.

Here are the key Android navigation concepts covered in this section:

> *Intent*: An abstract description of an operation to be performed, used to instantiate and display a new screen
>
> *Toolbar/action bar*: Top-of-screen navigation controls that can include a page title, an Up button, and a pop-up menu
>
> *Navigation bar*: Bottom-of-screen buttons that include the Back button
>
> *Bundle*: A dictionary within an intent that maintains state between screens
>
> *Fragment*: A mini-layout .axml with a code-behind class that is useful as a component to make modals, and can be combined to make larger layouts

Let's explore each concept in the context of UI navigation patterns.

Starting New Activities Using Intents

Intents create and navigate to new screens on Android. Instantiate an intent with the parameter of the desired new activity, such as IntentToActivity, and then call the Activity.StartActivity method, passing in the intent, as shown in Listing 6-21.

Listing 6-21. From IntentActivity.cs

```
Intent intent = new Intent(this, typeof(IntentToActivity));
StartActivity (intent);
```

This can be shortened to the following:

```
StartActivity(typeof(IntentToActivity));
```

StartActivity instantiates the specified new activity class (IntentToActivity) and loads it onto the screen, unloading the old activity.

New activities, such as IntentToActivity, are often spawned in response to a user action within an event handler. Here, IntentToActivity is created and called upon the click of a button:

```
Button button = FindViewById<Button> (Resource.Id.myButton);
button.Click += delegate {
        StartActivity(typeof(IntentToActivity));
};
```

■ **Tip**   The screen can be also changed without creating a new activity by using SetContentView.

Hierarchical Navigation Using the Toolbar

ANDROID

Hierarchical navigation on Android is now done using the toolbar, a featureful navigation bar with an Up button, icon, and current page name. The first page containing a toolbar usually displays a title and sometimes a pop-up menu icon used for choosing actions, as shown in Figure 6-18.

Figure 6-18. *Toolbar on a home page*

Deeper in the navigation tree, the toolbar generally sports an Up (or Home) button (<), as shown in Figure 6-19.

Figure 6-19. *Toolbar on a second page*

The toolbar was introduced in Android 5.0 Lollipop (API level 21) and replaced the action bar. Although the action bar still works on newer APIs, Google encourages the use of the toolbar. The toolbar can be found in the Android Designer's toolbox and can be dragged and dropped onto your layout. It can be used anywhere on the screen but is most often used at the top and, less often, at the bottom.

But there's a catch: *the new* Toolbar *class works only for API 21+*. So, I'll cover a backward-compatible approach to implement the toolbar using the Android.Support.V7.AppCompat library available as a NuGet. This allows us to target a range of API versions prior to Lollipop up to the present.

To recap, there are three ways to achieve up-and-back when using hierarchical navigation in Android:

- Toolbar: The new class for API 21+ (Lollipop)

- ActionBar: The older class replaced by Toolbar

- Toolbar using the Android.Support.V7.AppCompat library: Toolbar that is backward-compatible to API 4

For backward compatibility, I'll cover the third approach, Toolbar using the Android.Support. V7.AppCompat library, in the following example.

■ **Tip** If you're making an app with a minimum API of 21 or later, don't use the following approach with the Android.Support.V7.AppCompat library. Use the regular android.widget.Toolbar class covered in James Montemagno's blog post at http://blog.xamarin.com/android-tips-hello-toolbar-goodbye-action-bar/.

TOOL BAR VS. ACTION BAR

The action bar has been the standby navigation bar for some time now, and is built into an activity without the need for tagging in the XML layout. Google is encouraging us to upgrade to the more versatile, mature toolbar, which has a more focused feature set and supports the modern navigation aesthetic: a visually distinct color scheme for the top bar rather than leaning on the application icon as the main design element. The use of an application icon plus a title as a standard layout is discouraged on API 21 devices and later. Now it's about the styling of the toolbar, using style.xml coupled with liberal use of the Up button, page title, and action menu.

A couple of inconveniences are associated with the toolbar, however. First, it's not built into the activity and must be declared in the XML layout, generally as an include of a separate toolbar layout. Second, the standard new toolbar library works only on API 21 and later, so we're often required to use the backward-compatible Android.Support.V7.AppCompat library and its associated Support-prefixed keywords and methods in order to use the toolbar pre-Lollipop. If you want to heed Google's advice and start using the toolbar rather than the action bar, but you want your app to work on older APIs, then the Android.Support.V7.AppCompat approach is the way to go (available as a NuGet package or in the Xamarin Component Store).

Create an XML layout containing the toolbar, as shown in Listing 6-22.

Listing 6-22. Toolbar.axml

```
<?xml version="1.0" encoding="utf-8"?>
<android.support.v7.widget.Toolbar
    xmlns:android="http://schemas.android.com/apk/res/android"
    xmlns:local="http://schemas.android.com/apk/res-auto"
    android:id="@+id/toolbar"
    android:layout_width="match_parent"
    android:layout_height="wrap_content"
    android:minHeight="?attr/actionBarSize"
    android:background="?attr/colorPrimary"
    local:theme="@style/ThemeOverlay.AppCompat.Dark.ActionBar"/>
```

Several styles are available when using the Support Library:

- Theme.AppCompat: The "dark" theme

- Theme.AppCompat.Light: The "light" theme

- Theme.AppCompat.Light.DarkActionBar: The light theme with a dark action bar

The popupTheme here specifies ThemeOverlay.AppCompat, a dark theme, for use later with the pop-up menu.

Next, include the toolbar in your main layout, as shown in Listing 6-23. Add a button to navigate to page 2.

Listing 6-23. Main Layout in MainToolbar.axml

```
<?xml version="1.0" encoding="utf-8"?>
<RelativeLayout xmlns:android="http://schemas.android.com/apk/res/android"
    xmlns:local="http://schemas.android.com/apk/res-auto"
    android:layout_width="fill_parent"
    android:layout_height="fill_parent">
    <include
        android:id="@+id/toolbar"
        layout="@layout/toolbar" />
    <LinearLayout
        android:orientation="vertical"
        android:layout_width="fill_parent"
        android:layout_height="fill_parent"
        android:id="@+id/main_content"
        android:layout_below="@id/toolbar">
        <Button
            android:id="@+id/nextPageButton"
            android:layout_width="fill_parent"
            android:layout_height="wrap_content"
            android:text="Go to Second Page" />
    </LinearLayout>
</RelativeLayout>
```

■ **Important Note**   In the following activities, utilize the following using statements to reference the Android.Support.V7 library.

```
using Android.Support.V7.App;
using Toolbar = Android.Support.V7.Widget.Toolbar;
```

Create an activity, as shown in Listing 6-24, where you find the toolbar on the layout and initialize it by calling the SetSupportActionBar method. Inherit from ActionBarActivity.

Listing 6-24. Using the ToolBar in ToolBarActivity.cs

```
[Activity(Label = "ToolbarActivity")]
public class ToolbarActivity : ActionBarActivity
{
    protected override void OnCreate(Bundle bundle)
    {
        base.OnCreate(bundle);

        SetContentView(Resource.Layout.MainToolbar);
        var toolbar = FindViewById<Toolbar>(Resource.Id.toolbar);
        SetSupportActionBar(toolbar);
        SupportActionBar.Title = "Toolbar Home";
```

Set the toolbar's title by using the `SupportActionBar.Title` property.

In order to use the toolbar as the action bar, you need to disable the décor-provided action bar. As shown in Listing 6-25, the easiest way is to have your application theme in `AndroidManifest.xml` extend from `Theme.AppCompat.NoActionBar` (a dark theme, or the light variant, described shortly). Later you'll look at other ways to do this by customizing the theme.

Listing 6-25. Application Theme in AndroidManifest.xml

```
<?xml version="1.0" encoding="utf-8"?>
<manifest xmlns:android="http://schemas.android.com/apk/res/android"
    package="NavigationExamplesAndroid.NavigationExamplesAndroid"
    android:versionCode="1" android:versionName="1.0">
  <uses-sdk android:minSdkVersion="10" android:targetSdkVersion="21" />
  <application android:label="NavigationExamplesAndroid"
      android:icon="@drawable/Icon" android:theme=
      "@style/Theme.AppCompat.NoActionBar>
  </application>
</manifest>
```

Compile and run the application to create the `ToolbarActivity` with a toolbar, as shown in Figure 6-20.

Figure 6-20. *The toolbar*

Now it's time to create the second page with a toolbar and an Up button.

The second activity is virtually identical to the first, with the exception of the Up button, as shown in Listing 6-26. Find the toolbar on the layout and initialize it by calling the `SetSupportActionBar` method. Turn on the Up button with the toolbar's `SetDisplayHomeAsUpEnabled` method.

Listing 6-26. Second Activity in ToolbarActivitySecond.cs

```
[Activity(Label = "ToolbarActivitySecond")]
public class ToolbarActivitySecond : ActionBarActivity
{
    protected override void OnCreate(Bundle bundle)
    {
        base.OnCreate(bundle);

        SetContentView(Resource.Layout.MainToolbarSecond);
        var toolbar = FindViewById<Toolbar>(Resource.Id.toolbar);
        SetSupportActionBar(toolbar);
        SupportActionBar.Title = "Toolbar Second Page";
        SupportActionBar.SetDisplayHomeAsUpEnabled(true);
    }
}
```

The second XML layout, in Listing 6-27, is simpler than the first. It includes the same toolbar layout as before.

Listing 6-27. Second Layout in MainToolbarSecond.axml

```
<?xml version="1.0" encoding="utf-8"?>
<RelativeLayout xmlns:android="http://schemas.android.com/apk/res/android"
    xmlns:local="http://schemas.android.com/apk/res-auto"
    android:layout_width="fill_parent"
    android:layout_height="fill_parent">
    <include
        android:id="@+id/toolbar"
        layout="@layout/toolbar" />
</RelativeLayout>
```

Back in the main activity, ToolbarActivity, add a handler for the next-page button click that navigates to ToolbarActivitySecond.

```
var nextPageButton = FindViewById<Button>(Resource.Id.nextPageButton);
nextPageButton.Click += (sender, e) =>
{
    StartActivity(typeof(ToolbarActivitySecond));
};
```

Now when you get deeper into a navigation, you can get back by using the Up button (Figure 6-21).

Figure 6-21. *The toolbar on the second page with the Up button*

■ **Tip** Toolbars can also be made to stand alone anywhere on the screen, not just at the top. To do that, don't set `Toolbar` as the action bar by using `SetSupportActionBar`. Also, you won't need the `NoActionBar` theme for this unless you also have a top toolbar.

Handling the Up Button

ANDROID

Popping pages off the stack can be accomplished by either the Up or the Back button. Up is the less-than sign (<) in the top-left corner of the toolbar, and the Back button is on the bottom navigation bar. There are a few ways to handle the clicking of the Up or Home button: finish the activity and return to the previous one, return to a specified parent activity, or spawn a new intent and go to a specified activity. Let's cover all three.

Finish() the Activity

An easy way to back-navigate is to handle the Up button click by overriding `OnOptionsItemSelected` to call the `Finish()` method, which closes the current activity and returns to the previous activity (Listing 6-28).

Listing 6-28. Finish Method in ToolbarActivitySecond.cs

```
public override bool OnOptionsItemSelected (IMenuItem item)
{
    if (item.ItemId == Android.Resource.Id.Home)
        Finish();
    return base.OnOptionsItemSelected (item);
}
```

Other clickable options are available, but in this case we're concerned only with the Up button, identified by `Android.Resource.Id.Home`.

Using parentActivityName in AndroidManifest.xml

Specify the page that the Up button will travel to by declaring the parent of each activity in the `android:parentActivityName` attribute on the `<activity>` element of `AndroidManifest.xml` (beginning in Android 4.1, API level 16). The Up button will navigate to the parent specified on each activity.

Using an Intent

The Up button can also be manually coded to redirect to a particular page by using an intent (rather than popping the activity off of the stack). The Up button click event on the toolbar is handled with the `OnOptionsItemSelected` method:

```
public override bool OnOptionsItemSelected(MenuItem item){
    StartActivity(typeof(NewActivity));
    return true;
}
```

Adding a Pop-up Menu

ANDROID

The toolbar can be customized with additional menu and action icons, as shown in Figure 6-22. A pop-up menu is added by overriding the OnCreateOptionsMenu method and inflating the menu from an XML file. This is not hierarchical navigation. It's modal navigation, but because it's part of the toolbar, we'll cover it here.

Figure 6-22. *Toolbar with pop-up/action menu icon*

In your activity, override the OnCreateOptionsMenu, which inflates a menu called popupmenu, from ToolbarActivity.cs:

```
public override bool OnCreateOptionsMenu (IMenu menu)
{
    MenuInflater.Inflate (Resource.Menu.popupmenu, menu);
    return base.OnCreateOptionsMenu (menu);
}
```

Create a menu folder and build an XML file named popupmenu (in this case), as shown in Listing 6-29. Add your menu items and give them IDs and titles.

Listing 6-29. Menu XML File in popupmenu.xml

```
<?xml version="1.0" encoding="utf-8"?>
<menu xmlns:android="http://schemas.android.com/apk/res/android">
  <item android:id="@+id/item1"
  android:title="First Item" />
  <item android:id="@+id/item2"
  android:title="Second Item" />
  <item android:id="@+id/item3"
  android:title="Third Item" />
</menu>
```

Tap the pop-up menu icon to show the pop-up menu (Figure 6-23).

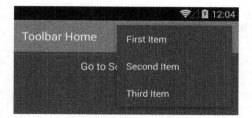

Figure 6-23. *Pop-up menu on the toolbar*

Back in the activity, handle the menu clicks (Listing 6-30).

Listing 6-30. Handle Menu Taps in ToolbarActivity.cs

```
public override bool OnOptionsItemSelected(IMenuItem item)
{
    switch (item.ItemId)
    {
        case Resource.Id.item1:
            Toast.MakeText(this, "Item1 tapped",
                ToastLength.Short).Show();
            return true;
        case Resource.Id.item2:
            Toast.MakeText(this, "Item2 tapped",
                ToastLength.Short).Show();
            return true;
        case Resource.Id.item3:
            Toast.MakeText(this, "Item3 tapped",
                ToastLength.Short).Show();
            return true;
    }
    return base.OnOptionsItemSelected(item);
}
```

■ **Tip**   Right-side navigation drawers are typically used for actions, not navigation.

Customize the Toolbar

ANDROID

The toolbar's colors can be customized with a custom theme. Style the toolbar's colors in styles.xml. In AndroidManifest.xml, change the android:theme to your custom theme name (MyTheme, in this case).

```
<application android:label="NavigationExamplesAndroid"
    android:icon="@drawable/Icon" android:theme="@style/MyTheme">
</application>
```

Create a folder called values and a new file called styles.xml (Listing 6-31) with the MyTheme theme, and a parent using one of the AppCompat themes mentioned earlier. The windowActionBar property must be set to false, and windowNoTitle must be set to true.

Listing 6-31. styles.xml in values Folder

```xml
<?xml version="1.0" encoding="utf-8" ?>
<resources>
  <style name="MyTheme" parent="MyTheme.Base">
  </style>
  <style name="MyTheme.Base" parent="Theme.AppCompat">
    <item name="android:windowNoTitle">true</item>
    <item name="windowActionBar">false</item>
    <item name="colorPrimary">#0066FF</item>
    <item name="colorPrimaryDark">#125393</item>
    <item name="colorAccent">#990000</item>
  </style>
</resources>
```

For API 21+ devices, add a values-v21 folder and create a styles.xml file (Listing 6-32), as required by Android. Note that this style is not compatible with the ActionBar tabs example later in this chapter.

Listing 6-32. styles.xml in values-v21 Folder

```xml
<?xml version="1.0" encoding="utf-8" ?>
<resources>
  <style name="MyTheme" parent="MyTheme.Base">
    <item name="android:windowContentTransitions">true</item>
    <item name="android:windowAllowEnterTransitionOverlap">true</item>
    <item name="android:windowAllowReturnTransitionOverlap">true</item>
    <item name="android:windowSharedElementEnterTransition">
        @android:transition/move</item>
    <item name="android:windowSharedElementExitTransition">
        @android:transition/move</item>
  </style>
</resources>
```

Even the pop-up menu can be themed and customized by adding a popupTheme in the toolbar XML declaration (Listing 6-33).

Listing 6-33. styles.xml in values-v21 Folder

```xml
<?xml version="1.0" encoding="utf-8"?>
<android.support.v7.widget.Toolbar
    xmlns:android="http://schemas.android.com/apk/res/android"
    xmlns:local="http://schemas.android.com/apk/res-auto"
    android:id="@+id/toolbar"
    android:layout_width="match_parent"
    android:layout_height="wrap_content"
    android:minHeight="?attr/actionBarSize"
    android:background="?attr/colorPrimary"
    local:theme="@style/ThemeOverlay.AppCompat.Dark.ActionBar"
    local:popupTheme="@style/ThemeOverlay.AppCompat.Light" />
```

Figure 6-24 shows the light-styled pop-up menu.

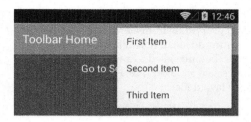

Figure 6-24. *Pop-up menu styled*

In addition to back navigation being handled in the toolbar, usually at the top of the screen, back navigation can also be handled at the bottom of the screen, in the navigation bar.

Using the Navigation Bar

ANDROID

The navigation bar (*nav bar*) shown in Figure 6-25 is the three-button bar at the bottom of the screen, or on some older devices, actual physical buttons. The buttons are Back, Home, and App Switcher.

Figure 6-25. *Android navigation bar*

Hide icons on the nav bar by using the `StatusBarVisibility` enum (`Hidden` or `Visible`):

```
text.SystemUiVisibility = StatusBarVisibility.Hidden;
```

Handling the Back Button

The Back button default behavior is to pop back to the previous activity or, if at the top-level activity, out of the app to the Android app menu. The Back button's click event can be explicitly handled by overriding the page's `OnBackPressed` method:

```
public override void OnBackPressed()
{
    // your code here
    base.OnBackPressed();
}
```

Fragments

ANDROID

The building blocks of mature Android apps, *fragments* are used for everything from alerts, to modal pop-up screens, to portions of screens, to views that can fill entire screens. Introduced in Android 3.0, fragments work like mini-layouts or custom controls, each with their own code-behind called a Fragment class. Just like regular Android layouts, they can be built with the UI designer and saved as .axml files. Fragment layouts can then be included within other layout files, allowing a nesting of layout files.

■ **Tip** Swap fragments in and out of a page dynamically by using FrameLayout in your main layout along with the FragmentTransaction Add(), Remove(), and Replace() methods in your main activity. See the tabs example in Listing 6-60.

This example shows how to display two fragments on a single main layout. First let's build the layouts, and then we'll make the code-behind classes.

Create three layouts: MainFragment (Listing 6-34), Fragment1 (Listing 6-35), and Fragment2 (Listing 6-36). Each fragment class refers to a fragment using its namespace and fragment class name (for example, FragmentExample.FirstFragment).

Listing 6-34. MainFragment.axml

```
<?xml version="1.0" encoding="utf-8"?>
<LinearLayout xmlns:android="http://schemas.android.com/apk/res/android"
    android:orientation="vertical"
    android:layout_width="fill_parent"
    android:layout_height="fill_parent">
    <fragment
        class="FragmentExample.FirstFragment"
        android:id="@+id/FirstFragment"
        android:layout_weight="1"
        android:layout_width="match_parent"
        android:layout_height="match_parent" />
    <fragment
        class="FragmentExample.SecondFragment"
        android:id="@+id/SecondFragment"
        android:layout_weight="1"
        android:layout_width="match_parent"
        android:layout_height="match_parent" />
</LinearLayout>
```

Listing 6-35. Fragment1.axml

```
<?xml version="1.0" encoding="utf-8"?>
<TextView xmlns:android="http://schemas.android.com/apk/res/android"
    android:layout_width="fill_parent"
    android:layout_height="fill_parent"
    android:text="FirstFragment"
    android:textStyle="bold"
    android:textSize="20dip" />
```

Listing 6-36. Fragment2.axml

```
<?xml version="1.0" encoding="utf-8"?>
<TextView xmlns:android="http://schemas.android.com/apk/res/android"
    android:layout_width="fill_parent"
    android:layout_height="fill_parent"
    android:text="SecondFragment"
    android:textSize="20dip"
    android:textStyle="bold" />
```

Now onto the classes. Create the main activity that references the MainFragment layout, as shown in Listing 6-37.

Listing 6-37. Begin with MainFragment Layout in FragmentsActivity.cs

```
public class FragmentsActivity : Activity
{
    public FragmentsActivity ()
    {
    }

    protected override void OnCreate (Bundle bundle)
    {
        base.OnCreate (bundle);
        SetContentView (Resource.Layout.MainFragment);
    }
}
```

Last, create the fragment classes, each inheriting from the Fragment base class and inflating their respective fragment layouts, Fragment1 and Fragment2, in their OnCreateView methods (Listings 6-38 and 6-39).

Listing 6-38. FirstFragment Inflates Fragment1.axml Layout

```
public class FirstFragment : Fragment
{
    public override void OnCreate (Bundle savedInstanceState)
    {
        base.OnCreate (savedInstanceState);
        // Create your fragment here
    }

    public override View OnCreateView (LayoutInflater inflater,
        ViewGroup container, Bundle savedInstanceState)
    {
        return inflater.Inflate(Resource.Layout.Fragment1, container);
    }
}
```

Listing 6-39. SecondFragment Inflates Fragment2.axml Layout

```
public class SecondFragment : Fragment
{
    public override void OnCreate (Bundle savedInstanceState)
    {
        base.OnCreate (savedInstanceState);
        // Create your fragment here
    }

    public override View OnCreateView (LayoutInflater inflater,
        ViewGroup container, Bundle savedInstanceState)
    {
        return inflater.Inflate(Resource.Layout.Fragment2, container);
    }
}
```

Running the app allows the MainFragment layout to instantiate both fragments on the screen at the same time, one above the other (Figure 6-26).

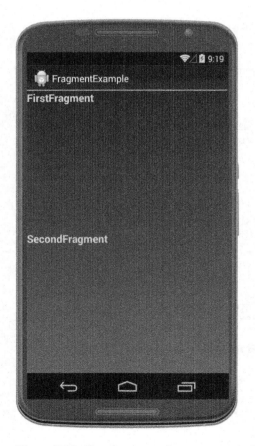

Figure 6-26. *Two fragments shown on one main layout*

■ **Tip** Fragments are particularly useful when an app must look good on widely varying screen sizes, specifically phone and tablet, as variations of the same app can be created depending on the screen real-estate size.

■ **Note** Several fragment class types, including `ListFragment`, `DialogFragment`, and `PreferenceFragment`, are used for particular UI functions: lists, dialog boxes, and preferences, respectively.

■ **Tip** Backward compatibility with pre-Android 3.0 devices can be achieved for most fragment functionality by using the `Android Support Library v4` component.

Modal Navigation

ANDROID

Modal navigation on Android is created by using a range of techniques, including the `DialogFragment`, `AlertDialog`, and `PopupMenu` class. `DialogFragment` is a specialized type of fragment that creates a pop-up modal that can contain a layout or wrap an `AlertDialog` (a dialog box containing text and/or controls). Pop-up menus are made by using the `PopupMenu` class.

Creating Modals Using DialogFragment

`DialogFragment` is used to create many types of modal dialog boxes. `DialogFragment` has largely replaced `AlertDialog` as the primary modal technique since Google deprecated the `ShowDialog` method. Create a layout XML to comprise the modal, and then build a `DialogFragment` subclass that inflates this layout in the `OnCreateView` method.

Create a layout XML called `Modal` that allows the entry of a name, using a `TextView`, an `EditView`, and a submit `Button`, as shown in Listing 6-40.

Listing 6-40. Modal Layout in Modal.axml

```xml
<?xml version="1.0" encoding="utf-8"?>
<LinearLayout xmlns:android="http://schemas.android.com/apk/res/android"
    android:orientation="vertical"
    android:layout_width="fill_parent"
    android:layout_height="fill_parent">
    <TextView
        android:text="Enter Your Name"
        android:textAppearance="?android:attr/textAppearanceLarge"
        android:layout_width="match_parent"
        android:layout_height="wrap_content"
        android:id="@+id/nameTextView" />
    <EditText
      android:id="@+id/nameEditText"
      android:textAppearance="?android:attr/textAppearanceLarge"
      android:layout_width="fill_parent"
      android:layout_height="wrap_content"/>
```

```
    <Button
        android:text="Submit"
        android:layout_width="match_parent"
        android:layout_height="wrap_content"
        android:id="@+id/submitButton" />
</LinearLayout>
```

Create a new fragment called DialogFragmentView and a subclass from DialogFragment. In the OnCreateView method, inflate the Modal layout. Find submitButton and handle the click event by calling the Dismiss() method to close the fragment, as shown in Listing 6-41.

Listing 6-41. Inflate Modal Layout in DialogFragmentView.cs

```
public class DialogFragmentView : DialogFragment
{
    public override View OnCreateView(LayoutInflater inflater,
        ViewGroup container, Bundle savedInstanceState)
    {
        base.OnCreate(savedInstanceState);
        var view = inflater.Inflate(Resource.Layout.Modal,
            container, false);
        view.FindViewById<Button>(Resource.Id.submitButton).Click +=
            (sender, args) => Dismiss();
        return view;
    }
}
```

■ **Tip**   DialogFragment can be dismissed from the activity in code by using the DialogFragment.Dismiss() method. This commits the transaction and fires the standard events in the destruction of a fragment.

In the main activity's OnCreate method, instantiate a transaction and DialogFragmentView. Call the Show method on the fragment and pass in the transaction and a string identifier, as coded in Listing 6-42.

Listing 6-42. Show the DialogFragment in DialogViewActivity.cs

```
var transaction = FragmentManager.BeginTransaction();
var dialogFragment = new DialogFragmentView();
dialogFragment.Show(transaction, "dialog_fragment");
```

This displays a modal that pops up over the main layout, as shown in Figure 6-27.

Figure 6-27. *DialogFragment modal layout*

Creating Alerts Using DialogFragment

DialogFragment can contain AlertDialog to create alerts and dialog boxes. These are built in the OnCreateDialog method.

Create a new Fragment class called DialogFragmentAlert (Listing 6-43) and inherit from the DialogFragment class. Inside the OnCreateDialog method, build a simple AlertDialog.

Listing 6-43. Using AlertDialog in DialogFragmentAlert.cs

```
public class DialogFragmentAlert : DialogFragment
{
    public override Dialog OnCreateDialog(Bundle savedInstanceState)
    {
        var builder = new AlertDialog.Builder(Activity)
            .SetMessage("This is an AlertDialog.")
            .SetPositiveButton("Ok", (sender, args) =>
```

```
        {
            // Handles button click
        })
        .SetTitle("DialogFragment");
    return builder.Create();
    }
}
```

In the OnCreate method of a main activity, such as DialogAlertActivity, instantiate and display the dialog fragment. The DialogFragment.Show method takes a transaction and a string as parameters (Listing 6-44).

Listing 6-44. Show DialogFragment in DialogFragmentAlert.cs

```
var transaction = FragmentManager.BeginTransaction();
var dialogFragment = new DialogFragmentAlert();
dialogFragment.Show(transaction, "dialog_fragment");
```

This pops up the dialog fragment on top of the main screen, until dismissed, as depicted in Figure 6-28.

Figure 6-28. *AlertDialog wrapped in DialogFragment*

Modal Layouts Using AlertDialog

Entire XML layouts can be created and displayed as modal dialog boxes by using AlertDialog. First, create the modal layout XML and then code AlertDialog in the activity to inflate that layout as an alert view, using alert.SetView.

In the activity's OnCreate method, instantiate AlertDialog and reference the Modal.axml layout in the alert.SetView method, and then alert.Create().Show() it. See Listing 6-45.

Listing 6-45. Inflate Modal Layout in ModalAlertActivity.cs

```
var alert = new AlertDialog.Builder(this);
alert.SetView(LayoutInflater.Inflate(Resource.Layout.Modal, null));
alert.Create().Show();
```

This displays a modal that pops up over the main layout, as shown in Figure 6-29.

Figure 6-29. *Enter Your Name dialog box using AlertDialog*

■ **Tip** Create user notifications via `AlertDialog` that elicit a response from the user by using `SetPositiveButton` and `SetNegativeButton`.

PopupMenu

The `PopupMenu` class provides a ready-made context-specific pop-up menu. Less popular than the navigation drawer discussed in the next section, the pop-up menu is still in use. The pop-up menu is created by making an XML menu file, using Android `<menu>` and `<item>` tags, which is placed in the `Resources/menu` folder. The `PopupMenu` class is instantiated and anchored to a control on the screen, and the XML menu file inflated.

■ **Tip** A lot of ugly navigation has been coded using pop-up menus. Keep your navigation elegant and consistent with industry UI patterns by heeding the Golden Rule of Mobile UI (du jour): *Nav on the left, action on the right.*

As shown in Listing 6-46, create the menu XML file and put it in the `Resources/menu` folder.

Listing 6-46. Menu Layout in Popuplayout.xml

```xml
<?xml version="1.0" encoding="utf-8"?>
<menu xmlns:android="http://schemas.android.com/apk/res/android">
  <item android:id="@+id/item1"
    android:title="First Item" />
  <item android:id="@+id/item2"
    android:title="Second Item" />
  <item android:id="@+id/item3"
    android:title="Third Item" />
</menu>
```

The layout can be simple, containing just a button for triggering the menu (Listing 6-47).

Listing 6-47. Main Layout in PopupLayout.axml

```xml
<?xml version="1.0" encoding="utf-8"?>
<LinearLayout xmlns:android="http://schemas.android.com/apk/res/android"
    android:orientation="vertical"
    android:layout_width="fill_parent"
    android:layout_height="fill_parent"
    android:minWidth="25px"
    android:minHeight="25px">
    <Button
        android:text="Show PopupMenu"
        android:layout_width="match_parent"
        android:layout_height="wrap_content"
        android:id="@+id/button" />
</LinearLayout>
```

In your activity, find the button called button. In the button.Click event, instantiate the PopupMenu class as a menu anchored to the button. Inflate the pop-up menu XML layout. Handle menu item clicks by using MenuItemClick and handle dismissal of the menu with DismissEvent, which also happens on an item click. Display the menu with the Show method (Listing 6-48).

Listing 6-48. Button to Trigger the Pop-up Menu in PopupActivity.cs (OnCreate Method)

```
SetContentView(Resource.Layout.PopupLayout);
Button button = FindViewById<Button>(Resource.Id.button);

button.Click += (s, e) => {
    PopupMenu menu = new PopupMenu (this, button);
    menu.Inflate (Resource.Menu.popupmenu);

    menu.MenuItemClick += (s1, e2) => {
        Console.WriteLine ("{0} Selected", e2.Item.TitleFormatted);
    };
    menu.Show ();
};
```

Clicking the Show PopupMenu button brings up the menu shown in Figure 6-30. The selected menu item title is written as output to the console by using the input parameter's Item.TitleFormatted property.

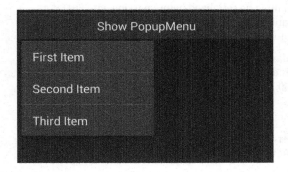

Figure 6-30. Context menus using PopupMenu

▓ **Note**   The DismissEvent event fires when the menu closes.

Managing State Using Bundles

ANDROID

Android uses a dictionary called a bundle, attached to an intent in the Extras property, to save object values and pass them between pages. Activities may not directly reference properties within one another. Bundles are passed between activities in two ways: either populated as individual fields by using PutExtra and GetExtra methods on the intent to pack and unpack the bundle, or as an entire bundle that is created stand-alone and then copied onto the intent's bundle by using putExtras. PutExtra is handy when passing a field or two, and bundle creation is useful when many fields must be managed. Objects from custom classes can be passed but must be serialized into strings.

Passing Strings

Pass strings to the new activity by using the `PutExtra` method on the second activity. In the first activity, declare the intent and pass in the string of data, as shown in Listing 6-49.

Listing 6-49. Pass String by Using PutExtra in PassStringActivity.cs

```
var intent = new Intent (this, typeof(DetailActivity));
intent.PutExtra ("MyData", "A string of data");
```

In the destination activity, retrieve the string by using `GetStringExtra`:

```
String text = Intent.GetStringExtra ("MyData") ?? "No Data";
```

■ **Tip** More than 20 `PutExtra` overloads and a similar number of `GetExtra` methods exist to handle different data types.

Passing Objects

Objects can be passed in the same manner as strings but must be serialized before passing with `PutExtra`. This can be done most easily with JavaScript Object Notation (JSON) and XML serialization. `System.Runtime.Serialization` and `IParcelable` are other options that are not covered here.

JSON is the easiest and more versatile approach, particularly using the Json.NET component in the Xamarin Component Store (or NuGet). This allows objects such as `object` of type `ObjectClass` to be serialized into JSON with the `SerializeObject` method. See Listing 6-50.

Listing 6-50. Pass Object Using PutExtra in PassObjectActivity.cs

```
String json = Newtonsoft.Json.JsonConvert.SerializeObject (data);
var intent = new Intent(this, typeof(PassToActivity));
intent.PutExtra("MyData", json);
StartActivity(intent);
```

And the objects can be deserialized with `DeserializeObject` in the activity called `PassToActivity`:

```
String json = Intent.GetStringExtra("MyData") ?? "No Data";
DataModel data =
    Newtonsoft.Json.JsonConvert.DeserializeObject<DataModel>(json);
```

XML serialization is another simple way to pass an object using the standard .NET `System.Xml.Serialization` library. We're not going to cover that here because it's a well-documented .NET technique. After serializing your object into a string via XML serialization, pass the string by using `putExtra`/ `GetStringExtra` in the same manner as a JSON string.

`System.Runtime.Serialization` and `IParcelable` are not covered here because the `[Serializable]` attribute is not supported in Portable Class Libraries (PCLs), making it unsuitable for many Xamarin architectures. `Java.IO.ISerializable` is a Xamarin-recommended alternative, and examples can be found on the Xamarin forums.

If you're not using a PCL, `System.Runtime.Serializable` can be implemented by using standard .NET practice, but `IParcelable` implementations run many times faster. `Serializable` uses reflection, which is slow and can produce many temporary objects, leading to more garbage collection. Use `IParcelable` (if you must) when handling a large number of objects (hundreds or more) or when you're concerned about performance. The `IParcelable` implementation is also beyond the scope of this book but is a useful option when performance is key and other options aren't working.

Creating a Bundle

When you have many fields to pass to another activity and need a way to manage them, creating a bundle can be useful. The `PutExtra` method used previously adds fields to a bundle that already exists on the intent. A bundle can be created explicitly, however, and overwritten onto the intent's bundle. It is useful to prepare them first and then write to the intent in one step.

Create the intent and the bundle, populate the bundle, and then copy it onto the intent by using `putExtras` before starting the new activity (Listing 6-51).

Listing 6-51. Build and Assign a Bundle in PassBundleActivity.cs

```
Bundle thisBundle = new Bundle();
thisBundle.PutString("MyData", "A string of data.");
thisBundle.PutString("MyData2", "Another string of data.");
var intent = new Intent(this, typeof(PassToBundleActivity));
intent.PutExtras(thisBundle);
StartActivity(intent);
```

Retrieving the bundle is exactly the same as retrieving data from `PutExtra` methods, using the `GetExtra` methods. This happens in the destination activity, as in Listing 6-52.

Listing 6-52. Get Fields from a Bundle in PassToBundleActivity.cs

```
String text = Intent.GetStringExtra ("MyData") ?? "No Data";
String text2 = Intent.GetStringExtra ("MyData2") ?? "No Data";
```

■ **Tip** Leverage the activity events `OnSaveInstanceState` and `OnRestoreInstanceState` to populate and read from the bundle when an activity is stopped and started.

Using Static Global Classes and StartActivityForResult

There are also a couple of other ways to pass data between activities:

- *Static global classes* can be used to share object instances instead of passing values, and were discussed in the "Using a Static Global Class" in the Xamarin.Forms section earlier.

- `StartActivityForResult` can be used to call an activity when return values are needed; then `SetResult` is used in the called activity, and `OnActivityResult` is overridden in the calling activity to handle the returned values.

Drill-down List

ANDROID

A *drill-down list* is a list of tappable items selected to navigate to a new page. The following recipes cover the two most common types of lists: by page and by item. Lists by page contain rows of menu pages that can be selected to navigate to different activities. Both of these recipes use ListView to bind to a data model to provide a dynamic list of tappable items. Lists by item can be viewed and selected to display more information about that item: the traditional master-detail pattern. In the interest of space, I'll provide details on implementing the first recipe and then general direction on the second one.

Drill-down lists often also have a toolbar at the top of the screen for back navigation, displaying the current screen title and action menus.

Using ListView by Page

A drill-down list in Android can be created using a ListView that binds to a data model containing the activity page types that you want to list and navigate to. This example covers navigation to a new activity.

Create a ListItem class that contains a PageType property, as shown in Listing 6-53. PageType will contain the activity type to navigate to.

Listing 6-53. List Data Model in ListItem.cs

```
public class ListItem
{
    public string Title { get; set; }
    public Type PageType { get; set; }
}
```

Create a list activity that populates a ListItem object with your navigation pages (Listing 6-54).

Listing 6-54. List Activity in DrilldownListActivity.cs

```
public class DrilldownListActivity : ListActivity
{
    List<ListItem> listItems;
    protected override void OnCreate(Bundle bundle)
    {
        base.OnCreate(bundle);
        listItems = new List<ListItem> {
          new ListItem {Title = "First Page", PageType=
              typeof(DrilldownActivity1)},
          new ListItem {Title = "Second Page", PageType=
              typeof(DrilldownActivity2)},
          new ListItem {Title = "Third Page", PageType=
              typeof(DrilldownActivity3)}
        };
        ListAdapter = new ListItemAdapter(this, listItems);
    }
}
```

Override `OnListItemClick` to start the new activity by using `StartActivity`, passing in the activity type that was clicked:

```
protected override void OnListItemClick(ListView l, View v,
    int position, long id)
{
    StartActivity(listItems[position].PageType);
}
```

`ListItemAdapter` inherits from `BaseAdapter` and works exactly like `ListItemAdapter` shown in Chapter 5, in Listing 5-11. Figure 6-31 shows the drill-down list with all three pages.

Figure 6-31. *Drill-down list using ListActivity*

Tap a page in the list, and the app navigates to the respective activity/layout, as shown in Figure 6-32.

Figure 6-32. *Navigate to the selected page by using StartActivity*

Using ListView by Item

Users want to drill down into a list of items to display more information about that item: the traditional master-detail pattern. Begin with the previous example of "Using ListView by Page." Add an item ID to the `ListItem` data model and remove the `PageType`. In the `OnListItemClick` `StartActivity` method call, navigate to a single activity type, a detail activity that shows detail on that item, and pass in the item ID by using the bundle on the new intent.

Using ListView with a Toolbar

Adding a toolbar above `ListView` requires the use of a layout XML containing `ToolBar` and `ListView`. Combine the `ListView` techniques in Chapter 5 with the toolbar recipes earlier in this chapter. Add a `<ListView>` tag to a layout (as shown in Listing 5-13) with an included toolbar (as in Listing 6-23), and bind the layout's `ListView` in your activity:

```
listView = FindViewById<ListView>(Resource.Id.listItems);
listView.Adapter = new ListCustomAdapter(this, listItems);
```

Navigation Drawer

ANDROID

The *navigation drawer* is the sliding side menu triggered by tapping an icon (usually the hamburger) at the top of the screen. Like the toolbar, the drawer layout is used as part of the Support Library to support older APIs (`android.support.v4.widget.DrawerLayout`). The available implementation solutions are too lengthy to include here. The following are some recommended sources for navigation drawer implementations:

- Effective Navigation in Xamarin.Android: Part 1—Navigation Drawer at MotzCod.es by James Montemagno

- And his GitHub example at `https://github.com/jamesmontemagno/Xam.NavDrawer`

Tabs Using ActionBar

ANDROID

Tabbed menus at the top of the screen allow switching screen content between different pages (Figure 6-33).

Figure 6-33. *Action bar tabs*

Android provides this functionality in the action bar, which handles tabs, but the page flipping must be coded manually by using fragments. There are a few steps to make this work:

1. Add a `FrameLayout` to the main layout XML to contain the tab fragments.

2. Create a fragment class and layout XML for each tab.

3. In the main activity, instantiate `ActionBar` and set its `NavigationMode` to `Tabs`.

4. Add tabs to the action bar by using `AddTab`.

5. Add event handlers for `TabSelected` and `TabUnselected` that invoke and destroy the tab fragments.

Let's go through the steps in detail.

Add a `FrameLayout` called `fragmentContainer` to the main layout XML, as in Listing 6-55, which will contain the dynamically loaded tab layout XML.

Listing 6-55. Main Layout in TabMain.axml

```
<LinearLayout xmlns:android="http://schemas.android.com/apk/res/android"
    android:orientation="vertical"
    android:layout_width="fill_parent"
    android:layout_height="fill_parent">
    <FrameLayout
        android:id="@+id/fragmentContainer"
        android:layout_width="match_parent"
        android:layout_height="0dip"
        android:layout_weight="1" />
</LinearLayout>
```

Create a fragment class for each tab. The first one is shown in Listing 6-56.

Listing 6-56. Tab Fragment in TabFirstFragment.cs

```
class TabFirstFragment : Fragment
{
    public override View OnCreateView(LayoutInflater inflater,
        ViewGroup container, Bundle savedInstanceState)
    {
        base.OnCreateView(inflater, container, savedInstanceState);
        var view = inflater.Inflate( Resource.Layout.TabFirst, container, false);
        var text = view.FindViewById<TextView>(Resource.Id.text);
        text.Text = "This is the first tab page.";
        return view;
    }
}
```

For each tag fragment, create a fragment layout that contains your tab page content, a TextView in this case (Listing 6-57).

Listing 6-57. Tab Fragment Page Content in TabFirst.axml

```
<?xml version="1.0" encoding="utf-8"?>
<TextView xmlns:android="http://schemas.android.com/apk/res/android"
    android:text="Large Text"
    android:textAppearance="?android:attr/textAppearanceLarge"
    android:layout_width="match_parent"
    android:layout_height="wrap_content"
    android:id="@+id/text" />
```

▪ **Note** Remember to create the layout and fragment class for the second tab (TabSecondLayout.cs and TabSecond.axml).

In the main activity's OnCreate method, set the layout to TabMain.axml and set the action bar's NavigationMode property to Tabs (Listing 6-58).

Listing 6-58. Display TabMain Layout and Set ActionBar to Tabs in TabMenuActivity.cs

```
SetContentView(Resource.Layout.TabMain);
ActionBar.NavigationMode = ActionBarNavigationMode.Tabs;
```

This creates a tabbed action bar, and the page below it is a frame layout ready for the tab fragments to be added and removed.

■ **Note** If you get a Null Object error on the action bar, make sure that you're not using the theme called MyTheme from earlier in this chapter, which is made for the Support Library v7 AppCompat library. Use an explicit theme declaration for this activity if you need to, as shown in Listing 6-60. If you need both an action bar and a toolbar in your app, consider using the Support Library v7 AppCompat library to implement both.

For each tab, instantiate the tab by using the ActionBar.NewTab() method, as coded in Listing 6-59. Then instantiate the tab's accompanying fragment. Use the TabSelected event to add and display the tab's fragment. Use the TabUnselected event for cleanup. Add the tab to the action bar by using AddTab.

Listing 6-59. Instantiate Tabs and Handle TabSelected Events in TabMenuActivity.cs

```
var tab = ActionBar.NewTab();
tab.SetText("First Item");
var tabFirst = new TabFirstFragment();
tab.TabSelected += delegate(object sender, ActionBar.TabEventArgs e)
{
    var fragment = this.FragmentManager
        .FindFragmentById(Resource.Id.fragmentContainer);
    if (fragment != null)
        e.FragmentTransaction.Remove(fragment);
    e.FragmentTransaction.Add(Resource.Id.fragmentContainer, tabFirst);
};

tab.TabUnselected += delegate(object sender, ActionBar.TabEventArgs e)
{
    e.FragmentTransaction.Remove(tabFirst);
};

ActionBar.AddTab(tab);
```

The null fragment check in the TabSelected event ensures that the fragment is not added twice.

■ **Tip** Remember to do this for the second tab as well, as shown in Listing 6-60.

Figure 6-34 shows the first tab selected.

Figure 6-34. *Action bar tabs in action*

Figure 6-35 shows the second tab selected.

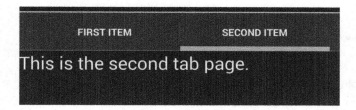

Figure 6-35. *Second tab selected, showing the second tab fragment layout*

Icons can be added to the tabs by using SetIcon:

```
tab.SetIcon(Resource.Drawable.tabFirstIcon);
```

When using more than a few tabs, the performance of tab event handlers may suffer. Manually implement ActionBar.ITabListener to handle each event. Xamarin.Android wraps the ActionBar.ITabListener with events on the ActionBar.Tab class. That means that ActionBar.ITabListener is created automatically when regular event handlers are used, but implementing it explicitly improves performance.

The tab pattern works naturally with the carousel pattern to allow sliding between tabs. Use the ViewPager class for slidable tab contents. Note that ActionBar works with Android.App.Fragment, while ViewPager works with Android.Support.V4.App.Fragment, so in order to rectify these two libraries, derive your main Activity from FragmentActivity.

■ **Tip**   The TabReselected event fires when a previously selected tab is selected again.

■ **Note**   The action bar was introduced in Android 3.0 (API level 11). Compatibility back to Android 2.1 (API Level 7) can be achieved by using the Android Support Library v7 AppCompat.

CODE COMPLETE: TabMenuActivity.cs

Listing 6-60 shows the complete main activity for the two-tab implementation of action bar tabs. See all of the files in the downloadable code solution NavigationExamplesAndroid.

Regarding the [Activity] attribute, an explicit declaration of this activity's theme is necessary only if you used the custom MyTheme theme in your app for the toolbar earlier in this chapter, which is incompatible with ActionBar.

Listing 6-60. TabMenuActivity.cs

```
[Activity(Theme = "@android:style/Theme.Material",
    Label = "TabMenuActivity")]
public class TabMenuActivity : Activity
{
    protected override void OnCreate(Bundle bundle)
    {
        base.OnCreate(bundle);
        SetContentView(Resource.Layout.TabMain);

        ActionBar.NavigationMode = ActionBarNavigationMode.Tabs;

        var tab = ActionBar.NewTab();
        tab.SetText("First Item");
        var tabFirst = new TabFirstFragment();
        tab.TabSelected += delegate(object sender, ActionBar.TabEventArgs e)
        {
            var fragment = this.FragmentManager.FindFragmentById(Resource.
            Id.fragmentContainer);
            if (fragment != null)
            e.FragmentTransaction.Remove(fragment);
            e.FragmentTransaction.Add(Resource.Id.fragmentContainer, tabFirst);
        };

        tab.TabUnselected += delegate(object sender, ActionBar.TabEventArgs e)
        {
            e.FragmentTransaction.Remove(tabFirst);
        };

        ActionBar.AddTab(tab);

        var tab2 = ActionBar.NewTab();
        tab2 = ActionBar.NewTab();
        tab2.SetText("Second Item");
        var tabSecond = new TabSecondFragment();
        tab2.TabSelected += delegate(object sender, ActionBar.TabEventArgs e)
        {
            var fragment = this.FragmentManager
                .FindFragmentById(Resource.Id.fragmentContainer);
            if (fragment != null)
                e.FragmentTransaction.Remove(fragment);
            e.FragmentTransaction.Add(Resource.Id.fragmentContainer,
                tabSecond);
        };
```

```
        tab.TabUnselected += delegate(object sender, ActionBar.TabEventArgs e)
        {
            e.FragmentTransaction.Remove(tabFirst);
        };

        ActionBar.AddTab(tab2);

    }
}
```

Using the Android navigation patterns we've covered, you should be able to build the skeleton of your app. If you're ready to learn more about Android, turn to Chapter 7, which covers data binding and data access.

If you're ready for iOS navigation patterns, read on!

iOS Navigation

iOS

iOS pages are built using UIView and UIViewController, the views and controllers in the MVC pattern. While UIView can be constructed by hand using code, it's typically built using iOS designer tools such as the Xamarin Designer for iOS or the Xcode Interface Builder in one of two ways: storyboards or nibs.

Storyboards are groups of UIView classes represented by XML layout files strung together into an application by using a designer tool. Each storyboard screen, called a *scene*, is made up of a UIView and a code-behind UIViewController. Each XML layout is typically instantiated into a UIView automatically without requiring code in the UIViewController to do that. Storyboard constructs called *segues* handle transitions to other layouts, also without code. When using storyboards, y*ou don't need to do much C# coding for basic navigation in iOS.*

An older method of constructing apps is using *nibs* (.xib files). A nib is a single XML layout file that is used separately from other nibs and instantiated into a UIView by its accompanying UIViewController. Nibs are typically constructed using the Xcode Interface Builder, and then a *little* C# coding is done to string them together.

■ **Important Note**   Most navigation in iOS development today is done using storyboards built with a designer tool, without much C#, leaving key aspects of iOS navigation beyond the scope of this code-first, non-tool-oriented book. Be certain to study appropriate designer tool resources, such as the Xamarin online docs, to learn about how that is done using Xcode Interface Builder or Xamarin Designer for iOS. *This is absolutely necessary for learning best-practice Xamarin.iOS development.*

You will explore how to code navigation by hand to give you an idea of what is happening behind the scenes and for the cases when you want more control. Use this chapter as a way to understand the underpinnings of iOS UI navigation and to help you out of tricky situations, but a tool-first approach is typically best practice here, and this is a code-first book. I'll cover code-first navigation approaches useful with both storyboards and nibs, but will mostly assume that you are using storyboards.

Now let's dive into the basics of iOS navigation. For each example, I'll first mention the standard approach using the designer, and then provide detail on the code-based approach.

Using Storyboards, Scenes, and Segues

Storyboards are constructed of *scenes* and the transitions between them, called *segues*. Scenes are made up of View and ViewController pairs, effectively single screens. iPhone scenes typically correspond to screens one-to-one. However, on an iPad multiple scenes may appear on one screen. Also, modal scenes can appear on top of other scenes. Segues define the navigation pattern, hierarchical or modal, and can handle animation and data passed between scenes.

Use storyboards to manage events for controls in the Properties Pad in the iOS Designer. Add the event handlers there and complete them in partial methods in the UIViewController class. Storyboards are stored as XML files. During the build, .storyboard files are compiled into nibs, screen-specific binary files. At runtime, nibs are initialized and instantiated to create new views.

In storyboard solution templates, storyboards are wired up to a project automatically via Options ➤ iOS Application ➤ Main Interface, which is set to the storyboard name.

Storyboard screens can also be instantiated programmatically within AppDelegate, as shown in Listing 6-61, where we instantiate the NavigationStory storyboard.

Listing 6-61. Instantiate a Storyboard in AppDelegate.cs

```
public partial class AppDelegate : UIApplicationDelegate
{
    UIWindow window;
    public static UIStoryboard Storyboard = UIStoryboard
        .FromName ("NavigationStory", null);
    public static UIViewController firstViewController;

    public override bool FinishedLaunching (UIApplication app,
        NSDictionary options)
    {
        window = new UIWindow (UIScreen.MainScreen.Bounds);
        firstViewController = Storyboard
            .InstantiateInitialViewController () as UIViewController;
        window.RootViewController = firstViewController;
        window.MakeKeyAndVisible ();

        return true;
    }
}
```

This AppDelegate initializes the first scene (view/view controller) in the storyboard as the first visible page, placed into the window's RootViewController as firstViewController.

Segues define the navigation type, animation details, and data passed between scenes. Storyboard projects begin, by default, with a Sourceless segue, the "lead-in" to the first scene that indicates which view the user will see first. The most common segues are Push, Modal, and Unwind:

- Hierarchical navigation is accomplished by using the *Push* segue or by-hand using the UINavigationController's PushViewController method.

- Modals are created with the *Modal* segue or the UIViewController's PresentViewController method.

- Back navigation can be accomplished using the *Unwind* segue or the DismissViewController method.

Create a segue by holding down the Ctrl key inside a button control and click-dragging from one scene to another; then define the segue type by choosing Root, Push, Modal, or Custom from the pop-up menu. Unwind segues are created by using the Segue Exit button at the bottom of the scene.

■ **Note**   Right-click for segues on VMware for your Windows virtual machine, or change your keyboard preferences to left-click.

Using Nibs

Before storyboards, there were nibs (.xib files): XML files representing a single screen's layout. You'll find many apps still using nibs. You may find occasion to use one yourself, as sometimes a storyboard is overkill. Whereas storyboards are groups of layouts, nibs are single XML layout files that are instantiated into UIViews by their accompanying UIViewControllers, often in the declaration of the UIViewController as part of the base class in quotes. ThisScreen.xib is loaded onto the screen in the UIViewController called ThisScreen.cs.

```
public ThisScreen () : base ("ThisScreen", null)
```

Nibs are typically constructed using the Xcode Interface Builder, and then strung together into applications using outlets or events in a designer tool or programmatically in their UIViewControllers.

Hierarchical Navigation

iOS

Hierarchical navigation in iOS uses the navigation controller, UINavigationController. Popping new pages onto the stack is achieved by using the navigation controller's PushViewController method and popped back off using DismissViewController. This is accomplished in storyboards by dropping a navigation controller onto the canvas and using the Push segue to add scenes, and then the Unwind segue to pop scenes off the stack (with Scene Exit).

Using UINavigationController

iOS

The primary navigation component in iOS is the navigation controller, or UINavigationController. This view controller provides a call stack and a fully customizable navigation bar with a screen title and navigation controls (Figure 6-36). A navigation controller object manages the currently displayed screens by using the *navigation stack*, which is represented by an array of view controllers. The first view controller in the array is the root view controller. The last view controller in the array is the view controller currently displayed.

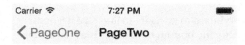

Figure 6-36.   *UINavigationController provides up navigation and titles for context*

First use your designer tool to create an initial page. Assign a view controller by clicking the bottom bar of that page in the designer and entering both the class name and view controller title as PageOne.

UINavigationController can be dragged and dropped onto a storyboard by using the designer or can be added manually by wrapping it around another view controller.

Manually add a navigation controller in your AppDelegate.cs, as in Listing 6-62, by wrapping it around the first view controller in your storyboard, which you can find using Storyboard. InstantiateInitialViewController().

Listing 6-62. Instantiate the Storyboard in AppDelegate.cs FinishedLaunching Method

```
firstViewController = Storyboard
    .InstantiateInitialViewController () as UIViewController;
UINavigationController navController = new UINavigationController
    (firstViewController);
```

Then assign the navigation controller as the root controller of the main window by using window. RootViewController:

```
window.RootViewController = navController;
```

Figure 6-37 shows page 1, which was created using a storyboard. The button called buttonGoToTwo was added to navigate to the second page (which we'll cover in a minute).

Figure 6-37. *Page 1 wrapped in UINavigationController*

Using the Push Segue or PushViewController

iOS

The Push segue adds a view controller onto the navigation stack within the same navigation controller. This presents a navigation bar with a Back button. The Push segue is functionally the same as using the UIViewController.PushViewController method. The UIViewController method PushViewController pushes a new view controller onto the stack.

First, use your designer tool to add a destination scene to your storyboard to navigate to and give it a name (PageTwoView, in this case). Also add a UIViewController by clicking the bottom of the PageTwoView scene and give the view controller a name, PageTwo. Set the Storyboard ID to PageTwo.

If you're building storyboards using the designer, create a Push segue in your designer by Ctrl-clicking inside a button on the source scene and then dragging the blue line to the scene to navigate to. Then pick the Push option from the pop-up menu.

To do the same thing by hand, add the code in Listing 6-63 to the PageOne view controller to navigate to this second page, in the button event in this case.

Listing 6-63. Navigate Using PushViewController in the ViewDidLoad Method of PageOne.cs

```
PageTwo pageTwo = this.Storyboard.InstantiateViewController ("PageTwo") as PageTwo;
NavigationController.PushViewController(pageTwo,true);
```

Listing 6-64 shows the entire button event handler.

Listing 6-64. TouchUpInside Event Handler

```
buttonGoToTwo.TouchUpInside += (sender, ea) => {
    PageTwo pageTwo = this.Storyboard.InstantiateViewController
        ("PageTwo") as PageTwo;
    NavigationController.PushViewController(pageTwo,true);
};
```

This code instantiates the second view controller by using Storyboard.InstantiateViewController and then pushes the second page on the stack by using NavigationController.PushViewController. Tap the buttonGoToTwo on the first page and navigate to page 2, as shown in Figure 6-38.

Figure 6-38. *Navigate to the second page by using UINavigationController*

UINavigationController allows the user to tap the left arrow and/or the PageOne text to return to the first page.

■ **Tip**   Back (or pop) can be coded manually with the Unwind segue or the DismissViewController method.

Customizing UINavigationController

Customizations can be made to UINavigationController directly (navController, in this case) or by referencing the navigation controller instance in UIViewController via the UIViewController. NavigationController property. The following customizations are made in navController directly.

The title used in the navigation bar comes from the Title property of each view controller:

```
navController.Title = "Page Title";
```

Change the style color of the navigation bar by using the BarStyle property:

```
navController.NavigationBar.BarStyle = UIBarStyle.Black;
```

Set the style back to the default:

```
navController.NavigationBar.BarStyle = UIBarStyle.Default;
```

Hide the navigation bar by using the SetNavigationBarHidden method:

```
navController.SetNavigationBarHidden (true, true);
```

Show the navigation bar:

```
navController.SetNavigationBarHidden (false, true);
```

■ **Note** The navigation bar has options for a customizable Back button icon, a right button, and a second toolbar at the bottom of the screen. For these and other options, consult the Xamarin online documentation for the iOS navigation controller.

Modal Navigation

iOS

There are two types of modals in iOS: full screen and pop-ups. Full-screen modals are created by using the Modal segue or the view controller's PresentViewController method. Pop-up modals, which include dialog boxes, user alerts, notifications, and pop-up menus, are created using UIAlertController. UIAlertController is a subclass of ViewController, and is displayed as a modal alert or *action sheet*, a pop-up menu.

■ **Tip** UIAlertController replaced both UAlertView and UIActionSheet in iOS 8. For tips on how to handle OS versioning, see Chapter 9.

Using the Modal Segue or PresentViewController

The *Modal segue* creates a relationship between two view controllers with an option for animation between the screens. The child screen will fill the entire visible page but will not provide a Back button. The Modal segue is functionally the same as using the UIViewController.PresentViewController method.

Add a scene to your storyboard by using your designer tool to drop a view controller into it, and give it a class name and view controller title of PageModalView. Also add a UIViewController by clicking the bottom of the PageModalView scene, and give the view controller a name and storyboard ID of PageModal.

If you're using the designer to build storyboards, create a Modal segue in your designer by Ctrl-clicking inside a button on the source scene and then dragging the blue line to the scene to navigate to. Then pick the Modal option from the pop-up menu.

To create a modal manually, code a button event in your source view controller, such as `PageOne.cs`. The `UIViewController` method `PresentViewController` calls your view controller modally and brings it into view, as shown in Listing 6-65.

Listing 6-65. Navigate Using PresentViewController in PageOne.cs

```
PageModal pageModal = this.Storyboard.InstantiateViewController
    ("PageModal") as PageModal;
this.PresentViewController(pageModal,true,null);
```

This navigates to a modal page *with no navigation bar*, even when `UINavigationController` is wrapping the current view controller (Figure 6-39).

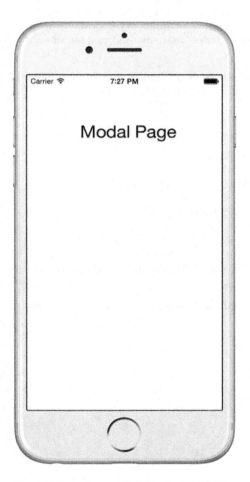

Figure 6-39. *PresentViewController in action*

No, there's no way for the user to go back in this app without clicking the Home button or restarting the app.

■ **Tip**   Back can be coded manually by using the Unwind segue or programmatically by using the
DismissViewController method.

```
buttonClose.TouchUpInside += (object sender, EventArgs e) => {
  DismissViewController(true, () => {});
        };
```

Alerts and User Notifications Using UIAlertController

Alerts and *user notifications* are typically small modal pop-up dialog boxes containing real-time feedback
to the user and one or more buttons to allow the user to dismiss or choose an option in response. Using
UIAlertController, a title and message are included in the alert with the Create method, and buttons are
added with the AddAction method.

Create an alert by specifying UIAlertControllerStyle.Alert in the Create method, as shown in Listing 6-66.
Add a button to it by using AddAction, and display the alert modally with PresentViewController.

Listing 6-66.   Using UIAlertController in PageOne.cs

```
var alert = UIAlertController.Create("Important",
    "Are you sure you want to do this irreversible thing?",
    UIAlertControllerStyle.Alert);
alert.AddAction(UIAlertAction.Create("Cancel", UIAlertActionStyle.Cancel,
    alertAction => {}));
alert.AddAction(UIAlertAction.Create("Yes", UIAlertActionStyle.Default,
    alertAction => {}));
this.PresentViewController(alert, true, null);
```

The alertAction lambda expressions here are empty (alertAction => {}) but would contain the code you
wanted to execute upon the user's choice of actions.

This UIAlertController presents a pop-up alert with important info and a couple of options (Figure 6-40).

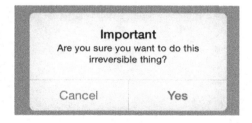

Figure 6-40.   *UIAlertController with the Alert style*

Pop-up Menus Using UIAlertController

Pop-up menus are modal dialog boxes containing several buttons that allow a user to choose from a list of options. This type of menu is sometimes called an *action sheet*.

Create an alert by specifying `UIAlertControllerStyle.ActionSheet` in the `Create` method (Listing 6-67). Add buttons to it by using `AddAction`, and display the alert modally with `PresentViewController`.

Listing 6-67. Using UIAlertControllerStyle.ActionSheet to Create a Pop-up in PageOne.cs

```
var popup = UIAlertController.Create("What is your choice?", null,
    UIAlertControllerStyle.ActionSheet);
var firstChoice= UIAlertAction.Create ("First Choice",
    UIAlertActionStyle.Default, alertAction => {});
popup.AddAction(firstChoice);
var secondChoice= UIAlertAction.Create ("Second Choice",
    UIAlertActionStyle.Default, alertAction => {});
popup.AddAction(secondChoice);
popup.AddAction(UIAlertAction.Create("Cancel", UIAlertActionStyle.Cancel,
    alertAction => {}));
this.PresentViewController(popup, true, null);
```

The `alertAction` lambda expressions here are empty (`alertAction => {}`) but would contain the code you wanted to execute upon the user's choice of actions.

This displays your pop-up menu at the bottom of the screen with a couple of choices (Figure 6-41).

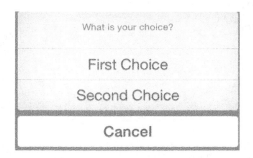

Figure 6-41. *UIAlertController with the ActionSheet style*

■ **Tip** It's often a good idea to provide a Cancel option.

Managing State

iOS

State is typically managed in iOS by passing data directly into UIViewController. This is usually done by using custom public properties on the destination view controller. When using segues, override the PrepareForSegue method to populate these properties before the segue, similar to coding transitions by hand by using PushViewController. Less commonly, values are passed through the view controller's constructor. All the approaches covered here scope data to a single view controller at a time, which is ideal from an architecture and memory use standpoint.

■ **Tip** Static global classes can be used to share object instances instead of passing values and were discussed in the Xamarin.Forms "Using a Static Global Class" section earlier.

Using the PrepareForSegue Method

You can use segues on your storyboard to pass values by overriding the PrepareForSegue method in the originating view controller and updating the public properties of the destination view controller before the segue takes place.

Add a destination view controller to the storyboard called DetailPageProperty. Add a public Item property (Listing 6-68).

Listing 6-68. Destination View Controller in DetailPageProperty.cs

```
partial class DetailPageProperty : UIViewController
{
    private ListItem _item;
    public ListItem Item
    {
        get { return _item;}
        set { _item = value;}
    }

    public DetailPageProperty (IntPtr handle) : base (handle)
    {
    }

    public override void ViewDidLoad ()
    {
        base.ViewDidLoad ();
        LabelTitle.Text = _item.Title;
        LabelDescription.Text = _item.Description;
    }

}
```

Create a Push segue in your designer by Ctrl-clicking inside a button on the source scene and then dragging the blue line to the scene to navigate to. Then pick the Push option from the pop-up menu.

Override PrepareForSegue in your parent view controller and populate your destination view controller's public properties, as shown in Listing 6-69.

Listing 6-69. PrepareForSegue Override in PageOne.cs

```
public override void PrepareForSegue (UIStoryboardSegue segue,
    NSObject sender)
{
    ListItem item = new ListItem();
    item.Title = "Item Title";
    item.Description = "Detailed Information about this item";

    base.PrepareForSegue (segue, sender);
    var detailPage = segue.DestinationViewController
        as DetailPageProperty;
    if (detailPage != null) {
        detailPage.Item = item;
    }
}
```

The DestinationViewController property of UIStoryboardSegue contains the instance of the destination view controller, and its public properties can be populated prior to the segue. After the segue is complete, the contents of public properties of the destination view controller (detailPage.Item, in this case) can be accessed.

Using UIViewController Public Properties

When pushing pages to the stack by hand, you can use a technique similar to the previous public property example, but using PushViewController instead of a Push segue. In the calling view controller, instantiate the detailPageProperty page, assign the public Item property, and push the new page to the stack, prepopulated with data (Listing 6-70).

Listing 6-70. Navigate to Detail Page Using PushViewController in PageOne.cs

```
detailPageProperty detailPageProperty = this.Storyboard.InstantiateViewController
("DetailPage") as
    detailPageProperty;
detailPageProperty.Item = item;
NavigationController.PushViewController(detailPageProperty,true);
```

When your pages are coded by hand with no storyboard, the view controller constructor parameters are useful for passing values.

Using the UIViewController Constructor Parameters

When calling a new page in code, you can pass in the variables that are defined in your page's constructor.

Define a destination page with a ListItem class as a constructor parameter, as shown in Listing 6-71. This example passes in the Item object and uses the Item.Title property.

Listing 6-71. Define Contructor Parameters in the Destination Page in DetailPage.cs

```
partial class DetailPage : UIViewController
{
    private ListItem item;

    public DetailPage(ListItem itemPassed)
    {
        item = itemPassed;
    }

    public override void ViewDidLoad ()
    {
        base.ViewDidLoad ();
        Title = item.Title;
    }
}
```

Instances of the ListItem class can then be passed directly into the page when it is called, as shown in Listing 6-72.

Listing 6-72. Pass Item into the Destination Page in PageOne.cs

```
DetailPage detailPage = new DetailPage(item);
NavigationController.PushViewController(detailPage,true);
```

■ **Tip**   C# events or callback methods with Action<string> are useful for returning data from a view controller.

Drill-down List Using UINavigationController

iOS

While building a list using UITableView (as shown in Chapter 5), the selectable list can become a drill-down list with hierarchical navigation.

Create a new UITableViewSource called DrilldownListSource beginning with our UITableView list source example from Chapter 5 (Listing 5-23). In the UITableViewSource constructor, pass in the parent UIViewController, as shown in Listing 6-73.

Listing 6-73. UITableViewSource Using Parent View Controller in DrilldownListSource.cs

```
UIViewController parentController;

public DrilldownListSource (List<ListItem> items, UIViewController parentController)
{
    listItems = items;
    this.parentController = parentController;
}
```

This allows the call from the parent `UIViewController` to pass in its own reference, allowing the list source's access to `tNavigationController:`.

```
table.Source = new DrilldownListSource(listItems, this);
```

Listing 6-74 is the full `UITableViewController` containing the list data population and the `Source` property setting. This is based on the list pattern covered in Chapter 5, in Listing 5-24.

Listing 6-74. UIViewController for a UITableView in DrilldownList.cs

```
public partial class DrilldownList : UITableViewController
{
    List<ListItem> listItems;
    public override void ViewDidLoad()
    {
        base.ViewDidLoad();
        UITableView table = new UITableView(View.Bounds);
        listItems = new List<ListItem> {
            new ListItem {Title = "First", Description="1st item"},
            new ListItem {Title = "Second", Description="2nd item"},
            new ListItem {Title = "Third", Description="3rd item"}
        };
        table.Source = new DrilldownListSource(listItems, this);
        Add (table);
    }
}
```

In the `UITableViewSource` subclass, instantiate the detail screen. Then use the `PushViewController` method to push that screen onto the stack by using the `NavigationController` on the parent `UIViewController`, as shown in Listing 6-75.

Listing 6-75. Navigate to the Selected View Controller by Using PushViewController in DrilldownListSource.cs

```
public override void RowSelected (UITableView tableView, NSIndexPath indexPath)
{
    var detail = new DetailScreen (listItems[indexPath.Row]);
    parentController.NavigationController.PushViewController(detail,true);
    tableView.DeselectRow (indexPath, true);
}
```

Use `indexPath` to locate the selected item in the `listItems` array, and then pass it into the detail page's constructor to use that `Item` object on the detail page. Figure 6-42 shows the resulting list.

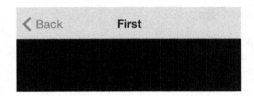

Figure 6-42. *Drill-down list using UINavigationController*

Clicking an item navigates to the specified page, passing though the item title, as shown in Figure 6-43.

Figure 6-43. *Drill-down list destination page*

■ **Tip** Create a drill-down list by page type by adding a page type field to the list data model and instantiating the detail page in the RowSelected method using that type.

Listing 6-76 is the complete code for the list source.

Listing 6-76. Drill-down List UITableViewSource in DrilldownListSource.cs

```
public class DrilldownListSource : UITableViewSource
{

    protected List<ListItem> listItems;
    protected string CellId= "TableCell";
    protected UIViewController parentController;

    public DrilldownListSource (List<ListItem> items,
        UIViewController parentController)
    {
        listItems = items;
        this.parentController = parentController;
    }

    public override nint RowsInSection (UITableView tableview, nint section)
    {
        return listItems.Count;
    }
```

```
public override UITableViewCell GetCell(UITableView tableView,
    NSIndexPath indexPath)
{
    UITableViewCell cell = tableView.DequeueReusableCell(CellId);
    if (cell == null) cell = new
        UITableViewCell(UITableViewCellStyle.Default, CellId);
    cell.TextLabel.Text = listItems[indexPath.Row].Title;
    return cell;
}

public override void RowSelected (UITableView tableView,
    NSIndexPath indexPath)
{
    var detail = new DetailPage (listItems[indexPath.Row]);
    parentController.NavigationController.PushViewController(detail,true);
    tableView.DeselectRow (indexPath, true);
}

}
```

Navigation Drawer Using Components

iOS

The *navigation drawer* is the sliding side menu triggered by tapping an icon (usually the hamburger) at the top of the screen. Unlike Xamarin.Forms and Android, Apple provides no out-of-the-box navigation drawer component at the time of this writing; it must be developed by hand. I suggest trying these components from the Xamarin Component Store:

- Flyout Navigation by James Clancey

- Sidebar Navigation by Jack Dehlin

GitHub also has options:

- MonoTouch.SlideoutNavigation by Dillon Buchanan

These include MVVM-friendly menus:

- MonoTouch.SlidingControls by Jonathan Stoneman

- MvxSlidingPanels.Touch by Big Frank

- SlidingPanels.Touch by Patrick Laplante

Tabs Using UITabBarController

iOS

Tabs are a group of screens that a user can navigate to via a set of folder-like buttons. In iOS, each tab screen is represented by a UIView/UIViewController pair (Figure 6-44). The tabs are at the bottom of the screen in iOS.

Figure 6-44. *UITabBarController*

Create tabs by dragging and dropping a tab bar controller onto a storyboard, or code them by-hand using the UITabBarController class.

When coding by hand, use UITabBarController to instantiate ViewControllers as tab menu screens and assign them to the ViewControllers property, as shown in Listing 6-77.

Listing 6-77. Tabbed Menu Using UITabBarController

```
public class TabBarController : UITabBarController {

    UIViewController tabFirst, tabSecond, tabThird;

    public TabBarController ()
    {
        tabFirst = new UIViewController();
        tabFirst.Title = "Purple";
        tabFirst.View.BackgroundColor = UIColor.Purple;
```

294

```
        tabSecond = new UIViewController();
        tabSecond.Title = "Black";
        tabSecond.View.BackgroundColor = UIColor.Black;

        tabThird = new UIViewController();
        tabThird.Title = "Blue";
        tabThird.View.BackgroundColor = UIColor.Blue;

        var tabs = new UIViewController[] {
            tabFirst, tabSecond, tabThird
        };

        ViewControllers = tabs;
    }

}
```

The result was shown earlier in Figure 6-43.

Tabs can be customized. The title and icon can be changed. Default values for these properties are available by using the TabBarItem property and UITabBarItem constructor.

■ **Tip**   Tab navigation usually appears at the bottom of the screen in iOS.

Create a Favorites tab by replacing the Title assignment of the first tab in Listing 6-77:

```
    tabFirst.TabBarItem = new UITabBarItem (UITabBarSystemItem.Favorites, 0);
```

Customize the second tab by setting the Image and Title properties. This image must be an alpha-channeled outline of an icon.

```
    tabSecond = new UIViewController ();
    tabSecond.TabBarItem = new UITabBarItem ();
    tabSecond.TabBarItem.Image = UIImage.FromFile ("second.png");
    tabSecond.TabBarItem.Title = "Second";
```

■ **Important**   Add second.png to the Resources folder of the project in Xamarin Studio, along with the high-resolution image named second@2x.png.

Badges are often used to reflect new content to be read in a tab screen. Badges may also be added to tabs by using the BadgeValue property:

```
    tabThird.TabBarItem.BadgeValue = "New";
```

Make the badge disappear by setting it to null:

```
    tabThird.TabBarItem.BadgeValue = null;
```

Summary

Congratulations! You have reached the end of the longest chapter in this book.

Navigation is a key topic in the creation of mobile apps. In web and desktop apps, single screens are so large and hold so much of the user workflow that navigation is often a small part of the user experience and is even sometimes added as an afterthought. Because of the economy of screen real estate in mobile apps, we must enable users to easily get around in an app in as short a time as possible. Consumer apps can engage a user for a long period of time, but success in business apps is not measured in the amount of time a user spends in the app but in the answer to this question: Did they find the information they were looking for? Menus can't be a catchall parking lot of drop-downs at the top of the page or (just as bad) a navigation drawer bursting with disorganized features.

The criticality of navigation in mobile apps leads us to this tenet: *Mobile navigation must closely match the user workflow.* If it doesn't, we risk confused and frustrated users.

In most of our apps, especially business apps, it is useful to try and match our user stories and use cases with these key navigation patterns: hierarchical, modal, drill-down list, navigation drawer, and tabs.

Hopefully, this chapter provides you with the ideas and patterns to map out the skeleton of just about any app you can imagine. The downloadable code samples can be mixed and matched to help you sketch out your app.

Now it's time for the foundation beneath all of our UI technique: the data. Let's explore data access and data binding in depth.

Please navigate to the next chapter.

CHAPTER 7

■ ■ ■

Data Access with SQLite and Data Binding

Data access in Xamarin apps often involves a local database and a remote data server accessed via web services. Local data access can be handled in many ways with many products, both open source and proprietary, but the Xamarin-recommended mobile database is SQLite, which is built into iOS and Android. Data can be queried from a SQLite database and manually populated into the UI, but a more sophisticated approach is to use data binding to transfer information automatically between the UI and your data models. In this chapter, you'll learn how to employ SQLite in your Xamarin apps as well as how to use data binding in your Xamarin.Forms apps.

What Is SQLite?

SQLite is a C-based relational database designed in the spring of 2000 by D. Richard Hipp for use in US Navy guided-missile warships. It is now a standby database engine included in many operating systems, including iOS and Android (but not in Windows Phone, so it must be shipped manually). SQLite implements most of the SQL standard and has no stand-alone database server process but instead is linked as a library-accessed datastore, providing an on-demand, app-specific database.

You will typically use SQLite with Xamarin in one of three ways:

- *SQLite.NET*: Using SQLite.NET to form CRUD transactions with `Insert`, `Get`, `Delete`, `Table`, and `Query`

- *ADO.NET*: Using a minimal ADO.NET implementation of SQLite to execute SQL statements with `Command` objects

- *Third-party MVVM libraries*: Data binding views to fields in the SQLite database by using a third-party MVVM framework such as MvvmCross or MVVM Light Toolkit

Third-party MVVM libraries are beyond the scope of this book. ADO.NET is covered at the end of the chapter, and SQLite.NET is a popular choice with developers.

What Is SQLite.NET?

To use C-based SQLite in C#, a binding library is required, which is why Frank Krueger founded SQLite.NET, an open source SQLite library in C#. SQLite.NET is an object-relational mapping (ORM) library. ORMs allow you to manipulate database objects instead of working with fields and tables. SQLite.NET provides both options. We can do data-object manipulations by using methods such as `Insert`, `Get`, and `Delete` acting on data classes that map to tables. We can also use SQL to query a table with the `Query` method and use LINQ to operate on a table's contents using the `Table` method. SQLite using SQLite.NET gives you everything you need from a local mobile database to build consumer, business, and enterprise native mobile apps.

DATA STORAGE OPTIONS

Many successful mobile apps use nondatabase storage options. You can use file-based data storage in addition to or even instead of using a SQLite database for data storage. This can involve serialized data in XML or JSON, HTML, or comma-delimited fields in text files stored in local folders on the device. *Preferences* is another data storage option. iOS, Android, and Windows Phone provide ways to store preferences as key-value pairs typically used to record user settings or other small bits of data. This chapter focuses on local database access and does not explore these or other nondatabase data storage techniques, but I encourage you to do so in the Xamarin online docs. Also, Chapter 6 touches on disk storage techniques involving XML serialization in the "Managing State" sections.

Data Binding

Keeping your UI in sync with your data model can be a lot of work if you do it by hand in code. Every time the user makes a change in the UI, you can implement event handlers (such as `TextChanged`) that update the contents of the data model, and each time the data model changes in code, you can notify the UI to refresh (by implementing `PropertyChanged`).

Data binding handles all of that for you by providing a framework to sync the views with a data model. Data binding manages views that need to modify the contents of their accompanying data model and the refresh of the UI from changes in the data model.

Data binding is built into Xamarin.Forms.

This real-time connection between the data layer and presentation layer is available to us in mobile development, because the presentation layer and data layer reside together on a single physical tier, the mobile device. Many similarities exist with the development of Windows Presentation Foundation (WPF) desktop apps. The design pattern used frequently in WPF development is *MVVM* (Model-View-ViewModel). MVVM and data binding involve the coupling of the presentation and data layers to create a rich, responsive user experience.

Xamarin apps can use third-party data-binding libraries such as MvvmCross or MVVM Light. A range of platform-specific techniques are also available. Android provides the data-binding adapter approaches discussed in Chapter 5, such as subclassing `BaseAdapter`. Android also provides adapter classes for data binding to SQLite databases by using `SimpleCursorAdapter` and `CursorAdapter`, which are beyond the scope of this book. iOS provides adapters such as `UITableViewSource`, which was also covered in Chapter 5.

■ **Important Note**   This chapter covers cross-platform SQLite techniques such as SQLite.NET and ADO.NET, as well as Xamarin.Forms data binding. If you need a SQLite solution set up with Xamarin.Android or Xamarin.iOS, refer to the Xamarin online docs and recipes.

This chapter does not focus on platform-specific data access techniques, but delves into cross-platform SQLite techniques and data binding using Xamarin.Forms.

Xamarin.Forms Data Binding

XAMARIN.FORMS

Xamarin.Forms has data binding built in, allowing you to bind views to models easily and elegantly. XAML is often used to implement data binding in Xamarin.Forms. This chapter covers the C# approach, and you can follow the XAML in the downloadable code examples. Xamarin.Forms data binding supports the binding of one view to another as well as a view to a variable. This section focuses primarily on the most common business app use case: binding a view to a data model.

Xamarin.Forms data binding is done by binding a data source property to a target UI element property. The target property must be a bindable property (derived from `BindableObject`), which can be specified by using the view's `SetBinding` method. Bindable properties are indicated in the online Xamarin.Forms API documentation for each class. The data source can be a variable or data model class property and may be set by using the `BindingContext` property on a page or view.

It's worth noting that data binding can be done manually by using a view's `PropertyChanged` or `TextChanged` event to synchronize with the source.

However, Xamarin.Forms data binding is largely automatic after the setup is complete. You need to create and configure the target view and pair it with a source. You also need to prepare that source by implementing the `INotifyPropertyChanged` interface to make changes to that source observable via `PropertyChanged` event handlers. Xamarin.Forms lays in the remaining event handlers under the covers to carry out the transfer of data to and from the source and target. The following examples focus on this automatic approach, using the `BindingContext` property and `SetBinding` method.

Trivial data binding involves views that contain initial values from the data model (source), and changes to the UI (target) are reflected in the model. However, no refresh of the UI occurs to reflect changes to the data model. Refreshing of the UI requires *nontrivial data binding*, covered later, in "Using INotifyPropertyChanged."

Let's walk through a few examples of automatic data binding in Xamarin.Forms. You will begin with a trivial example, in which the UI updates a data model. Next you'll proceed into nontrivial examples, in which changes to the data model are refreshed in the view. You'll explore the MVVM design pattern, wrapping your data model in a view model (or ViewModel). Then you will revisit data-bound lists, except you will make them editable instead of read-only.

In trivial, automatic data binding, changes to the UI are reflected in the data model in real time. Here is a common way (but not the only way) to approach trivial data binding in C#:

1. Specify the source data model by using the `BindingContext` page (or view) property:

   Ex. `this.BindingContext = listItem;`

2. Pair the source property with the target view property by using the `SetBinding` method:

   Ex. `titleEntry.SetBinding(Entry.TextProperty, "Title");`

These two steps bind the Entry view to the Title property of the Item model (listItem is an instance of Item).

Nontrivial data binding, in which the target must be refreshed to reflect changes made to the contents of the source in real time, requires an implementation of the INotifyPropertyChanged interface's observer event called PropertyChanged, which fires when the view model detects a change to the data (in a property's Set accessor method).

■ **Tip** Do you want to data bind using Xamarin.iOS or Xamarin.Android? Check out the third-party MVVM data-binding libraries such as MvvmCross or MVVM Light. More-traditional data binding techniques include BaseAdapter, SimpleCursorAdapter, and CursorAdapter on Android, and UITableViewSource on iOS. Refer to Chapter 5 to get started with Android BaseAdapter and iOS UITableViewSource.

Let's look at a trivial Xamarin.Forms data-binding example.

Binding to a Data Model

XAMARIN.FORMS

Using the two-step data-binding approach in the preceding section, bind an Entry view to the Title property of a data model called Item. This is trivial binding: changes to the view result in an update to the data model.

Create a data model called Item with a Title and Description string property, as shown in Listing 7-1.

Listing 7-1. Item Data Model in Item.cs

```
public class Item
{
    public string Title { get; set; }
    public string Description { get; set; }
}
```

Create a ContentPage that instantiates and then populates Item (Listing 7-2). Set the BindingContext property of the page to the item object. Create the Entry view, and then use the SetBinding method to tie its Text property to the Title property in Item. Entry.TextProperty in the SetBinding method call is a data-binding property that provides a reference to the Entry view's Text property.

Listing 7-2. Bind a View to a Model in ItemPage.cs

```
public ItemPage()
{
    var item =  new Item {Title = "First", Description="1st item"};

    this.BindingContext = item;

    var titleEntry = new Entry()
    {
        HorizontalOptions = LayoutOptions.FillAndExpand
    };
```

```
        titleEntry.SetBinding(Entry.TextProperty, "Title");

        Content  = new StackLayout {
            Children = { titleEntry }
        };
    }
```

In the SetBinding call, the "Title" string parameter is used to create a Binding object.

BindingContext can be set at the page or view level. In most cases, the page-level property will suffice, but be certain to set BindingContext at the view level if you are using more than one source. In MVVM apps, a single source (the ViewModel) is typical. More on this in a moment.

Any value that you type into the Entry view is populated into the item.Title property because of the binding. Prove this by adding a button view with an event handler that shows the value of the item object, as shown in Listing 7-3.

Listing 7-3. Button Click Displays the Value of the Title Property

```
Button buttonDisplay = new Button
{
    Text = "Display Item Value",
    FontSize = Device.GetNamedSize(NamedSize.Large, typeof(Button)),
    HorizontalOptions = LayoutOptions.Center,
    VerticalOptions = LayoutOptions.Fill
};

buttonDisplay.Clicked += async (sender, args) =>
{
    await DisplayAlert("Item Object", "Title property:" +  item.Title.ToString(), "OK");
};
```

Remember to add the new button to StackLayout:

```
Content  = new StackLayout {
    Children = { titleEntry, buttonDisplay }
};
```

Fire up the app and you'll see your Entry view with data prepopulated (Figure 7-1).

Figure 7-1. *Trivial data binding populates the target with an initial source value*

Change the entry value to something else and click the button to see the data binding in action, as shown in Figure 7-2.

Figure 7-2. *The data-bound Entry view changes the Item property when edited*

The data model was automatically updated by the user's change to the Entry view's Text property.

The BindingContext used here is at the page level. This could just as easily have been set at the view level:

```
titleEntry.BindingContext = item;
```

On pages with multiple views that require separate bindings, set BindingContext at the view level.

■ **Tip**   If you want to see the limitations of trivial binding firsthand (not using INotifyPropertyChanged), put the following line of code into your button.Clicked event. When you click the button, you'll see that the UI is *not* updated by this change to the data model.

```
item.Title = "Trivial binding";
```

All of the previous examples are trivial data-binding examples; the data model and variables will reflect changes to the UI. In order for the UI to be refreshed from the data model, you will need to use the INotifyPropertyChanged interface to implement nontrivial data binding.

Using INotifyPropertyChanged

INotifyPropertyChanged is a .NET interface used to notify binding clients that a property value has changed. Use INotifyPropertyChanged when your data-bound UI must refresh to reflect changes to the data model in real time (above and beyond just displaying the initial data in the UI).

Here is the definition of the INotifyPropertyChanged interface:

```
public interface INotifyPropertyChanged
{
    event PropertyChangedEventHandler PropertyChanged;
}
```

Implement INotifyPropertyChanged in a view model (or ViewModel), a class built to serve data to a particular screen. The INotifyPropertyChanged interface is found in the System.ComponentModel namespace, and the CallerMemberName attribute resides in the System.Runtime.CompilerServices namespace, so remember to add them to your class:

```
using System.ComponentModel;
using System.Runtime.CompilerServices;
```

Implement INotifyPropertyChanged to create a simple view model with one property called Title, as shown in Listing 7-4. The Set accessor on the Title property invokes the OnPropertyChanged event to notify the UI of a data change so it can refresh.

Listing 7-4. INotifyPropertyChanged Implementation in a View Model in TitleViewModel.cs

```
public class TitleViewModel : INotifyPropertyChanged
{
    public event PropertyChangedEventHandler PropertyChanged;
    String title;

    public string Title
    {
        set
        {
            if (!value.Equals(title, StringComparison.Ordinal))
            {
                title = value;
                OnPropertyChanged("Title");
            }
        }
        get
        {
            return title;
        }
    }

    void OnPropertyChanged([CallerMemberName] string propertyName = null)
    {
        var handler = PropertyChanged;
```

```
                    if (handler != null)
                    {
                        handler(this, new PropertyChangedEventArgs(propertyName));
                    }
            }
      }
}
```

When the Title property is set, a call is made to the OnPropertyChanged event to fire, with the calling property passed in by the [CallerMemberName] attribute. The PropertyChangedEventHandler event is the Xamarin.Forms mechanism for notifying the view that is bound to that property to refresh and reflect the updated data model.

Note that this simplified approach does not use the Item data model. You'll do that soon.

Back in your ContentPage, update the binding:

```
var titleViewModel = new TitleViewModel();
titleViewModel.Title = "First";
this.BindingContext = titleViewModel;
```

Since the property name (Title) hasn't changed, SetBinding remains basically the same as the previous example. So you can see how the method is working, here I use an alternative overload of SetBinding, which takes a Binding object, new Binding("Title"), instead of just a "Title" string.

```
titleEntry.SetBinding(Entry.TextProperty, new Binding("Title"));
```

In your buttonDisplay.Clicked event, change the display property to titleViewModel.Title.

Add a button to modify the data model's property and demonstrate the nontrivial data binding:

```
Button buttonUpdate = new Button
{
    Text = "Update the Data Model",
    FontSize = Device.GetNamedSize(NamedSize.Large, typeof(Button)),
    HorizontalOptions = LayoutOptions.Center,
    VerticalOptions = LayoutOptions.Fill
};

buttonUpdate.Clicked += async (sender, args) =>
{
    titleViewModel.Title = "Data Model Updated";
    await DisplayAlert("Item Object", "Title property:" + titleViewModel.Title.
                       ToString(), "OK");
};
```

Remember to add the new button to StackLayout:

```
Content = new StackLayout
{
    Children = { titleEntry, buttonDisplay, buttonUpdate }
};
```

Figure 7-3 shows the updated `ContentPage`.

Figure 7-3. *ContentPage for nontrivial data binding*

Click `buttonUpdate` to change the `Title` property and see that change propagated back into the `Entry` view (Figure 7-4).

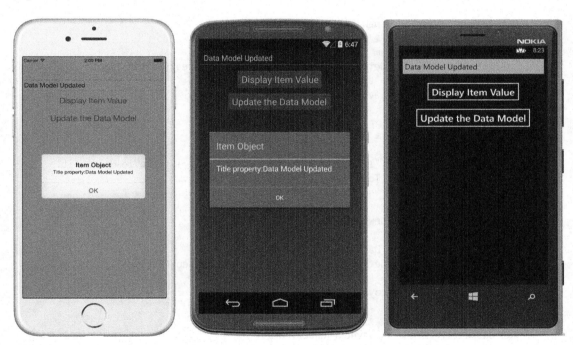

Figure 7-4. *The Entry view has refreshed to match the model.*

CODE COMPLETE: Using INotifyPropertyChanged

XAMARIN.FORMS

Listing 7-5 is the complete code for the `INotifyPropertyChanged` implementation against `TitleViewModel`.

■ **XAML**   All of the Xamarin.Forms data-binding code solutions in this chapter, including the XAML versions of these C# examples, can be found at Apress.com (from the Source Code/Downloads tab, access the title of this book) or on GitHub at `https://github.com/danhermes/xamarin-book-examples`. The Xamarin.Forms XAML folder for the data-binding samples in Chapter 7 is `DataBindingExamples.Xaml`.

Listing 7-5. ItemPageUsingTitleViewModel.cs

```
public ItemPageUsingTitleViewModel()
{
    var titleViewModel = new TitleViewModel();
    titleViewModel.Title = "First";
    this.BindingContext = titleViewModel;

    var titleEntry = new Entry()
    {
        HorizontalOptions = LayoutOptions.FillAndExpand
    };

    titleEntry.SetBinding(Entry.TextProperty, new Binding("Title"));

    Button buttonDisplay = new Button
    {
        Text = "Display Item Value",
        FontSize = Device.GetNamedSize(NamedSize.Large, typeof(Button)),
        HorizontalOptions = LayoutOptions.Center,
        VerticalOptions = LayoutOptions.Fill
    };

    buttonDisplay.Clicked += async (sender, args) =>
    {
        await DisplayAlert("Item Object", "Title property:" + titleViewModel.Title.
                           ToString(), "OK");
    };

    Button buttonUpdate = new Button
    {
        Text = "Update the Data Model",
        FontSize = Device.GetNamedSize(NamedSize.Large, typeof(Button)),
        HorizontalOptions = LayoutOptions.Center,
        VerticalOptions = LayoutOptions.Fill
    };

    buttonUpdate.Clicked += async (sender, args) =>
    {
        titleViewModel.Title = "Data Model Updated";
        await DisplayAlert("Item Object", "Title property:" + titleViewModel.Title.
                           ToString(), "OK");
    };

    Content = new StackLayout
    {
        Children = { titleEntry, buttonDisplay, buttonUpdate }
    };

}
```

■ **Tip** Avoid repeating boilerplate `PropertyChanged` code by creating a `BindableBase` class that implements `INotifyPropertyChanged`. Then you can subclass `BindableBase` in your models or view models to make them ready for nontrivial binding.

```
public abstract class BindableBase : INotifyPropertyChanged
{
    public event PropertyChangedEventHandler PropertyChanged;

    void OnPropertyChanged([CallerMemberName] string propertyName = null)
    {
        var handler = PropertyChanged;
        if (handler != null)
        {
            handler(this, new PropertyChangedEventArgs(propertyName));
        }
    }
}
```

With your implementation of `INotifyPropertyChanged`, your app can now notify the UI when data has changed, and Xamarin.Forms will refresh the UI. By creating a class that serves data to a particular view (`TitleViewModel`), you have just created a view model.

Understanding ViewModels and MVVM

A ViewModel (the VM in MVVM) is a class built to serve data to a particular screen by using one or more models (the M in MVVM, or data models). The ViewModel is decorated with view-specific properties and bound to the view (the V in MVVM, referring to the presentation layer, or UI, not to be confused with a Xamarin.Forms View class). A ViewModel is like a data model except that it is customized to a particular view (or screen) by using helper classes and handler events necessary to populate the data on that page or manage changes to the data model. In a traditional MVVM app, you create a view model for each view (screen), imbuing your view model with the constructors and helper methods needed to serve up and save data on each screen.

MVVM apps typically use data models (not just a few variables added as properties to a view model). This requires wrapping the data models within the view models with the notion that views should not use models directly but should interact only with view models.

Binding to ViewModels and Data Models

ViewModels can implement `INotifyPropertyChanged`, as discussed earlier, but data models can also implement `INotifyPropertyChanged`. These are the two standard approaches for implementing `INotifyPropertyChanged` for nontrivial data binding, in order of popularity. There are heated arguments for why one or the other is the only way to do things, but I'll show you both ways and let you decide. I'll also show a third way that avoids some of the problems of the other two:

- *Create a view model that implements INotifyPropertyChanged.* Inherit from `INotifyPropertyChanged` and encapsulate the necessary variables and data models within your view model class and, within each editable property Set accessor, raise the `OnPropertyChanged` event. This approach is strict MVVM.

- *Implement INotifyPropertyChanged in your data model.* Every time you use your model in a data-binding context, it will be ready for nontrivial binding and provide notifications to the bound UI via its OnPropertyChanged events.

- *Wrap your data model in an observable class.* More on this in a moment.

The first two approaches are functionally similar but architecturally different.

The first approach, creating a view model that implements INotifyPropertyChanged, means including an instance of the data model in the view model and wrapping the top-level model class as a property as well as all of the data model's properties that must be exposed in the view model. This gives complete control to the view for instantiating, assigning, and changing the encapsulated data model and all of its relevant properties. If the view model implements INotifyPropertyChanged, and OnPropertyChanged is called in the Set method of each public property, this class can provide nontrivial binding. (See Listing 7-6.)

The second approach to implementing INotifyPropertyChanged happens in your data model even before you use it in the view model. See Listing 7-7 for an example of implementing INotifyPropertyChanged in the Item class to create an observable collection of items. For MVVM apps, this approach still requires the extra step of embedding the resulting data model in a view model.

Some developers don't like the first approach because it can lead to code duplication with multiple INotifyPropertyChanged implementations of the same properties in different view models, and some developers don't like the second approach because it clutters up the data model.

A *third* approach avoids both of those problems, and that is to wrap your data model in a class that implements INotifyPropertyChanged to make it observable (at the cost of creating yet another subclass). This is done for us in .NET for classes such as ObservableCollection, and you'll do it in a moment for your Item model to create an ObservableItem. It's a little extra work but keeps your models clean. We'll get to the third approach in the section "Binding an Editable ListView," in Listing 7-10.

Here are examples of each of the first two approaches:

Create a ViewModel That Implements INotifyPropertyChanged

Implement INotifyPropertyChanged in your ViewModel by using an encapsulated data model for a straightforward MVVM approach.

Create a view model based on the Item data model, as shown in Listing 7-6. It's basically the same as the TitleViewModel view model in Listing 7-4 except that an Item class is instantiated and used to hold the Title property value instead of a string. (This is an architectural change, not a functional one.)

Listing 7-6. View Model Based on the Item Data Model (ItemViewModel.cs)

```
class ItemViewModel : INotifyPropertyChanged
{
    public event PropertyChangedEventHandler PropertyChanged;

    Item item;

    public ItemViewModel ()
    {
        item = new Item();
    }
```

```csharp
public string Title
{
    set
    {
        if (!value.Equals(item.Title, StringComparison.Ordinal))
        {
            item.Title = value;
            OnPropertyChanged("Title");
        }
    }
    get
    {
        return item.Title;
    }
}

void OnPropertyChanged([CallerMemberName] string propertyName = null)
{
    var handler = PropertyChanged;
    if (handler != null)
    {
        handler(this, new PropertyChangedEventArgs(propertyName));
    }
}
}
```

Note that you didn't wrap the Description property, since that was not needed by the view in this case. View models typically contain only what is needed by their view.

Implement the view model as before by using ItemViewModel:

```csharp
var itemViewModel = new ItemViewModel();
itemViewModel.Title = "First";
this.BindingContext = itemViewModel;
```

Even the Entry view is bound the same way:

```csharp
titleEntry.SetBinding(Entry.TextProperty, new Binding("Title"));
```

The rest of the ContentPage is the same as the previous example ItemPageUsingTitleViewModel, in Listing 7-5, with renaming to use itemViewModel instead of titleViewModel. See the downloadable code ItemPageUsingItemViewModel.cs for details.

The functionality of the app is exactly the same as the previous example except that instead of using the Title string variable, you're using the Item data model, which is a more real-world implementation (and MVVM).

Now for the second approach to INotifyPropertyChanged.

Implement INotifyPropertyChanged in Your Data Model

INotifyPropertyChanged can be implemented in your data model instead of in your view model. This data model can then be bound directly to the view, as in the following example, or you can include the data model in a view model in an MVVM app.

Create a class called ItemModel.cs, as shown in Listing 7-7. Implementing the OnPropertyChanged event and calling it in the Set method of each property, Title and Description, ensures that changes to the list data are reflected in the UI in real time.

Listing 7-7. Implementing INotifyPropertyChanged in a Data Model

```
class ItemBindable: INotifyPropertyChanged
{
    public event PropertyChangedEventHandler PropertyChanged;

    string title;
    string description;

    public string Title
    {
        set
        {
            if (!value.Equals(title, StringComparison.Ordinal))
            {
                title = value;
                OnPropertyChanged("Title");
            }
        }
        get
        {
            return title;
        }
    }

    public string Description
    {
        set
        {
            if (!value.Equals(description, StringComparison.Ordinal))
            {
                description = value;
                OnPropertyChanged("Description");
            }
        }
        get
        {
            return description;
        }
    }
```

```
    void OnPropertyChanged([CallerMemberName] string propertyName = null)
    {
        var handler = PropertyChanged;
        if (handler != null)
        {
            handler(this, new PropertyChangedEventArgs(propertyName));
        }
    }
}
```

This ItemBindable class can now be implemented to bind its properties to any view:

```
var itemBindable = new ItemBindable();
itemBindable.Title = "First";
this.BindingContext = itemBindable;
```

Use the Entry view binding once again with the Title property:

```
titleEntry.SetBinding(Entry.TextProperty, new Binding("Title"));
```

This direct use of the model in the view (which I've used to simplify the demonstration) is not consistent with the MVVM pattern, which encourages a separation between the model and the view. Include ItemBindable within a view model to utilize the MVVM pattern.

Those are some techniques for building view models and data models for nontrivial, two-way binding in Xamarin.Forms. Now let's explore data binding as it applies to lists.

Binding a Read-Only ListView

XAMARIN.FORMS

Binding to a ListView was covered extensively in Chapter 5, but we did only trivial, read-only binding. That means that the initial values of the data model are displayed in the list for viewing or selection, but no changes to the UI or model take place. Nontrivial, editable list binding means that the initial values of the data model are displayed in the list, and controls are provided to allow the user to add or delete rows or change row properties displayed in the list.

I'll begin with a review of trivial binding to a ListView before moving on to nontrivial binding.

In the ContentPage, instantiate and populate the data model as shown in Listing 7-8. Assigning the model to the list's ItemSource property is the equivalent of setting BindingContext. Use ItemTemplate.SetBinding to assign each field in a row.

Listing 7-8. Trivial, Read-Only ListView Binding from Chapter 5

```
class ListViewPage: ContentPage
{
    public ListViewPage()
    {
```

```
        var listView = new ListView();
        var items = new Item[] {
            new Item {Title = "First", Description="1st item"},
            new Item {Title = "Second", Description="2nd item"},
            new Item {Title = "Third", Description="3rd item"}

        };
        listView.ItemsSource = items;
        listView.ItemTemplate = new DataTemplate(typeof(TextCell));
        listView.ItemTemplate.SetBinding(TextCell.TextProperty, "Title");
        listView.ItemTemplate.SetBinding(TextCell.DetailProperty, "Description");

        listView.ItemTapped += async (sender, e) =>

        {
            Item item = (Item)e.Item;
            await DisplayAlert("Tapped", item.Title.ToString() + " was selected.", "OK");
            ((ListView)sender).SelectedItem = null;

        };

        this.Padding = new Thickness(0, Device.OnPlatform(20, 0, 0), 0, 0);

        Content = listView;

    }

}
```

This approach works well for read-only, selectable lists (and can even be extended to include editing of data model properties in the list UI, such as Entry views, though that is beyond the scope of this book). If you want to read more about building and customizing read-only lists by using Xamarin.Forms, turn to the beginning of Chapter 5.

If your list needs to change dynamically, with rows added or deleted or properties changed in real time in the code, then nontrivial data binding may be required.

Binding an Editable ListView

XAMARIN.FORMS

The standard ways that a user can edit a list are to add or delete list rows, or modify properties of list rows. These types of list edits require nontrivial data binding, when list rows are added or deleted from an array or collection, or when changes to list properties take place in code. We need those data model changes to be reflected in the UI.

Nontrivial list binding requires the implementation of an INotify interface to notify the UI to refresh when changes to the model take place. There are two ways to do this: using a manual implementation of INotifyPropertyChanged or using an ObservableCollection. ObservableCollection *already* implements the INotifyCollectionChanged interface. Which approach you use (either or both) should depend on the types of changes to the list that you want to reflect in the list UI.

Here are the two main list-editing scenarios and a standard way to handle them:

- *Adding and deleting rows*: Use an ObservableCollection as the list data source.

- *Editing properties in the ListView*: Create a view model implementing INotifyPropertyChanged that exposes the editable properties in the list data model (such as Title).

■ **Tip** If you need to replace the entire list, you'll likely need to rebind the list by reassigning ItemsSource to get the UI to refresh.

Let's begin with adding and deleting rows.

Adding and Deleting Rows

XAMARIN.FORMS

Nontrivial data binding while adding and deleting rows from ListView can be handled using ObservableCollection, which has a built-in implementation of INotifyCollectionChanged. A ListView bound to an ObservableCollection will automatically install a handler for the CollectionChanged event.

Using ObservableCollection as the bound data type for ListItem ensures that changes to the list rows are reflected in the UI in real time.

Create and populate ObservableCollection, as shown in Listing 7-9. Set the ItemsSource property of ListView to the collection.

Listing 7-9. List Binding Using an ObservableCollection (ListObservablePage.cs)

```
var items = new ObservableCollection<Item> {

    new Item {Title = "First", Description="1st item"},
    new Item {Title = "Second", Description="2nd item"},
    new Item {Title = "Third", Description="3rd item"}
};
listView.ItemsSource = items;
```

The ListView's ItemTemplate implementation is the same as in the previous example in Listing 7-8:

```
listView.ItemTemplate = new DataTemplate(typeof(TextCell));
listView.ItemTemplate.SetBinding(TextCell.TextProperty, "Title");
listView.ItemTemplate.SetBinding(TextCell.DetailProperty, "Description");
```

The complete code can be found in the downloadable code file ListObservablePage.cs.

Test this approach by adding a button that adds or deletes rows in the ObservableCollection called items, and you'll see your model changes reflected immediately in the list UI.

```
items.RemoveAt(0);
```

Upon execution of our `RemoveAt` method, the first list row is immediately deleted in the UI, as shown in Figure 7-5. Note that without an `items.Count > 0` check, our simple demo code can break with multiple deletes.

Figure 7-5. *The deleted first item disappears from the list*

This approach does not use a view model, so it is not an MVVM implementation. We'll get serious about MVVM for editable lists soon.

■ **Tip**   Adding and deleting list rows by using `ObservableCollection` works especially well with context actions, the Xamarin.Forms approach for providing a Delete and/or More button on each list row. Turn to Chapter 5 for more on context actions.

An `ObservableCollection` tracks only the addition or removal of rows. Reflecting changes to properties within those rows is another matter.

Editing Properties

XAMARIN.FORMS

Editing list properties in code and reflecting those changes in the list UI can be handled in any of the three ways discussed earlier, binding the list to one of the following:

- Create a view model that implements `INotifyPropertyChanged`.
- Implement `INotifyPropertyChanged` in your data model.
- Wrap your data model in a class that implements `INotifyPropertyChanged`.

The first approach is a popular choice, but since you already saw that earlier in Listing 7-6, and the second approach in Listing 7-7, here you'll use the third approach: wrapping your data model in an observable item class using `INotifyPropertyChanged`. Then bind this observable class to your list (directly or via a view model).

Create a class called `ObservableItem.cs`, as shown in Listing 7-10. Implementing the `OnPropertyChanged` event and calling it in the `Set` method of `ListItems` ensures that changes to the list data are reflected in the UI in real time. Note that this class alone isn't MVVM unless you encapsulate it in a view model, which you'll do in a moment.

Listing 7-10. Wrap Your Data Model in an Observable Class (ObservableItem.cs)

```csharp
class ObservableItem: INotifyPropertyChanged
{
    public event PropertyChangedEventHandler PropertyChanged;
    Item item;

    public ObservableItem()
    {
        item = new Item();
    }

    public string Title
    {
        set
        {
            if (!value.Equals(item.Title, StringComparison.Ordinal))
            {
                item.Title = value;
                OnPropertyChanged("Title");
            }
        }
        get
        {
            return item.Title;
        }
    }

    public string Description
    {
        set
        {
            if (!value.Equals(item.Description, StringComparison.Ordinal))
            {
                item.Description = value;
                OnPropertyChanged("Description");
            }
        }
        get
        {
            return item.Description;
        }
    }

    void OnPropertyChanged([CallerMemberName] string propertyName = null)
    {
        var handler = PropertyChanged;
        if (handler != null)
        {
            handler(this, new PropertyChangedEventArgs(propertyName));
        }
    }
}
```

This ObservableItem class can now be implemented to create a nontrivial data-bound list:

```
var items = new List<ObservableItem> {
    new ObservableItem {Title = "First", Description="1st item"},
    new ObservableItem {Title = "Second", Description="2nd item"},
    new ObservableItem {Title = "Third", Description="3rd item"}

};
listView.ItemsSource = items;
```

The ListView's ItemTemplate implementation is the same as in the (two) previous examples covered in Listing 7-8:

```
listView.ItemTemplate = new DataTemplate(typeof(TextCell));
listView.ItemTemplate.SetBinding(TextCell.TextProperty, "Title");
listView.ItemTemplate.SetBinding(TextCell.DetailProperty, "Description");
```

See the downloadable file ListPropertiesPage.cs for the complete ListView code listing.

Changes to any of the properties in code will be reflected in the list UI in real time. You can see this for yourself by creating a button or context action that edits a property in the items list—the Title, for example:

```
items[0].Title = "First Edited";
```

Upon execution of this statement, the first list row is immediately updated in the UI, as shown in Figure 7-6.

Figure 7-6. *The first row is edited in code, and the UI is refreshed automatically*

■ **Note**   If editable views in your list rows, such as Entry views, are bound to properties in your data model, then trivial data binding described earlier may be sufficient, and this INotifyPropertyChanged approach may not be needed.

Binding List<ObservableItem> directly to the list didn't use a view model either, so it's not MVVM.

Next you will see how to use the observable item class in tandem with the observable collection to create a view model for an editable list.

Binding to a View Model

XAMARIN.FORMS

Building MVVM apps requires the use of view models. When using MVVM, it's an antipattern to implement data models directly in your view. You'll need to create a view model and wrap your data models inside it to bind to your editable list.

Create a ListViewModel class that includes all the features in the previous list-binding examples. The Items property is an ObservableCollection, so the UI can reflect rows that are added or deleted, and the base item class is ObservableItem, so property changes can also be reflected in the list UI. See Listing 7-11.

■ **Note** Listing 7-11 is an unusual example of a view model, as there is no explicit implementation of INotifyPropertyChanged. INotifyPropertyChanged was already implemented in all the encapsulated models: ObservableCollection and ObservableItem. Additional implementation of INotifyPropertyChanged in this view model would be redundant or extraneous.

Listing 7-11. ListViewModel for an Editable List in ListViewModel.cs

```
class ListViewModel
{
    ObservableCollection<ObservableItem> items;

    public ListViewModel()
    {
        items = new ObservableCollection<ObservableItem> {
        new ObservableItem {Title = "First", Description="1st item"},
        new ObservableItem {Title = "Second", Description="2nd item"},
        new ObservableItem {Title = "Third", Description="3rd item"}
        };
    }

    public ObservableCollection<ObservableItem> Items
    {
        set
        {
            if ( value != items)
            {
                items = value;
            }
        }
        get
        {
            return items;
        }
    }
}
```

Bind the Items property in your view model to your list source:

```
var items = new ListViewModel();
listView.ItemsSource = items.Items;
```

The ListView's ItemTemplate implementation is the same as in previous examples and shown in Listing 7-8:

```
listView.ItemTemplate = new DataTemplate(typeof(TextCell));
listView.ItemTemplate.SetBinding(TextCell.TextProperty, "Title");
listView.ItemTemplate.SetBinding(TextCell.DetailProperty, "Description");
```

And *that* is a nontrivial, fully editable list using MVVM. Add and delete rows from the list, edit properties in code, and all will be reflected in the list UI in real time.

Create a ContentPage demo app that includes row editing, property editing, and replacing the entire list. Bind it to your ListViewModel. Figure 7-7 shows how this listing data-binding demo app might look.

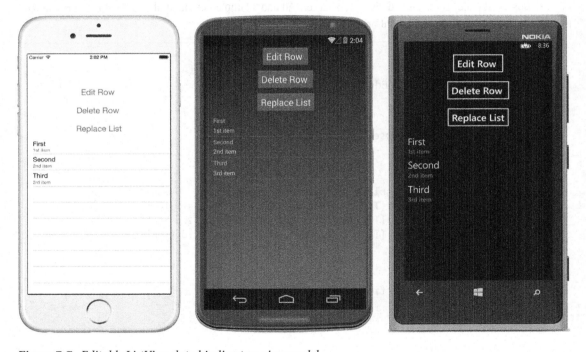

Figure 7-7. *Editable ListView data binding to a view model*

This basic example of editable list binding is for demo purposes only. For a professional-looking UI, consider using context actions, the Xamarin.Forms approach to providing a Delete and/or More button on each list row. Turn to Chapter 5 for more on context actions.

See the ContentPage for this example, called ListPageUsingListViewModel.cs, in Listing 7-12.

■ **Tip** Replacing the entire list requires the list to be rebound (this example is a `Replace` method in the ListViewModel).

```
public void Replace()
{
    Items = new ObservableCollection<ObservableItem> {
        new ObservableItem {Title = "Primero", Description="First"},
        new ObservableItem {Title = "Segundo", Description="Second"},
        new ObservableItem {Title = "Tercero", Description="Third"}
    };
}
```

CODE COMPLETE: Binding an Editable ListView

XAMARIN.FORMS

Listing 7-12 shows the complete `ContentPage` that binds to the view model `ListViewModel` in Listing 7-11. This demonstrates row editing, property editing, and replacing the entire list.

Listing 7-12. ListPageUsingListViewModel.cs

```
public ListPageUsingListViewModel()
{
    var listView = new ListView();

    var items = new ListViewModel();
    listView.ItemsSource = items.Items;

    listView.ItemTemplate = new DataTemplate(typeof(TextCell));
    listView.ItemTemplate.SetBinding(TextCell.TextProperty, "Title");
    listView.ItemTemplate.SetBinding(TextCell.DetailProperty, "Description");

    listView.ItemTapped += async (sender, e) =>
    {
        ObservableItem item = (ObservableItem)e.Item;
        await DisplayAlert("Tapped", item.Title.ToString() + " was selected.", "OK");
        ((ListView)sender).SelectedItem = null;
    };

    Button buttonEdit = new Button
    {
        Text = "Edit Row ",
        FontSize = Device.GetNamedSize(NamedSize.Large, typeof(Button)),
        HorizontalOptions = LayoutOptions.Center,
        VerticalOptions = LayoutOptions.Fill
    };

    buttonEdit.Clicked += async (sender, args) =>
    {
        items.Items[0].Title = "First Edited";
        await DisplayAlert("Edited", "First row edited", "OK");
    };
```

```
    Button buttonDelete = new Button
    {
        Text = "Delete Row ",
        FontSize = Device.GetNamedSize(NamedSize.Large, typeof(Button)),
        HorizontalOptions = LayoutOptions.Center,
        VerticalOptions = LayoutOptions.Fill
    };

    buttonDelete.Clicked += async (sender, args) =>
    {
        items.Items.RemoveAt(0);
        await DisplayAlert("Delete", "Row deleted", "OK");
    };

    Button buttonReplace= new Button
    {
        Text = "Replace List",
        FontSize = Device.GetNamedSize(NamedSize.Large, typeof(Button)),
        HorizontalOptions = LayoutOptions.Center,
        VerticalOptions = LayoutOptions.Fill
    };

    buttonReplace.Clicked += async (sender, args) =>
    {
        items.Replace();    // see previous Tip
        await DisplayAlert("Replace", "List replaced con Español", "OK");
        listView.ItemsSource = items.Items;
    };

    Content = new StackLayout
    {
        Children = { buttonEdit, buttonDelete, buttonReplace, listView }
    };

    this.Padding = new Thickness(0, Device.OnPlatform(20, 0, 0), 0, 0);

}
```

buttonReplace invokes Replace(), a method added to ListViewModel and not shown here. Replace() is shown in the previous tip, is viewable in the downloadable code ListViewModel.cs, and replaces the list with Spanish rows before the list must be rebound to reflect the changes.

Views can also be bound to other views.

Binding a View to Another View

XAMARIN.FORMS

The focus of this book is data-driven applications, which means binding views to models and view models. However, views can be bound to one another. A slider can be bound to a label. A switch can be bound to an entry view, and so forth.

The target of a data binding must be backed by a `BindableProperty` object, and most Xamarin.Forms views have many properties that fit this requirement. Explore the Xamarin API documentation to learn about these. Many view properties are also bindable as sources.

Single views are easily bound, as each view must have one `BindingContext`. Multiple views require mapping using the `BindingModes: OneWayToSource` and `TwoWay`, which are beyond the scope of this book. Refer to the Xamarin online docs for details.

Although data binding is platform-specific, database access is truly cross-platform in Xamarin development. Using SQLite is basically the same regardless of what platform you're developing for.

Using SQLite.NET

CROSS PLATFORM

Data models are often populated from and synchronized with a local database. SQLite.NET is the mobile, cross-platform database library of choice for many Xamarin developers using Xamarin.Forms, Xamarin.Android, or Xamarin.iOS.

Xamarin.Forms is used in the UI portion of the following SQLite.NET examples for the sake of demonstration, but these techniques can be used equally well in Xamarin.Android and Xamarin.iOS apps. SQLite.NET is a cross-platform technology.

How you install SQLite.NET in your solution depends on the solution type. A PCL setup differs from a shared project setup:

> *PCL Setup*: The best option for using SQLite.NET with PCLs is the NuGet package called SQLite.NET PCL. There are a few of these with similar names, so be certain to use the package with these attributes:
>
> - Name: SQLite-Net PCL
> - Created by: Frank A. Krueger
> - ID: sqlite-net-pcl
> - NuGet link: sqlite-net-pcl
>
> *Install SQLite*-Net PCL in the projects where you'll need it, usually most if not all of them in your solution. Do not manually add the `SQLite.cs` file to your project(s). See the downloadable code solution `SQLiteNetPCL`.
>
> *Shared project setup*: Add a file to your shared project called `SQLite.cs` from the sqlite-net GitHub project by downloading it and then clicking your application solution and selecting Add File. See the downloadable code solution `SQLiteNETSharedProject`.

Many of the SQLite.NET examples in this section use a PCL because it's clearer in a demonstration, but I'll cover shared projects too. PCL and shared project SQLite.NET implementations are similar except for how they handle platform-specific implementations of the database path and connection. More about that in the section "Building the Database Path."

Now that you have SQLite.NET installed in your solution, reference the library in your data access layer classes with a `using` statement:

```
using SQLite;
```

Constructing a data access layer using SQLite.NET requires the creation of a database connection, a locking object, and CRUD transaction methods (get, insert, update, and delete) that are specific to your table data.

■ **Important Note**   Inserting, getting, updating, and deleting rows should be done using locks in order to avoid conflicts. The following examples exclude the lock for simplicity until the section "Locking Rows." Review the code with locks in Listing 7-19 or Listing 7-22.

Installing SQLite on Windows Phone
WINDOWS PHONE

The SQLite database engine ships with iOS and Android but not with Windows Phone, so you must ship it with your own app. Download the Precompiled Binaries for Windows Phone 8 (`sqlite-wp80-winrt-xxxxxx.vsix`) from sqlite.org. Install this Visual Studio extension and restart Visual Studio. Add this reference to your project: the Windows Phone Extension called SQLite for Windows Phone.

Now that SQLite.NET is installed, let's create a SQLite database.

Creating a Database

Create a new SQLite database by establishing a database connection to a database filename that includes the folder path. You can open a SQLite connection and use it throughout your app without closing it.

First locate the folder that the database should go into and create the database folder path:

```
string folder = Environment.GetFolderPath (Environment.SpecialFolder.Personal);
databasePath = Path.Combine(documents, "ItemsSQLite.db3");
```

Create a database connection by specifying the database path and name:

```
var database = new SQLite.SQLiteConnection(databasePath);
```

No check is needed to see if the file already exists. It will be created if it does not yet exist; otherwise, it will simply be opened.

■ **Tip**   Avoid using a single connection on different threads. Using locks helps avoid conflicts, as described in the section "Locking Rows."

In real apps, building database paths is often the only platform-specific code in the data access layer.

Building the Database Path

The database path is typically platform-specific, requiring an implementation for each platform to retrieve it.

The implementation of the database path and database connection is the primary difference between the PCL approach and shared project approach to building a data access layer. In PCLs, use dependency Injection (DI) to create platform-specific implementations of the database path and connection. In shared projects, create the database path by using *conditional compilation*, which is a way to implement platform-specific code at compile-time.

■ **Tip** For more detail on cross-platform architecture approaches such as conditional compilation and DI, see Chapter 9.

Let's begin with the shared projects database connection implementation before moving on to PCLs.

Connect by Using Shared Projects

The trick with SQLite database connections in Xamarin apps is that the database path is usually platform-specific. For example, iOS iCloud requirements specify that files not created by the user should not reside in the personal documents folder, but can reside in a subfolder such as /Library.

In a shared project, use conditional compilation as in Listing 7-13 to specify platform-specific folders.

Listing 7-13. Database Path in a Shared Project

```
string databasePath {
    get {
        var dbName = "ItemsSQLite.db3";
        #if __IOS__
        string folder = Environment.GetFolderPath (Environment.SpecialFolder.Personal);
        folder = Path.Combine (folder, "..", "Library");
        var databasePath = Path.Combine(folder, dbName);
        #else
        #if __ANDROID__
        string folder = Environment.GetFolderPath (Environment.SpecialFolder.Personal);
        var databasePath = Path.Combine(folder, dbName);
        #else
        // WinPhone
        var databasePath = Path.Combine(Windows.Storage.ApplicationData.Current.
         LocalFolder.Path, dbName);;
        #endif
        #endif

        return databasePath;
    }
}
```

■ **Tip** Shared projects can't have references added to them, so you'll need to add the SQLite.cs code from GitHub.

Connect by Using Portable Class Libraries

In a PCL, acquiring a connection to your SQLite database will require dependency injection (DI), which can be done using the Xamarin.Forms DependencyService.

In the Xamarin.Forms project, create an interface for platform-specific database functionality called IDatabase containing a connection method, DBConnect:

```
public interface IDatabase {
    SQLiteConnection DBConnect();
}
```

To connect to the SQLite database, call out to the connection method, DBConnect, using DependencyService:

```
database = DependencyService.Get< IDatabase > ().DBConnect ();
```

The rest of the examples in this section on SQLite will use this database connection type in a PCL.

Next you need to implement the IDatabase interface on each platform.

■ **Tip** PCLs require a special SQLite.NET NuGet library installed called SQLite-NET PCL that was created by Frank A. Krueger with an ID of sqlite-net-pcl. Do *not* manually add the SQLite.cs file to your project(s).

Connect in Android

Create a database path for Android in the Android project by implementing the IDatabase interface in a class called Database_ Android (Listing 7-14). Begin the class with an [assembly] attribute declaring the class as a dependency injection for use in a DependencyService back in the PCL project. Set the folder name to System.Environment.GetFolderPath (System.Environment.SpecialFolder.Personal).

Listing 7-14. Database Path in the Android Project of a PCL Solution

```
[assembly: Dependency(typeof(Database_Android))]
namespace SQLiteNetPCL.Android
{
    public class Database_Android : IDatabase
    {
        public Database_Android() { }
        public SQLiteConnection DBConnect()
        {
            var filename = "ItemsSQLite.db3";
            string folder =
                System.Environment.GetFolderPath(System.Environment.SpecialFolder.Personal);
            var path = Path.Combine(folder, filename);
            var connection = new SQLiteConnection(path);
            return connection;
        }
    }
}
```

Connect in iOS

Create a database path for iOS in the iOS project by implementing the IDatabase interface in a class called Database_iOS (Listing 7-15). Meet iCloud requirements of not placing files directly in the user's personal folder by finding the user's /Library folder. Start with the user's personal folder at System.Environment. GetFolderPath (System.Environment.SpecialFolder.Personal) and locate /Library.

Listing 7-15. Database Path in the iOS Project of a PCL Solution

```
[assembly: Dependency(typeof(Database_iOS))]
namespace SQLiteNetPCL.iOS
{
    public class Database_iOS : IDatabase
    {
        public Database_iOS() { }
        public SQLiteConnection DBConnect()
        {
            var filename = "ItemsSQLite.db3";
            string folder =
                Environment.GetFolderPath (Environment.SpecialFolder.Personal);
            string libraryFolder = Path.Combine (folder, "..", "Library");
            var path = Path.Combine(libraryFolder, filename);
            var connection = new SQLiteConnection(path);
            return connection;
        }
    }
}
```

Now for the Windows Phone implementation of IDatabase.

Connect in Windows Phone

Create a database path for Windows Phone in the Windows Phone project by implementing the IDatabase interface in a class called Database_ WinPhone (Listing 7-16). Set the folder name to ApplicationData. Current.LocalFolder.Path.

Listing 7-16. Database Path in the Windows Phone Project of a PCL Solution

```
[assembly: Dependency(typeof(Database_WinPhone))]
namespace SQLiteNetPCL.WinPhone
{
    public class Database_WinPhone : IDatabase
    {
        public Database_WinPhone () { }
        public SQLiteConnection DBConnect()
        {
            var filename = "ItemsSQLite.db3";
            string folder =
                ApplicationData.Current.LocalFolder.Path;
            var path = Path.Combine(folder, filename);
```

```
                    var connection = new SQLiteConnection(path);
                    return connection;
                }
            }
        }
```

Once you get your implementations of IDatabase wired up correctly, your call to retrieve the SQLite database connection will work: DependencyService.Get< IDatabase > ().DBConnect (). If you're running into difficulty, check your references and using statements. Platform-specific solutions need to reference the PCL project containing your data access layer, and using statements (or direct namespace references) are needed when referring to those libraries. Once in a while, Visual Studio appears to fail when adding new libraries, and it's then helpful to close and reopen the solution.

The rest of this chapter uses a PCL instead of a shared project, for simplicity of demonstration only, but the code is basically the same between these approaches except for the database path and initial connection. If you want to understand the basic differences in a SQLite.NET implementation between PCL and shared project, refer back to the section "Building the Database Path."

Once the connection to your SQLite database is made, you can add tables to our new database and start inserting, getting, updating, and deleting rows.

Creating a Table

Create a new table in a database by defining the table in a data model and then using the database's CreateTable method. Use attributes such as [PrimaryKey, AutoIncrement] to specify keys, max lengths, and other properties of the table and its fields (Listing 7-17).

Define the Item data model. Using the PrimaryKey and AutoIncrement attributes, specify an integer primary key to help facilitate queries. Unless specified otherwise (using attributes), SQLite will use the class name as the table name and the property names as column names.

Listing 7-17. Table Class Declaration Using SQLite Attributes (Item.cs)

```
public class Item {
    [PrimaryKey, AutoIncrement]
    public int ID { get; set; }
    [MaxLength(15)]
    public string Name { get; set; }
    [MaxLength(50)]
    public string Description { get; set; }
}
```

Create the table by using the CreateTable method:

```
database.CreateTable<Item>();
```

The table now exists and is ready for rows to be inserted. CreateTable won't overwrite an existing table (use DropTable to drop a table).

The bracketed attributes tell SQLite.NET how to regard the properties in the data model in relation to the database table.

Using Attributes

The following commonly used attributes for SQLite data models help you define the table in the database:

- [Primary Key]: Specifies the table's primary key when applied to an integer property (no composite keys).

- [AutoIncrement]: Automatically increments an integer property when each object is inserted into the database.

- [Column(name)]: Specifies the column name. Useful for when it should differ from the property name.

- [Table(name)]: Specifies the table name. Useful for when it should differ from the data model class name.

- [Ignore]: SQLite.NET will disregard this property. Useful for properties that cannot be stored in the database.

- [MaxLength(value)]:Limit the size of a text field on inserts and updates by rejecting longer text objects. Remember to validate the length before committing text to this field.

Once the table is created and fields defined, you can add data to the database.

Inserting and Deleting Rows

Insert a new row into a table by populating the data model and then calling the Insert method.

Populate the Item data model with data:

```
var item = new Item { Name = "First" , Description = "This is the first item"};
```

Call the database connection's Insert method to attempt to add a row to the table:

```
database.Insert (item);
```

Delete rows by using the Delete method:

```
database.Delete<Item>(id);
```

■ **Tip** SQLite supports transactions using the SQLiteTransaction object with the BeginTransaction, Commit, and Rollback methods.

Getting Rows

Retrieve rows from a table by using the Get, Table, or Query methods. Get returns a single row, Table returns the entire table, and Query returns multiple rows using SQL.

Pass the integer key ID into the Get method to return a row from the Item table:

```
var item = database.Get<Item>(1);
```

Return the entire table by using the Table method:

```
var itemList = database.Table<Item>();
```

Use SQL to filter the table's contents by using the Query method:

```
var firstItem = database.Query<Item>("SELECT * FROM Item WHERE Name = 'First' ");
```

Use LINQ to filter the table's contents:

```
var firstItem = from i in database.Table<Item>()
    where i.Name == "First"
    select i;
```

Or to specify parameters in the FirstOrDefault method to filter:

```
var itemList = database.Table<Item>().FirstOrDefault(x => x.ID == id);
```

Updating Rows

Update rows in the table by using the Update method. This changes data on an existing row.

First populate the Item data model with data:

```
var item = new Item { Name = "First" , Description = "This is the first item"};
```

Call the Update method to populate the new data in the existing row:

```
database.Update(item);
```

Check whether the ID exists so you know whether you should update or insert a new row:

```
if (item.ID != 0) {
    database.Update(item);
    return item.ID;
} else {
    return database.Insert(item);
}
```

If you're not sure that the row exists, use a combination Insert/Update. The Insert method will return a nonzero value if it fails, allowing the Update to proceed.

```
if (database.Insert(item) != 0)
    database.Update(item);
```

Locking Rows

To avoid database collisions, all transactions should be locked. Use the lock keyword against a static object.

Here's a locking example using the Delete method:

```
static object locker = new object ();
lock (locker) {
    database.Delete<Item>(id);
}
```

To avoid a deadlock, do not lock a method that calls another method that creates a lock.

Those are all the basic techniques you need to use the SQLite.NET ORM! Now you're ready to build a data access layer (DAL) for your app by using these techniques. Since it's not good architectural form to use SQLite.NET inside your UI layer, you can encapsulate SQLite.NET calls in the repository pattern to create a more elegant and decoupled architecture.

Creating the Data Access Layer

The *data access layer* (DAL) is an industry-standard architecture for data access in a C# app. This group of classes encapsulates the data layer, and includes the database connection, the database path, and the CRUD transactions, exposing data access methods that reflect the specific data in a particular app (for example, GetItem, SaveItem methods). Depending on the level of architectural rigor, the data access layer can offer a simple group of loosely arrayed access classes and methods to a highly structured and decoupled layer with limited access points (which often uses the repository pattern). This approach decouples the data layer implementation from the business and presentation layer of your app.

■ **Note** Create, read, update, and delete (CRUD) transactions running against a local database typically make up the foundation of mobile application data. Some apps don't require local database access and run entirely using web services, but I'm not covering those in this book.

Creating a Repository

At the heart of many enterprise-grade Xamarin data access layers is an implementation of the repository pattern. This abstraction placed between the business layer and the data layer (the SQLite.NET ORM) provides app-specific CRUD methods using object collections, without exposing details of data source implementations (databases, XML, JSON, flat files, and so forth). Use this pattern to abstract away the details of SQLite implementation, including locking. Later you can couple your repository with the singleton pattern to maintain the database connection.

■ **Note** The definition of the repository pattern has evolved since its inception. It was originally intended as an abstraction to decouple the data layer implementation (for example, SQLite) from the rest of the app with the added benefit of providing in-memory data-object collections. Over the years, many C# apps needed the decoupling but not the in-memory data objects, so those collections have evolved to become data objects returned by methods in many cases, not kept in repository properties. This is true in most Xamarin apps as well.

Create table-specific data access methods (GetItems, SaveItem, and so forth) that encapsulate and employ the generalized SQLite CRUD methods described earlier (Get, Insert, Update, and so forth.):

```
public IEnumerable<Item> GetItems ()
public IEnumerable<Item> GetFirstItems ()
public Item GetItem(int id)
public int SaveItem(Item item)
public int DeleteItem(int id)
public void DeleteAllItems()
```

Make methods that are specific to the kind of data you're using, the Item table in this case. Avoid generic methods like Get and Insert and instead employ data-specific methods like GetItem and InsertItem (generic-sounding but specific to your Item table). There is a place for generic repository components, and we'll get to that soon.

A basic repository that represents a single database with a single table will typically look like the class outline in Listing 7-18.

Listing 7-18. Repository Class Outline (ItemDatabaseBasic.cs)

```
Public Class ItemDatabaseBasic
    {
        protected static object locker = new object ();
        protected SQLiteConnection database;

        public ItemDatabaseBasic()
        {
            database = DependencyService.Get<IDatabase>().DBConnect();
            database.CreateTable<Item>();
        }

        public IEnumerable<Item> GetItems () { ... }
        public IEnumerable<Item> GetFirstItems () { ... }
        public Item GetItem(int id) { ... }
        public int SaveItem(Item item) { ... }
        public int DeleteItem(int id) { ... }
        public void DeleteAllItems() { ... }

    }
```

Create a Portable Class Library (PCL) solution for this example called SQLiteNetPCL. See the earlier section "Connect by Using Portable Class Libraries" for implementations of DBConnect() and IDatabase.

■ **Tip** If you want to create a repository using a shared project, virtually everything is identical to what you would do with a PCL except the initial connection. For details on shared project implementations, see the earlier section "Connect by Using Portable Class Libraries," and the downloadable solution example SQLiteNETSharedProject.

Listing 7-19 shows the full code for this basic repository based on the outline in Listing 7-18. Create a static locker object that is used within the data access methods for avoiding concurrency issues on different threads, as discussed earlier. Encapsulate the SQLiteConnection object and instantiate it in the constructor. The databasePath is created using the method described earlier in "Connect by Using Portable Class Libraries."

Listing 7-19. Single-Table Repository in ItemDatabaseBasic.cs

```csharp
public class ItemDatabaseBasic
{
    protected static object locker = new object ();
    protected SQLiteConnection database;

    public ItemDatabaseBasic()
    {
        database = DependencyService.Get<IDatabase>().DBConnect();
        database.CreateTable<Item>();
    }

    public IEnumerable<Item> GetItems ()
    {
        lock (locker) {
            return (from i in database.Table<Item>() select i).ToList();
        }
    }

    public IEnumerable<Item> GetFirstItems ()
    {
        lock (locker) {
            return database.Query<Item>("SELECT * FROM Item WHERE Name = 'First'");
        }
    }

    public Item GetItem(int id)
    {
        lock (locker) {
            return database.Table<Item>().FirstOrDefault(x => x.ID == id);
        }
    }

    public int SaveItem(Item item)
    {
        lock (locker) {
            if (item.ID != 0) {
                database.Update(item);
                return item.ID;
            } else {
                return database.Insert(item);
            }
        }
    }

    public int DeleteItem(int id)
    {
        lock (locker) {
            return database.Delete<Item>(id);
        }
    }
```

```
        public void DeleteAllItems()
        {
            lock (locker) {
                database.DropTable<Item>();
                database.CreateTable<Item>();
            }
        }
    }
}
```

■ **Important Tip**   This basic repository works for only a single table: Item. You can access additional tables either by adding more methods to this repository or by refactoring the class using generics, both of which you'll do in a moment in the section "Adding Methods to the Repository."

Let's get back to the database connection.

Managing the Repository

In Xamarin apps using SQLite, the database connection is often kept in memory so it can be reused throughout the user session. Because static classes remain in memory, they are a likely candidate for helping to build a repository and store the connection. You can also open and close the connection for each transaction, but because SQLite is a serverless database, there is less of a need, and keeping a single connection open is common practice.

The connection is typically handled in one of two ways, either encapsulated in the repository, or passed in as a parameter. In these examples, the SQLite database connection is encapsulated in the repository. (You may want to move the connection out of the repository and pass it in as a parameter if you wish to have more control over the connection instance, for testability, for instance.) Since the connection resides in our repository in this example, we need to keep the repository in memory.

A common location to maintain a repository is in a static property on the Application class, as shown in Listing 7-20. The following code references the earlier ItemDatabaseBasic repository in Listing 7-19.

Listing 7-20. Static Database Property Declared in the Application Object

```
    public class App : Application
    {

        static ItemDatabaseBasic database;

        public static ItemDatabaseBasic Database {
            get {
                if (database == null) {
                    database = new ItemDatabaseBasic ();
                }
                return database;
            }
        }
        ...
    }
```

Use this self-instantiating repository by referring to it via the `Application` object:

```
App.Database.SaveItem (item);
```

The `ContentPage` UI is found in downloadable code files `App.cs` and `DataAccessPageDatabase.cs`.

Often, you have to access more than one table in your database, or you have multiple data sources, such as files, XML, JSON, or multiple databases. These situations warrant a more advanced repository approach.

Adding Methods to the Repository

Accessing multiple tables or multiple data sources requires some thinking about how the DAL architecture should grow to accommodate that. Here are the two common options for multisource repositories:

- Add data access methods directly to your repository class.

- Refactor your repository into a repository class and a generic database access class.

The first option is quick and dirty, whereas the second option is more suitable for enterprise-grade business apps. Let's look at each option.

Add data access methods directly to your repository class. If you want to access a new table, a `Person` table, for example, you need to create `GetPerson` and `SavePerson` methods somewhere. You could just add these methods to your repository.

```
public Person GetPerson (int id) { ... }
public IEnumerable<Person> GetPeople () { ... }
public int SavePerson(Person person) { ... }
public int DeletePerson(int id) { ... }
public int DeleteAllPeople() { ... }
```

That will work just fine. It's even moderately testable. Use it if it works for you.

The problem with this approach is all the code that's not shown: the implementation of these methods is virtually identical for every table. This approach smells of code duplication. If you need to access a third or fourth table, you'll wind up with dozens of methods that look more or less like this:

```
public int GetOrSaveOrDeleteSomething(int id)
{
    lock (locker) {
        return database.GetOrSaveOrDelete<TableName>(id);
    }
}
```

Very smelly, indeed. If you're lucky, that's all that will be in there. In some cases, a mash-up of table-specific logic and SQLite implementation will provide additional smells. It's time for a refactoring, and the second option is the obvious choice.

Refactor your repository into a repository class and a generic database access class.

A more advanced approach to the repository pattern separates the repository class from the DAL implementations. This approach is useful if you have multiple tables, or mixed types of data access, such as file-based, XML, and JSON, as well as a SQLite data layer, or multiple databases (rare). Each data source can have its own implementation; then the repository ties them all together with one interface. SQLite implementations can all be encapsulated into a single generic database class.

Create a generic database class that handles the SQLite data layer and then create an advanced repository class that handles all the data access calls to that generic database and to other sources.

Begin with the generic database class, as shown in Listing 7-21. Take your original ItemDatabaseBasic class, make a copy, and call it ItemDatabaseGeneric.cs. Replace all references to specific tables, data models, and data classes such as Item or Person with T. In a liberal use of generics, create methods that could transact with *any* table, depending on the data type passed into them.

Listing 7-21. Generic Database Class (ItemDatabaseGeneric.cs)

```
public class ItemDatabaseGeneric
{
    static object locker = new object ();

    SQLiteConnection database;

    public ItemDatabaseGeneric()
    {
        database = DependencyService.Get<IDatabase>().DBConnect();
        database.CreateTable<Item>();
        database.CreateTable<Person>();
    }

    public IEnumerable<T> GetObjects<T> () where T : IObject, new ()
    {
        lock (locker) {
            return (from i in database.Table<T>() select i).ToList();
        }
    }

    public IEnumerable<T> GetFirstObjects<T> () where T : IObject, new ()
    {
        lock (locker) {
            return database.Query<T>("SELECT * FROM Item WHERE Name = 'First'");
        }
    }

    public T GetObject<T> (int id) where T : IObject, new ()
    {
        lock (locker) {
            return database.Table<T>().FirstOrDefault(x => x.ID == id);
        }
    }

    public int SaveObject<T> (T obj) where T : IObject
    {
        lock (locker) {
            if (obj.ID != 0) {
                database.Update(obj);
                return obj.ID;
            } else {
                return database.Insert(obj);
            }
        }
    }
```

```
    public int DeleteObject<T> (int id) where T : IObject, new ()
    {
        lock (locker) {
            return database.Delete<T> (id);
        }
    }

    public void DeleteAllObjects<T> ()
    {
        lock (locker) {
            database.DropTable<T>();
            database.CreateTable<T>();
        }
    }

}
```

Since the ID field is needed in these methods, it must be added as a constraint to the type parameters of some of the methods. This means you need to upgrade to your data model(s) with an interface that requires an ID (Listing 7-22).

Listing 7-22. Generic Model Interface That Includes an ID Field (IObject.cs)

```
public interface IObject
{
    int ID { get; set; }
}
```

Apply the interface to your models, inheriting from IObject:

```
public class Item : IObject
```

You already have an ID field in the Item class, so there's no need for further changes to it.

Add a Person class as a new data model, inheriting from IObject and including an ID field to implement IObject (Listing 7-23).

Listing 7-23. Person Data Model Class (Person.cs)

```
public class Person : IObject
{
    [PrimaryKey, AutoIncrement]
    public int ID { get; set; }
    [MaxLength(25)]
    public string FirstName { get; set; }
    [MaxLength(25)]
    public string LastName { get; set; }
}
```

Create an advanced repository class that consumes the generic database class. Use methods that are specific to the types of data being handled, as shown in Listing 7-24. Avoid any SQLite implementation in this repository, as the purpose of this class is to act as a layer between the business logic and the data access implementation.

Listing 7-24. Advanced Repository Calls Generic Database Class Methods (ItemRepository.cs)

```
public class ItemRepository {
    ItemDatabaseGeneric itemDatabase = null;

    public ItemRepository()
    {
        itemDatabase = new ItemDatabaseGeneric();
    }

    public Item GetItem(int id)
    {
        return itemDatabase.GetObject<Item>(id);
    }

    public IEnumerable<Item> GetFirstItems ()
    {
        return itemDatabase.GetObjects<Item>();
    }

    public IEnumerable<Item> GetItems ()
    {
        return itemDatabase.GetObjects<Item>();
    }

    public int SaveItem (Item item)
    {
        return itemDatabase.SaveObject<Item>(item);
    }

    public int DeleteItem(int id)
    {
        return itemDatabase.DeleteObject<Item>(id);
    }

    public void DeleteAllItems()
    {
        itemDatabase.DeleteAllObjects<Item>();
    }

    public Person GetPerson(int id)
    {
        return itemDatabase.GetObject<Person>(id);
    }

    public IEnumerable<Person> GetPeople ()
    {
        return itemDatabase.GetObjects<Person>();
    }
```

```
    public int SavePerson (Person person)
    {
        return itemDatabase.SaveObject<Person>(person);
    }

    public int DeletePerson(int id)
    {
        return itemDatabase.DeleteObject<Person>(id);
    }

    public void DeleteAllPeople()
    {
        itemDatabase.DeleteAllObjects<Person>();
    }

}
```

Three components are in this more advanced repository: the generic database instance, the item methods, and the person methods. Item objects are passed into the item methods, and Person objects appear in the person methods. The generic database class resolves all of its SQLite.NET methods by using those data types via generics, deciding which tables to read and write to/from.

That is how to refactor your basic repository into an advanced repository, using generics and a data model interface.

If you're looking at the repositories in this chapter and asking where the model properties and caching mechanisms are, you're asking the right questions. Using a repository to maintain in-memory data models is a common technique in web development, but it can be risky given the limited memory of mobile devices and is beyond the scope of this book. The repositories shown here are basic ones designed only to create an app-specific abstraction around the SQLite ORM.

■ **Note** A third option exists for adding methods to a repository: create a generic repository. This is similar to the second option, the generic database class, but without the encapsulating repository class. This exposes a generic DAL interface to your views and view models and is considered by many to be lazy coding and a leaky abstraction.

CODE COMPLETE: Creating a DAL by Using SQLite.NET

Listings 7-21, 7-22, 7-23, 7-24, 7-25, 7-26, and 7-27 contain the complete data access layer code for the advanced repository example invoking the generic database class. The Application object containing the static Repository property is found in Listing 7-25. This example uses the advanced repository we refactored in Listing 7-24 instead of the basic database repository (Listing 7-18).

The ContentPage demo UI in Listing 7-26 walks through various methods in the DAL. The List data model with IObject implemented is in Listing 7-27.

This example is a PCL Xamarin.Forms project, which uses dependency injection for retrieving the database connection with the DBConnect() method as described in "Connect by Using Portable Class Libraries" and as seen in the downloadable code solution called SQLiteNetPCL.

If you're using a shared project instead, skip the DI and use conditional compilation to create DatabasePath, as mentioned earlier in "Connect by Using Shared Projects" and as seen in the downloadable code solution called SQLiteNETSharedProject.

Listing 7-25. App.cs Using a Static Application Property for the Repository

```
public class App : Application
{
    static ItemRepository repository;
    public static ItemRepository Repository {
        get {
            if (repository == null) {
                repository = new ItemRepository ();
            }
            return repository;
        }
    }

    public App()
    {
        MainPage = new NavigationPage(new HomePage());
    }
}
```

Figure 7-8 shows the UI output of the ContentPage called DataAccessPageRepository (Listing 7-26), a quick demo of the data access layer using the advanced repository.

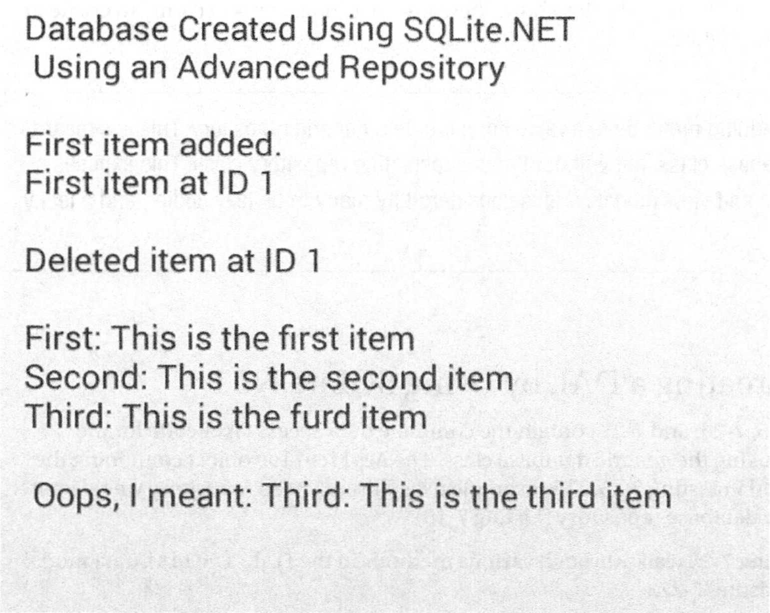

Database Created Using SQLite.NET
 Using an Advanced Repository

First item added.
First item at ID 1

Deleted item at ID 1

First: This is the first item
Second: This is the second item
Third: This is the furd item

 Oops, I meant: Third: This is the third item

Figure 7-8. *UI display in the demo data access page shown in Listing 7-27*

Listing 7-26. DataAccessPageRepository.cs Is a Xamarin.Forms ContentPage That Uses ItemsRepository

```
public class DataAccessPageRepository : ContentPage
{
    public DataAccessPageRepository()
    {
        var label = new Label { Text = "Database Created Using SQLite.NET\n" };

        label.Text += " Using an Advanced Repository\n\n";

        App.Repository.DeleteAllItems (); // clear out the table to start fresh

        var item = new Item { Name = "First" , Description = "This is the first item"};
        App.Repository.SaveItem (item);

        var firstItem = App.Repository.GetFirstItems();
        label.Text += firstItem.First().Name + " item added.\n";

        var id = 1;
        item = App.Repository.GetItem (id);
        label.Text += item.Name + " item at ID " + id.ToString () + "\n\n";

        App.Repository.DeleteItem(id);
        label.Text += "Deleted item at ID " + id.ToString () + "\n\n";

        item = new Item { Name = "First" , Description = "This is the first item"};
        App.Repository.SaveItem (item);
        item = new Item { Name = "Second" , Description = "This is the second item"};
        App.Repository.SaveItem (item);
        item = new Item { Name = "Third" , Description = "This is the furd item"};
        App.Repository.SaveItem (item);

        var items = App.Repository.GetItems ();
        foreach (var i in items) {
            label.Text += i.Name + ": " + i.Description + "\n";
        }

        label.Text += "\n Oops, I meant: ";

        item.Description = "This is the third item";
        App.Repository.SaveItem(item);

        id = 4;
        item = App.Repository.GetItem (id);
        label.Text += item.Name + ": " + item.Description + "\n";

        this.Padding = new Thickness(10, Device.OnPlatform(20, 0, 0), 10, 5);
```

```
        Content = new StackLayout
        {
            Children = {
                label
            }
        };
    }
```

Listing 7-27. Item.cs Contains the Item Class Implementing IObject

```
public class Item : IObject
{
    [PrimaryKey, AutoIncrement]
    public int ID { get; set; }
    [MaxLength(15)]
    public string Name { get; set; }
    [MaxLength(50)]
    public string Description { get; set; }

}
```

Using ADO.NET

CROSS PLATFORM

Xamarin provides an ADO.NET implementation of SQLite that provides all of the necessary SQL transactions using the familiar ADO.NET Command and DataReader objects (mapped to SqliteCommand and SQLiteDataReader).

Create an ADO.NET database by using the SqliteConnection object. Take care to open and close the connection for every use, just as you're used to with ADO.NET. Use ADO.NET Command objects for the creation and execution of SQL statements. Create Command objects by using the connection's CreateCommand method, and then assign SQL to the command by using its CommandText property.

First, add these references to your platform-specific project and to your database class:

```
using System.Data;
using Mono.Data.Sqlite;
```

■ **Important Note** A Xamarin ADO.NET implementation is not supported by PCLs, as they do not offer System.Data or Mono.Data.Sqlite. The Xamarin project options available with ADO.NET are using a shared project or using a PCL, but implement the data layer almost entirely in platform-specific projects (for example, Android and iOS), which is a less-than-ideal architecture. Certain third-party libraries, such as MvvmCross, provide these missing libraries for use in a PCL.

Determine the database path by using techniques described earlier in this chapter. Here is the shared projects approach again:

```
var dbName = "ItemsSQLite.db3";

#if __IOS__
string folder = Environment.GetFolderPath (Environment.SpecialFolder.Personal);
folder = Path.Combine (folder, "..", "Library");
var databasePath = Path.Combine(folder, dbName);
#else
#if __ANDROID__
string folder = Environment.GetFolderPath (Environment.SpecialFolder.Personal);
var databasePath = Path.Combine(folder, dbName);
#else // Windows Phone
var databasePath = Path.Combine(Windows.Storage.ApplicationData.Current.LocalFolder.
                               Path, dbName);
#endif
#endif
```

Next, create the database.

Creating a Database

Create a new database by using the `CreateFile` method. You may need to check whether the file exists first (using `File.Exists`) because this statement will *overwrite an existing database*.

```
Mono.Data.Sqlite.SqliteConnection.CreateFile (databasePath);
```

Once the database is created, you'll need to establish a connection to it. Instantiate a `SqliteConnection` object and call the `Open` method:

```
var connection = new SqliteConnection ("Data Source=" + databasePath);
connection.Open();
```

Conduct your SQL operations and then close the connection:

```
connection.Close();
```

As mentioned earlier, a connection should never be reused across threads.

Now you can use SQL to create tables, insert and delete their rows, and query the data.

Creating a Table

Create a new table by using ADO.NET with SQLite; use the `CREATE TABLE` statement in SQL with a command object and call its `ExecuteNonQuery` method.

Create a Command object by using the connection's CreateCommand method, and then assign the CREATE TABLE SQL to the command by using its CommandText property. Create an Items table containing Name and Description fields. Use the command's ExecuteNonQuery to execute the SQL, because you don't want a data result.

```
using (var command = connection.CreateCommand ()) {
    command.CommandText = "CREATE TABLE [Items] ([ID] INTEGER" +
        " PRIMARY KEY AUTOINCREMENT, [Name] ntext, [Description] ntext)";
    var rowcount = command.ExecuteNonQuery ();
}
```

The ID field is created to AUTOINCREMENT so SQLite can create and maintain this value.

Populate your table with data by creating an array of SQL INSERT statements. Loop through them with a foreach, creating a Command object for each one:

```
var sqlStatements = new [] {
    "INSERT INTO [Items] ([Name], [Description]) VALUES ('First', 'The first row')",
    "INSERT INTO [Items] ([Name], [Description]) VALUES ('Second', 'the second row')",
    "INSERT INTO [Items] ([Name], [Description]) VALUES ('Third', 'the third row')"
};
foreach (var sqlStatement in sqlStatements) {
    using (var command = connection.CreateCommand ()) {
        command.CommandText = sqlStatement;
        var rowcount = command.ExecuteNonQuery ();
    }
}
```

Now that there is data in the table, you can query it by using SELECT statements.

Executing SQL Statements

Execute SQL statements by assigning them to the command's CommandText property and calling one of three methods: ExecuteNonQuery for nondata results, ExecuteReader for queries, and ExecuteScalar to return a single numeric value.

Create a command object and populate it with a SQL query. This SELECT statement queries the Items table for ID, Name, and Description:

```
using (var command = connection.CreateCommand ()) {
    command.CommandText = "SELECT [ID], [Name], [Description] from [Items]";
    var results = command.ExecuteReader();
    while (results.Read ())
        rows += String.Format ("\t ID={0}\t Name={1}\t Desc={2}\n",
            results ["ID"].ToString (),
            results ["Name"].ToString (),
            results ["Description"].ToString ());
}
```

The command.ExecuteReader() call returns a SqliteDataReader populated with data in the results variable. rows is a string containing the results for display.

The using statement keeps the scope of the Command object brief and on an as-needed basis. This approach encourages good data access layer design and cuts down on memory-hogging data classes.

Here are the three ways to execute ADO.NET commands containing SQL. Which you use will depend on the nature of your SQL and what you want to return:

- ExecuteNonQuery: Writes operations to the table, such as CREATE, INSERT, or DELETE, and returns a count of the number of rows affected:

```
using (var command = connection.CreateCommand ()) {
    command.CommandText = "CREATE TABLE [Items] ([ID] INTEGER" +
        " PRIMARY KEY AUTOINCREMENT, [Name] ntext, [Description] ntext)";
    var rowcount = command.ExecuteNonQuery ();
}
```

- ExecuteReader: Executes read-only SQL statements, such as SELECT, and returns a SqliteDataReader object populated with data:

```
command.CommandText = "SELECT [ID], [Name], [Description] from [Items]";
var dataReader = command.ExecuteReader ();
```

  Other useful properties of the SqliteDataReader include RowsAffected, a count of affected rows, and HasRows, a Boolean specifying whether any results were returned.

- ExecuteScalar: Reads a single value of type object from a SQL statement, such as a row count or a single field value:

```
command.CommandText = "SELECT COUNT(*) FROM [Items]";
count = "There are " + command.ExecuteScalar().ToString() + " rows.";
```

The following section contains all the ADO.NET examples deployed in a single Xamarin.Forms ContentPage.

CODE COMPLETE: Using ADO.NET

Listing 7-28 contains all the previous ADO.NET examples placed inside a Xamarin.Forms ContentPage called ConnectionPage.cs in a shared project. The UI displays a single label view that gives simple status updates of all the ADO.NET operations. Figure 7-9 shows the output of the ConnectionPage ADO.NET demo.

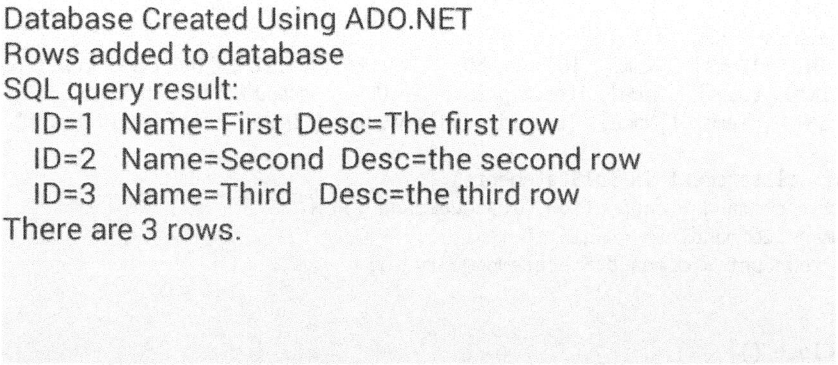

Database Created Using ADO.NET
Rows added to database
SQL query result:
  ID=1 Name=First Desc=The first row
  ID=2 Name=Second Desc=the second row
  ID=3 Name=Third Desc=the third row
There are 3 rows.

Figure 7-9. *ADO.NET demo called ConnectionPage*

Listing 7-28. ADO.NET Implemented in Xamarin.Forms (ConnectionPage.cs)

```
public class ConnectionPage : ContentPage
{
    public ConnectionPage ()
    {
        var dbName = "ItemsSQLite.db3";

        #if __IOS__
        string folder = Environment.GetFolderPath (Environment.SpecialFolder.Personal);
        folder = Path.Combine (folder, "..", "Library");
        var databasePath = Path.Combine(folder, dbName);
        #else
        #if __ANDROID__
        string folder = Environment.GetFolderPath (Environment.SpecialFolder.Personal);
        var databasePath = Path.Combine(folder, dbName);
        #else // Windows Phone
        var databasePath = Path.Combine(Windows.Storage.ApplicationData.Current.
        LocalFolder.Path, dbName);
        #endif
        #endif

        Mono.Data.Sqlite.SqliteConnection.CreateFile (databasePath);
        var connection = new SqliteConnection ("Data Source=" + databasePath);

        connection.Open();
        using (var command = connection.CreateCommand ()) {
            command.CommandText = "CREATE TABLE [Items] ([ID] INTEGER" +
                " PRIMARY KEY AUTOINCREMENT, [Name] ntext, [Description] ntext)";
            var rowcount = command.ExecuteNonQuery ();
        }
        connection.Close();

        var label = new Label { Text = "Database Created Using ADO.NET\n" };

        connection.Open ();
        var sqlStatements = new [] {
            "INSERT INTO [Items] ([Name], [Description]) VALUES ('First', 'The first row')",
            "INSERT INTO [Items] ([Name], [Description]) VALUES ('Second', 'the second row')",
            "INSERT INTO [Items] ([Name], [Description]) VALUES ('Third', 'the third row')"
        };
        foreach (var sqlStatement in sqlStatements) {
            using (var command = connection.CreateCommand ()) {
                command.CommandText = sqlStatement;
                var rowcount = command.ExecuteNonQuery ();
            }
        }
        connection.Close ();

        label.Text += "Rows added to database\n";

        var rows = "SQL query result:\n";
```

```
            connection.Open ();
            using (var command = connection.CreateCommand ()) {
                command.CommandText = "SELECT [ID], [Name], [Description] from [Items]";
                var results = command.ExecuteReader();
                while (results.Read ())
                    rows += String.Format ("\t ID={0}\t Name={1}\t Desc={2}\n",
                        results ["ID"].ToString (),
                        results ["Name"].ToString (),
                        results ["Description"].ToString ());
            }
            connection.Close ();

            label.Text += rows;

            var count = "";
            connection.Open ();
            using (var command = connection.CreateCommand ()) {
                command.CommandText = "SELECT COUNT(*) FROM [Items]";
                count = "There are " + command.ExecuteScalar().ToString() + " rows.";
            }
            connection.Close ();

            label.Text += count;

            Content = label;
        }
    }
```

This implementation is for concise demo purposes only. The mingling of a presentation layer with a data access layer is not recommended in a professional-grade app.

Database Creation Options

The three most common options for creating your SQLite database are as follows:

- *Use SQLite.NET*: Use the SQLite.NET API to create the database and tables as described in "Creating a Database" in the section "Using SQLite.NET." Use SQL for features not covered in the ORM, such as foreign keys and indexes.

- *Use SQL*: Create your database and tables when the app first runs, using SQL as described in "Creating a Database" in the section "Using ADO.NET."

- *Include a database*: You can include a fully created database with your app, a good option if you want complete control over details of the tables and their relationships. Use a tool such as the MonoDevelop database editor or the SQLite Manager Firefox extension. Then remember to have your app copy the database into a writable directory before using it with code like this:

```
if (!File.Exists (databasePath))
{
    File.Copy (dbName, databasePath);
}
```

SQLite provides a local database to help you maintain state between user sessions and have important data on demand. Many apps also require interaction with a server-side data source, such as a SQL server or other data source on a remote data server.

Web Services

Web services facilitate communication with a remote data store and synchronization with the local SQLite database. They allow the Xamarin app to pull down data from the remote data source and push it back up when needed.

Many options are available for building web services when using the Xamarin platform, but here are a few of the most common:

- **REST:** A common approach, RESTful services can use `HttpWebRequest`, `WebClient`, or one of many third-party libraries, including RestSharp, Hammock, or ServiceStack often coupled with JSON or LINQ.

- **Windows Communication Framework (WCF):** The standard Microsoft web service approach is supported in a limited fashion by using `BasicHttpBinding` in the Silverlight library.

- **SOAP:** An older, standards-based approach for data transmission over the Web, Xamarin supports SOAP 1.1, Microsoft's SOAP implementation, and ASP.NET Web Services (ASMX), albeit with an incomplete implementation.

Detailed exploration of web services is beyond the scope of this book, but the fundamentals are similar to web services used in web, and especially desktop, apps. If you're interested in how the data access layer fits into mobile app architecture, you'll find more on that topic in Chapter 9.

There are heavier-weight options that provide out-of-the box data solutions, handle the fine points of security, and can save on development time. These enterprise cloud data solutions are the industrial-grade platforms for remote data integration.

Enterprise Cloud Data Solutions

A range of enterprise solutions provide authentication, security, cloud storage, data synchronization, push notifications and a host of other features. Here are a few of the most popular.

Microsoft Azure

The Azure Mobile Services Xamarin component provides a way to get started with Microsoft's premiere cloud platform for mobile data storage, authentication, and push notifications. Mobile Services, including the SQL Database and Push Notifications, are configurable on the Azure portal without any coding. Authentication, including Single Sign-On (SSO), is available using Azure Active Directory (AAD). Offline data sync saves changes locally and then uploads them to the cloud database when the app is back online. These features are accessible using the `Microsoft.WindowsAzure.MobileServices` namespace in the Azure Mobile Services Xamarin component. Azure services can also be coded by hand on the server to give greater control and broaden the features available. Consume REST or Web API cloud services and use `OAuth` authentication and authorization to access any required functionality in an Azure service. The newer Azure App Services provide an additional platform for configuring services for use in Xamarin apps and includes Mobile Apps (in preview at the time of this writing). You can find more information at `azure.microsoft.com/mobile`.

IBM MobileFirst Platform Foundation

The IBM MobileFirst SDK in the Xamarin Component Store provides a bridge into IBM's enterprise-grade mobile application platform product as part of a suite of enterprise mobile solutions. IBM MobileFirst Platform Foundation (formerly IBM Worklight) provides a range of mobile app development features including security, cloud data access, enterprise integration, and application management. MobileFirst Platform Foundation security offerings include secure authentication using SSO and multi-factors. Transactions can use SSL encryption, local data can be encrypted, and there is some protection against reverse-engineering. The platform's cloud data access feature set provides remote data access, storing user preferences, and data synchronization. Enterprise integration features include unified push, SMS notifications, and optimized access to enterprise services, such as Web Services, REST Services, SAP, and more. Application management functionality provides a full range of app release management features including distribution, versioning, analytics, push notifications, remote disabling of apps, and error logging. These are some of these features available using the `WL.Client` namespace in the IBM MobileFirst SDK. You can find more information at `xamarin.com/ibm`.

Amazon Web Services (AWS)

Use Amazon services for authentication (Amazon Cognito), cloud storage (Amazon S3), and other features. Get started with AWS Mobile SDK at AWSLabs (in beta at the time of this writing). The SDK provides access to features such as authentication, Amazon S3 cloud data storage, user preference persistence, NoSQL database service, push notifications, and encryption. You can find more information at `aws.amazon.com`.

Those are a few of the enterprise-grade options available for cloud data services in Xamarin apps. Other popular options include Couchbase and Parse.

Summary

Xamarin.Forms data binding was built upon the foundation and experience of the third-party MVVM libraries used with Mono for years, MvvmCross and MVVM Light Toolkit, and was also inspired by WPF XAML data binding. Although it's a relatively young product, in this way, Xamarin.Forms is an advanced and mature API.

Data binding gets data into and out of your data model through your views. Moving that data into and out of your database can be accomplished with SQLite.NET or ADO.NET. Some Xamarin developers prefer SQLite.NET because of the ease of the built-in ORM. The SQLite.NET ORM wraps all the standard CRUD transactions in handy LINQ-friendly methods. The ADO.NET approach is bare-bones but functional. Neither option supports foreign keys, and those have to be done in SQL or in an included database.

That's everything you'll need to populate your data models and couple them with a local SQLite database.

In the next chapter, we will return to the mobile UI for the final and catalyzing topic in Xamarin.Forms development: custom renderers. Custom renderers allow you to use *almost all* of the UI functionality covered in this book (and more) within the context of a Xamarin.Forms app. You can include platform-specific code, which employs Xamarin.iOS and Xamarin.Android, in your Xamarin.Forms pages by using custom renderers.

Turn to Chapter 8 to see how to use custom renderers.

CHAPTER 8

Custom Renderers

When you're ready to extend the capability of Xamarin.Forms views beyond their out-of-the-box functionality, then it's time to start customizing them using custom renderers. Platform-specific controls and layouts have scores of features unavailable using only the Xamarin.Forms abstraction. Fortunately, Xamarin.Forms exposes the mechanism whereby cross-platform views are made into platform-specific views, called *renderers*. By creating your own custom renderers, you get full access to platform-specific features buried deep within each view!

Custom renderers are a bridge between Xamarin.Forms and Xamarin platform-specific libraries, Xamarin.iOS, Xamarin.Android, as well as the Windows Phone SDK.

Xamarin.Forms controls are drawn on the screen using two primary components: *elements* and *renderers*. Throughout this book you've been working with the elements: views, pages, or cells defined within Xamarin.Forms. The renderers take a cross-platform element and draw it on the screen using the platform-specific UI library. All Xamarin screens use renderers! For example, if you create a Label view using Xamarin.Forms, this element is rendered in iOS using UILabel, in Android using TextView, and in Windows Phone using TextBlock. However, Xamarin.Forms provides only a partial binding to these platform-specific views. If you want to gain access to all of the properties and methods within platform-specific elements (such as UILabel, TextView, and TextBlock), then you need to create a custom renderer.

Think of a custom renderer as a way to access and extend the binding between Xamarin.Forms and the platform-specific elements.

Tip   You can create custom renderers for these elements: Views, Cells, and Pages.

At the end of this chapter I'll list most of the Xamarin.Forms elements covered in this book, their platform-specific equivalents, and which renderers to use when customizing them.

When to Use a Custom Renderer

When might you want to use a custom renderer?

You may want to make a slight change to a view and Xamarin.Forms isn't obliging you. For example, you know for a fact that iOS does text decorations or shadows on a particular view and this isn't available in Xamarin.Forms, so you create a custom renderer to access a Xamarin.iOS control. Use a custom control when you need direct access to an element's platform-specific properties and methods or when you need to replace a Xamarin.Forms element with your own custom platform-specific element.

■ **Note**   A Xamarin.Forms *customized control* uses a custom renderer to access native functionality in a single control. A *custom control* is typically a group of controls composited into a single reusable component using ContentView (Chapter 3) (but you can also create a custom control using a custom renderer and replace the view with a group of views). Sometimes developers will say "custom control" to refer to a customized control.

Let's explore how to create a custom renderer for Android, iOS, and Windows Phone.

Creating and Using a Custom Renderer

XAMARIN.FORMS

A custom renderer is created to implement the visual representation of a custom element. You create a custom element class that inherits from a standard Xamarin.Forms element, such as Button. Then you use that custom element in the UI. You can implement the custom renderer for each platform to use platform-specific members of that element, such as Android's SetBackgroundColor method, or the iOS BackgroundColor property.

There are several steps in the creation and implementation of a custom renderer, but I'll break them into two tasks: preparing the custom element in the Xamarin.Forms project and creating a custom renderer in each platform-specific project.

Prepare the custom element in your Xamarin.Forms project by creating an element subclass and then using it in your UI. The following steps only happen once.

1. Create an element subclass. Create an empty subclass of the element you want to customize, such as Button, in your Xamarin.Forms project.

   ```
   public class CustomButton : Button {}
   ```

2. Use the element. Use the subclassed element, such as this CustomButton, in a layout in your Xamarin.Forms project.

Create a custom renderer in each of your platform-specific projects (iOS, Android, Windows Phone) using these three steps. The following steps occur *once for each platform*.

1. Create a custom renderer. Add a custom renderer class to each platform-specific project where you want to make customizations.

   ```
   public class CustomButtonRenderer : ButtonRenderer
   ```

2. Add [assembly]. Add the [assembly] attribute outside of the namespace declaration to declare the new renderer.

3. Add using. Add using statements to the renderer class so that the renderer types are resolved.

That's the upshot for creating a custom renderer.

In the next example, you will create a custom button that has custom renderers for each platform. Start by preparing your custom view in the Xamarin.Forms project before moving onto the renderers.

Preparing the Custom Element

XAMARIN.FORMS

A custom renderer first requires a custom Xamarin.Forms element, which can be a View, a Cell, or a Page. In this example, you will use custom renderers to change the background color of a button view to some variant of orange, as this is not possible using the Xamarin.Forms Button view at the time of this writing. The custom view will be called CustomButton and inherit from the Button view.

Now, to make your CustomButton orange…

Create a Xamarin.Forms PCL solution called CustomRenderer; then I'll go through these steps in more detail.

1. Create an element subclass. Create an empty subclass of the element you want to customize, the Xamarin.Forms Button in this case, and place it in CustomButton. cs in your Xamarin.Forms project.

    ```
    public class CustomButton : Button {}
    ```

2. Use element. Use the subclassed element, such as this CustomButton, in a layout in your Xamarin.Forms project.

Create a new ContentPage in a file called Mainpage.cs. Instantiate an instance of the CustomButton view, create a click handler, and place the button on a StackLayout, as shown in Listing 8-1.

Listing 8-1. Invoke the CustomButton in Mainpage.cs (in the Forms Project)

```
public class MainPage : ContentPage
{
    public MainPage()
    {
        CustomButton button = new CustomButton
        {
            Text = "Custom Button",
            FontSize = Device.GetNamedSize(NamedSize.Large, typeof(Button)),
            HorizontalOptions = LayoutOptions.Center,
            VerticalOptions = LayoutOptions.Fill
        };

        button.Clicked += (sender, args) =>
        {
            DisplayAlert("Congratulations",
                "This button was rendered in a platform-specific class.", "OK");
        };

        Content = new StackLayout
        {
            VerticalOptions = LayoutOptions.Center,
            Children = {
                button
            }
        };
    }
}
```

Remember to assign this `MainPage` class to the `MainPage` property of your `Application` constructor. In the `StackLayout`, your use of the custom view, `CustomButton`, is exactly the same as the use of a regular Xamarin.Forms `Button` view.

Creating the Custom Renderer

Now that you have created a custom element and used it in your UI, you'll need to create the custom renderer. You'll need to determine the name of the renderer for your element, and I'll show you how to do that later in this chapter in the section "Which Renderer and View Do You Customize?" In this example, you'll use `ButtonRenderer`.

There are two main ways to customize a control: by property or by replacing the entire control. Customizing a control's properties involves accessing platform-specific properties unavailable via the Xamarin.Forms view (such as a button's background color). A Xamarin.Forms control can also be *completely replaced* by a platform-specific control of the developer's choice. I'll cover property customization in depth in this chapter and touch upon control replacement in the notes.

Here are the custom renderer's key methods:

- `OnElementChanged`: This main method fires upon changes to the element and is used for control initialization. Set the initial control value and its properties.

- `OnElementPropertyChanged`: This method fires upon changes to element properties and is useful for data binding.

- `SetNativeControl`: Call this method manually to replace the entire element with a custom platform-specific control. (such as `SetNativeControl(new YourCustomizedControl());`)

Here are the custom renderer's important properties:

- *Control:* A reference to the platform-specific element (such as `UIButton`) displayed by the renderer. Platform-specific properties are available here. This object can also be replaced with an entirely new (and customized) platform-specific control.

- *Element:* A reference to the Xamarin.Forms subclassed element (such as `CustomButton`). Xamarin.Forms element properties are available here.

Customize controls and their properties by using the `Control` property within the `OnElementChanged` method.

Implement data-bound customized controls by assigning `Control` properties from their corresponding `Element` properties in the `OnElementPropertyChanged` method.

Now create a custom renderer on each platform. Begin with the Android platform, then do iOS and Windows Phone.

Android Custom Renderer

ANDROID

Renderers realize a view on the native platform. Create your own renderer by inheriting from the standard renderer, such as `ButtonRenderer`. Then call into the native view's platform-specific API to customize the view using the renderer's `Control` property. In `OnElementChanged`, you'll assign your `Control`'s background color property.

Do the first of three platform-specific steps.

1. **Create a custom renderer.** Add a custom renderer class to the platform-specific project, which is `ButtonRenderer` in this case.

■ **Tip**   Refer to the section "Which Renderer and View Do You Customize?" at the end of this chapter to help you determine the renderer and platform-specific control(s) to use for the element you want to customize.

Create `CustomButtonRenderer.cs` as a class in the Droid project. Inherit from the `ButtonRenderer` class and modify the `Control` property to affect your button as needed. The platform-specific view is assigned to the `Control` property, in this case an Android `Button` control, and its native properties and methods are made available. Listing 8-2 shows an Android renderer where the background color is set using the `SetBackgroundColor` method.

Listing 8-2. Customized ButtonRenderer in CustomButtonRenderer.cs (in the Droid Project)

```
public class CustomButtonRenderer : ButtonRenderer
{
    protected override void OnElementChanged (ElementChangedEventArgs<Button> e)
    {
        base.OnElementChanged (e);

        if (Control != null) {
            Control.SetBackgroundColor (global::Android.Graphics.Color.Chocolate);
        }
    }
}
```

■ **Tip**   `OnElementChanged` is where to replace the entire control with your own customized platform-specific control.

```
if (Control != null) {
    SetNativeControl(new YourCustomizedControl());
}
```

■ **Note**   If you don't add a platform-specific renderer, the default Xamarin.Forms renderer will be used.

Complete the final two platform-specific steps. In order to make the custom renderer visible to the Xamarin. Forms project, an attribute on the class is required. Then add the `using` statements.

2. Add the `[assembly]` attribute outside of the namespace declaration to declare the new renderer.

```
[assembly: ExportRenderer (typeof (CustomButton), typeof (CustomButtonRenderer))]
```

3. Add using statements to the renderer class so that the renderer types are
   resolved.

```
using Xamarin.Forms.Platform.Android;
using Xamarin.Forms;
using CustomRenderer;
using CustomRenderer.Droid;
```

Figure 8-1 shows the result: a "chocolate"-colored button that looks orange. Setting a button's background color is only possible using a custom renderer with the current version of Xamarin.Forms.

Figure 8-1. *Orange CustomButton via an Android custom renderer*

■ **Tip** Color is close-captioned in this chapter for all of you black-and-white print readers.

CODE COMPLETE: Android Custom Renderer

ANDROID

Listings 8-3, 8-4, and 8-5 contain the complete code listing for the Android custom button renderer. Listing 8-3, `CustomButton.cs`, and Listing 8-4, `MainPage.cs`, are in the Xamarin.Forms project and Listing 8-5, `CustomButtonRenderer.cs`, is from the Droid project in the same solution, `CustomRenderer`.

■ **XAML** The XAML version of this example can be found at the Apress web site (`www.apress.com`), or on GitHub at `https://github.com/danhermes/xamarin-book-examples`. The Xamarin.Forms solution for Chapter 8 is `CustomRenderer.Xaml`.

Listing 8-3. CustomButton.cs

```
public class CustomButton : Button {}
```

Listing 8-4. MainPage.cs

```
public class MainPage : ContentPage
{
    public MainPage()
    {
        CustomButton button = new CustomButton
        {
            Text = "Custom Button",
            FontSize = Device.GetNamedSize(NamedSize.Large, typeof(Button)),
            HorizontalOptions = LayoutOptions.Center,
            VerticalOptions = LayoutOptions.Fill
        };

        button.Clicked += (sender, args) =>
        {
            DisplayAlert("Congratulations",
              "This button was rendered in a platform-specific class.", "OK");
        };

        Content = new StackLayout
        {
            VerticalOptions = LayoutOptions.Center,
            Children = {
                button
            }
        };

    }
}
```

Listing 8-5. CustomButtonRenderer.cs (Droid Project)

```
using Xamarin.Forms.Platform.Android;
using Xamarin.Forms;
using CustomRenderer;
using CustomRenderer.Droid;

[assembly: ExportRenderer (typeof (CustomButton), typeof (CustomButtonRenderer))]

namespace CustomRenderer.Droid
{
    public class CustomButtonRenderer : ButtonRenderer
    {
        protected override void OnElementChanged (ElementChangedEventArgs<Button> e)
        {
            base.OnElementChanged (e);

            if (Control != null) {
                Control.SetBackgroundColor (global::Android.Graphics.Color.Chocolate);
            }
        }
    }
}
```

Now we'll do an orange button in iOS.

iOS Custom Renderer

iOS

Creating an iOS renderer for the Button view is similar to making the Android one. Create a custom renderer that inherits from a standard renderer, such as ButtonRenderer. Then call into the native view's platform-specific API to customize it using the renderer's Control property. In OnElementChanged, you'll assign your Control's background color property.

Begin with the first platform-specific step.

1. Create a custom renderer. Create CustomButtonRenderer.cs as a class in the iOS project. Inherit from the ButtonRenderer class and modify the Control property to affect your button as needed. The platform-specific view is assigned to the Control property, in this case an iOS UIButton control, and its native properties and methods are available. Listing 8-6 shows an iOS renderer where the background color is set using the UIButton's BackgroundColor property.

Listing 8-6. Customized ButtonRenderer in CustomButtonRenderer.cs (iOS Project)

```
public class CustomButtonRenderer : ButtonRenderer
{
    protected override void OnElementChanged (ElementChangedEventArgs<Button> e)
    {
        base.OnElementChanged (e);

        if (Control != null) {
            Control.BackgroundColor = UIColor.Brown;
        }
    }
}
```

Next, do the final two steps. In order to make the custom renderer visible to the Xamarin.Forms project, you need to add an attribute on the class and the two using statements.

2. Add [assembly]. Add the [assembly] attribute outside of the namespace declaration to declare the new renderer.

```
[assembly: ExportRenderer (typeof (CustomButton), typeof (CustomButtonRenderer))]
```

3. Add using statements to the renderer class so that the renderer types are resolved.

```
using Xamarin.Forms.Platform.iOS;
using Xamarin.Forms;
using UIKit;
using CustomRenderer;
using CustomRenderer.iOS;
```

Figure 8-2 displays the result: another orange button (orangish-brown), only possible using a custom renderer with the current version of Xamarin.Forms.

Figure 8-2. *Orange CustomButton via an iOS custom renderer*

CODE COMPLETE: iOS Custom Renderer

iOS

Listing 8-7 shows the complete code listing for the iOS custom button renderer. This goes with Listings 8-3 and 8-4 in the Xamarin.Forms project.

Listing 8-7. CustomButtonRenderer.cs for the iOS Project

```
using Xamarin.Forms.Platform.iOS;
using Xamarin.Forms;
using UIKit;
using CustomRenderer;
using CustomRenderer.iOS;

[assembly: ExportRenderer (typeof (CustomButton), typeof (CustomButtonRenderer))]

namespace CustomRenderer.iOS
{
```

```
public class CustomButtonRenderer : ButtonRenderer
{
    protected override void OnElementChanged (ElementChangedEventArgs<Button> e)
    {
        base.OnElementChanged (e);

        if (Control != null) {
            Control.BackgroundColor = UIColor.Brown;
        }
    }
}
```

Now let's make the button orange in Windows Phone.

Windows Phone Custom Renderer

WINDOWS

A Windows Phone custom renderer is also a renderer class inheriting from a standard renderer with an [assembly] tag and platform-specific implementation of views. Here's the detail for customizing the Button view renderer.

■ **Note** The following Windows Phone custom renderer is made using the Silverlight API, not WinRT. WinRT namespaces will differ slightly but the approach remains the same.

Begin with the custom renderer, as usual:

1. Create a custom renderer. Create CustomButtonRenderer.cs as a class in the WinPhone project. Inherit from the ButtonRenderer class and modify the Control property to affect your button as needed. The platform-specific view is assigned to the Control property, in this case a Windows Phone Button control, and its native properties and methods are made available. Listing 8-8 shows a Windows Phone renderer where the background color is set using the Button's Background property.

Listing 8-8. Customized ButtonRenderer in CustomButtonRenderer.cs (WinPhone Project)

```
public class CustomButtonRenderer : ButtonRenderer
{
    protected override void OnElementChanged(ElementChangedEventArgs<Button> e)
    {
        base.OnElementChanged(e);

        if (e.OldElement == null)
        {
            var customButton = (System.Windows.Controls.Button)Control;
            customButton.Background = new SolidColorBrush(Colors.Orange);
        }
    }
}
```

> ■ **Note**   In the null check, the `OldElement` property is used instead of `Control` on Windows Phone.

> ■ **Note**   For WinRT, use `Windows.UI.Xaml` instead of `System.Windows`.

Now complete the two final steps. Add the `[assembly]` attribute to make the custom renderer visible to the Xamarin.Forms project then add the `using` statements.

    2.   Add `[assembly]`. Add the `[assembly]` attribute outside of the namespace declaration to declare the new renderer.

```
[assembly: ExportRenderer (typeof (CustomButton), typeof (CustomButtonRenderer))]
```

    3.   Add `using` statements to the renderer class so that the renderer types are resolved.

```
using System;
using System.Windows.Media;
using Xamarin.Forms.Platform.WinPhone;
using Xamarin.Forms;
using CustomRenderer;
using CustomRenderer.WinPhone;
```

> ■ **Note**   Here are the WinRT `using` statements.
>
> ```
> using Windows.UI;
> using Windows.UI.Xaml.Media;
> using Xamarin.Forms;
> using Xamarin.Forms.Platform.WinRT;
> ```

Figure 8-3 shows a Kool-Aid-orange-colored button, on a Windows Phone this time.

Figure 8-3. *Orange CustomButton via a Windows Phone custom renderer*

CODE COMPLETE: Windows Phone Custom Renderer

WINDOWS

Listing 8-9 shows the complete code listing for the Windows Phone custom button renderer. This goes with Listings 8-3 and 8-4 in the Xamarin.Forms project.

Listing 8-9. CustomButtonRenderer.cs for the WinPhone Projectusing System;

```
using System.Windows.Media;
using Xamarin.Forms.Platform.WinPhone;
using Xamarin.Forms;
using CustomRenderer;
using CustomRenderer.WinPhone;

[assembly: ExportRenderer(typeof(CustomButton), typeof(CustomButtonRenderer))]
```

```
namespace CustomRenderer.WinPhone
{
    public class CustomButtonRenderer : ButtonRenderer
    {
        protected override void OnElementChanged(ElementChangedEventArgs<Button> e)
        {
            base.OnElementChanged(e);

            if (e.OldElement == null)
            {
                var customButton = (System.Windows.Controls.Button)Control;
                customButton.Background = new SolidColorBrush(Colors.Orange);
            }
        }
    }
}
```

That's how to build a custom renderer on all three mobile OS platforms!

The first trick in building a custom renderer is figuring out what the renderer is called and the native element name. Here's a quick guide to help with that.

Which Renderer and View Do You Customize?

XAMARIN.FORMS

Table 8-1 shows most of the Xamarin.Forms elements covered in this book, their renderers, and their platform-specific equivalents that can be customized.

Table 8-1. Elements, Their Renderers, and Platform-Specific Elements

Xamarin.Forms	Renderer	Android	iOS	Windows Phone
Chapter 2				
ContentPage	PageRenderer	ViewGroup	UIView	Panel
Label	LabelRenderer	TextView	UILabel	TextBlock
Button	ButtonRenderer	Button	UIButton	Button
Entry	EntryRenderer	EditText	UITextField	PhoneTextBox
Image	ImageRenderer	ImageView	UIImageView	Image
BoxView	BoxRenderer, BoxViewRenderer(WP)	ViewGroup	CGContext	Rectangle
ScrollView	ScrollViewRenderer	ScrollView	UIScrollView	ScrollViewer
Chapter 3				
Frame	FrameRenderer	Drawable	UIView	UIElement
Chapter 4				
Picker	PickerRenderer	TextView, AlertDialog, NumberPicker	UIPickerView, UIPickerViewModel, UIToolBar, UIBarButtonItems, UITextField	ListPicker
DatePicker	DatePickerRenderer	TextView, AlertDialog	UIDatePicker, UIToolbar, UITextField, UIBarButtonItems	DateTimePickerBase
TimePicker	TimePickerRenderer	TextView, AlertDialog	UIDatePicker, UIToolbar, UITextField, UIBarButtonItems	DateTimePickerBase
Stepper	StepperRenderer	LinearLayout, Button	UIStepper	Border, Button
Slider	SliderRenderer	SeekBar	UISlider	Slider
Switch	SwitchRenderer	Switch	UISwitch	ToggleButton

(continued)

363

Table 8-1. (*continued*)

Xamarin.Forms	Renderer	Android	iOS	Windows Phone
Chapter 5				
ListView	ListViewRenderer	Not yet available	UITableView	LongListSelector
TextCell	TextCellRenderer	LinearLayout, TextView, ImageView	UITableViewCell	DataTemplate
EntryCell	EntryCellRenderer	LinearLayout, TextView, EditText	UITableViewCell, UITextField	DataTemplate
SwitchCell	SwitchCellRenderer	Switch	UITableViewCell, UISwitch	DataTemplate
ImageCell	ImageCellRenderer	TextView, ImageView	UITableViewCell, UIImage	DataTemplate
Chapter 6				
NavigationPage	NavigationRenderer, NavigationPageRenderer(WP)	None with View pages	UINavigationController, UIToolbar	None with FrameworkElements
MasterDetailPage	MasterDetailRenderer, tMasterDetailRenderer(iPad)	DrawerLayout	custom(iPhone), UISplitViewController(iPad)	Panel
TableView	TableViewRenderer, TableViewModelRenderer(A)	ListView, View	UITableView	LongListSelector
TabbedPage	TabbedRenderer, TabbedPageRenderer(WP)	None with View pages	UIViewController, UIView	Pivot
CarouselPage	CarouselPageRenderer	View	UIScrollView	PanoramaItem

(A) = Android

(WP) = Windows Phone

Xamarin.Forms Layout renderers are not exposed for customization at the time of this writing.

The Windows Phone classes listed in Table 8-1 are from the Silverlight API and many (not all) are unchanged in WinRT.

That should be sufficient to get you started with custom renderers.

Summary

Custom renderers complete the Xamarin.Forms picture, extending the reach of Xamarin.Forms deep into the platform-specific APIs using Xamarin.iOS, Xamarin.Android, and the Windows Phone SDK. The Xamarin.Forms abstraction provides immeasurable value as a cross-platform tool, but the platforms do differ, and developers need a way to bridge the gap. The custom renderer is that bridge.

It is time that the design of the book you are reading be laid bare (although I'm fairly certain you had this figured out already):

This entire book is architected around Xamarin.Forms and how to extend it using custom renderers. That is partly why so many of the chapters begin with the Xamarin.Forms approach, and then continue with the Android and iOS equivalents.

For that reason, this chapter on custom renderers is the bow on your present. A big orange bow. Hopefully you've found this gift to be useful, as it is drawing to its end.

If you recall the Xamarin.Forms versus platform-specific implementation discussion in Chapter 2, you should now have a thorough understanding of the decisions to be made when setting out to build a Xamarin app and the options available to help you do it using Xamarin.Forms, Xamarin.Android, and Xamarin.iOS.

Custom renderers are the main approach used in platform-specific UI in Xamarin.Forms apps. There are, however, a number of other ways to slice and dice platform-specific bits of code in the data access layer, business logic, and other non-UI functionality. This brings you to Xamarin application architecture.

In the next and final chapter, you'll look at how to architect cross-platform apps.

CHAPTER 9

Cross-Platform Architecture

At the outset of this book, I mentioned the unicorn of mobile development: *write once, deploy anywhere*. In the quest for this unicorn, the fair maiden that might entice this beast to appear is cross-platform design.

The entirety of the Xamarin platform already provides a foundation of cross-platform design, but you can further the cause by understanding and thoughtfully implementing *cross-platform architecture*.

What is cross-platform architecture?

It begins with two kinds of code.

Shared Code and Platform-Specific Code

A Xamarin app can be broken down into the two types of code found in it:

- *Shared code*: Used by all platforms in the app solution; also called cross-platform code.

- *Platform-specific code*: Used by one OS platform in the app solution, such as iOS or Android, but not both.

There are a number of ways to divide an application solution between shared and platform-specific code. It can be done top-down by project, or bottom-up using individual lines of code; then there are middle ways using specific files or classes. Many good apps are divided into shared and platform-specific code at all these levels.

The options available for slicing and dicing an application top-down are *Portable Class Libraries* (PCL), projects compilable into a single DLL used by multiple platforms, and *Shared Projects*, which are recompiled in different platform contexts. Bottom-up options include *conditional compilation*, which is a platform-specific compilation demarcation around small blocks of code in a Shared Project. Conditional compilation is not available in a PCL, since the DLL is pre-compiled, so Dependency Injection (DI) can be used instead to create platform-specific classes against a common interface. Custom renderers, covered in Chapter 8, use DI to split out platform-specific UI classes in a Xamarin.Forms solution. *File linking* is used to share specific files between projects.

All of these techniques are used to solve the problem of platform-specific differences in a cross platform app, which is called *divergence*.

Handling Divergence

Divergence describes the need for platform-specific implementations in a cross-platform app because platform-specific differences cause their implementations to diverge from the main code in a solution. Examples include custom renderers in Xamarin.Forms apps where platform-specific UI diverges from the cross-platform approach, and when networking or push notifications implemented in a core library reach a point where they require local OS API access.

The following are the primary techniques for handling divergence in a cross-platform application at different levels of granularity.

- At the *project* level, use platform-specific projects.

- At the *file* level, use file linking, sometimes with partial classes or methods.

- At the *class* level, use dependency injection in PCLs. In Shared Projects you have more options, including DI, partial classes, and conditional compilation.

- At the *method* level, use partial methods.

- At the *code* level, use conditional compilation for individual lines of platform-specific code.

Due to their encapsulated nature, PCLs can only use a couple of the preceding techniques without recompiling a new DLL for each platform: platform-specific projects and dependency injection. Recompiling a cross-platform PCL DLL for each platform implementation is not recommended. If you must recompile, consider using a Shared Project. Shared Projects can use all of the previously mentioned techniques as they are designed to be recompiled for each platform. I'll say more about PCLs and Shared Projects shortly.

■ **Tip** There is also divergence within single platforms due to variations between platform versions, such as Android API or iOS release versions, for example. Version divergence may include divergence between screen sizes or features in APIs that are added or deprecated.

These techniques lead to a few standard architectures for Xamarin cross-platform apps that you'll look at now. With the acknowledgment that *architecture overlaps but isn't the same as solution structure*, let's begin with the Xamarin.Forms solution.

Xamarin.Forms Solution Architecture

Xamarin.Forms apps have a base solution pattern that was mentioned in Chapter 2. These are the main projects.

Xamarin.Forms: Cross-platform UI code in a PCL or Shared Project, which is called by one of the platform-specific projects.

Xamarin.Android: Android-specific code, including Android project startup.

Xamarin.iOS: iOS-specific code, including iOS project startup.

Windows Phone application: Windows Phone–specific code, including Windows Phone project startup.

Core Library: Shared code such as Business Logic Layer (BLL) and DAL using a PCL or Shared Project. (A core library may not be necessary in a small or prototype app since shared code can reside in the Xamarin.Forms project.)

All these projects can be created automatically by the project template except the core library, which must be added manually when needed. Figure 9-1 shows the projects in question.

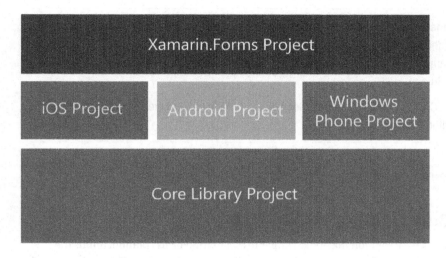

Figure 9-1. *Xamarin.Forms solution projects*

Figure 9-2 shows another way of looking at the Xamarin.Forms solution that includes the app and architecture layer axes.

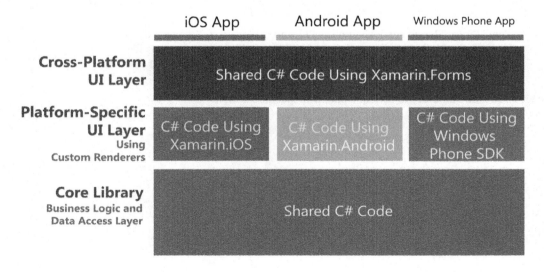

Figure 9-2. *Xamarin.Forms solution architecture of iOS, Android, and Windows Phone apps*

There are two types of shared code in a Xamarin.Forms solution: the shared UI code in the Xamarin.Forms project and the DAL and BLL in the Core Library project.

The platform-specific projects (Xamarin.Android, Xamarin.iOS, and Windows Phone) house startup code, custom renderers, and other platform-specific functionality such as services, notification, sensors, or networking. In a Xamarin.Forms solution, most of the UI is housed in the Xamarin.Forms project and only in platform-specific projects when there are custom renderers. Platform-specific projects handle divergence at the project level.

■ **Note on Windows Phone Projects**   Creating a Xamarin.Forms Solution on Windows will not create a Windows Phone project without having the Windows Phone SDK installed. Windows Phone apps cannot be developed using a Mac. Xamarin Studio does not support the creation of Windows Phone projects and these must be created in Visual Studio.

■ **Note on iOS Projects**   Creating a Xamarin.Forms Solution on a Windows machine will create an iOS project, but it will not be usable without a Mac build host.

Entirely platform-specific solutions keep most or all of the UI in platform-specific projects.

Platform-Specific Solution Architecture

Platform-specific apps have a base solution that looks similar to a Xamarin.Forms solution, minus the Xamarin.Forms project, and all the platform-specific projects contain a lot more code. Here are the projects in a typical platform-specific solution.

> *Xamarin.Android*: Android-specific code.
>
> *Xamarin.iOS*: iOS-specific code.
>
> *Windows Phone application*: Windows Phone–specific code.
>
> *Core Library*: Shared app logic such as BLL and DAL using a PCL or a Shared Project. (For a lighter-weight solution without a core library, you can use file linking to connect shared code that resides in a single platform's project to each of the other platform's projects.)

Figure 9-3 shows the Xamarin projects for a platform-specific solution.

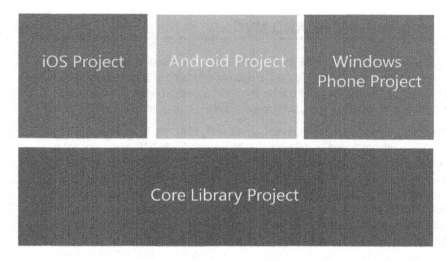

Figure 9-3. *Xamarin projects in a platform-specific solution*

Figure 9-4 shows another way of looking at the platform-specific solution that includes the app and architecture layer axes.

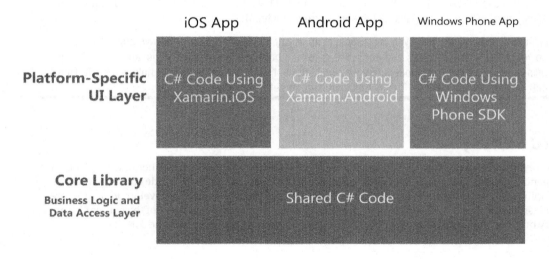

Figure 9-4. *Xamarin solution architecture for Xamarin.iOS, Xamarin.Android, and Windows Phone apps*

The platform-specific projects here (all projects except Core Library) handle divergence at the project level. In many situations, these are created one at a time. For example, first the iOS version of an app is written, then the Android version. This is a useful way to build an app because the core library can be tested with a single platform and the UI can be worked out entirely on one platform before adding a second or third platform.

```
                          MVVM AND MVC
```

Xamarin.Forms is strongly modeled after the MVVM pattern with built-in data binding (as discussed in Chapter 7). For MVVM with platform-specific apps, there are open source options such as MvvmCross and MVVM Light. Both MvvmCross and MVVM Light can be used with Xamarin.Forms. However, many features of MvvmCross overlap with Xamarin.Forms, providing diminishing returns on using them together.

Regarding MVC in platform-specific solutions, Xamarin apps are largely MVC-ish. You create data models by-hand (M in MVC), which are bound as data sources to fields and lists. XML layouts make up the View (the V in MVC), and Android `Activities` and iOS `UIViewControllers` can act as controllers; however, due to native OS UI architectures, the lines between the View and Controller can be somewhat blurry. Although iOS is touted as MVC-based, if you are accustomed to the strict separation of concerns (SOC) found in an ASP.NET MVC solution, you may find iOS's idea of MVC to be diluted. Since storyboard-generated `UIViews` define mainly static aspects of the screen, the logic defining dynamic content is pushed down into the `UIViewController` (the Controller, or C, in MVC). Much of the storyboard-generated `UIView` is about as View-like as .aspx files were before the release of ASP.NET MVC, that is, not very View-like at all. There isn't an equivalent of Razor in native mobile development (building HTML templates in Xamarin using Razor notwithstanding). The same is true of Android development. Layout XML files create largely static layouts and leave the job of populating the dynamic content into the page to the `Activity`, which can become enmeshed with business logic. Xamarin's mission is to provide direct access to these APIs, not to change their fundamental pattern. So, for a lot of us, iOS and Android development will be a step back architecturally from stricter MVC.

Having this knowledge, however, is power. It is up to you to impose SOC in your own apps. You can use your `UIViewControllers` and `Activities` to hold primarily view-related logic, and separate out business logic into true controllers of your own construction. Don't let the toolset hold you back. That's what classes are for, after all. This is the advantage of getting to do all this in C#!

Core Library

The *core library* is a dedicated project in your solution where the DAL, BLL, and other non-UI platform-independent code can reside. Enterprises use the core library for professional-grade code separation, decoupling the presentation layer from the BLL and DAL, and to facilitate team development. The core library isn't necessary for some prototype apps, small projects, or small teams. All of the content in the core library project *could* instead be placed in the Xamarin.Forms project to simplify the solution.

■ **Tip** If you're just starting out with Xamarin.Forms, consider putting your data access, business logic, and shared code in the Xamarin.Forms UI project, and hold off on using a core library for now. You can use folders inside the Xamarin.Forms project to organize your non-UI code (for example, /data, /utilities, etc.) If you're just starting out with platform-specific apps, you can use file linking (explained later in this chapter) as a lightweight alternative to a core library.

In large-scale and/or enterprise-grade apps, non-UI shared code should go into a core library project, separate from the UI projects. Core libraries are typically implemented using PCLs or Shared Projects. Here's what you might put in the core library:

- *DAL*: Data access layer that may include SQLite access, data models, view models, repositories, cloud data access, and web services. See Chapter 7.

- *BLL*: Business logic that cuts across and is independent of platforms.

- *Miscellaneous*: Utilities, interfaces, cross-platform resources, and sundry necessities. The core library is a cross-platform catch-all for non-UI files, folders, and classes.

In a nutshell, put platform-independent, non-UI code in your core library.

It is natural for core library components to be moved into platform-specific projects if it becomes clear that they are not sharable. There are quite a few functions, such as certain types of local file access or OS services, which are platform-specific functions that must be placed in the platform-specific projects. If only a few lines of code in the core library need to be platform-specific, then conditional compilation can be employed in Shared Projects or dependency injection in PCLs. File linking is also a useful option in Shared Projects for creating partial classes with platform-specific files. More on these shortly.

Core libraries are sometimes created using shared libraries or, less commonly, using file linking in platform-specific apps instead of creating a dedicated core library project (usually by sharing BLL or DAL files from a platform-specific project to all the other platform-specific projects). An increasing number of core libraries and Xamarin.Forms projects use PCLs.

Portable Class Libraries (PCL)

PCLs are code projects that provide a built-in subset of the .NET Framework based on the selection of target platforms, such as Xamarin.Android and Xamarin.iOS (or .NET 4.5 or even Xbox!). PCLs can be compiled into a DLL once and then run on all target platforms, so they are ideal for cross-platform code sharing.

Shared code in a solution—such as a Xamarin.Forms project, business logic, or data access code—can be compiled into a PCL DLL for use with platform-specific projects or in other solutions altogether. Because of its decoupled nature, the PCL is particularly useful when it is distributed to other developers rather than used by a single developer.

Create a PCL in Visual Studio while on the Add New Project screen by selecting the Portable Class Library option. In Xamarin Studio, on the New Project screen, select the Portable Library option.

PCLs are configured at compile-time in Visual Studio or Xamarin Studio to target particular platforms using a profile. Profiles are configured to allow a PCL to run with Xamarin.iOS, Xamarin.Android, or Windows phone, as well as with other platforms. PCLs allow you to target these platforms:

- Microsoft .NET Framework

- Silverlight

- Windows Phone

- .NET for Windows Store apps

- Xamarin.Android

- Xamarin.iOS

- Xbox

PCLs provide a convenient, decoupled component for holding shared code in a solution. The cost of using a PCL is that once the DLL is compiled, platform-specific customization requires a bit of extra work.

■ **Important Note**   In a PCL, you cannot add or link files nor use partial classes, partial methods, or conditional compilation for platform-specific implementations.

Because PCLs are constructed to avoid recompiling, platform-specific customization is usually done outside of the PCL in the platform-specific projects using dependency injection.

Dependency Injection

Dependency Injection (DI) is a design principle that helps developers include platform-specific functionality into an otherwise cross-platform class using Inversion of Control (IoC). IoC patterns are framework calls to specific implementations of general classes provided by the application. DI does this by passing the implementation into a constructor/setter.

DI is useful for platform-specific functions such as custom renderers, file handling, background services, and sensors. In your shared code (usually a PCL, but this will also work in a Shared Project or file), create an interface to define the methods and patterns to be implemented in each platform. Implement platform-specific subclasses of the base class in each respective platform-specific project. Then you can inject these platform-specific implementations into your shared code. DI handles divergence at the class level.

There are a few ways to implement the DI design principle, including interfaces, abstract classes, and inheritance. Built into Xamarin.Forms is a DI implementation called DependencyService, which implements DI using interfaces.

■ **Note**   DI is a way to implement the Gang of Four (GoF) Strategy and/or Bridge patterns. Microsoft added to this in Windows Presentation Foundation (WPF) and called it the Provider pattern. Xamarin.Forms implements a variation of the Provider pattern in DependencyService.

Using DependencyService

Xamarin.Forms provides a built-in DI implementation called DependencyService that allows you to create a base interface, and then build platform-specific implementation classes to be invoked in shared code. This involves three steps:

1. *Interface*: An interface in the shared code declares the class for platform-specific implementation.

2. *Implementation*: Platform-specific implementations of the interface are registered using [assembly] tags.

3. *Invocation*: The platform-specific code is invoked from the shared code using DependencyService.Get<InterfaceName>.MethodName.

Let's look at an example that passes a simple string into a custom class, concatenates the name of the OS onto the beginning, and returns the string to the shared code caller.

I'll begin with the interface.

Creating an Interface

Using DependencyService first requires an interface of the functionality you want to implement. Interfaces help to create a consistent architecture for specifying cross-platform feature sets with platform-specific implementations.

Create an interface for your cross-platform class, ICustomClass, with a GoNative method.

```
public interface ICustomClass
{
    string GoNative(string param);
}
```

The second step is to create platform-specific implementations.

■ **Important Note**   Remember to provide an implementation of your interface in all platform-specific projects. The DependencyService.Get method requires this in order to resolve the reference; otherwise, a NullReferenceException error will be thrown at runtime.

Let's begin with Android.

Android Implementation

ANDROID

In your Android project, create a platform-specific implementation of ICustomClass called CustomClass_Android.cs. This version of the CustomClass.GoNative returns the value "Android".

```
class CustomClass_Android : ICustomClass
{
    public CustomClass_Android() { }

    public string GoNative(string param)
    {
        return "Android " + param;
    }
}
```

Register the class for use in DependencyService above the CustomClass_Android and namespace declarations.

```
[assembly: Xamarin.Forms.Dependency(typeof(CustomClass_Android))]
```

Remember to reference the current project to resolve CustomClass_Android.

```
using DependencyServiceExample.Android;
```

Now for the iOS implementation.

iOS Implementation

iOS

In the iOS project, create a platform-specific implementation of CustomClass called CustomClass_iOS.cs. This version of the CustomClass.GoNative returns the value "iOS".

```
class CustomClass_iOS : ICustomClass
{
    public CustomClass_iOS() { }

    public string GoNative(string param)
    {
        return "iOS " + param;
    }
}
```

Register the class for use in DependencyService above the CustomClass_Android and namespace declarations.

```
[assembly: Xamarin.Forms.Dependency(typeof(CustomClass_iOS))]
```

Remember to reference the current project to resolve CustomClass_iOS.

```
using DependencyServiceExample.iOS; And next is the Windows Phone version.
```

And next is the Windows Phone version.

Windows Phone Implementation

WINDOWS PHONE

Lastly, in your Windows Phone project, create a platform-specific implementation of CustomClass called CustomClass_WindowsPhone.cs. This version of the CustomClass.GoNative returns the value "Windows Phone".

```
class CustomClass_WindowsPhone : ICustomClass
{
    public CustomClass_WindowsPhone () { }

    public string GoNative(string param)
    {
        return "Windows Phone " + param;
    }
}
```

Register the class for use in DependencyService above the CustomClass_WindowsPhone and namespace declarations.

```
[assembly: Xamarin.Forms.Dependency(typeof(CustomClass_WindowsPhone))]
```

Remember to reference the current project to resolve CustomClass_WindowsPhone.

```
using DependencyServiceExample.WinPhone;
```

Now you'll use these platform-specific implementations in the shared code.

Invocation of the Platform-Specific Class

Invoke the platform-specific implementation in your Shared Project or PCL.

```
var text = DependencyService.Get<ICustomClass>()
    .GoNative("platform-specific implementation complete!");
```

Create a button on your main page and use this DI invocation in the button's Clicked event.

```
class MainPage : ContentPage
{
    public MainPage()
    {
        var button = new Button
        {
            Text = "Go Native!",
            VerticalOptions = LayoutOptions.CenterAndExpand,
            HorizontalOptions = LayoutOptions.CenterAndExpand,
        };
        button.Clicked += (sender, e) =>
        {
            var text = DependencyService.Get<ICustomClass>()
                .GoNative("platform-specific implementation complete!");
            DisplayAlert("GoNative Called", text, "OK");
        };
        Content = button;
    }
}
```

Figure 9-5 shows the button waiting to call CustomClass.GoNative.

Figure 9-5. *Button ready to call platform-specific implementations using DependencyService*

When the button is clicked, DependencyService calls the platform-specific GoNative method of the ICustomClass implementation, passing in the text "platform-specific implementation complete!". The registered platform-specific version of CustomClass takes the text param, adds the name of the OS at the beginning of the passed-in text string, and returns it to the calling class in shared code. The calling class then displays the entire string in a DisplayAlert, as shown in Figure 9-6.

Figure 9-6. *Platform-specific implementations of CustomClass*

■ **Tip** Other ways to implement Dependency Injection include abstract classes and inheritance.

CODE COMPLETE: Using DependencyService

Listings 9-1, 9-2, 9-3, 9-4, and 9-5 contain the complete code for this DependencyService example. Listing 9-1 contains the interface. Listing 9-2 contains the callout to the platform-specific implementation of CustomClass.GoNative using DependencyService. Listings 9-3, 9-4, and 9-5 contain the OS-specific implementations of ICustomClass.

This example can be found in the downloadable code in the DependencyServiceExample solution.

Listing 9-1. The Interface Resides in CustomClass.cs in the Xamarin.Forms Project

```
public interface ICustomClass
{
    string GoNative(string param);
}
```

Listing 9-2. The DependencyService Callout Is in MainPage.cs in the Xamarin.Forms Project

```
class MainPage : ContentPage
{
    public MainPage()
    {
        var button = new Button
        {
            Text = "Go Native!",
                VerticalOptions = LayoutOptions.CenterAndExpand,
            HorizontalOptions = LayoutOptions.CenterAndExpand,
        };
        button.Clicked += (sender, e) =>
        {
            var text = DependencyService.Get<ICustomClass>()
                .GoNative("platform-specific implementation complete!");
            DisplayAlert("GoNative Called", text, "OK");
        };
        Content = button;
    }
}
```

Listing 9-3. The Android Implementation Is in CustomClass_Android.cs in the Android Project

```
using System;
using DependencyServiceExample.Droid;

[assembly: Xamarin.Forms.Dependency(typeof(CustomClass_Android))]

namespace DependencyServiceExample.Droid
{
    class CustomClass_Android : ICustomClass
    {
        public CustomClass_Android() { }

        public string GoNative(string param)
        {
            return "Android " + param;
        }
    }
}
```

Listing 9-4. The iOS Implementation Is in CustomClass_iOS.cs in the iOS Project

```
using System;
using DependencyServiceExample.iOS;

[assembly: Xamarin.Forms.Dependency(typeof(CustomClass_iOS))]
```

```
namespace DependencyServiceExample.iOS
{
    class CustomClass_iOS : ICustomClass
    {
        public CustomClass_iOS() { }

        public string GoNative(string param)
        {
            return "iOS " + param;
        }
    }
}
```

Listing 9-5. The Windows Phone Implementation Is in CustomClass_WindowsPhone.cs in the Windows Phone Project

```
using System;
using DependencyServiceExample.WinPhone;

[assembly: Xamarin.Forms.Dependency(typeof(CustomClass_WindowsPhone))]

namespace DependencyServiceExample.WinPhone
{
    class CustomClass_WindowsPhone : ICustomClass
    {
        public CustomClass_WindowsPhone() { }

        public string GoNative(string param)
        {
            return "Windows Phone " + param;
        }
    }
}
```

There are third-party alternatives to using DependencyService and to coding your own DI implementation.

Third-Party and Open Source DI Containers

A number of useful third-party and open source DI containers exist to help you do Dependency Injection. Here are a few of them used by many developers:

- TinyIoC: Simple open source IoC solution
- Unity: Microsoft's DI solution
- AutoFac: Another useful open source IoC solution

■ **Tip** Dependency Injection (DI) is a subset of the Inversion of Control (IoC) design principle.

When more flexibility is required in the shared code than a PCL affords, a Shared Project can be useful.

Shared Projects

Shared Projects contain shared code that can be recompiled into different applications (in the same solution or in different ones). Like the PCL, this is where a core library or Xamarin.Forms project can be housed for use in different platform contexts. The Shared Project is particularly useful when it is used by a single developer, as it produces only a shareable code project, not a DLL.

Create a Shared Project in Visual Studio by navigating to File ➤ New Solution and choosing a name for the project and solution. In Xamarin Studio, navigate to File ➤ New Solution and choose a name.

■ **Tip**   The Shared Project solution template requires Visual Studio 2013 Update 2 (or Xamarin Studio).

There are many techniques available for handling divergence in Shared Projects: Dependency Injection (DI), conditional compilation, file linking, partial classes, and partial methods. I've already discussed DI, so let's look at the rest of these common approaches:

- *Conditional compilation*: Compiler directives for small, code-level amounts of divergence

- *File linking*: Project file include for file or class-sized levels of divergence

- *Partial classes*: Using the partial keyword for class divergence

- *Partial method*: Using the partial keyword for method divergence

These approaches can be used loosely, as needed, without much structure. Use them carefully, because implementations of any of them can become an anti-pattern, tightly linking cross-platform and platform-specific classes without proper organization.

An architecturally disciplined approach might instead use the Strategy pattern with the Bridge pattern. The Strategy pattern encapsulates the various platform behaviors in a class to abstract away the platform-specific implementations. The Bridge pattern is used to decouple the class or method declarations in the shared code from the platform-specific implementations using an interface, abstract classes, or inheritance. You can also use DI, as discussed earlier.

Let's look at each of the techniques in turn, starting with conditional compilation. The Shared Project is an ideal place to put code that requires slight variations between platforms using conditional compilation.

Conditional Compilation

When shared code requires slight platform-specific variations (that cannot be accounted for using the Xamarin.Forms OnDevice command), you can create compiler directives that compile code conditionally by platform. This is a useful way to inject small pieces of platform code into an otherwise shared block of code. This is a way to handle divergence at the smallest granularity: line-by-line.

Xamarin solution templates predefine three compilation symbols: __IOS__, __ANDROID__, and __MOBILE__ (two underscores before and after each term). Use these compilation symbols with the #if/#endif compiler directives to include and exclude code based on the project platform.

Specify an iOS-specific block of code using #if __IOS__.

```
#if __IOS__
// iOS-specific code
#endif
```

Specify Android using #if __ANDROID__.

```
#if __ANDROID__
// Android-specific code
#endif
```

Specify either iOS or Android using #if __MOBILE__.

```
#if __MOBILE__
// iOS or Android-specific code
#endif
```

Android API level can also be specified in the conditional. This is a way to manage platform-version divergence.

```
#if __ANDROID_22__
// code for Android API 22 or newer
#endif
```

Conditional compilation is useful for platform-specific exceptions in a cross-platform class. If there are too many exceptions, you should divide your features into platform-specific implementations and put them into their respective projects, that is, in the Xamarin.iOS project. You can do this in an architecturally sound manner by using interfaces to define the feature set before creating platform-specific implementations using the Strategy and/or Bridge pattern (or DI).

File Linking

You can bring individual files into projects from other projects using *file linking*. This can be used to bring platform-specific implementations into Shared Projects or shared code into platform-specific projects.

Simply right-click a project and choose Add (in Xamarin Studio) or Add Files (in Visual Studio). Pick the desired file or folder and choose Link when prompted to virtually include it in your current project.

A common use of file linking is for small or prototype platform-specific apps where a lightweight alternative to a core library is needed. You can put all of your shared files (business logic, data access, utilities, and so on) into a single project (such as the Android or Xamarin.Forms projects), and then link to those files from the other platform-specific projects (such as the iOS and/or Windows Phone projects). File linking instead of a core library is a quick and dirty approach that probably shouldn't be used on enterprise-grade or team projects.

■ **Tip** Overuse of bottom-up, fine-grained approaches such as file linking and conditional compilation can lead to architecturally undisciplined code, so consider your top-down alternatives first (like PCLs and Shared Projects).

Partial Classes and Methods

Partial classes are useful for extending a shared, cross-platform class with platform-specific functionality. *Partial methods* are useful for implementing platform-specific functionality at the method level, though without a base cross-platform implementation. These techniques work in Shared Projects and linked files, but not PCLs.

Create a partial class in your Shared Project.

```
public partial class Utility
{
    public void DoCrossPlatformThing()
    {
    }
}
```

Then extend that class in your platform-specific project.

```
public partial class Utility
{
    public void DoPlatformSpecificThing()
    {
    }
}
```

Partial methods are similar to partial classes, although they don't provide a cross-platform implementation, only a platform-specific one.

Define a partial method in your Shared Project, but do not provide an implementation.

```
partial void DoThing();
```

Then implement that method in your platform-specific projects.

```
partial void DoThing()
{
}
```

Partial classes are a common method for architecting for divergence in Shared Projects and linked files. Divergence isn't just for platforms, though; it happens with OS versions as well.

Handling Version Divergence

As new releases of mobile OSs take place and new devices are released, changes such as screen size and feature deprecation must be accounted for. Old features must be gracefully deprecated and new features are eagerly embraced. All this can happen on a single platform, such as iOS or Android, creating a process called *version divergence*.

In order to account for this type of divergence, your apps must be aware of the active OS version in certain situations and respond accordingly. This requires version detection. Here are a few ways to do that.

On Android, you can use the following:

```
if (((int)Android.OS.Build.Version.SdkInt) >= 22)
{
  // code for Android API 22 or newer
}
```

And when using conditional compilation, there is an option on Android.

```
#if __ANDROID_22__
  // code for Android API 22 or newer
#endif
```

On iOS, you use CheckSystemVersion.

```
if (UIDevice.CurrentDevice.CheckSystemVersion(8, 0))
{
  // code for iOS version 8.0 or newer
}
```

Those are some techniques for handling OS version divergence. Remember to gracefully degrade deprecated functions and provide a lowest-common denominator functionality when necessary.

Summary

After you've decided whether you're going with Xamarin.Forms or a platform-specific approach, you need to craft an architecture. Split your cross-platform apps into two types of code: shared and platform-specific. Divide your app into these two groups starting with the largest divisions and working down toward the smaller ones.

A core library is useful in a professional-grade Xamarin app for holding your BLL, DAL, utilities, interfaces, and other back-end, non-UI, cross-platform classes.

Platform-specific code should go into its respective platform-specific projects—into a Xamarin.Android project, for example. Custom renderers in Xamarin.Forms projects are placed in these platform-specific projects.

Cross-platform projects include Xamarin.Forms projects and core libraries. These are typically built using Portable Class Libraries (PCL) or Shared Projects. PCLs result in pre-compiled cross-platform DLLs, which are ideal for sharing between developers. Shared Projects produce shared code projects designed to be recompiled for each platform and are generally more useful for a single developer.

Plenty of cross-platform classes call for platform-specific code and the decision must be made as to how to handle these exceptions. Granularities that are smaller than an entire project require special treatment in the handling of shared versus platform-specific code. Useful design principles include Dependency Injection (DI) and Inversion of Control (IoC). Useful design patterns include the Provider, Strategy, and Bridge patterns.

When using cross-platform PCLs, Dependency Injection (DI) is the platform-specific weapon of choice, and Xamarin.Forms provides a handy DependencyService class for easy DI implementation. Because Shared Projects are more tightly coupled to platform-specific projects than PCLs and must be recompiled per platform, they afford more options, including DI, conditional compilation, partial classes and methods, and file linking. These techniques can be used to create loosely-constructed explicit implementations of platform-specific tasks, so be on the lookout for anti-patterns when using Shared Projects.

Those are the fundamental principles, patterns, and divergence-handling techniques in Xamarin mobile app architecture. I hope you find everything you need here to go forth and build!

███

The Art of Xamarin App Development

"The Latin phrase Gradus ad Parnassum means "Steps to Parnassus." The name Parnassus was used to denote the loftiest part of a mountain range in central Greece, a few miles north of Delphi, of which the two summits, in Classical times, were called Tithorea and Lycoreia. In Greek mythology, one of the peaks was sacred to Apollo and the nine Muses, the inspiring deities of the arts, and the other to Dionysus. The phrase has often been used to refer to various books of instruction, or guides, in which gradual progress in literature, language instruction, music, or the arts in general, is sought."

Wikipedia entry for "Gradus ad Parnassum"

For many of us, software development is a calling as well as a vocation. We labor to create things of beauty even as we deliver functional code. In this way, Xamarin mobile application development is an art form.

Respectable art forms require tremendous dedication and skill to master. Step-by-step, we practice each little technique and seek to comprehend minor concepts until we incorporate them into our repertoire, then on to more complex techniques and loftier concepts, and on and on as we ascend each step up the mountain of mastery.

The notion that we are pursuing knowledge and skill in our ascent toward mist-veiled peaks is a very old one, as evidenced by the reference to Parnassus, the home of the Muses. While climbing, we might not expect to reach the summit, but along the way we become more knowledgeable and more skilled developers and architects, and we afford ourselves the opportunity to build better mobile apps. There is also the simple pleasure of the climb, and the stopping now and again to enjoy the view.

The first steps toward mastery of the Xamarin platform involve creating basic solutions in Xamarin.Forms, Xamarin.iOS, and Xamarin.Android. Next, we must explore the mobile UI using layouts, building screens using views, and placing them in relation to one another. Data-bound lists are the mainstay of the mobile app data UI, so we need to understand how to bind lists to our data models and customize the look and feel of the list. Our users must move between screens and this requires navigation, during which we must manage state. Displaying and editing data is the purpose of many apps, so data access and binding are a necessity. The catalyzing technique in Xamarin.Forms UI is the custom renderer, which allows us to customize our cross-platform views by using the platform-specific libraries. Lastly, we must understand cross-platform architecture in order to manage the use of shared and platform-specific code.

Those are the steps in this book, which was crafted with the intent of giving you most of what you require most of the time while building your apps, with emphasis on C# and the mobile UI.

I sincerely hope that I have helped you to climb just a bit closer to the peaks most important to you and to write your next Xamarin killer app.

Index

Get the eBook for only $5!

Why limit yourself?

Now you can take the weightless companion with you wherever you go and access your content on your PC, phone, tablet, or reader.

Since you've purchased this print book, we're happy to offer you the eBook in all 3 formats for just $5.

Convenient and fully searchable, the PDF version enables you to easily find and copy code—or perform examples by quickly toggling between instructions and applications. The MOBI format is ideal for your Kindle, while the ePUB can be utilized on a variety of mobile devices.

To learn more, go to www.apress.com/companion or contact support@apress.com.

Apress®
THE EXPERT'S VOICE™

CPSIA information can be obtained at www.ICGtesting.com
Printed in the USA
LVOW03s2204010715

444612LV00007BB/237/P

9 781484 202159